Food
is not the
Problem:
Deal With What is!

Michelle Morand, M.A.

Note for Librarians: A cataloguing record for this book is available from Library and Archives Canada at www.collectionscanada.ca/amicus/index-e.html
ISBN 1-4251-0519-X

PUBLISHING™
Offices in Canada, USA, Ireland and UK

Book sales for North America and international:
Trafford Publishing, 6E–2333 Government St.,
Victoria, BC V8T 4P4 CANADA
phone 250 383 6864 (toll-free 1 888 232 4444)
fax 250 383 6804; email to orders@trafford.com
Book sales in Europe:
Trafford Publishing (UK) Limited, 9 Park End Street, 2nd Floor
Oxford, UK OX1 1HH UNITED KINGDOM
phone +44 (0)1865 722 113 (local rate 0845 230 9601)
facsimile +44 (0)1865 722 868; info.uk@trafford.com
Order online at:
trafford.com/06-2277

10 9 8 7 6 5 4 3 2

Contents

With Gratitude

First and foremost, I would like to thank my mother, Linda Patton. Not only did you offer spelling and grammatical suggestions, thereby ensuring my readers would get the most benefit and enjoyment from this book, but you also provided me with the gift of your emotional support and encouragement throughout this project. I couldn't have done it without you, Ma! I feel so blessed by the precious gift of your love and caring in all areas of my life. I appreciate you so! I am also deeply touched by your consent to share your story with my readers so that they may understand my experience better. Thank you for your openness and courage. I love you.

Steve-O, thanks so much for all your support over the years. I am so very lucky to have you for a step-father and as a grandfather for Ben. And thank you for the wonderful photo you took for the book. You definitely have talent!

Peter Bion, you have been a true friend in all ways. This project would not be coming to fruition at this time if not for your support of the Centre and of my work.

Karen Stein, you are my dear friend, mentor and colleague. Without your constant support and passion for our Centre and the work we do, this book may not have seen the light of day. You are a daily blessing in my life, and I thank you for all of the gentle ways you invite me to challenge myself and to grow.

Brooke Finnigan-Holst, your enthusiasm for the Centre and its purpose helped me to see that what we were doing had the potential to make a great difference in many people's lives. Your ingenuity and creativity played a large role in bringing the Centre to where it is today. Thank you.

Virginia Preston, for keeping us organized. You brought an air of respect, integrity and professionalism to our Centre that has taken us to a new level. I am supremely grateful for the connection we share.

Beth Burton-Krahn, your sense of humour has been such a great gift in my life; thank you for the lightness. And thank you for your gentle communication and the integrity that you bring to your work and to our friendship. Namaste.

And last but by no means least, to my clients. Your courage, strength and determination to grow and to heal have been such a great honour to witness. Thank you for sharing your journey with me.

INTRODUCTION

a.k.a. Why do I want to read this book?

Do you often eat when you are not hungry? Do you eat beyond the point of comfortable fullness? Do you fantasize about what you are going to eat when you next get to be alone with food? Do you feel shame and guilt for eating certain types of foods, or for eating at certain times of the day? Perhaps you restrict yourself from eating when you are hungry. Do you imagine what you would like to eat, maybe even prepare it for others, and then get off on the experience of not allowing it for yourself? If you answered *yes* to any of these questions, you are using food to cope. If this is the case, this book is for you. Welcome to the start of a new way of being in relationship with food and with your body.

The purpose of this book is to provide you with the education and skills you need to heal from your use of food as a coping strategy. It will also greatly benefit you if you use alcohol, drugs, cigarettes, sex, relationships, self-harm, rage, and any other coping behaviours to help you numb or soothe painful thoughts or feelings.

If you would like to get an immediate sense of how you will benefit from our work together, flip to Chapter 7, and have a look at the coping strategy flow chart. If any of those patterns of thoughts, feelings, or behaviours seem familiar to you, know that you will gain an opportunity to heal those patterns by exploring and implementing the tools outlined in the chapters to follow.

As a clinician with over a decade of experience specializing in the field of disordered eating, depression, and trauma, I have come to identify three key areas of focus in supporting clients to heal: your relationship with food; your relationship with yourself; and your relationships with others. My intention is that by the time we have completed our work together, you will be confident in your ability to address these three key areas in a way that continually enhances your sense of confidence and trust in yourself, and that provides you with a life which is free of food and body-image focus.

If you are one of the millions of men and women who use food to cope in one of the ways I described above, take a moment and ask yourself the following questions:

- What exactly is it that you do with food right now?
- How does it impact your feelings about your body at this time?
- How do you feel when you engage in that way of being with food?
- What are the thoughts that you have when you engage in this behaviour?
- What are the things that you do or don't do in your life because of how you think and feel about your relationship with your body and food?
- What is the impact on your life of thinking and feeling and behaving this way?
- What is the price that you and others around you pay for your current behaviours, thoughts, and feelings about food and about your body?

Given your answers to these questions, you might feel reinforced in your belief that it truly is your behaviour around food, and your non-compliant body, that are to blame for how you feel about yourself and for what is not working in your life at this time. You may feel that you have just proven to yourself yet again that food *is* the problem, and, if you could just change this, everything else would shift; you wouldn't feel so crappy, sad or angry; you wouldn't think so negatively of yourself and believe that you truly are undeserving of happiness and peace in your life; you wouldn't hate your body; you'd be getting out more; you'd feel safe engaging in relationships more fully and deeply; you wouldn't be afraid to say what's on your mind; you wouldn't be thinking about harming yourself; you'd exercise more; you'd take better care of yourself overall.

Based on this story, everything seems to hinge on you getting a solid handle on your relationship with food. No wonder food is such a powerful force in your life. No wonder there is such an emotional charge around your current relationship with food and so much self-judgement.

What we are going to explore together in the pages to come, and what you are about to learn and to quickly prove to yourself, is that the issue is not food. And it's not about your body either. Food and body focus are just symptoms of a deeper concern. As with isolation, anxiety, depression, fear, procrastination, and negative self-talk, food and body focus stem from something deeper and do not arise in and of themselves.

You cannot focus your emotional, psychological, and behavioural efforts on changing your relationship with food and body image and expect any lasting change to occur. If you have picked up this book, it means that on a gut level you know that dieting, or restriction of any kind, is not going to get you where you want to go.

You may be coming to this process with a great deal of judgement of yourself and the assumption that if you only tried harder; if you only had more willpower; if you only were more committed or less lazy; if you really, really wanted things to change, you would be able to make that diet or exercise program stick. Given the line of thinking that is so prevalent in our society, namely, that it is something wrong or lacking in you that prevents your success with diet and exercise, it would be perfectly appropriate for you to be entering this process of lasting growth and transformation with some self-judgement.

Regardless of the judgement and self-recrimination you may be carrying about your perceived past failures, the important thing is that you are willing to allow for the possibility, however remote it may seem, that there is something beyond food and body image that is triggering you to use food and body focus to cope. The process outlined in this book will identify what that underlying trigger is and what you can do to begin to heal and overcome that pattern so you can come to a place of never again thinking of using food to cope.

My goal for you is a free and easy relationship with food and with your body. The pages that follow will provide you with a step-by-step approach to identifying and healing not just your relationship with food but also the underlying trigger. This will allow you to let go of your food and body focus once and for all.

Let's begin the journey.

NB: In the interest of simplicity, I have chosen to use the pronoun "she". Please know that we do have male clients at the CEDRIC Centre, and we respect that these issues pertain to men as well as women.

SECTION I

EXPLORING YOUR READINESS
FOR CHANGE

Food is not the Problem

From the time I was a little girl, I used food to cope. I ate when I wasn't hungry, ate more than I needed to when I had a meal, and sometimes I would not allow myself to eat when I *was* hungry. For years I played around with food in these ways, using it for pleasure and punishment, nurturing and neglect. It served its purpose because I was so focused on what I was eating, what I was going to eat, what I shouldn't have eaten, and the physical ramifications of it all (my weight!) that I hardly noticed how incredibly insecure and unsafe I felt all the time. I was so accustomed to feeling anxious that I began to chalk it up to the lack of satisfaction I felt with my body. If I just looked the way I wanted to and could just control myself around food, I certainly wouldn't feel so insecure and anxious all the time. Right?

Well, not exactly. You see, like you, I had a damn fine reason for feeling anxious. I had a reason to feel unsafe and insecure in myself and in my world. My focus on food and body image was only a coping strategy that I learned very early in life to help me "numb out" to the lack of safety and security I felt in my home. I say "like you," because I know that, even if you didn't have an abusive home environment or can't put your finger on any specific event which would be a "reason" to use food to cope, you do have a legitimate reason. I know it. You may doubt it or question what it might be. You may even be reading this saying, "Yeah, yeah. I know this happened to me when I was ten, but it doesn't impact me now!" Regardless of your perspective at this moment, my own recovery and my 13 years of professional experience specializing in the area of compulsive eating leaves me with absolutely no doubt that, **if you use food to cope in any of the ways I described above, you have reason to, and it's time to stop judging yourself and start seeking to understand.**

The title of this book is *Food is not the Problem: Deal With What Is!* Food is *not* the problem. Even though it may now have become its own problem, it is not the underlying problem in and of itself. Coming to understand what the underlying trigger is for you, and what can be done about it now, is what will allow you to finally free yourself from food and body-image obsession and come to a natural relationship with food.

Often, people who engage in the process of recovery from the Diet Mentality initially feel frustrated and as though they are not making progress. This happens because you come to the process of recovery thinking that it is all about your body. You believe that you would be acceptable and nothing would stand in your way, if only your body looked normal or weren't so fat/thin. Therefore, if you do not see immediate change in your physical form (some change that is tangible), you feel stuck, hopeless, and become so discouraged that you will give up and return to the old patterns of restriction/ overeating and feelings of guilt and shame. You don't know what else to do, and even though the old way has never worked before, it is something!

So allow yourself to consider the thought that you will forever be vulnerable to your old way of thinking, and it will sabotage you and the change you are seeking to create if you remain fixated on external signs of physical change as the only true indication of progress. This is the irony of the situation; it's the old way of thinking of yourself and food that you are seeking to change, and yet it's the old way of thinking which you allow yourself to believe in and return to when the going gets tough!

And when I say *you*, I mean all of us who have become so confused about our behaviour around food and its true cause that we keep replaying the same scene in our lives, hoping for a different outcome. The pop-psychology definition of insanity is: *doing the same thing and expecting different results.* Well, what would you call dieting? Isn't one diet like any other, after all? Calories in. Calories out. One of my favorite authors, Barbara Sher, writes in her book *I Could Do Anything If Only I Knew What It Was*: "When too many people fail a requirement, there is nothing wrong with them, there is something wrong with the requirement!"

I love this quote because she makes a key point that resonates deeply with those of us who have been struggling to "meet the requirement" of our society of the ideal physical form, to be the good girl, or to feel and think the "right" way. When we are forced to ignore the natural signals from our body about what we need—whether it is food, safety, or a connection with others or with ourselves in order to meet the needs of our society or the key people in our lives—there is clearly something wrong with the requirement of those relationships.

In the early stages of recovery from the Diet Mentality, you are still looking for physical change as the indicator of your progress or success. This physical change can only come from a marked change in your relationship with food; however, **your relationship with food exists as it does because you have not yet found a way to feel safe in the world**. What must come before any noticeable change to your relationship with food, and subsequently your body shape and size, is a strengthening of your Self to the point that you are able to trust in your ability to handle the ups and downs that life throws your way. You must come to trust your perception of your feelings and of life events, knowing that you will respond appropriately to those feelings. As you come to trust yourself to have integrity, meaning your words and actions are aligned, and to feel safe being authentic in all situations, you will naturally be able to experience thoughts, feelings, and life events without the use of food as a crutch.

In this book I will use the terms Compulsive Eating, Diet Mentality, and Disordered Eating interchangeably. In my professional experience, they are one and the same. Each one speaks to a relationship with food which is not being driven or dictated by our bodies but by messages from outside ourselves about what we should be, do, think, feel and eat. When you are focused outside of yourself for cues about what your body needs and wants, you are robbing yourself of the power that comes from being connected to your body and to yourself, and the power to trust that you know what you need and want. In these instances, you are setting yourself up to be vulnerable to the needs and perspectives of other people who may not be aligned with what you truly want or need. Therefore, your needs continue to be unmet, and your need for food grows to cope with this increasing sense of insecurity.

Stop and think for a moment about how frequently you allow yourself to trust the signals from your body. Let's say it is 11 a.m. You had breakfast at 8:30, even though you weren't hungry (but it was breakfast time after all!), and yet it is now 11 a.m. and your body is sending you signals of hunger. How do you respond? Do you mistrust that signal and question how you could possibly be hungry? Do you judge these signals as good or bad? Do you feel frustrated and annoyed at your body for being hungry so soon after eating? Do you feel excited because now you get to eat "legitimately"? Do you force yourself to wait until "lunch time"? And at whatever point you *do* allow yourself to eat something, do you force yourself to stop before you are full, or do you eat everything, even though you are feeling full part way through?

An affirmative to any of the above responses to a natural cue from your body that you are hungry is an indicator that your relationship with food has taken a turn to the unhealthy. It doesn't matter how those symptoms manifest themselves. Whether you overeat, binge and purge, or use more of a restrictive pattern with food, the cause is the same and so is the cure. And yes, I did say cure. The

Diet Mentality is not something that you have for life as if it were some incurable disease. It is a naturally and appropriately occurring set of symptoms that is present in your life because of some underlying event or series of events. As you attend to the underlying cause of those symptoms and its manifestation in your present life, you will find that your need for food as an aid to coping naturally fades away.

You can think of it this way. Let's say you have a sinus infection, but you don't know it yet. You are aware that you have a headache. You are aware that your nose runs a lot. You are aware that you are feeling tired. You take a pill for the headache, and you blow your nose. You feel annoyed at your fatigue and frustrated with your body for demanding so much attention and for not functioning optimally. You work yourself into quite a tizzy, focusing on your fatigue— maybe it's cancer! And the headache... brain tumor! That's just too scary. Better not look further. Let's just keep doing what we're doing and hope it goes away. Eventually, you are going to find yourself at the doctor because you will get tired of those headaches, nasal drip and fatigue, and the doctor will immediately put two and two together and hand you a prescription for an antibiotic for your sinus infection. You breathe a sigh of relief. You say, "I knew there was some reason for those headaches. Thank God it's just a sinus infection!" You attend to the underlying cause of those symptoms that had you so frustrated and scared, and soon you are well again.

But how much extra emotional, psychological and physical stress did you unnecessarily put yourself through? By not trusting that your body was telling you about some legitimate problem which required your attention, you experienced much more stress and strain than necessary. This is exactly what you are doing with food. Your relationship with food is a naturally and appropriately occurring symptom of some underlying trigger or concern. It is not *the* problem! It is trying to tell you that something else requires your attention—pronto!

I promise, as you begin to understand more about your underlying trigger and what you can do to heal this in your present day life, your use of food to cope will naturally ease and eventually diminish entirely. When this happens for our clients at the CEDRIC Centre, they find themselves coming to a natural weight for their bodies without dieting or any specific focus on weight or fitness. This means they have come to have a natural relationship with food; they eat when they are hungry, they stop when they are full. It's this simple. The "what to eat" ceases to be an issue when the signals of hunger and fullness are consistently responded to.

If you have struggled with overeating, purging, restriction, or a mixture of the three, take heart. There is nothing wrong with you. You have simply been taught to focus on the symptoms or, as I did, found the symptoms of your problem a lot easier to focus on than the problem itself! Well, you are a grownup now. You may not feel as though you are most of the time. You may even resent that you have to take care of yourself. That's okay. We are going to work on this together.

I know you are capable of understanding and attending to the underlying trigger of your Diet Mentality. In the chapters to come, I will support you to have a complete understanding of the trigger(s) for your compulsive or restrictive eating. In case you are wondering, we are not going to spend much time reliving the past. We are going to focus on how this initial trigger continues to impact you today in your relationship with food, your relationship with yourself, and your relationship with others.

By the time you have completed this book, you will have a solid grasp on the two key components for healing the use of food as a coping strategy: empathy and compassion. You will soon see that from these two components, all else flows. You will have experimented with the use of a variety of tools. You will have witnessed yourself finding many different ways of resolving stress and conflict within and with others which don't involve self-criticism, food, or bad body thoughts. You will know, beyond a shadow of a doubt, that food focus is just a coping strategy, and you will no longer spin your wheels focusing on what, when, and why you have just eaten. You will immediately identify the trigger of your desire to use food to cope, and you will then be in a position to make a choice between using food in the old way or to use one of your new tools. This is all we can ask of ourselves in any behavioural change: the intellectual ability to understand why we do what we do and the compassion to support ourselves to find new ways to cope that are more respectful and life-enhancing.

As you begin to explore your use of food to cope, know this: **there is always a reason for why you do what you do**. You are *not* weak. You do *not* lack willpower. You are *not* stupid or lacking in deservedness. I repeat, there is always a reason for why you do what you do, and the key is in trusting this. For now, if you are skeptical but willing, trust me, and you will soon prove this to yourself. In addition to trusting that there is always a reason for why you do what you do with food, trust this equally as well: **there is always a solution**. It may not be your dream or ideal solution at first glance, but there is always a solution. There is always a way to resolve every situation that will enhance your self-esteem and maintain the dignity of yourself and of the others involved.

Are you ready for a life which is free from a focus on food and body image? Follow the steps in this book and you will begin to experience a natural lessening in your use of food to cope, and in your 24/7 thoughts of food and body image. You also will experience the greatest gift of all—PEACE (something that you may not have thought you wanted or needed, and something that you never allowed yourself to dream was achievable). The empathy and compassion that you develop for yourself and others through this process will bring you to a relationship with yourself and with the key people in your life that is more intimate, safe, and more beautiful than anything you have imagined. Let us journey together, and gently explore new ways of responding to life that remove your need for food to cope and bring you closer to yourself and to a peaceful, secure, and passionate existence. Welcome to a new way of life.

2

Readiness For Change

Often, as much as you truly believe you are ready to change an old pattern of behaviour, you find yourself coming up against some resistance to this change in a variety of ways. Most of your resistance is unconscious and can be pretty slippery when you are trying to find it initially. What follows is some key information on why you might be resisting change in your use of food to cope, as well as information on some of the other coping strategies you will identify later in this book. Once you understand the *why* and have a stronger sense of empathy and compassion for this part of yourself which is resistant to change, you will identify thoughts, feelings, and behaviours that you have used or are currently using which prevent you from making beneficial changes.

You see, when you truly understand that there is a reason for why you do what you do, it is a lot harder for your Drill Sgt. (that critical, contemptuous voice within) to criticize and shut you off to your authentic feelings and needs in that moment. Understanding your true motivation provides you with many opportunities to acknowledge and validate your thoughts, feelings, and behaviours, while seeking respectful and dignified solutions that will allow you to meet your ultimate goal: a peaceful, secure, and passionate life that is free from using food as a coping strategy!

First, we will take a look at what the process of lasting change looks like. Second, we will explore a model for assessing your current stage of readiness for change and identifying the various stages you will be visiting throughout this process. Finally, we will look at specific thoughts, feelings, and behaviours which you will witness in yourself as indicators you are in resistance to something that is going on in that moment. Remember, unless you are aware of what you are doing, you cannot change your behaviour; therefore, supporting yourself to be aware of some of your common indicators of resistance is key to moving through them and making it possible for you to change your behaviour around the use of food to cope.

■ THE PROCESS OF LASTING CHANGE

Repeated patterns are a window to your needs. For every pattern you repeat, such as: overeating, purging, or restriction, there is a need which is being met within you. Your inability to change the undesirable pattern has nothing to do with lack of willpower or discipline. The pattern is merely a symptom of a deeper problem. As we discussed earlier, if you direct your efforts only at attempting to eliminate the symptom without putting effort into understanding and dissolving its cause, you are setting yourself up for a very fatiguing and defeating battle.

Awareness is the first step in changing any behaviour, so you must first become aware that you are doing something which is detrimental to your values and life plan before you can implement a change. Resistance is often your immediate reaction to becoming aware of what you are doing and why. This makes perfect sense. You have lived your life with a certain set of behaviours and beliefs. Given this, change, even if desired on some level, often feels less like innovation and more like annihilation of your entire existence as you know it. You wonder what will be left of you, your relationships, and the life you know, when you have made the changes necessary to free yourself of this debilitating behaviour. This really means: when you are fully aware of the underlying need that led you to execute this behaviour, will you still choose the people and things you chose before? From this perspective, change can look very scary and the outcome very lonely. This is why so many of us have to hit our own personal "rock bottom" before we are ready to challenge old, harmful patterns of thoughts and behaviours. You must reach a place where you say, "I don't care what the outcome is. Just make it stop!"

And yet, questioning what life will look like when you are "done" is a wise and significant thing to do. It implies that you know you can change, and on some level you know that your current behaviour is providing you with a way of remaining in an uncomfortable situation without having to fully feel the discomfort being generated. In other words, you know that you are numbing yourself to certain aspects of your life, and, because you have chosen this approach to problems for so many years, it is a little scary to imagine being fully present and aware. You are saying that you want your life to be different, but you are fearful of how this change might appear. This sounds reasonable, from the perspective of the person who has yet to experience the benefits of the change and can only imagine the void which will remain by the removal of the old behaviour. Until you have experienced the pleasure and freedom that is created by letting go of the old pattern, you are naturally going to have some discomfort and doubt about the change.

It is human nature to seek familiarity and feel comforted by it. Often, even when the familiar behaviour is harmful to your essence and prevents you from fulfilling your dreams, you will cling to it because of the comfort provided by the familiarity. This very normal tendency in all humans is why lasting change must happen gradually. When you demand immediate and complete change, you deny yourself time to learn the lessons that the problem or situation you have created is meant to teach. And you certainly don't have a solid base or foundation in place to feel secure as you move into unfamiliar territory. This means you are likely to flounder and find yourself returning to your old familiar behaviour when things get a little challenging. This can leave you feeling defeated and hopeless.

Just think of any diet or "nutritional plan" you have tried. You no doubt discovered that your attempts to heal your relationship with food and body-image focus, prior to understanding the cause, set you up to have short-term success. Your success could last only for as long as you did not require those coping strategies, that is, as long as nothing in day-to-day life upset your apple cart! This is why, at the pinnacle of our Diet Mentality, many of us can stick to a diet or some form of restrictive behaviour for only about 12 hours! Max! You can be "good" during the day when you are busy, out and about, or in front of others, but when you get home or the chores of the day are mostly attended to, you decompress with food, and the whole cycle repeats itself. If the underlying trigger that leads you to use food to cope is unattended, you will be in trouble when something happens that you hadn't planned for, or it didn't happen the way you had hoped. The feelings and unmet needs, which naturally and appropriately get triggered in those life situations, currently drive you to restrict, binge, or purge to cope.

To be successful in changing an old coping strategy, you must have the confidence of knowing that a nurturing force is standing by, ready to catch you when you start to naturally default into those old patterns. And this force must be predominantly found within. Building a solid, nurturing, supportive, and understanding relationship with yourself can take some time, as it would with others; however, you will begin to see the immediate benefits of this stronger and more supportive internal relationship, in your awareness of what you are thinking, feeling, and needing in that moment, and in your ability to respond to those thoughts, feelings, and needs respectfully and appropriately.

With a greater sense of trust, security, and awareness of yourself rather than the impatience your Drill Sgt. was throwing your way, you will feel a sense of relief which allows you to relax and trust yourself to make life-enhancing and dignified choices around food, yourself, and others.

And know this as well: you own this process of change. It does not own you. You can take it as fast or as slow as you like, and as you have time and space for. You can look at as much "stuff" and be as aware as you want at any given time, and you can make as many changes as you wish; furthermore, you can return to your previous comforting behaviour whenever you feel the need for the old numbing peace that it brings. Soon, you will naturally find that the old, comfortable coping behaviour no longer fits. It just doesn't feel right any more. It is not who or where you want to be, nor will you really feel the need to find "security" this way. You will naturally choose not to use it, opting to engage in thoughts, feelings, and behaviours which you have had some practice with and that are coming to feel so much more respectful, natural, and "right" on a gut level than that old coping strategy ever did or ever could. You have found yourself. You have found peace.

Stages of Readiness for Change

In 1982, psychologists Prochaska and DiClemente published a model that outlines the stages of readiness for change that we all travel through when we are changing an old thought, feeling, or behavioural pattern. This model applies to recovery from the Diet Mentality, as well as: alcoholism, abusive relationships, co-dependency, depression, anxiety disorders, bad body thoughts, and any other harmful coping strategy. As you read over the stages outlined below, ask yourself to be honest about where you truly are in your readiness to change your use of food to cope. And remember, it's okay to be doubtful and to wonder if you will really be able to change this old pattern. In fact, considering how long you have likely been trying without success to get a handle on the coping strategies of food and body focus, it would be natural for you to feel some skepticism.

Knowing where you are currently in your stage of readiness to change will help greatly in ensuring that, as you approach the information and tools in this book, you do so with understanding, compassion, and a realistic expectation for yourself, given where you are in your readiness for change. I absolutely expect that, as you read through the chapters and explore the tools in this book, you will have many experiences which support you to feel safer and more prepared to change old patterns of coping, and you will naturally find yourself in the action stage before you know it! Until then, be respectful of where you truly are and what you are truly able to ask of yourself. Trust that, as you build a stronger relationship with yourself in the chapters to come, you will be able to comfortably do more.

The model of *The Stages of Readiness of Change* by Prochaska and DiClemente is as follows:

1. **Pre-contemplation**

    All change must begin here. At this stage you are not even considering change. If someone tells you that you have a problem, you may be more surprised than defensive. You are not even considering that there might be a problem or that change is possible. This is not denial: this is true unconsciousness.

2. **Contemplation**

    You are somewhat ambivalent, often communicating about the problem with a "yes, but..." approach. Part of you wants to change and part doesn't. You rock back and forth between motivations to change on one side and a desire to stay the same on the other. This is where we might find ourselves in denial: knowing there's something going on but not wanting to acknowledge the scope of it or that we might benefit from doing something about it.

3. **Determination**

    Here the seesaw balance has tipped in favor of change. This can occur suddenly, as when a major health or relationship risk is at hand. It can also occur gradually, as the scale tips further and further in favor of change. At some point the decision is made that it is time to change. *Something's* got to change. You can't go on like this. What can you do? If you take action, you move forward on the healing journey. If something prevents you from acting at this time, you will return to contemplation until something else triggers you back to determination.

4. Action

Here you are engaged in actively doing something about the problem. You choose a strategy for change, such as the tools in this book, and you pursue it! For example, this would be the point in the past at which you chose a diet or weight loss program. Old ways of experimenting with change that were unsuccessful in the long term create the necessity to look at your problem in a new and different way. Successful navigation of the action phase of change requires that, instead of seeing yourself as a failure and lacking willpower, you must be willing to accept that there are subconscious needs which are motivating your use of food when you are not hungry, and you can then begin to identify and attend to them as they arise. In other words, you must be willing to trust that there is a reason for why you do what you do—beyond what is obvious at a glance. This will provide you with the motivation to attend to your problem in a new way, even when the Drill Sgt. is in there saying, "You've tried to change this before, and you couldn't do it. Why are you bothering this time?" Trusting that there is a reason for your actions will allow you to respond respectfully to the Drill Sgt. that there is more to the issue than you had previously thought and that you had been only attending to the symptoms in the past. This time you are attending to the underlying trigger; therefore, everything is different!

5. Maintenance

This is the real challenge in all addictive behaviours. It is not difficult to stop one binge when you are frustrated and disgusted with yourself and determined to change. However, underlying triggers are not ministered to, it is difficult op binging completely when the day-to-day stresses of pile upon the mountain of unexpressed emotion and unmet needs that already exist. If food is an old, tried and true way for you to numb out to these stresses and unmet needs, it will be very difficult, when you are already stressed out, to choose a new way of coping that isn't yet proven. In order to avoid regressing to the old coping strategy in moments of distress, you must have a fulfilling and safe way of coping with these feelings and needs which allows you to stay present and work them through rather than seeking sanctuary in food. And while this is being established, you will undoubtedly and appropriately continue to seek support and distance from life through your old coping strategy. Expect this. Relax and focus on the things that you are doing which are new and are intended to bring about change to your use of food to cope.

6. **Relapse**

Relapse is a very common phenomenon in addictive behaviours. It takes time to develop the familiarity and trust required to implement new methods of coping. In a pressure situation, you will learn to use your new tool rather than reverting to your old coping strategy. Until you have the strength and trust in yourself to cope effectively in the new way, you will often utilize the coping strategy which has worked best for you in the past, even if you have a strong desire to behave differently. What is most important is that you appreciate that **relapse is a part of the healing process and not a failure or sign of inability to change**. Relapse is to be expected and welcomed, because it provides you with clear information about the situation at hand. The goal, when you experience relapse, is to use it as a tool for identifying stressors that are still challenging and for which you need to reinforce new, more healthful ways of coping. It is also an opportunity to offer yourself compassion, prove that you appreciate and accept your humanness, and that you desire to learn to respond differently to your successes and your challenges.

It is to be expected that each of us will revisit each of these stages several times before we exit the cycle permanently through maintenance. The more readily you compassionately learn from your relapses, the quicker you will find yourself experiencing stable recovery.

Make a mental note of where you perceive yourself to be at this time, and check in about this throughout your growth with this book, particularly when you notice yourself resisting a certain exercise or hearing a lot of criticism from the Drill Sgt. There is no single stage that is more correct or better than any other. They are what they are, and you are where you are. Trying to pretend that you are anywhere else will only sabotage your success. For now, in the comfort and privacy of your own internal world, let down the need to be perfect; let go of your need to have all the answers, and let yourself be exactly where you are in your process right now.

■ RESISTANCE TO CHANGE

Now let's take a look at the different ways that resistance to change might manifest itself for you. As you look at the lists below, allow yourself to consider behavioural patterns with food, with yourself and with others, and see if you can identify any patterns in terms of the kinds of situations which will trigger you to feel resistance.

Regardless of what you discover in terms of your individual indicators of resistance, it is important not to let your resistance prevent you from making the changes you desire. Having said this, we absolutely must acknowledge the trigger(s) which cause us to feel resistance, and we must determine why this might be. For example, I might feel great resistance to going out for dinner with a particular person. On the surface, I might judge myself for being anti-social or think I'm just being lazy. Perhaps, though, if I asked myself where my resistance was coming from or, in other words, what I was telling myself about dinner with this person that had triggered me to feel resistant, I would discover quite readily that this person has a habit of putting me down or making rude comments which undermine my sense of security and/or value system. In this light, no wonder I'm resistant to spending time with this person—and more power to me!

Please do not consider identifying your resistance for the sole purpose of pushing on at all costs. There is a reason why you do what you do, remember? When you notice any of the following common indicators of resistance, take time to ask yourself what it is about this situation or person which triggers the resistance, and then look—really look—at the reality of the story you are telling yourself about that person or situation. Is it true? Your thought or feeling will certainly feel real, and it is, but is it arising out of truth or out of fiction? You will know which is which, and then it is up to you to respectfully and compassionately respond either by validating your perception and taking action in this regard, or by acknowledging your fear and educating yourself on what is the truth.

We will talk much more about this in the chapters to come. For now, just make a mental note (this would indicate the determination or contemplation stages of change). Even better, make a list on paper (this would indicate a step in the action stage of change) of the forms of resistance you find yourself using most frequently. If you wish, make three separate lists:

1. Ways I demonstrate my resistance around food and body image.
2. Ways I demonstrate my resistance in relationship with myself.
3. Ways I demonstrate my resistance in relationship with others.

No doubt, you will see some crossover. Remember, the two key components to healing your use of food to cope are empathy and compassion. So, the more you understand why you might seemingly sabotage your process, the more you can respond to this behaviour with patience and compassion rather than judgement and frustration. And this means that you will actually learn and grow from these experiences rather than shutting yourself down and using food to cope all the more!

■ Non-Verbal Cues That I Am In Resistance

Your actions often show your resistance, for example:
- Changing the subject.
- Leaving the room.
- Going to the bathroom.
- Being late.
- Getting sick.
- Procrastinating by:
  a) Doing something else.
  b) Doing busywork.
  c) Wasting time.
- Looking away or out the window.
- Flipping through a magazine.
- Refusing to pay attention.
- Eating, drinking or smoking.
- Creating or ending a relationship.
- Creating breakdowns with cars, appliances or plumbing, and so forth.

■ Assumptions We Make To Sustain Our Resistance

You may assume things about others to justify your resistance. If so, you might catch yourself making statements, such as:
- It wouldn't do any good anyway.
- My husband/wife won't understand.

- I would have to change my whole personality.
- Only crazy people go to therapists.
- They couldn't help me with my problem.
- They couldn't handle my anger.
- My case is different.
- I don't want to bother them.
- It will work itself out.
- Nobody else does it.

Some Beliefs You May Hold Which Create Resistance To Change

- It's just not done.
- It's just not right.
- It's not right for me to do that.
- That wouldn't be spiritual.
- Spiritual people don't get angry.
- Men/women just don't do that.
- My family never did that.
- Love is not for me.
- That's just silly.
- It's too far to drive.
- It's too much work.
- It's too expensive.
- It will take too long.
- I don't believe in it.
- I'm not that kind of person.

Giving Your Power To Others

- God doesn't approve.
- I'm waiting for the stars to tell me it's okay.
- This isn't the right environment.
- They won't let me change.
- I don't have the right teacher/book/class/tools.
- My doctor doesn't want me to.
- I can't get time off work.
- I don't want to be under their spell.
- It's entirely their fault.

- They have to change first.
- As soon as I get _____, I'll do it.
- You/they won't understand.
- I don't want to hurt them.
- It's against my upbringing, religion, philosophy.

■ Limiting Self-Concepts

You generate and sustain resistance to change with thoughts, such as, "I am. . .
- Too old
- Too fat
- Too thin
- Too short
- Too tall
- Too lazy
- Too strong
- Too weak
- Too dumb
- Too smart
- Too poor
- Too worthless
- Too frivolous
- Too serious
- Too stuck.

Maybe it's just all too much.

■ Delaying Tactics

Your resistance often expresses itself as delaying tactics. You use excuses, such as:
- I'll do it later.
- I can't think right now.
- I don't have the time right now.
- It would take too much time away from my work.

- Yes, that's a good idea. I'll do it some other time.
- I have too many other things to do.
- I'll think about it tomorrow.
- As soon as I get through with _____.
- The time isn't right.
- It's too late or too soon.

■ Denial

This form of resistance shows up in denial of the need to do any changing:
- There is nothing wrong with me.
- I can't do anything about this problem.
- I was all right last time.
- What good would it do to change?
- If I ignore it, maybe the problem will go away.

■ Fear

By far the biggest category of resistance is fear—fear of the unknown. How many of these can you identify with?
- I'm not ready yet.
- I might fail.
- They might reject me.
- What would the neighbors think?
- I don't want to open that can of worms.
- I'm afraid to tell my husband/wife.
- I don't know enough.
- I might get hurt.
- I may have to change.
- It might cost me money.
- I would rather die or get a divorce first.
- I don't want anyone to know I have a problem.
- I'm afraid to express my feelings.
- I don't want to talk about it.

- I don't have the energy.
- Who knows where I might end up?
- I may lose my freedom.
- It's too hard to do.
- I don't have enough money now.
- I might hurt my back.
- I wouldn't be perfect.
- I might lose my friends.
- I don't trust anyone.
- It might hurt my image.
- I'm not good enough.

You may be feeling a little overwhelmed with your present awareness of the many ways you exhibit resistance. Isn't it amazing how many ways we have of getting our attention and how much we have perfected our ability to ignore those same cues? The fact that most of the items on the lists above are indicators of a contemplation stage of readiness for change need not be cause for concern, even if you had previously judged yourself at being more in the determination or action stages of readiness. Despite your desire for things to be different, this book is geared toward the aspect of yourself that is sitting on the fence. We will explore the underlying reasons for your use of food to cope, and why you would resist changing or attending to them, in such a way that you understand completely why you have done so. Through this understanding come forgiveness and compassion, followed by the freedom to change.

In other words, the purpose of this book is to walk you through the contemplation stage (and even pre-contemplation, as you explore the underlying cause of your use of food to cope), teach you how to clarify what you really want (determination stage), and then show you how to go about achieving this in a way which is lasting (action and maintenance). Consequently, if you can associate with a number of the above points, you are exactly in the right place!

Now that you have come to a greater sense of awareness of your readiness and resistance to change, you have begun to possess more empathy and compassion for yourself. You truly have taken a significant step toward healing your Diet Mentality. Let's now look at your relationship with food in more detail, see how you use it to cope, and determine what you can do to begin to implement change.

SECTION II

YOUR RELATIONSHIP WITH FOOD

This stage of our work together is centred around two key pieces of the healing journey:
1. Deepening your awareness of what is really triggering you to use food to cope.
2. Beginning to experiment with new ways of responding to these triggers.

We will be exploring fundamental concepts, for example: coping strategies, basic needs, and unfinished business. We will also explore some of the primary coping strategies you employ, including: the Diet Mentality, the Drill Sgt., post traumatic stress disorder, alexithymia, and intrusive ideation. Next, we will explore the concept of Natural Eating, what it is, and how to do it. We will conclude this section with a fundamental tool for your recovery: the *List of Stressors*. All of these pieces figure quite prominently in your use of food to cope, and they must be acknowledged, understood, and attended to in order for you to successfully challenge your use of food to cope in a lasting way.

I will be providing you with as much information as I can, as well as any tools and exercises that I believe will deepen your understanding and enhance your recovery experience. Allow yourself to remember what you have just learned about your stage of readiness for change and your cues of resistance, so that you can be aware of any assumptions, beliefs, procrastinations, and denials which may surface. You can then ask what the story is that you are telling yourself right now about that situation, person or thing. And check it out for reality versus "perceived" reality status. Remember, whatever you discover, be gentle. If you are telling yourself a story which creates resistance, there is a reason for it. Blasting your way through this resistance is only going to create a greater sense of insecurity within yourself and with this process. Thus, let it be okay for yourself to respond with dignity and respect to the messages you receive from yourself about what you need and want as you explore your use of food to cope in greater detail. Do unto you what you would do unto others.

You may also notice that, as we explore some of the pieces in this section, you occasionally feel a need for food to cope. It may seem ironic and feel a little frustrating or even inappropriate, but it's perfectly normal. It's okay. Nothing is "wrong". It simply means that we are getting close. We are triggering some needs and feelings, and this means something is happening. So let it be okay for now to use food to cope in whatever way you feel the need. I ask for your faith and trust in this process. And, I assure you, that any need to use food to cope will diminish as you proceed. For now, do your best to give yourself permission to use food to cope, and allow yourself to experiment as best you can with some of the new ways of responding to life that we will discuss in the chapters to come. Eat, restrict, purge: whatever you would normally do. And to those old coping behaviours, add some new tools. This is the gentle, nurturing, and safe way to transition from the old, harmful but familiar patterns to the new, life-enhancing thoughts and behaviours you are inviting yourself to create through your participation in this process.

So do what you need to do to care for yourself; just invite yourself to add some new thoughts and behaviours, too! Now, let's get started.

3

Fragmentation And The Drill Sgt.

Let's begin by exploring two fundamental concepts in the recovery process: Fragmentation and the Drill Sgt.

Fragmentation Versus Integration

The concept of fragmentation is an important one to explore in the recovery process because it is one of the key symptoms and coping strategies of those of us who use food to cope. When you are able to notice the symptoms of your fragmentation and in what situations you feel the need to fragment, you will be in a much better position to keep yourself in the present moment and take care of what is triggering you to separate from the essence of who you are.

What does it mean to be fragmented? It means that you have a few different personae or personalities within you which you draw upon depending on whom you are with, what you are doing, and how comfortable you are there. People who have had childhood experiences in their homes or with their peer group of judgement, ostracism, or abusive behaviour (whether verbally, emotionally, physically, sexually, or a climate of neglect) typically fragment as children. This is done to protect certain aspects of their core Self from the ridicule and potential judgement of others. The only problem is that we, who fragmented as children, never stop when we reach adulthood and say, "Okay. I'm safe now. I can stop using these different personae to hide aspects of myself from others. It's safe to be fully me, anywhere, anytime, because I can take care of me now." Instead, we are so accustomed to feeling insecure and only letting certain aspects of ourselves show that it feels normal. We never consider that there is anything wrong or that we could feel safer and happier in our relationships. As we mature, we create increasingly fragmented relationships, that is, connections with people who can only accept certain aspects of ourselves or with whom we are willing to only share small bits and pieces.

We keep building fragmented relationships where it is only safe to bring certain parts of ourselves but not all; we don't know that the relationships we are building are actually only partial or pseudo relationships and not whole, healthful ones. We don't know that there is such a thing as a relationship which can sustain and nurture the whole of who we are. Hence, we simply continue to develop our skills of fragmentation and bring only specific bits and pieces out with certain people. We feel unknown and lonely, even in a significant, long-term relationship. This serves as proof of our core belief that we are unlovable and unacceptable as we are.

We approach relationships from the perspective that we had best protect ourselves and keep those pieces hidden because, if someone really knew what makes us tick, they wouldn't like us. We feel fraudulent, phony and fake. We absolutely feel like imposters and fear that, at any time, we will be exposed for the frauds we are.

How Can You Tell If You Are Fragmented?

Consider the following question: If you were to host a party attended by all the people you consider to be friends or acquaintances, how comfortable would you be with the experience of having your work folks hanging with your friends, your friends chatting with your family, and mingling those groups with any extracurricular or other acquaintances? Does the thought make you cringe? Do you imagine that one group would have nothing in common with the other? Does it make you worry about whether *this* person may talk about something which you have kept secret from *that* person? If so, you have learned the art of fragmentation. You have learned to be one person with one group and one person with another.

As fragmenters, we might feel proud of this talent: w*e can get along with anyone* is the way we see it. Hey, that's great. You can get along with anyone. At what cost to you? What is the payoff if you must keep your Authentic Self hidden and feel that you cannot truly bring all of yourself to a relationship? What benefit is there to being friends with someone who you believe won't accept you as you are. Well, here we are running smack dab into the issue of core beliefs. On some level, if you fragment, it is because you believe that who you really are is unacceptable. You would rather have this person in your life and be inauthentic and squash your true self than have them possibly reject you. The problem with this is twofold:

First, you can only have relationships which are fairly surface. It is impossible to have deep connections with some- one when you don't bring all of yourself to the relationship, because your holding back sends them the message that you can only receive so much of *their* Authentic Self as well. So they begin to hold back too, and soon you have a stilted, surface, one-dimensional relationship which may have been, and in many cases still can be, deep and authentic and beau- tiful. Now let me add here that just because you may have a girlfriend with whom you share "everything" that's going on, it doesn't mean you truly allow yourself to be authen- tic with her. How much do you let her see your heart? Your fears? Your sadness? How free and trusting do you feel to call her on her behaviour or set boundaries? Any reservation in these areas indicates a fragmented connection and doubts of whether she would accept all of you.

Second, the key problem with choosing to be inauthentic is that you perpetuate your old core beliefs whenever you spend time with someone who you believe won't accept you if you were your true self. You are drilling this message deeper into your subconscious, which then leads you to continue to seek out connections with people who are fragmented themselves and who reinforce your belief of being unacceptable... enter the Drill Sgt.

The Inner Family

Each of us at the beginning of the recovery process feels as though there is more than one person inside of us calling the shots— the person who says, "I want food!" and the one who says, "Yeah, this is all you need. If you eat that, you will be..." (fill in the blank with one of your Drill Sgt.'s standard threats). We have become fragmented as a way of protecting ourselves and making sense of our life experiences because of stressful or traumatic experiences as a child and/or young adult. Most of us fragment into three pieces: a critical self (the Drill Sgt.); our Authentic Self (also known as our Inner Child—perfect and ready to live life to the fullest); and a Nurturing Parent who wants to comfort and care for us, inspire and support us to be the best we can be, and wants to share our innate gifts with the world. You may think that you don't have a Nurturing Parent. You do. It's just less developed and gets a lot less air time than the Drill Sgt. currently does.

What I would like you to know is that through the process of recovery, you will learn to integrate these three pieces of yourself into one, healthy, boundaried individual with high self-esteem and positive self-regard. You will go from feeling as though you have no power or control and are blown about by the wind to feeling on top of and in control of all aspects of your life. You will have the experience of feeling integrated, whole and united. As a result, you will feel strong, grounded and confident. While you may feel a degree of skepticism about this statement, could you at least allow for the *possibility* that you may be able to reach a state of integration and self-awareness which allows you to feel as if you are calling the shots and that you only choose life experiences which honour you?

Currently, you may feel as though you are working against yourself when the voice that keeps you "on track" (the Drill Sgt.) seemingly gets undone at the end of the day by your Authentic Self who says, "I don't care if I get fat. Just get me the food!" We then feel even more confused, because the Drill Sgt. kicks in and contradicts himself. After pressuring us all day not to have this or to only have so much of that, he both criticizes and supports us to use food to cope: "Well, you have ruined the day now, he says. You may as well pig out. But tomorrow..." He goes on to establish another set of rigid guidelines that are bound to be compromised simply because they are unrealistic given the fact that, at this point, you don't possess any new tools to enable you to do anything differently. You still have not addressed your need to use food to cope, nor have you attended to the underlying triggers impelling you to do so. The only possible outcome of another set of restrictive goals is to find yourself using food to cope. And around you go again.

This experience of the Drill Sgt. changing sides (on the one hand berating your use of food to cope, and on the other saying that you may as well eat as much as you want because you won't be doing this tomorrow) is clear evidence that you can override the Drill Sgt. any time you choose.

You can see from this example alone, and there are many more, that the Drill Sgt. will always try to get away with pretending that he is the one running the show, giving you his "permission" to do what you will anyway, or what you are already doing. **The truth is that you—the authentic, intuitive, inner you—are in control of your behaviour**. The Drill Sgt.'s only method for controlling you is through threats about what will happen in the future and beratement about what has occurred in the past. He's all about fear tactics, punishment, and "power over". And, of course, the Drill Sgt. will say that those past events occurred because you failed to listen to his wise counsel. If the Drill Sgt. were so powerful, always right, and always running the show through such oppressive behaviour, then why have you been able to act (use food to cope) without his consent? The Drill Sgt. can't have it both ways. Either he's in control and running the show, or he's not. And I think the evidence shows that he's not! So, who is?

The little voice that says *I want food* is coming from your Authentic Self. She's all about feeling good and being happy in the moment, and she'll do whatever is necessary to get there, even if it means sabotaging your physical health and opening yourself up to criticism from the Drill Sgt. and from others. Currently, your Authentic Self knows that the best way to feel good is to numb herself so she won't be obligated to listen further to the Drill Sgt.'s reminders of everything that's "wrong" with her and with her life.

Yes, your Authentic Self is currently all about immediate gratification and soothing the thoughts and feelings she is having now—not tomorrow, next week or any other time, but *now*! The only problem is that the majority of her feelings aren't really about what's happening in this moment, and your Drill Sgt. would have you believe that they are not "rational" or "logical". The feelings of your Authentic Self are derived from assumptions she is making. These assumptions are based on the worst-case scenarios which the Drill Sgt. is threatening are bound to happen in the future, or on past experiences that the Drill Sgt. is throwing in her face. These scenarios trigger your Authentic Self to feel frightened and overwhelmed with life and to feel very immediate in her need for food and comfort. But it isn't a *now* feeling she is soothing, with the exception of any feelings surfacing in the *now* from the nasty and threatening things the Drill Sergeant is saying.

To prove my point, check in with yourself right now. What are you feeling? Just approximate or guess at the feeling if you can't exactly put your finger on it. Does anger come close? How about sadness, joy or fear? Which one resonates with you right now? You will probably find that there is at least a little bit of anxiety or distress (what I call "the permeating level of anxiety"). This distress is constant and lies just below your current level of awareness, always reinforcing the feeling/thought that something isn't right, even if you can't put your finger on it.

Ask yourself right now, in this moment, if you are physically and emotionally safe? Or are you being threatened, judged or pressured by anyone or any outside influence—not five minutes ago or possibly in one hour, but right now. The answer will very likely be no. Okay then, why the anxiety? Why the distress? Why the level of **dis**-ease that you are feeling right now?

The answer is that your Drill Sgt. and Authentic Self live life in the past and the future—not the present moment. The past was painful and scary, and you were powerless. And on some level you felt overwhelmed by the behaviour of others. Your Authentic Self's approach to the future, as well as that of the Drill Sgt., is all about the past and trying to control every possible permutation and contingency so you won't be hurt as you once were. You don't have any control over the future; therefore, you live life in fear of the past and unknowingly put your energy into those traumatic events. Even if you never come close to having anything like this happen again, you are living your life in such a state of distress and anxiety that you are suffering as if they were happening right now, regardless of whether they ever happen again or not. This pattern of catastrophic or worst-case-scenario thinking is also called "intrusive ideation," which we will talk more about in a while.

For the record, your pattern of worrying, planning and holding on to the anxiety is definitely not protecting you or keeping you safe. It is sustaining a life of fear and suffering, and enhancing your need for food to cope. It is also keeping your controlling and verbally-abusive Drill Sgt. firmly entrenched. This undermines your self-esteem, and it limits the energy available to you that could be put to better use by moving forward in life with ease and success.

You come by this pattern of being honestly. The majority of the people on the planet live life this way. No doubt someone close to you modeled this behaviour for you and you are merely continuing to put into action what you have learned so well. You are taking steps, through reading this book, to implement a change in the constant fighting and incessant chatter within and to bring the Drill Sgt. and your Authentic Self together as an integrated whole. The way to do this is to begin to enhance your ability to understand and feel compassion for both parts. The piece within you that will be responsible for this is your Nurturing Self.

This part of you, which is so very able to love and care for others, will learn to express this love and care for herself. Clients know when they have achieved this state of integration. It is an obvious feeling within, and you begin to feel and behave differently in the world. I call it the "Cha-Ching!" You need to say it as though it's a little bell ringing, like an old time cash register opening its drawer, and then it works! "Cha-Ching!" It's a feeling of everything falling into place within; a felt sense of things coming together. And the sensation you get is one of being whole, being strong, being grounded and secure in yourself. From this place of integration, you are able to safely and comfortably share anything you want with others. You create healthful relationships where all of yourself can grow and flourish, and thoughts of settling for the old fragmented thing are nonexistent. It's far too unfulfilling and stressful to work this hard and get so little.

The tools acquired in this process of recovery from food to cope will provide you with the experience of feeling, perhaps for the first time in your life, as though you are an integrated, whole, secure person. From this place of trust and groundedness in yourself, you will no longer desire or need to use food to cope.

As we work together in the chapters to come, I will be inviting you to explore a number of different ways for speaking with and integrating your Drill Sgt. and Authentic Self. Try each of them a few times, and see which ones feel most right for you.

Now let's learn a little bit more about the characteristics of the inner family. This will assist you in our work together and provide a greater sense of and ability to identify certain Drill Sgt. thoughts, feelings, and behaviours. You will also be more readily able to connect with your Authentic Self and your Nurturing Self, and these are two key players in the journey to integration and a life that is free from food and body-image stress and strife.

The Origin Of Your Inner Family

The inner parent is the result of all the parenting you received from your parents or parental substitutes. It is the part of you which reflects the programming you received from your caregivers, as well as experiences you had with siblings, grandparents, relatives, peers, teachers and other important people in your life.

The inner parent is responsible for raising and caring for your Authentic Self. The Authentic Self is the part of you which is alive and present. It houses your feelings, and only when you are aware of and connected with the Authentic Self in the present can you fully feel your feelings and therefore fully feel alive. The Authentic Self could also be described as your intuition. Some of you may be familiar with this aspect of yourself as the Inner Child. It is the core of who you are—your essence.

Your Authentic Self is innocent, forgiving, and full of love. If your Authentic Self is being neglected or treated badly, you will feel distanced from your feelings—almost as though you are disconnected from yourself. When overwhelming situations force you to be aware of your feelings, you will feel unable to cope with the sadness, fear and loneliness which arise from your neglected Authentic Self. You will seek to distance yourself from your feelings and will turn to using coping strategies, such as, overeating or bad body thoughts to take your mind off what is truly stressing you at that time.

The Drill Sgt.

Depending on the models you had as a child for nurturing and support, you will most likely associate strongly with either a Nurturing Parent or a critical parent (the Drill Sgt.). Until we learn to integrate each of these pieces into a united whole, we will continue to feel fragmented—sometimes feeling more like the critical parent, sometimes the Authentic Self, and sometimes the Nurturing

Parent but never whole and strong. The Nurturing Parent supports us to find honouring ways to acknowledge and meet our needs. The Nurturing Parent never leads us to use food to cope. Just as when you feel truly loved and accepted by someone, you are less likely to feel the need to eat, restrict or purge.

The Drill Sgt., on the other hand, believes in the "motivation through criticism" model of support. He continuously reinforces negative thoughts and judgements and leaves our intuitive Authentic Self feeling beaten and bruised, doubting her perception of the world and her capabilities, therefore turning to food to cope. The Drill Sgt. typically exhibits the same type of non-nurturing and neglectful behaviour that key people in your past may have used to support or motivate you. Here are some examples of this behaviour:

- He is quick to judge and lecture.
- It is common for the Drill Sgt. to warn, advise and berate the Authentic Self's feelings.
- He will frequently make major decisions without asking the Authentic Self how she feels.
- He can act very irrationally and get caught up in petty, unimportant thoughts. This pattern can sometimes leave us feeling as though we are obsessive or compulsive.
- He can be very persnickety and a perfectionist.
- He can be overly critical, threatening, and frequently thinking in terms of **"should"**.
- He engages in all-or-nothing thinking. Everything is black or white, otherwise known as "concrete" thinking. The Drill Sgt. is very, very uncomfortable with ambiguity.
- In a conflict with the Authentic Self, the critical parent will overpower the Authentic Self with its position of power and authority. This is done at the expense of your Authentic Self's sense of trust in her perspective and undermines her respect for her needs.
- The Drill Sgt. will invalidate, misunderstand, and/or ignore the needs and desires of your Authentic Self. This leads to an

increased lack of security within and greater need for fragmentation and food.

- He can be abusive by being selfish, demanding, and too much of a perfectionist, which applies too much pressure to the Authentic Self. This leads to the coping strategy of procrastination. The Authentic Self is fearful of contemplating the beginning of something because of the all-or-nothing thinking of the Drill Sgt. Her experience is that nothing will ever be good enough for the Drill Sgt.

Any one of these behaviours can rob your Authentic Self of a sense of inner strength, groundedness and connection. In other words, any one of these behaviours has the potential to keep you fragmented and insecure. They steal your joy and enthusiasm for life. Imagine having three or four or five or six behaviours. What might that do to your sense of joy and zest for life?

Integrating The Drill Sgt.

It can be a challenge to be willing to trust that the voice in your head that says such harsh, demeaning things has only the best of intentions; however, my experience has absolutely shown this to be true. You will have many opportunities in our work together to prove this to yourself. The Drill Sgt.'s whole purpose in being is to *protect* you from the painful ache of feelings, such as: fear, loss, failure and rejection. He desires you to meet your needs for love and belongingness and for safety and security—those needs which were not met for you as a child. The way he seeks to protect you now is likely the way you were "supported" at the time of those initial painful experiences.

If your caregivers were unable to support you in a nurturing and accepting way, it makes sense that you would have developed the idea that it is acceptable to give yourself criticism and judgement, or neglect yourself, when you need nurturing and love. If we return to the point that the critical voice within is only seeking to support you, it becomes apparent that the method he uses to get his message of caring and concern across is ineffective. In fact, this method of "caring" does more harm than good. The intent of the message is to protect and care for you, to generate only the best for you, and to inspire you to be the best that you can be. Yet, the true intention of the Drill Sgt. is most often lost because of the harshness of the words which are used and the tone that is used to convey them.

It is difficult to stay present and hear all of a message when it is delivered in a critical fashion. You may find yourself seeking distraction in food, television, legal and/or illegal drugs, and relationships (focusing on other people) to avoid hearing this barrage. This avoidance results in the Drill Sgt. having to get louder and more critical to deliver his well-intentioned message. The end result of this pattern of inner relating is a sense of separation from your Self, lowered self-esteem, and a lack of trust in your perception of the world, your thoughts, feelings, and behaviours.

The key to doing away with this critical voice is not to banish the Drill Sgt. eternally. He is a part of you and truly does have some wonderful qualities—tenacity being one of them! The key is to teach yourself to **seek to understand the intent** of the Drill Sgt.'s message. Focus on the delivery, only for as long as you need, in order to identify that the Drill Sgt. has surfaced and is giving you a hard time. Then don't just buy in to or rebel against his message. Take some time to ask several questions of the Drill Sgt., and prove to yourself in that moment that his intention is positive. Then educate the Drill Sgt. on how to share with you more effectively. The key to integrating your Drill Sgt. (and therefore never having to hear those harmful inner messages again) is this: *never let him have the last word*. Gently seek to understand what he is really trying to say, and stay with the conversation until your Nurturing Self is able to acknowledge the true intent of the Drill Sgt.

This is done by:

- Noticing the critical message.
- Letting the Drill Sgt. know that you appreciate that his intent is good and that the way he communicated with you just now

makes it difficult for you to stay present and really hear the message.

- Invite the Drill Sgt. to share with you his intent. For example, what was his intent in calling you stupid? What is he trying to achieve by saying that?

- Then to whatever the Drill Sgt. replies, you say, "What is important about...?"

- The Drill Sgt. will tell you what he believes is important regarding the thing, situation, or trait for which you were being judged. Then you ask the same question again with the new answer from the Drill Sgt.: "And what is important about that?"

- After a few rounds of gathering information, seeking to understand, and identifying what was important to the Drill Sgt., you will come to the core of it. Initially, this usually takes anywhere from three to six rounds of *what's important?*, but after a handful of times, you will know the answer and, as soon as you hear the Drill Sgt. attempting to motivate you with criticism, you will be able to say, for example, "I know that your intention in saying this is to support me to be happy, but the way you're going about it doesn't make me feel very good about myself. Would you be willing to simply say that you don't think that choice is going to help me achieve the goals that I have for my life?"

- The Drill Sgt. will receive a message like this quite well. If he comes back at you with something, such as: "You need my style of motivation or you will just be lazy and do nothing," take a moment and repeat the process. "What is your intention in saying I will be lazy and do nothing?" And to whatever he responds, even if it is harsh and nasty, such as, "Well, then you will be a big fat pig forever!" stay grounded, trusting that beneath his nasty comment is a misguided, positive and loving intention. You say, "Okay. What's important about me not being lazy and fat forever?" Yes, I know, the answer may seem obvious. But ask it anyway. The Drill Sgt.

is so deeply ingrained right now that, if you don't have full dialogues and instead allow yourself to assume you know the answers, you are simply allowing the Drill Sgt. to have the last word, and your healing journey will take longer. Soon, if you ask him *what's important about...?* a few times, you will return to the Drill Sgt.'s affirmation that he wants you to be happy or feel safe or loved, and you can reiterate the key message of, "Thanks for the concern. If you really want me to hear this message and feel motivated to make any changes, would you please just say that you want me to be happy instead of criticizing me?"

- Now you will no longer feel attacked and angry; you will likely feel understanding and relieved that the two of you truly are on the same side. Each time you do not allow the Drill Sgt. to have the last word and instead seek to understand his intention, you are building a stronger, more integrated you. You will feel more confident and secure; more trusting of your worth and deservedness of good things. And, from this one tool alone, you will absolutely have a greatly lessened need for food to cope.

Eventually, the Drill Sgt. will become one with the Nurturing Parent as you continue to set boundaries and attend to the intent, while inviting the critical parent to learn more effective ways of sharing.

I recommend that you schedule five minutes, two times a day for the next week, to try this for yourself. Write it in your day-timer or on your calendar. Make a sticky or whatever will work to trigger you to do this. The critical voice is so deeply ingrained and so habitual, it will be difficult to hear if you don't stop and invite yourself to listen. So schedule some time to do this, and use these steps as a structure for the dialogue that will occur. You will definitely notice within a weeks' time of performing this exercise that your Nurturing Parent grows, and you are more able to be conscious of the Drill Sgt. and notice when he is "motivating through criticism". Then you are in a place of consciousness and able to invite him to change his delivery. This means that you no longer need to continue to undermine yourself, and your self-esteem can flourish. Self-actualization, here we come!

Those of you at the contemplation or determination stage of readiness for change may simply want to invite yourself to notice the Drill Sgt.'s "motivation through criticism" and just name it: "Hey, that's my Drill Sgt." This is a great start! And for those of you who are going to do the homework of a few scheduled conversations a day, this is a great little tool because you can do it anywhere, anytime. It helps to reinforce that the Drill Sgt. is not all of who you are, and *you* can have the last word rather than feeling undermined and just buying hook, line, and sinker into the Drill Sgt.'s painful message.

I guarantee that you will not be overwhelmed by the feedback of the Drill Sgt. if you stay tuned to the intent. If you feel yourself shutting down, it is because you have lost sight of the intent of the words and are taking them at face value. Just keep asking *what's important about that*? and you will stay on track.

Just so you know where you are ultimately headed, I have included some information on the Nurturing Parent here. This is the payoff for your efforts with the Drill Sgt. Please don't go all-or-nothing here and expect yourself to do this all the time right away. I truly believe that a successful start is being able to notice the Drill Sgt. a few times a day and having a dialogue with him, from the Nurturing Parent, once a day during the first week. Expect that you will build your awareness of the Drill Sgt. and your ability to come from the Nurturing Parent gradually over the next few months. This is a new skill, and it takes time to learn new things and become proficient.

Just in case it isn't abundantly clear how this homework will benefit your relationship with food, let me recap. When your Drill Sgt. isn't running the show and motivating through criticism, you will feel more confident and secure in yourself. This confidence will support you to begin to handle life situations as they arise, so stressors won't accumulate. Therefore, you won't need to turn to food to cope because you won't be feeling so overwhelmed and anxious in the first place. So, as you can see, there is great benefit to integrating and understanding the Drill Sgt.

The Nurturing Parent

Most of us at the start of our healing journey don't yet believe we have a Nurturing Parent. We may not have heard from her for a long time. She may not be all that well developed internally—this will depend completely on your role models for caregiving, and on how much you were encouraged to treat yourself with dignity and respect as a child and adolescent. Take a moment to think about how you support key people in your life when they are hurting or down. How do you motivate others and invite them to see their strengths? I am certain that at least some of the time you do this with loving kindness, and you authentically offer compassion and empathy. This is your Nurturing Self or Nurturing Parent. Most of us who use food to cope rarely allow ourselves, or even think to offer, the same gentle, compassionate nurturing to ourselves which we so naturally offer to someone else. The reason? Again, this was not modeled for us very often, and the support we offer to others is frequently coming from a place of seeking to meet needs for safety and security in the relationship, and for love, acceptance and belongingness. The love and support you will be offering to yourself will be meeting your needs for esteem. It will also meet some needs for safety and security, and love, acceptance and belongingness within, so it really is far, far more effective than looking outside for this validation.

Currently, the Drill Sgt. is most prominent, and he believes that, if you offer yourself nurturing and love as you are now, you will become complacent and settle for your present Self, which he believes is unacceptable. Why is this? Because once upon a time, you gave him the message, based on what you learned from key role models and media, that you must look a certain way to gain the approval of others. Only then could you be happy.

As long as he is stuck in his former belief that you need the external validation of others to be okay, he is going to keep beating his head and yours against the same old brick wall. The Nurturing

Parent, with her acceptance, strength and compassion, is your ticket to freedom from the tyranny of the Drill Sgt. and from food as a coping strategy. Below are some key characteristics of the Nurturing Parent. Whenever you find that you are behaving this way to yourself, take the time to really acknowledge this and to congratulate yourself. *Really*. Stop and celebrate the new and loving ways you attend to your Authentic Self.

Nothing expedites your healing process more than acknowledging the small steps you are taking to reach your ultimate goal. Don't let the Drill Sgt. have the last word here. He still believes his approach is best and will pooh-pooh anything that might undermine him. You must remind him that his approach hasn't been successful after all these years, regardless of his intention, and that it is time to try something new.

- The Nurturing Parent is the ideal outer parent internalized.
- It is patient and respectful in its listening and sharing.
- It always comes from a place of dignity and respect for the Authentic Self.
- It is an excellent teacher.
- It sets healthful examples, in terms of choices, regarding self-care and relationship with others.
- It provides a strong sense of caring and support for the Authentic Self to develop its own talents and skills.
- It has a calming and soothing voice during times of stress.
- It makes decisions, but considers the Authentic Self's needs before deciding what is right.
- It nurtures the Authentic Self when it is scared or angry, by asking what its needs are and then providing for them—not judging or criticizing them.
- It is the highly-developed, rational-thinking part of ourselves.
- It takes time to determine the consequences and ramifications of your behaviours and only acts when it feels peaceful and grounded. The Nurturing Parent never "reacts".
- It is good at making difficult decisions.

- Much of our outer communication comes from the Nurturing Parent, especially our polite or formal conversation.
- Overall, the Nurturing Parent is supportive and loving toward the Authentic Self.
- It guides and encourages the Authentic Self to explore its interests and talents.
- It provides an atmosphere of comfort, warmth, security, and safety for the Authentic Self to grow and flourish.

The ultimate role and purpose of the Nurturing Parent is to effectively love, support, and nurture the Authentic Self.

The Authentic Self

Many of you have heard of the Authentic Self. You may even have done some Authentic Self work. Depending on your success with this in the past, your Drill Sgt. may have some judgement of anything that sounds as if it might be a repeat of that "failed" attempt to heal. Keep in mind, it was the Drill Sgt. and his "motivation through criticism" that would have undermined your attempts to connect with and nurture the Authentic Self in the past. So, if there is resistance to even acknowledging that you have an Authentic Self, you may ask the Drill Sgt. the same series of questions we ran through earlier: "What is your intention in resisting this concept?" "What is important about that?" Soon you will come to a similar response, as above. You will have proven to your Nurturing Parent, your Authentic Self, and your Drill Sgt. that the message really is about your being successful in your bid to meet your needs for safety and security, love, acceptance, belongingness and, in due course, esteem and self-actualization. Then you can say, "Well, let's try this new approach to our use of food to cope because the old one isn't working all that well!" Seek to understand the intention of the Drill Sgt., and you will always come away feeling stronger, healthier, more integrated, and knowing that the situation is not all-or-nothing; there are other ways of approaching the situation that will lead to success.

The Authentic Self is the part of you which houses your feelings and your true essence. She is the real you. She is the one who is speaking when you are answering a question authentically about what you feel or what you need at any given time. It has the potential to be confident, courageous, secure and internally motivated. And she has the potential to be insecure, meek, fearful, and a procrastinator. It all depends on how much trust your Authentic Self has in her worth and her right to have what she wants—peace and happiness. This is why the communication you offer yourself internally is so important. Simply by changing the way you communicate with yourself, you alone have the power to instantly change your world. This is a lot of power, and it is definitely worth learning how it can be accessed and utilized.

The moment the restraints of your current limiting thoughts and behaviours are removed, your Authentic Self is ready to rise up and realize her full potential. She knows exactly what she wants and how to go about getting it. She just needs the freedom to act. Right now, because of the Drill Sgt. and his reinforcement of old stories about your lack of worth and deservedness, your Authentic Self is stuck feeling small and unworthy—fundamentally flawed. But trust me; she has not lost her sense of purpose!

All that your Authentic Self really needs right now to realize her full potential is a Nurturing Adult presence to protect her from the verbal barrage of the Drill Sgt. and to attend to her needs and feelings. When you begin to consistently demonstrate to your Authentic Self that you are stepping in to care for and protect her in a loving way, you will begin to build a strong sense of trust between your Authentic Self and your Nurturing Self. The Drill Sgt. will become a part of that sense of trust, as you consistently prove that his intention is positive and teach him how to support you. You will become an integrated, solid, secure individual through the process of demonstrating loving and caring for yourself. You will be living from a place of true self-esteem and be on your way to the realization of your life's purpose. I'd say that's worth a little conscious effort and some self-care. Wouldn't you?

As we go through our work together, you will discover many ways in which you currently undermine and "numb out" to your Authentic Self and her feelings and needs. You will begin to experiment with new ways of perceiving yourself. And you will learn new, self-honouring ways of responding to yourself and others in present day circumstances which would otherwise be overwhelming and lead you to use food to cope.

If you are experiencing feelings of concern, doubt, and resistance (particularly to the concept of "self-love" and "self-care"), remember that this is your Drill Sgt. who is desperate to maintain the status quo. He fears your contemplation of self-love because, to him, this is akin to complacency and means you are going to give up. From his perspective, it is an excuse to be lazy, and you are not permitted to be lazy or to rest until you have met the Drill Sgt.'s criteria for acceptability. And this is only because he really does think he knows best. What he knows is "motivation through criticism" and not motivation through love and compassion. In a nutshell, this is why you are where you are today.

So, gently invite him to allow for the possibility that there is another way to support you. Then ask him for this support and to journey with you. Reinforce that your intention is not to be rid of him or to tune him out. Your intention is to truly be the best that you can be. You will need his strength and support in order to do this, just not in his current critical and defeating way.

We will be speaking a great deal in the chapters to come about authenticity and integrity, which really means connecting with and responding to your Authentic Self. Through our work together, you will come to be very aware of what you are truly feeling and needing in any moment, and how to go about responding in a life-enhancing way to those cues from your Authentic Self. This will create a strong, integrated whole you who no longer feels any desire or need to use food to cope.

4

The Matrix

Let's explore a simple but profound model for understanding where you stand in terms of your awareness of and comfort with your experience of life as you know it. The purpose of this is to support you to have a greater awareness of any blind spots you might have about the past, present or future that may be impacting your use of food to cope.

The diagram below is called The Bennett-Hastings Process of Counselling Matrix (also known as The Matrix). It was created by two professors from my master's program at Gonzaga University in Spokane, Washington. Dr. Elisabeth Bennett and Dr. Paul Hastings created this model to provide us students with a simple way of identifying: (a) where our clients were in their process as we worked with them through a session; (b) where they spent most of their conscious time; and (c) what areas they needed to enhance in order to have a full experience of life. I love this model for its simplicity. Its obvious truth makes it easy for everyone to "get" it and to identify with immediately.

What you are seeing is what I call a model of the human experience. At any given time, you are somewhere on this Matrix. You are either more focused in the past, the present, or the future, and you

Figure 1:
THE Bennett-Hastings Process of Counseling Matrix

	Thoughts	Feelings	Behaviours
Past			
Present			
Future			

are more in your thoughts, feelings or behaviours—or a mixture of the three. In an ideal life experience, you are comfortably and securely able to navigate all possible states of being as depicted by the Matrix. Meaning, you are ideally equally comfortable thinking about past experiences and behaviours, planning for future endeavours, and feeling your feelings in the present moment.

The concept of the Matrix, if you think of it as a mental checklist, can be a great way to determine if, for example, you have a piece of work to do around comfort with thoughts or feelings about past experiences. Any judgement of past behaviours, thoughts, or feelings, or general resistance to thinking about the past, would be an indication to me, and likely to you as well, that there is a piece of healing yet to do there. Likewise, any internal criticism or condemnation of present thoughts, feelings, and behaviours is an indicator of some healing that needs to occur in the present. You may also notice a resistance to or an avoidance of any thoughts of future events. You may resist planning for retirement, getting ready for a special event, and so on, all of which would indicate that you are telling yourself a story about the future which undermines your ability to embrace it openly and fully.

You have no doubt heard much about the concept of "the now". Many fabulous books have been written about the value of being in the present moment as fully and as frequently as we can manage.1 And I am a believer of this philosophy. Living predominantly in a state of peace and contentment in the present moment is, in my belief, our natural state, which poses the question: If the peaceful experience of the present is our natural state, why the heck do so few actually experience it?

Most of us have been conditioned out of this state by the modeling we have received from key people in our lives and messages from society at large. And, even though we are now adults and can truly choose to think, feel and do anything that feels right, most of us continue to unconsciously follow the old patterns of thinking, feeling, and behaving which were modeled for us.

An exploration of the ways we might be buying into these old messages and modeling doesn't start with a look to the past and a condemnation of those key people. It starts in the present with this question: If it's possible to live in a state of peaceful contentment in the present moment, what is happening in my current life experience which prevents me from doing just this?

Don't worry if it's tough to come up with any answer other than something relating to your Diet Mentality right now, for example: my body, my weight, my obsession with food. Of course this would come to mind as the key issue which prevents you from feeling happy. It's your primary coping strategy, and it still seems like *the* problem. For now, just take my word for it that it's not!

If you are not feeling peaceful and content in the present moment, you can rest assured that you have a need which is unmet. The feeling of unrest or disease you are experiencing is a signal from your Inner Self, calling your attention to this unmet need and inviting you to take care of it. This need may manifest itself as a thought, feeling, and/or behaviour. For example, a thought, such as, I am hungry, could be drawing your attention to true physical hunger (a need for food), or it could be drawing your attention to the desire to numb out with food (a need for space or security, perhaps). Either way, if you are having this thought, you are not likely feeling peaceful and content in the present; you have an unmet need of some sort, and, until it is acknowledged and attended to, you will feel anywhere from a little unsettled to outright distressed, depending on the strength of the need.

Any thought, feeling, or behaviour that takes you out of the peaceful experience of the present moment is there to draw your attention to needs you have which are unmet. The more you remind yourself of this when you notice that you are not feeling peaceful and grounded, which I am aware will be almost all of the time for you in the early stages of recovery, the more rapidly you will come to this peaceful place as your "default setting" or natural state. You may be skeptical of this concept, or you may just have felt overwhelmed with the magnitude of the task of meeting all of your unmet needs. Either way, take a deep breath and offer yourself this reassurance:

> *You are currently engaged in a process of learning and self-discovery which will provide you with all the tools and support you need to identify what your needs are and how to meet them in a safe, respectful and dignified way. It's not imperative that you know how to do this now or tomorrow, just trust that you will learn, and you will come to a place of being able to identify what you need as each need arises and how to attend to it in a life-enhancing way. And trust me; you don't have as many unmet needs as you think you do!* (We will talk more about this soon, when we explore needs fully.)

Take a moment and consider the following:
1. Where, on the Matrix, do I spend the most time, typically?
2. Am I focused on thoughts of the future or what I'm going to be "doing" in the future, or more on what has happened in the past?
3. How much time do I spend in the present moment, and how much of this time am I conscious of not only what I'm doing but what I am thinking and feeling as well?

Make a mental note of the areas with which you would like to find yourself spending more time.

Notes:
[1]For more reading on the concept of "the now," I highly recommend any and all of the following transformative books:

Byron Katie: *Loving What Is*

Eckhart Tolle: *The Power of Now* and *A New Earth*

Don Miguel Ruiz: *The Four Agreements* and *The Mastery of Love*

5

Basic Needs

Before we take a deeper look at the concept of coping strategies and identify what your "favorites" or primary coping strategies are, it is absolutely imperative that we fully explore the concept of needs. In order to begin to offer yourself a more empathic and compassionate approach to your use of food to cope, you must be able to know, without a doubt, that there is a reason why you do what you do. This, in turn, builds a stronger more secure relationship with yourself and provides you with the confidence and strength to address life events in the moment without food as a buffer. In fact, if you do not understand on a gut level that legitimate, valid needs are behind your use of food to cope, there will be no change in your Diet Mentality. So, I guess you could say that this is a pretty important topic!

Abraham Maslow was a psychologist who, in the late 1960's, developed a model he called *The Hierarchy of Basic Human Needs*. The purpose of the model was to simply explain what Maslow was seeing in his research as a behavioural psychologist: human beings were capable of many great things, yet many humans lived most of their lives merely subsisting, just getting by, or stuck in old harmful patterns of behaviour. He wondered what prevented these people from achieving the greatness that he believed each one of us was

Abraham Maslow: Hierarchy of Basic Human Needs

Figure 2:
Abraham Maslow's Hierarchy of Basic Needs

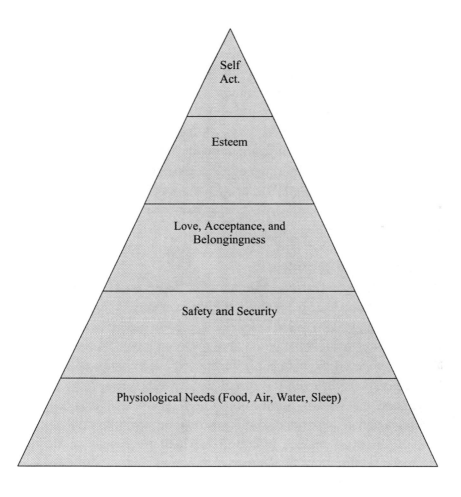

capable of. As he continued his research, he determined that there were five levels of basic human needs[1] and, most significantly, that the lower level need must be consistently met in order for the individual to be able to ascend to the attainment of the next level.

Physiological Needs

To illustrate this point, Maslow drew his model as a pyramid with the most basic physiological needs, such as, *Food, Air, Sex (reproduction) and Water* creating the base. It is clear that we humans would cease to exist as individuals and as a race if we were lacking any of those pieces for too long. Yes, this is a little drastic, but you get the point. These basic physiological needs are, therefore, the most fundamental levels of human need. In order to meet our needs for food, air, sex and water, we will compromise our self-esteem and our sense of community. The need for approval and love will take a back seat, and we will even compromise our personal safety and security.

Safety and Security

Next, Maslow spoke to the need for *Safety and Security*. When we know that our needs for food, air and water are being met consistently, we then begin to consider our needs for safety and security—first on a physical level, then on an emotional level. Those of us who have experienced the loss of our home or have experienced physical or sexual abuse, or even the threat of physical harm, have had our basic needs for security undermined by those experiences. Those of us who have had experiences of emotional or psychological abuse or have experienced neglect, will, until we heal this wound in the present, feel a lack of emotional security and question our ability to keep ourselves safe in relationship with others. This means that it will be virtually impossible for us to truly ascend to focusing on our needs for love, acceptance and belongingness—to say nothing of needs for esteem or self-actualization.

Until we attend to the underlying sense of a lack of security, whether it is an old wound or something which is happening in our present life, we will be unable to establish healthful, loving relationships; a sense of community; and a sense of positive self-regard. What can be so nasty about this state of being is that, typically, we've never known anything else, and so it feels, well... normal! Yes, feeling anxious and being harmed physically or verbally by others can feel perfectly normal. I'm not saying it feels good, but, on some very fundamental level, it feels normal, and until we have the gift of experiencing something other than harm in our relationship with others, we will continue to perceive this state of being as normal and be largely unconscious to its impact on our quality of life in the present.

A person who is stuck at this stage of their development is vulnerable to abusive relationships and to self-harming behaviours, such as, sexual promiscuity, suicide, drug and alcohol addiction, and cutting. They often experience financial difficulties. There is a sense of being anxious or on guard at all times and an anticipation of the worst-case scenario, which only serves to further enhance our lack of safety in the present and raise our anxiety level. And what do we do to cope with our uncomfortable feelings? We use our overeating or restrictive behaviours around food, among other coping strategies. So you can see how important it is to create a sense of safety in the present and to create a relationship with yourself and with the key people in your life which enhances your sense of security in the world rather than detracts from it. *Your recovery from the Diet Mentality depends on it.*

Love, Acceptance and Belongingness

Maslow then spoke to the need for *Love, Acceptance and Belongingness*. At this stage of need, we are focused on a sense of being loved and accepted by others. We are looking outside ourselves for a sense of community and for the reassurance that we are accepted and okay as we are. Imagine a child in a family where there is an expectation of perfection or where there is no demonstration of affection? This child would have a challenging time getting his needs for love, acceptance and belongingness met at home, and he would likely begin to develop some undermining beliefs about his worth and acceptability as a person. Until this child, as a child or later as an adult, finds a way to get those needs for acceptance and community met consistently, he will find himself thwarted in his attempts to build a healthful sense of self-esteem—if it even occurs to him that he is allowed to do so. This is a very dangerous place in which to be stuck. It leaves us very vulnerable to abusive relationships, self-harm, and the debilitating experience of co-dependent relationships in our misguided attempts to find someone to love us and confirm that we are okay.

The good news for those of you who are beginning to identify with needs for safety and security, and/or love, acceptance and belongingness is that, as an adult, you can meet these needs yourself. You no longer need to look outside of yourself for them, although you certainly can develop healthful relationships with others and offer each other safety and love which enhance your own sense of connectedness and security in the world. The key is that you can ascend to the level of esteem and beyond, through your own empathy and compassion. So regardless of the state of your current social scene and intimate relationship status, you are truly able to provide for yourself all the safety and love that you could ever need.

My experience of life as a child and young adult was filled with crushing blows to my self-esteem that, at the time, I just interpreted as normal life experiences. They were all I'd ever known, so why on earth would I think they weren't the same experiences which everyone else had? I grew up thinking that hitting and yelling at children and other adults was normal in a relationship. I grew up believing that sexual abuse wasn't abuse, it was normal, and it happened to everyone. I grew up believing that you can pretty much do whatever you fancy to the people you "love," as long as you don't do it in public. My sense of security in the world was so non-existent that, when I left home at the age of 15, it didn't occur to me that perhaps moving in with two twenty-five-year-old ex-cons was not the smartest thing to do. I had been taught to disregard my own feelings and needs, and to focus my life exclusively on making other people happy, particularly men. And I didn't even have a clue that what I had been taught was not the way it had to be.

I was so accustomed to feeling unsafe—to feeling this anxiety in the pit of my stomach yet still moving forward as though everything was normal—that I thought this was how life was supposed to feel. So anything which made me feel unsafe was interpreted by me at that time as normal. My training as a child taught me well that I could do, think, and feel whatever I wanted inside, just as long as I kept up the good front. You can imagine the situations I put myself in, based on the interpretation of my childhood experiences as normal relationship behaviour and anxiety as a normal state of being. There was no way I could have had a healthful relationship with this perspective on life.

Some of you will empathize with my story; some will have experienced other circumstances that, although different, were equally as undermining of your sense of safety and security, love, acceptance and belongingness. Whatever your own personal experience, it was significant. It was real, and it had an impact on you. This is where you are at: this is what matters. It is time to acknowledge this and give yourself the love, acceptance and belongingness, and the security and safety that you deserved then and that you absolutely without a doubt deserve now! As much as it pains you to acknowledge this, no one is going to do this for you. Yes, some might come close, but no one can consistently and completely meet your needs in the way you can. And believe me, as you begin to explore this concept fully and experience the feeling of attending to your needs for love and security, you will know that it is not a second-best to meet your own needs, it is *the* best. It is absolutely, fabulously, wonderful to love and respect yourself fully. Life takes on a whole new perspective when we approach it from loving and accepting ourselves, and trusting that we will keep ourselves safe.

Esteem

This brings me to the gift of the next level of basic needs. After love, acceptance and belongingness, Maslow determined that the need for e*steem* must be met. Esteem, from Maslow's perspective, spoke somewhat to how others, beyond our immediate family and community, regard us and our accomplishments. Mostly, it speaks to how we as individuals regard ourselves. What is my perception of my worth? How do I value myself?

Most of us who have been hanging out for years, however unconsciously on the level of seeking security or love and acceptance, would gladly settle for attaining a solid sense of positive self-esteem. In fact, most of us who are trapped at those lower levels wouldn't really have a clue what self-esteem is! We can catch a glimpse of it in someone who appears confident in their body: an individual whom we witness confronting someone, being authentic about their feelings, or asking directly for a need to be met. Any of those instances which we might have had the gift of witnessing will likely trigger those of us at the level of security or love to feel a yearning to have this sense of confidence for ourselves. We are at the contemplation level then—thinking about what we would like, but still often unaware of how our old patterns of thinking and behaving are impacting us. From this perspective, if we received even a sliver of what that individual has, we would feel such an enhanced sense of peace and contentment in our lives that we probably wouldn't even desire anything more. Most of us in recovery, as we find ourselves increasingly in this state of peace and security and internal acceptance of our thoughts, feelings and needs, are content to stay here for some time. And then it seems that naturally we begin to find ourselves drawn to experiences which enhance our sense of passion and fulfillment in life. This is what Maslow spoke to as self-actualization.

Self-Actualization

At the level of self-actualization, our focus is the attainment of our full potential; the realization of what it is we were meant to do in this world; the fulfillment of our life's purpose. This is self-actualization. And to whatever extent you are not experiencing this right now in your life, my goal for you is that you attain a solid sense of positive self-esteem that drives you to self-actualization and the realization of your full potential. You have a gift which you are meant to impart to the world. Our work together is about attending to these unmet needs for safety and security, and for love, acceptance and belongingness, to whatever extent they remain unmet for you, and helping you move on with living a passionate, exuberant existence for the remainder of your days!

The questions that follow, and any other exercises you will find in this book, are meant to be attended to in a way that feels right for you in this moment. Do you wish to read them and ask yourself to think about the answer? Do you want to skip them and get on to the next piece? Would you like to write both the questions and your answers down to deepen your understanding and awareness of what's inside of you? Whichever method you choose, do what feels right to you, always.

Remember the stages of readiness for change? A contemplation stage would perhaps have you reading the questions and answering them in your head or maybe skipping them altogether. An action stage would have you pulling out paper and pen, writing out your answers, and perhaps even observing yourself for the next few days to see which level of need you spent most of your time in. If this fits for you, when you notice you have a need for safety and security, or love, acceptance and belongingness, just acknowledge this. Name it. Get familiar with identifying which situations trigger you to feel that your needs for security or for acceptance are unmet. You will be using this key information soon to begin to make behavioural changes to your Diet Mentality.

Where do you think you sit on Maslow's hierarchy? Are your basic needs for health, food, safety and security being met at all times? Remember, if you are restricting yourself around food, either with quantity or what your body truly wants, you are not meeting your most basic physiological need; therefore, you are not free to experience your full potential.

- Can you think of experiences in your past when your basic needs for safety and security, and/or love, acceptance and belongingness were unmet?

- How old were you?
- What did you experience?
- What basic need(s) was/were not met at that time?
- What impact has that experience had on your feelings of safety or belonging?
- How does that sense of lacking safety or acceptance impact you in your present-day life?

The degree to which you feel your basic needs are unmet will be the degree to which you feel the need for something outside of yourself, for example, another person, alcohol, and/or food, to help you cope with life's stresses. This is why I say that a trusting relationship with yourself, one in which you feel that you can be counted on to deal with life's problems successfully and with dignity, is the most important relationship you will ever have.

When you know that you can trust yourself to look out for and meet your needs to the best of your ability at all times, you can peacefully attend to advancing yourself in all areas of your life.

Right now you may be more aware of needs for safety and security or for love and acceptance that take precedence over your need for esteem and self-actualization. This makes perfect sense. Although you no doubt have some positive regard for yourself and may even have a sincere desire to be self-actualized, you must acknowledge that your need for the more basic needs of love, acceptance, safety and security will always outweigh the higher-level needs. This is why, although you may find that you berate yourself for eating when you are not hungry or for looking as you do, you have a hard time actually changing anything in terms of your behaviour or desire for that harmful coping strategy—until now, that is!

At these times, it is of paramount importance to *gently* acknowledge your Diet Mentality thoughts or behaviours (which we'll address shortly) as coping strategies, and to *gently* remind yourself that these behaviours do not enhance your self-esteem. It is then equally important to ask yourself, "What needs are being met at this time with this behaviour or thought, and what need is it that I am seeking to meet with food?"

When you take the time to ask this question, your conscious awareness that you are seeking to meet your need for love, acceptance, or safety and security will provide you with the capacity for compassion for yourself and naturally produce a redirection of your behaviour. In essence, the simple act of acknowledging you have a need for security or acceptance, and of seeking to understand what triggered this need, naturally enhances your self-esteem. You have just taken action. And any action you take toward compassion for yourself or in understanding that there is always a reason for doing what you do will enhance your self-esteem and therefore attend to your needs for safety *and* acceptance. You gotta love it! Killing three birds with one stone!

The more conscious you become of your use of food to cope and the underlying needs you are seeking to meet with this coping strategy, the more it becomes abundantly clear, in the moment, that you will not find lasting love and security in food, and you will get much closer to fully meeting these needs if you allow yourself to look to the situation which triggered them. You can then take steps to create a greater sense of security and love in that situation. At some point in your recovery, you will find yourself initiating the old coping behaviour, and you will stop and ask yourself why you would do this. And this gentle enquiry—this conscious awareness that it is truly a *choice*—will be enough for you to find another way that feels more respectful, dignified, and mature for resolving whatever unmet need was originally triggered.

Remember earlier that I said you don't have as many unmet needs as you think you do. Now you likely see for yourself that you really only have a few. To some extent, if you are using food to cope, you have unmet needs for security, for love, and for esteem. So your list is pretty short. This makes it much, much easier for you to identify what need is feeling unmet when you find yourself using your food coping strategies.

- Take a moment and make a list of things in your life that feel overwhelming or out of control right now, such as: work, relationships, finances or health.

- Now make a list of all the things you would like to change about your life experience, past and present. (If it fits, you can even make a list of all the things you would like to change about your future, based on assumptions you have made about what it's going to look like.)
- In what situations or in what ways do you feel that you cannot count on yourself to do what is right or best for you?
- What do you believe would have to happen for the feeling of anxiety/unease that you feel within to dissipate or lessen significantly?

You can use the information just gathered in your answers to provide you with more ways of knowing when you may have unmet needs for safety or acceptance. So, for example, if you wrote down that a particular aspect of your work feels overwhelming right now and the next time you are engaged in that activity at work you feel the urge to eat or start having strong negative self-talk or bad body thoughts, you know you are using your primary coping strategies and that your needs for safety and security, and/or love, acceptance and belongingness are feeling unmet at that time. This is powerful information to have in the moment, because you can immediately ask yourself: "What would need to happen in order for me to feel peaceful and secure right now?" In essence, you are asking how you can meet your need for security and acceptance right now. But when you ask, "What needs to happen in order for me to feel more peaceful?" the answer is much clearer.

Once you know what it is that would support you to feel more peaceful and at ease in that scenario, you will either take action to make that a reality or you will not. If you don't take action, it is time to speak to a counsellor/support person who can help you to see what is preventing you from acting in support of yourself, and the can give you some tools to change those old thoughts and behaviours. We'll talk more throughout our work together about this concept of identifying needs and what to do to meet them in a way that strengthens your esteem and gets you poised and ready for self-actualization.

By offering yourself compassion, love, acceptance, security and safety to the best of your ability, you will begin to identify and attend to your unmet needs, and this will have a dramatic and immediate impact on your use of food for coping and comfort, and on your experience of the feelings of guilt and anxiety. It will deepen your connection with yourself. This will then enhance your ability to identify your needs as they arise. You will come to have absolute trust in your ability to meet your needs in ways that enhance your self-esteem. This means you will spend far more time feeling peaceful and secure in the present, and your use of the Diet Mentality as a coping strategy will become a thing of the past. Wahoo!

[1]Later in life Maslow expanded on his model, adding another level of need between Esteem and Self-Actualization which he called *Aesthetic Needs*. From Maslow's perspective, Aesthetic Needs were met by attending to creating beauty in our surroundings and in our world. You can add this level to your concept of needs as we work, if it suits you. For simplicity sake, I have chosen to omit it from our discussion.

6

Coping Strategies Defined

You have heard me talk a great deal about coping strategies. Perhaps you are already beginning to find yourself naturally referring to your Diet Mentality as a coping strategy. No worries if you are not there yet! By the time you are finished with this section, you will be.

In the following pages we will explore the formal definition of a coping strategy, why we have them, and what yours are. Then the remainder of our work together will centre on exploring ways to:

1. Use your awareness of your use of these coping strategies to deepen your relationship with yourself and enhance your trust in your ability to respond respectfully and appropriately to life's circumstances.

2. Improve your repertoire of life-enhancing coping strategies! So let's begin.

The formal definition of a coping strategy is: *any thought, feeling, or behaviour that allows you to remain in an uncomfortable situation without being aware of how uncomfortable you are.*

Coping strategies can be adaptive or maladaptive. In other words, coping strategies can be life-enhancing or they can be harmful. Most life-enhancing coping strategies can become harmful, to some extent, if we use them too much or if they are our only option! Some examples of common coping strategies which we would consider adaptive or life-enhancing would be: laughter, sleep, positive self-talk, meditation, yoga, and exercise.

Maladaptive, also known as harmful coping strategies, have the characteristic of impacting our psychological and physical health in a negative way. They can seemingly take on a life of their own, and we become dependent on them to avoid being conscious of the discomfort we are feeling in other areas of our lives. Typically, the harmful coping strategies we choose to use in our lives are the same ones that were modeled for us by key people in our childhood. You will notice, as we begin to explore more fully the definitions of the Diet Mentality and co-dependency, that you can likely identify a role model from your past who "taught" you to cope this way by modeling their own similar behaviour.

As children, we are extremely vulnerable. We are physically smaller than most others; therefore, we do not have a lot of physical power. We are also a clean slate, in terms of our understanding of how the world works and how things are supposed to look in a healthful environment. This means that we are constantly looking outside ourselves for feedback about what to think, feel, and do in order to be accepted and loved, safe and secure. Because we do not yet have an inner frame of reference to assess ourselves, we need constant external reassurance that we are okay. If something that we *are* doing is harmful to us or others, we need a gentle and understanding redirection in a way which makes it clear that it is not we who are wrong but the behaviour itself.

If the key people in our lives are not able to permit us to make mistakes and do not have the patience or time to educate us on the proper way to handle situations, we can become confused about the "right way" to proceed and become fearful of doing anything at all lest we upset or disappoint these key people. Or we may learn to go "underground"; doing what we want to do but sneaking or lying in order to do it. In either of these situations, we do not learn to develop our own sense of right and wrong, integrity, and conscience.

We are not given the chance to learn how to assess situations from the perspective of what feels right for *us*. Instead, we focus increasingly on others' feelings and needs, and on how we should behave in order to avoid upsetting them. We have been taught to believe that pleasing them, even if it feels stifling or compromising to ourselves, will create greater security in our relationship and help us to avoid punishment.

This pattern is what we call co-dependency. It is very difficult to confront, when experienced as a child or adolescent, because our primary role models expect us to behave this way and get upset when we don't; therefore, it becomes "normal" to do whatever it takes to gain external approval. For the most part, we are unaware that there is anything wrong with this pattern, except for the feeling in the pit of our stomach which we have been taught to ignore in order to avoid punishment and gain acceptance. Also, as children, our small size and dependency make it difficult to effect change in an adult who does not see their own dysfunctional behaviour.

If co-dependency is one of the coping strategies we learned as children, we must begin to change this as soon as we become conscious that we are being undermined by this harmful pattern. If we do not challenge it as adults, our co-dependency will keep us stuck on the level of needs for love, acceptance and belongingness, and it will undermine our sense of security in the world. In other words, we will likely find ourselves somewhat dependent and insecure in our relationships, and this leads to the use of food as a coping strategy when our needs for security, acceptance, esteem and self-actualization are unmet.

As children, the sense of feeling secure in our world, particularly in our home environment, is fundamental to our being able to focus on our relationship needs and subsequently our esteem needs. If we feel safe and secure, and know that we are loved and accepted just as we are, we will be free to focus on developing an authentic relationship with ourselves. Coming to a clear understanding of who we are and what we require to feel strong and peaceful in our environment is our primary goal as children, yet it is surprising how few children actually reach the age of majority with a strong sense of self-esteem.

In fact, many twenty-, thirty- and forty-somethings still feel as though they are children inside. Their co-dependent training of looking outside themselves for validation and approval has prevented them from developing a strong sense of trust and connection with themselves. As such, they feel fraudulent much of the time, as though they are acting the role of an adult, and at any moment their ruse will be uncovered—they will be exposed. This sense of being a phony creates a great deal of anxiety and distress in and of itself. Add to this the day-to-day stresses of life, and, even if nothing particularly "big" is happening that day, you may find yourself feeling quite overwhelmed and unable to cope without your primary coping strategy—the Diet Mentality and food.

The good news is that through the process of recovery which centres around building a strong, trusting relationship with yourself, you will naturally come to feel that you are an adult. In essence, you have grown into yourself. You have a right to be here and to do what feels right for you, if only because *it feels right for you.*

You may recall that in Chapter 4 we explored a model called the Matrix. In that model we looked at how our conscious experience as humans is spent either in the past, present or future. We also identified that, at any given time, we will be in our thoughts, feelings, or behaviours, or a mixture of the three. When we have unmet needs for safety and security; love, acceptance and belongingness; esteem and even self-actualization, we will attempt to meet these needs in whatever way we know. For you, this includes using food to cope, which, at the point of overeating, purging, or restricting, is a coping *behaviour.* So, what about our thoughts and feelings? What role do they play in our use of food to cope at this behavioural level?

As it turns out, our thoughts play the leading role. Our feelings are nothing more than a natural appropriate response to our unmet needs and the thoughts that they elicit. They impact us, for sure. Feeling anxious or depressed, for example, will have a dramatic impact on our thoughts, our behaviour, and on our overall quality of life in the present. It will also shade our view of the past and prevent us from seeing the future as anything but a continuation of the darkness and fear we are currently experiencing. But it was our thoughts about a certain situation which triggered us to feel depressed and anxious initially. And if our feelings naturally and appropriately flow from our thoughts, our behaviours are simply a natural if harmful reaction to our thoughts and to the feelings they create within us.

The Power Of Thought

For thousands of years many cultures have held a belief in a very powerful philosophy, the gist of which is: w*e create our thoughts, and our thoughts create our life as we know it*. Because our thoughts are our very own creation, we alone have the power to change them and therefore to change our entire experience of life as we know it.

Yes, with the act of simply choosing to believe something other than what you have believed in the past, you create an entirely new existence for yourself. For example, if you have been choosing to believe that you need others to be happy with you in order for you to be happy, and you allow yourself to believe that you no longer need anyone's approval in order to be happy, your perspective on every situation in your life will be changed instantly, as will your behaviour in those situations. You have changed your life completely, simply by allowing yourself to put your faith in a new thought rather than the old one.

I happen to know first hand that this philosophy is absolutely valid. Human beings are incredibly powerful in their ability to create whatever it is they want for themselves, once they know that they can. There was a time when I believed I had no right to my body, but everyone else did; that no one would be the slightest bit interested in anything I had to say; that I couldn't look or smile at anyone I saw on the street because they might get mad or wonder *who the hell does she think she is*? I thought that because I had a few extra pounds on my body, I was less important and deserved to be treated this way. I could go on, but you get the point. Once, I believed all of those things fully, without question; therefore, I lived my life accordingly.

Those thoughts, which I was so willing to believe, generated feelings of sadness, fear and isolation. And those feelings maintained in me a constant state of anxiety and distress. Everything was scary. From the perspective of those beliefs I was carrying, every situation had the potential for criticism, ostracism and humiliation. This made me feel even more frightened, sad and isolated. I was stuck in the pre-contemplation stage of change; I did not even know there was something wrong let alone what it was. I absolutely believed my perspective on the world was accurate, so why would I think there was anything "wrong," even though I was feeling perpetually anxious? This was my normal experience, remember? Those thoughts of being not good enough or acceptable, and the scary and sad feelings they generated, led me, from a young age, to use a variety of behaviours in an attempt to soothe myself and tune out to situations which I believed were beyond my control.

As a child I became quite attached to food and would eat whether I was hungry or not. This generated quite a lot of shame and judgement in my family and in myself, but in the moment, I only cared about feeling soothed. (My nickname in my family as a child was Miss Moo! While I now receive this as a term of endearment, it felt more like ridicule and derision at the time, which did nothing for my self-esteem.)

I also developed the coping strategy of lying. It certainly wasn't safe to be honest about what I thought or felt or needed, and it wasn't safe to come clean about what I "did". In one instance, as a child of about ten, I was beaten by my father because I spilled milk on the kitchen floor. Certainly, this was not an environment which made me feel safe being authentic or honest or even conscious!

Later in life, I became obsessed with relationships with men. I needed this relationship, and, when I got one, I was completely preoccupied with what was wrong with it and what I needed to do to make it work. I spent many years in unfulfilling and sometimes abusive relationships because I still believed that I was the problem and just needed to try harder to be acceptable. My lying behaviour continued as a penchant for exaggeration because, although I desired honesty in myself and in my relationships, I still believed that I wasn't enough on my own and that I had to enhance my stories of the day's events, or life in general, in order to measure up. Of course, this behaviour only served to make me feel anxious of being discovered and maintained the feeling of isolation and separation I felt with others.

I experimented with drugs of various natures and for many years smoked marijuana almost daily. I went through bouts of depression and had 24/7 bad body thoughts, and thoughts of suicide on numerous occasions. I shopped! Yes, even though I really had no money to speak of, I shopped to cope. If I were feeling sad and isolated or anxious, I would go to the mall and spend some money. For a moment, for the most part, I felt better. Sometimes I would feel a qualm at the time of the purchase; something inside me trying to get my attention; some hint that maybe this was not a good idea and that it might ultimately generate more stress, but I always tuned this voice out and went ahead, sometimes only because I didn't want the check-out girl to be mad at me for changing my mind! Yes, I learned to take a co-dependent stance in even the most casual and transient relationship and to put everyone else's needs first, which meant that I rarely came close to getting what Michelle really needed. Instead, I was still operating on trying to feel safe and loved by others.

I certainly was not consciously in charge of my life for those first twenty-something years. The person who happened to be in front of me at any given moment had the power to dictate what I did and said, and whether or not I was safe or accepted. This made me very vulnerable to the moods and whims of the people I came in contact with throughout the day, and it made the world feel quite overwhelming much of the time, leading me to again use my coping strategies: bad body thoughts; passive thoughts of suicide, such as, *this would be so much easier if I weren't here to deal with it*; negative self-talk; anxiety; depression; sadness; isolation; lying; co-dependency and relationship addiction; shopping; drugs; and food.

This was my life experience for the first twenty-five years (and some of those coping strategies lingered beyond that for a time). And it wasn't my behaviour which kept me stuck in this way of life, nor was it my feelings around my body. It was my thoughts. It was my belief system and the amount of trust, energy and faith I was placing in my harmful, distorted perception of how the world worked and my place in it. I could try any diet in the world, and frankly I did. I could take any drug I wanted, obsess, and try to control everyone and everything in my life, but until I attended to my thoughts and became clear on what was truth and what was bunk, I was only ever going to be able to put band-aids on my behaviours. They would always resurface with a vengeance when something happened which triggered me to feel unsafe or unloved. And because of the negative thoughts I had about my worth and acceptability, this was pretty much all the time.

You know all too well how distressing and overwhelming it can be when you observe yourself doing something you don't want to do, for example, overeating, because this action will be of no assistance to you in reaching your ultimate goal. But you can't stop yourself; you feel as though you have no control and that your life is out of your hands. You feel simultaneously comforted and soothed, in that anxious and strangely familiar way, and frustrated. You feel as if you are going crazy. You feel stuck and hopeless, and you begin to make plans for what you are going to do differently next time because this gives you a sense of power and makes you feel a little better in the moment, even though you know you are not likely to be successful then, either!

This whole scenario used to play itself out countless times a day for me at the height of my compulsive eating. Never once did I stop to think that there may be something else going on. I never once asked myself what just happened (past, present, future, thoughts, feelings, behaviours) to make me want to use food to cope. I did not have a clue that anything other than my own weakness and lack of willpower was at work. I had bought so fully into the Diet Mentality message that it is about food and you just have to change your food behaviour and everything else will be fine that I never even thought something else *could* be going on. Yes, this is the pre-contemplation stage. I was miserable, feeling hopeless and stuck. It never occurred to me that the way I was attending to the problem of compulsive eating was perhaps not effective. No, instead, I bought fully into the story that it was I who was ineffective.

After all, they had all those "before and after" shots of people for whom this diet stuff actually worked. So I *must* be the problem. In fact, when I would weigh in, the people who weighed me reinforced this belief frequently. Some would be harsh and judgemental in their tone and words: "Well you're up ¼ of a pound. What did you eat this week?" "Are you following the plan properly?" "Next week, try eating less." Others would be clearly sympathetic and try to make excuses for me: "Oh, it must be close to your period." "It can be tough at first to only choose things from the Plan." "I'll bet you had a busy week and didn't have time to plan your food choices." Their sympathetic excuses made me feel equally as bad as the judgemental ones. I was a failure, regardless of how you sliced it or how you framed it. I had failed. I had gained ¼ of a pound instead of losing the three pounds they said I could lose each week. What was wrong with me? Why couldn't I stick to a diet? Didn't I want to look good? Didn't I want to stop overeating? Absolutely! But I now understand completely that focusing on the symptom of my problem could never create anything other than distress and failure. I also realize that ¼ of a pound is not the end of the world; however, it sure seemed like it when my self-worth was hanging on what I weighed and how I looked!

I am shocked that no one at any of the myriad diet centres I attended in those years ever said anything about emotional eating. Not once. The message was always clear: "You are the problem." "This works for everyone else." "You are just not trying hard enough." I already had enough self-judgement and blame within me from the co-dependency of my childhood to sink a ship. I believed that everything that happened in my home was clearly my fault, so why wouldn't I blindly accept that this "failure" to succeed at diets was my fault too. Imagine the pain and suffering I could have saved myself if only I had known that my overeating and body focus were coping strategies: they were symptoms of deeper needs for safety and love.

Imagine if you were able to catch yourself thinking about or actually overeating, purging, or restricting, and rather than believing you are weak and can't stop this behaviour, you could say, "Oh, I'm doing the food thing." "What is the unmet need which I have right now that's making me want to use food to cope?" Imagine that! In moments, you have gone from blaming yourself for needing a coping strategy to empathy and compassion for the fact that you have a need which isn't being met, and now you are in a position to actually find a solution to the unmet need and meet it in ways which make you feel stronger and more trusting in yourself. Oh, it is really so beautiful and empowering to see yourself meeting your own needs in a life-enhancing way. This is when the world begins to take on a different perspective—and all because you have allowed yourself to put your faith in a different thought: food is not the problem!

We will be talking more about thoughts and beliefs in detail when we explore our relationship with ourselves and when we look at core beliefs and other key pieces. For now, allow yourself to consider the possibility that, although your behaviour around food seems like the most obvious "problem" and the thing that really needs to be changed, it is actually your thoughts which need to be attended to. It is your thoughts which trigger your feelings, and your feelings which trigger your behaviours. Attend to the thoughts and unmet needs which are triggering them, and voilà!—no discomfort, no need for harmful coping behaviours.

Your Drill Sgt. may be inwardly groaning and saying, "Oh no, not another book about affirmations and positive thinking; been there, done that!" Allow me to offer your Drill Sgt. some reassurance. This book is not about trying to brainwash yourself into believing good things instead of bad things. What you will find is *information*. You will be educated on what your personal coping strategies are, what triggers them, and what you can do about it. The "what" is not about replacing one coping strategy for another, that is, a positive thought for a negative thought, it is about providing enough information for you to make a decision as to whether you want to continue your former belief or whether you would like to just let it go. There is no need to replace your old truth with anything specific in the way of a mantra or new belief. It is enough that you no longer blindly follow the old way of thinking. This, in and of itself, provides you with consciousness which allows you to make new and different choices in your thoughts, feelings, and behaviours which, in turn, change your experience of life.

A Brief Look At Feelings

We will be exploring feelings in greater detail as we progress in our work together, but it is important, for a full exploration of the concept of coping strategies, for you to hear a bit about them now.

Feelings are signals from your body about what you need or want. They are not good or bad, right or wrong. They just are. You have a need which triggers a thought, and immediately a feeling arises. A spiritual leader, whom I know by the name of Ramana, refers to this pattern as "thought/feeling bundles". The thoughts arise from the sense of an unmet need, and immediately, with seemingly no space in between, a feeling is elicited, and to the extent that we are conscious of them, the feeling is felt! It is practically impossible to have a thought without a feeling attached to it. And it is not necessary to the healing process to try to separate them. What is important is that we begin to trust—to know on a gut level—that **what we are feeling has arisen from a thought which was triggered by a need**. That's all. When we absolutely know this, we no longer spin our wheels and harm ourselves by judging the feeling. Instead, we just ask ourselves, "What need do I have that is unmet right now, and what can I do about it?"

So, have I made my point? Feelings are normal, healthful, natural, appropriate responses to what you are thinking. Even if someone else may judge your feeling or emotional response as "too much," "too sensitive," "too drama queenish," and so on, your emotional response is absolutely perfect, based on your perception (thought) of the circumstance at that time. Now, it is possible that your perception is a bit skewed, as we acknowledged above, but the key point is that your reaction is never "too much". It is always exactly right for your understanding of the situation. So, remember this the next time a key person in your life judges your authentic emotional response to a situation or if you find *yourself* judging your natural and appropriate reaction to your perception of the situation. At the same time, begin to allow for the possibility that your perception may be coloured by old, distorted beliefs about how the world works and your right to peace and happiness.

At this time, while your goal is to establish a strong, healthful, trusting relationship with yourself, I beg you to err on the side of trusting what you are feeling versus trusting what others say you should be feeling. If you give yourself the benefit of the doubt rather than giving it to others, you will make great and quicker progress with this process. For even if, upon reflection, you can see that your emotional response was coloured by an old false story, you can still give yourself the experience of validating yourself in the moment and of then acknowledging that your response was appropriate, based on what you believed to be true at that time. Then you can go to this person and let them know that you felt justified in your reaction at the time, and, upon reflection, you can see that you did not have all the information. Then ask if the two of you can talk about this some more. I promise, anyone who is at all interested in having a healthful relationship with you will be eager to share what they were trying to convey, and you will hear it differently because you are no longer blinded by this old belief. We will explore this to a greater extent in our work on relationships with others. For now, err on the side of your own immediate, authentic experience, and trust that there is a reason for why you feel what you feel.

The Permeating Level of Anxiety

A key feeling which I want you to be tuning in to now (rather than a few chapters from now when we explore feelings in depth) is the Permeating Level of Anxiety (also known as the PLA).

The PLA is a constant, low-grade feeling of unease or unrest. In my own recovery experience and the past 13 years as a specialist in this field, I have never once met anyone who uses food to cope who does not also have the PLA. Now, you may have been tuning out to your feelings and your PLA for so long that it feels natural, so it may be a little slippery to identify at first. But most likely, identifying your PLA will be as simple as stopping and turning your attention within and inviting yourself to be aware of it.

The PLA is, in my opinion, a leading trigger of your use of food to cope. If you are feeling constantly uneasy but don't know why or where it's coming from, it makes sense that you would try to find something to do to take your mind off this sense of unease. We know that you use food to cope, whether you restrict, binge or purge. We then know that you must have some unmet need(s) and some undermining thought-level coping strategies which trigger you to feel the need to use food to cope.

You can prove the presence of the PLA to yourself in one hour by checking in with yourself, that is, focusing your attention around your abdomen and asking within, "What am I aware of feeling right now?" Repeat this procedure again in one hour. You will find that you are feeling anxious and that you likely would not have noticed it if you had not looked. If you choose to check in this way a few times a day over the next week, you would find that most of the time, right now, that feeling is present.

The PLA is a constant, low-grade level of distress which is ever-present within (until we heal it!) and frequently leads us to feel something is wrong, but we just can't put our finger on what, so we eat! It is what I call a blanket feeling. It covers the feelings of sadness, fear, anger and resentment: all the feelings that we believe we are not allowed to feel or that we believe are unsafe to feel. The PLA can feel a little muddy, unclear, and difficult to attach to any one specific trigger, confusing us further about what we are feeling and why. Typically, we physically sense the PLA as a case of "evil butterflies" in our tummies. Unless we actively look for it, we will only know it is there when we try to take a break from some chore or task, and, for some reason, even though we can't think of anything that is left undone or really needs to be attended to, we just can't relax. There is a sense of unease—of something being not "quite right". This is the PLA. Is it any wonder that so many of us who use food to cope have such a hard time sitting still and taking a break without television, food or drugs!? Who wants to "rest," when we are only going to be more conscious of our distress by doing so! Ah-ha! Another behavioural coping strategy has just been identified—busy-work! If you keep yourself busy, you don't have to be aware of the discomfort you are feeling.

Now, remember that feelings, including the PLA, arise in those thought-feeling bundles; hence, if you are feeling the PLA, you can rest assured that you have just had a thought which was triggered by a sense of an unmet need. The only thing is, this need could be and frequently is a past or future need. It is not necessarily anything which is actually happening in the present. So, if you have ever tried to figure out what is bothering you or leading you to use food to cope, and you have only allowed yourself to explore the present or very recent past in your search for triggers, you have very likely overlooked the two key areas which provide the greatest amount of our distress—the past and the future.

What you will discover in the weeks to come is that, most of the time, your use of food to cope is predominantly influenced by thoughts and feelings about the past or future rather than anything that is actually happening in the present. The reason this is so hard to "get" is that the present behaviour of Disordered Eating stands out like a sore thumb and seems obviously to be the problem. So we get stuck there. We focus on food and what needs to change around that, why we are so weak or bad, or what life will be like when we implement a change.

Now imagine yourself just stopping, whenever you notice yourself thinking about or actually engaging behaviourally in your food coping strategy, and saying, "This is just a coping strategy. What is the thought/feeling that I just had, and what is the need I have that triggered the thought and feeling?" What do you think would happen if you approached each use of food to cope in this manner? How much time do you think you would spend spinning your wheels and berating yourself for needing to cope? What do you think would happen to your self-esteem and quality of life when you proved to yourself that there is a reason for why you were using food to cope and that there is actually something, usually quite simple, which you can do about this need to meet it in a respectful and dignified way? I guarantee that almost immediately you will not be feeling the PLA nearly as much, and you won't be creating any unfinished business! "What's this?" you say.

Unfinished Business

The PLA is often triggered by what I call "unfinished business". Your unfinished business is comprised of your unmet needs from the past and present as well as projections about the future. Mostly, it speaks to *past* experiences which feel, well... unfinished! Most of us at the start of our recovery process have a mountain of unfinished business, such as: conversations which need to take place; relationships which have no closure; tasks left undone; and life-experiences that feel unresolved or incomplete. Most of us, when we begin coming to consciousness through recovery from Disordered Eating, have been adding to our mountain of unfinished business each day through the reinforcement of those old beliefs (thoughts) which trigger us to feel overwhelmed, anxious, and to use our behavioural coping strategies of procrastination, isolation, self-criticism, co-dependency, lying/exaggeration, food and more.

In the cycle of addiction, you have legitimate unmet needs but are unaware of them. You then use various thoughts, feelings, and behaviours to try and feel okay. But feeling okay for long is not possible when there is something legitimate that needs to be taken care of *before* you will feel peaceful and okay. This also describes the cycle of Disordered Eating. Attending to your unfinished business—those legitimate, underlying needs—has a profound impact on your entire life experience (past, present and future) and on your thoughts, feelings, and behaviours. This is a grand statement, I know. But I assure you it is true, and you will come to prove it to yourself. You see, the simple task of beginning to identify and list your unfinished business is enlightening. It would be typical and appropriate to hear yourself say, "I didn't realize this was still impacting me." Or, "Wow! No wonder I feel so stressed all the time; look at everything I'm dealing with!"

Once you have this list of the things which may be impacting you, you can begin to use the tools in this book to attend to this unfinished business. Some of your unfinished business will be specifically focused on your own behaviour and treatment of yourself. Some will be about events which occurred in relationship with others. This is why our work together is set out in three sections: (1) Your Relationship With Food; (2) Your Relationship With Yourself; and (3) Your Relationship With Others. It is my goal to create as much awareness within you as possible to determine what leads you to use food to cope and what you can do, in the present, to change this. We are going to work on identifying your unfinished business, because it creates that feeling of unease called the PLA and subsequently leads you to want to "tune out" to the present moment with food and body obsession.

Without ever having met you, one of the things I know for certain from my professional experience is that you are intelligent. People who are drawn to use food to cope are smart people. You are so smart and so intuitive that you have had to deaden almost all of your senses and inner awareness in order to be able to stay in the uncomfortable situations in your life without being aware of how uncomfortable they are making you. No doubt the intelligent being that you are is beginning to feel as if I am repeating myself a fair bit in this section. I am. And I am doing so for a very good reason.

Your Diet Mentality is so deeply ingrained that it feels as though it were a tried and true perspective on the world. Your Drill Sgt. needs to be repeatedly educated and challenged right now, or, regardless of how much you want to experience change in your Disordered Eating, you will revert to the old unconscious patterns as soon as any unmet need surfaces or any thought triggers you to feel the good old PLA! So I am inoculating you! You must be able to remember that there is another way to approach the situation of wanting to use food to cope—other than just going for it and telling yourself you will sort it out later. I've been there, done that. It does not generate any change except for an increase in our pant size or lessened self-esteem, perhaps.

No, you must be so familiar with the concept that food is just a coping strategy that, when you do notice yourself reaching for food to cope; heading to purge; disallowing yourself to eat when you are hungry or to have what you would really like, you immediately say, "Oh, I'm using the food-coping strategy. This must mean I have a need that is unmet. What's going on? What just happened (thoughts/feelings/behaviours/past/present/future) to trigger me to want to use food to cope?" Initially, you may sometimes say that to yourself and hear a voice from within reply, "Who cares, just give me the food!" Don't worry about it. It happens to the best of us and is just the resistance to change we talked about earlier. All you need to do then is to say to that voice, "It's okay. You can use your food coping strategy, *and* we are going to take some time to figure out what is going on." Most of our resistance will be attended to by simply acknowledging that it is okay to feel resistant and that you are going to let the old coping behaviour be used while you are becoming more familiar and trusting in the ability of the new behaviour to bring a lasting solution—not just a band-aid, as food provides.

Let's try an exercise. Those of you at the action stage of readiness for change can grab a pen and piece of paper (can be toilet paper, paper towel, napkin, or the real MacCoy, as long as it is something for you to write on). Now briefly, in point or bullet form, make a list of all the things which you can think of that could possibly be impacting your experience of life in this moment and/or on the whole these days. Make sure you cover all the bases: any thoughts, feelings, and/or behaviours (physical experiences) from the past, present and future. Just take a moment and make your list. Then come right back.

Those of you at the contemplation or determination stages will want to skip the actual writing part, and that's okay for now; however, do allow yourself to take a few minutes to think about the question and get your brain headed in this direction. The next time we talk about the mountain of unfinished business, you will then have a sense of how it applies specifically to you.

Okay. Now you have your list, or you have at least given it some thought. You are going to be referring to this list over the next few weeks and adding to it as you think of more things or have more experiences of unfinished business. When we explore the tool of the List of Stressors at the end of this section, you will find it is much easier to identify the things which are triggering you to use food to cope when you have a sense of the unfinished business you may be dealing with.

For now, take a moment and offer yourself some empathy and compassion. Give yourself some acknowledgement for all that you have experienced—for the load that you have been carrying in the form of those past experiences or fears about the future. If you can, now is also the perfect time to express your newfound appreciation for your strength and resiliency in the face of all that you are carrying. It may be too soon for you to have a full appreciation for this; however, if it feels at all authentic to do so, take this opportunity to acknowledge the magnitude of what you are dealing with in terms of unfinished business and that it makes sense for you to feel overwhelmed and want to tune out with food.

For those of you who are not quite ready to be so generous with yourselves or perhaps fear that offering yourself some validation and support will make you weak and complacent, it is okay. Let yourself hang on to your resistance to this self-compassion. Just let it be okay to be as resistant as you are to cutting yourself any slack at all. And read on.

7

The Coping Strategy Flow Chart

Let's explore coping strategies from a more visual perspective.

The following diagram is what I call the Coping Strategy Flow Chart.[1] You will notice that it starts at the bottom with unmet needs and flows up through thought-level coping strategies, on to feeling-level coping strategies, and finally to behavioural-level coping strategies. It can be helpful to support your newfound awareness of the concept of needs and coping strategies to have a clear understanding of why behaviours are at the top, after thoughts and feelings. To do so, let's explore this model through the concept of energy.

It is widely accepted in scientific circles that there is an energetic force around all objects in the world. You have an energetic force flowing in and around your body, as does the building you are in and the car you drive. Your thoughts, feelings, and behaviours also have energy. Consider that your unmet needs begin in your awareness as a little bubble of energy: a little nudge or inkling that stirs something in you and triggers you to have a thought.

Ideally, when you get that little inkling of energy, you will have the thought that there is a need which is unmet. Ask yourself what it may be, and take action to meet the need if required. That's all. You will notice the energy, you will identify it as meaning you have an unmet need, and you will then set to work identifying what the need is and how to meet it. No stress or judgement of yourself for having a need, or of the energy as being bad or wrong. That is the ideal, and that is what you are working toward as the ultimate outcome of this recovery process.

What is most likely to happen now is that you feel this inkling of an energy indicating your unmet need, and you judge it. Worse, you judge yourself by asking, "What is wrong with me?" "Why can't I ever be happy and peaceful?" "Why am I so needy?" And that's if you even have a sense of what *is* going on at the moment. What is even more realistic right now is that most of the time you will notice this vexing feeling and begin to delve into your coping strategy repertoire to distance yourself from it as quickly as you can.

At the thought level, you will use negative coping strategies, such as: bad body thoughts, negative self-talk (put downs and harmful core beliefs), all-or-nothing thinking, and intrusive ideation (worst-case-scenario thinking), all of which fall under the umbrella of your Drill Sgt. So, as we attend to the education and integration of your Drill Sgt., all of these thought-level coping strategies will naturally be attended to.

As I mentioned before, if the need you have is unmet at the level of thought, the energy will increase and you will find yourself experiencing a feeling. Feeling-level coping strategies, which you probably experience to some extent at this time, are: alexithmyia (a disconnect from and an inability to process feelings—more about this in a bit); depression; anxiety; anger; sadness; frustration; resentment; insecurity; overwhelm; hopelessness and despair. While you are possibly experiencing a number of these feelings most of the time right now, at this stage the feeling that you are most likely to be aware of when you check in will be the PLA.

Currently, it might seem that suddenly, apropos of nothing, you feel uneasy or uncomfortable. In reality, you have already had an inkling of a need, and you have by now made a judgement about it or about yourself for having the need. Because of your skill at tuning out to your own thoughts and feelings, you are unaware that you have already missed the signs of an unmet need at the thought level. Instead, you will assume (think), for no reason, that you are just suddenly feeling anxious. That assumption will trigger you to feel fearful. It is scary to think that, for no reason, you are feeling anxious! We have a need to understand and to be in control of what is happening, and, if we can't figure out why something is happening, we will make up a story to be able to make sense of things.

The story you have been making up and buying in to for years is that the PLA you are "suddenly" feeling, which you believe arose from nothing, is really about the fact that you are unacceptable, someone is judging you, you need to be thinner or better or smarter, or that you just can't cope like everyone else. These are your core beliefs, and you will currently default to them whenever you experience a feeling whose source you can't readily identify. And even when you can identify the source of the emotion, you will quickly find a way to make sense of the situation in such a way that it has something to do with you in a negative rather than positive way!

So you spin around and around, having a thought about the feeling you are experiencing, which triggers stronger feelings, which triggers more negative core beliefs and defeating thoughts. All of which, at this stage, will be geared toward judging and blaming yourself and not toward the identification of the need that triggered you to use those thought- and feeling-level coping strategies originally. With all the cycling around from thought to feeling to thought to feeling, is it any wonder that people frequently speak to the feeling of living in a tornado when they begin the process of recovery from disordered eating? There is a constant storm whirling within, and our patterns of coping through self-judgement and fear only serve to perpetuate this tornado. As you move through your recovery process, you will notice your tornado naturally slowing down. You will begin to notice the power you have over the tornado, how fast or slow it goes, and whether you ever experience it again.

Imagine that! You have the power to decide for yourself if you will ever again feel the PLA that has been such a constant companion. The more conscious you become about what your primary coping strategies are, the more you will be able to notice when you are wanting to use one. You will be able to consciously choose to use an old coping strategy and keep the tornado raging, or to take action toward coping in a way which slows this tornado down, ultimately eliminating it forever. The choice will truly be yours, and through the experience of realizing that you alone have the power to create your reality, you will begin to feel drawn to the new feeling of peace and enhanced self-esteem.

Until this time, you will become increasingly aware that the tornado of thoughts and feelings creates such an uncomfortable and powerful energy that, if you want to remain unconscious of the fact that you have a need which is unmet, you must desensitize yourself in a more powerful way than misleading thoughts or numbing feelings. You must use a behaviour to create greater distance from your discomfort. The behavioural coping strategies you will likely find yourself using are strategies such as: overeating; restriction; purging through exercise, laxatives or vomiting; shopping; drinking; drugs; sex; relationship addiction; co-dependency; isolation; avoidance; procrastination; sleeping (a lot); busywork; passiveness or aggressiveness; raging; blaming; and cutting.

So let's plot those primary coping strategies of thought, feeling, and behaviour on the Coping Strategy Flow Chart. Keep in mind that we are exclusively focusing on harmful coping strategies for the present, so this list will be speaking to all of the thoughts, feelings, and behaviours which harm you, if used to any extent as a consciousness blocking tool.

This list of harmful coping strategies may seem overwhelming to you (the feeling of being overwhelmed is a coping strategy in and of itself, remember?). If you do feel any sense of distress, hopelessness, despair, frustration, fear, or any other similar feeling when looking at the list and noticing how many of these patterns are alive in you, it is because you are telling yourself a story.

Your thought-level coping strategy of all-or-nothing thinking has kicked in because your needs for safety and security, love, acceptance, and belongingness feel challenged or threatened. The truth is, your security and acceptance are not really being threatened: it's just that your old, harmful beliefs about yourself have you going to a place of doubt where you question your ability to successfully change these patterns of thinking, feeling, and doing. That's okay. You have the right to be doubtful right now because you have yet to prove that you can change these patterns (which I know you can!). But please, don't let this doubt stop you from moving forward.

Chances are that if you were able to be completely truthful with yourself, you would identify with many of the coping strategies listed on this chart. Unquestionably, a few from each section would ring true for you. That's great! Your consciousness of your old coping strategies will provide you with two key benefits: (1) to employ more life-enhancing coping strategies in their place, and (2) to identify, in the moment, what is not meeting your needs. You can then take action to meet those needs so that that experience does not go underground and add to your mountain of unfinished business which, in turn, can lead to further use food to cope!

The process of recovery is dependent on: (1) your being able to notice when you are using an old coping strategy and then identifying what triggered this thought, feeling, or behaviour; and (2) what action you need to take, internally or externally, to meet the need which was triggered. That's it in a nutshell! Our work together has already helped you to understand why you might use the coping strategy of food and other coping strategies as well. By now, it has clarified how those coping strategies impact you in terms of unfinished business, the permeating level of anxiety, and the hopelessness and despair of feeling out of control and powerless to do anything about it. In the pages to come, we will look at each of the coping strategies which I have listed on the Coping Strategy Flow Chart, and we will explore ways to tune in to them, as well as ways to effect change and let them go.

Much of your work with this process over the next few months will be happening "after the fact," meaning, you will notice—sometimes days later—that you have used an old coping strategy. It really doesn't matter right now. Invite the Drill Sgt. to relax and to know

BEHAVIOURAL-LEVEL COPING STRATEGIES   **Behaviour(s)**

- Overeating; Restriction; Purging through exercise, Laxatives or Vomiting
- Shopping
- Drinking
- Drugs
- Television, Internet, Computer Games
- Sex
- Relationship Addiction
- Co-dependency
- Isolation
- Avoidance
- Procrastination
- Perfectionism
- Sleeping (a lot)
- Busywork
- Passive-aggression
- Raging
- Blaming
- Cutting

FEELING-LEVEL COPING STRATEGIES   **Feeling(s)**

- Alexithymia (disconnection from our feelings)
- Permeating Level of Anxiety
- Depression
- Anxiety
- Anger
- Sadness
- Frustration
- Resentment
- Insecurity
- Being Overwhelmed
- Hopelessness and Despair

THOUGHT-LEVEL COPING STRATEGIES   **Thought(s)**

The Drill Sgt.

- Bad Body Thoughts
- Negative Self-talk (put downs and harmful core beliefs)
- All-Or-Nothing Thinking
- Intrusive Ideation (worst- case-scenario thinking)
- Discounting, Dismissing, and Denying

Unmet Needs

- Food, Air, Water
- Safety and Security, Love, Acceptance, and Belongingness
- Esteem
- Self-Actualization

that it is unimportant that you catch the behaviour, thought, or feeling in that very moment. What is important to your recovery is that when you do identify that you have used your coping strategy, take the time to acknowledge this. It means you have unmet needs in that particular situation. Then, explore life-enhancing ways of meeting these needs and of resolving the situation.

The process of looking beneath the coping strategy and proving to yourself how truly capable you are of handling its triggers (your unmet needs) in life-enhancing ways is what leads to freedom from the coping strategy itself. This is important because, as soon as you begin to feel capable of meeting your needs in ways that maintain your respect and dignity, you will no longer choose to harm yourself with your old coping strategies. It won't be a struggle. You just won't want to engage in those old thoughts, feelings, and behaviours because you now have so many life-enhancing ways of handling situations.

If you notice yourself using any of your old coping strategies over the next while, I encourage you to cut yourself some slack. Let it be okay. For the time being, expect to tune in only after the fact of using an old coping strategy. This is normal and understandable. Remember, the key here is to look beneath your coping strategies to the underlying trigger. Your coping strategies are only signposts. They are meant to make you aware of your unmet needs in that moment. Don't spin your wheels focusing on the coping strategies themselves. Always look to the underlying need which triggered them initially.

A Coping Strategy Flow Chart Example

Let's take a look at what my coping strategy flow chart would have looked like at the start of my recovery process.

I began my recovery with a fairly sizeable mountain of unfinished business and some very nasty and undermining core beliefs, as I have mentioned earlier. Because of my limiting beliefs and the weight of the unresolved past issues I was carrying, I could not get out of bed in the morning without feeling anxious and fearful of what the day might bring. Also, I was most likely waking up feeling sick or bloated from a night of having used food to cope. Typically, once awake, I would immediately be anxious about food: what to eat; what not to eat; how much; would I be able to refrain from binging today, and so on. I would begin to feel disgusted and frustrated with my body and its various parts and their external appearance.

Then, of course, I would head to the kitchen for my breakfast, which I would usually have "too much" of according to my Drill Sgt.'s standards. Or, if I managed not to overeat at breakfast, inevitably I would be so overwhelmed with the discomfort I felt about the thoughts I was having (and was sure everyone else was having) about my body that I would use my morning coffee break as an excuse to eat something more, hungry or not: something that was usually not on my diet nor what my Drill Sgt. would consider a "good" choice. Then I would physically feel icky because I was probably overfull, and my head would kick in yet again about how ugly I looked, how fat I was, and how everyone saw this in me. Eventually, I would feel so sad and scared and stuck, so overwhelmed, that I had to distance myself from this with some behaviour.

So... yes, I'd probably eat some more! Or I would begin to judge others and focus my distress on them, maybe even blaming them or exaggerating circumstances in my head, sometimes even to others, in an attempt to make myself feel better and not be so focused on my self-loathing. And it's not even lunch time yet! Whew! I'm exhausted just thinking about this being my daily existence for so many years. The rest of the day was exactly the same, but my distress and disgust grew throughout the day as I continuously "failed" to do what my Drill Sgt. thought I should. By the time I returned home from work, I was so exhausted from the stress of my day (which was really the stress of my internal thought processes and coping strategies) that I flopped on the couch, watched television, and ate for the rest of the night even though I had told myself that morning that I would definitely go to the gym!

I really would try to keep myself as busy as I could so that I had as little time as possible to do the flopping and eating combination, but at some point, the couch would win out and the food would accompany it—no matter how hard I tried to resist. I would numb myself as much as I could with my foods of choice and with the television, and then, feeling sick and way, way too full, I would crawl into bed. Naturally, I would first have to touch my stomach, just to reinforce how incredibly fat I was and to feel just that little bit more gross and disgusted with myself. Then I would lie there, imagining what would be different the next day... Somehow, I would miraculously awake and not eat anything I wasn't "allowed" to that day; and I wouldn't continuously think about food or feel so crappy about my body. I would fantasize about losing weight and what my life would be like then, until sleep claimed me.

In reality I would awaken the next day and repeat the process almost exactly as I had the day before, feeling even more hopeless and overwhelmed. And so it went until I began to explore the possibility that there was another issue beneath my food and body focus—a larger issue—something I could actually change!

The above story, very likely a story much like yours, about my typical day as a person who used food to cope can be stated a different way. Let's look at it in terms of coping strategy thoughts, feelings, and behaviours.

For instance, I awaken and have the physical sensation of being bloated from overeating the night before. Needs for esteem (comfort/ease/health) are definitely unmet. My thought-level coping strategy of the Drill Sgt. and his critical, all-or-nothing thinking would kick in good and strong. He would say things such as: "Oh, you've gone and done it again." "You will always be fat." "You have no willpower." This will trigger feelings of fear and being overwhelmed. As I head to the kitchen, I am feeling heavy, anxious and depressed. These feelings trigger me to eat, even though I am still stuffed from eating last night. This again triggers the coping strategy of the Drill Sgt., and more critical thoughts ensue. These thoughts of how fat and ugly I am, and how everyone I see today will undoubtedly think so too, trigger me to feel disgusted and ashamed. I am fearful as I leave my house for work, anticipating judgement and rejection. So I use the coping strategies of isolation and avoidance. I sit on my own on the bus; I do not make eye contact with anyone; I do not talk to anyone.

By the time I get to work I have been cycling rapidly through the coping strategies of negative self-talk, feelings of fear and self-loathing, and the behaviours of avoidance and isolation. Once I arrive at work, I must hide those feelings and behaviours because I can't interact with co-workers or clients in a way which suggests I have any problems whatsoever. So the façade of perfectionism masks my true emotions. Rigid, all-or-nothing thinking and an ocean of self-contempt lie just beneath the veneer of the happy-go-lucky, competent, reliable employee. Keeping up the façade for any length of time is very draining. At the insistence of my Drill Sgt., I must pretend to be what I think other people would accept, or maybe even like, because I am certain they wouldn't like the real me.

After a day of cycling through negative thoughts, painful feelings, and my behavioural coping strategies of food, perfectionism, avoidance and isolation, I am bagged! I have nothing left to give anyone, and I absolutely must relieve myself from the stress I am feeling. Throughout the day I have been crammed into clothes which are uncomfortable or that draw my attention to parts of my body that I am dissatisfied with (that would be everything, with the possible exception of my hair!). As soon as I arrive home, I rush to shed the clothes of the day and throw on my sweat pants and a baggy T-shirt. Yes, I know I promised myself I would go to the gym, but I am so tired and do not want to go out again (coping strategies of the PLA, avoidance, and isolation are being used here).

I know that as soon as I sit down in front of the television, I am done for. So I use the behavioural coping strategy of busywork. (By the way, it goes without saying that the Permeating Level of Anxiety has been present from before I opened my eyes this morning). I use my food coping strategy and numb out with television, too. When my Drill Sgt. realizes I have eaten everything in front of me, I hear more criticism and feel more hopeless, depressed and anxious. On the way to bed, I experience more thought-level coping strategies of the Drill Sgt. He tells me how I have failed yet again and how I am going to have to do things differently tomorrow. My anxiety rises, as I hop into my pj's and see my stomach sticking out much farther than the Drill Sgt. believes it should (more negative body-image coping strategy). As I fall asleep, I welcome the experience of being able to fully shut out that critical voice in my head and to experience a peaceful moment, perhaps.

An entire day of my life lived in hell. Countless days lived this way. From the outside, I appear happy and "together". From the inside, I feel as though I could fall apart at any moment—my entire day being dependent on how much I ate the day before and how gross I'm feeling in my body. And never once in those days did I allow for the possibility that this experience was not normal; that it was not necessary; that I did not have to be living this way. It was just the way it was, and, until I lost weight, it would remain the same. I could not lose weight until I got control of my food, and every single day only served to prove how incapable of this I was. I was stuck, overwhelmed, paralyzed, depressed, anxious and isolated.

I did not know that what was really going on for me was that I felt unsafe from past experiences—so unlovable and unacceptable to others. This created a desperate need for safety, security, love, acceptance, and belongingness—a need that could never be filled at the rate I was going. Each of my coping strategies only served to make me feel less safe and acceptable to myself and, I thought, to others. How could I feel safe in the world when I was so full of criticism and contempt for myself? How could I feel safe in the world when I could not trust myself to ask for what I needed or to assert myself if something was happening that I didn't want or like? How could I possibly feel accepted in the world when I felt so insecure within and was constantly telling myself how unacceptable I was?

No, it wasn't the food or what I weighed that had to change. It was how incredibly unsafe I felt just being in the world. At any moment I believed that someone could just waltz right in and take over my life, and that made just stepping out my front door a scary proposition, requiring the use of some pretty heavy-duty and harmful coping strategies.

That cycle of the day of hell was doomed to repeat itself until I began to trust that I could keep myself safe, that I had worth, that I was acceptable and began to regard myself as such. Imagine what pain I could have spared myself if only I had known that each of those thoughts, feelings, and behaviours was nothing in and of itself. It was only a coping strategy, and, if I were using a coping strategy, that meant I had a legitimate need which was unmet. Imagine!

My list of coping strategies at the time I began my recovery is quite average. Most people at the beginning of their recovery process have been tuned out to themselves for so long that they, too, have established many ways of being in an uncomfortable situation without being aware of how uncomfortable they are. You will likely identify with many of the ones I have mentioned already.

Imagine the pain and distress you will spare yourself, as you begin to notice your use of a key or primary coping strategy. Instead of focusing on that use, as I did, you will say, "That is just a coping strategy. It means that I have needs which are unmet. What are they, and what can I do about it?"

The identification of your primary coping strategies is key to your recovery process, so be really clear with yourself about which ones pertain to you. This will put you in the position of being conscious that you are using a coping strategy. Then you are in the most important position of being able to identify the needs you have in that moment and how to meet them in ways which make you truly safe and accepted. You will then hold yourself in high regard.

As we move on in our work together, we will be defining and exploring these coping strategies more clearly in terms of how they might manifest themselves in your life and what you can do to let go of them permanently. Remember, letting go of a coping strategy typically requires very little focus on the coping strategy itself, except to notice that you are doing it. The actual letting go of the coping strategy occurs quite naturally. When you eliminate the mountain of unfinished business or underlying unmet needs, you will no longer feel the need to use a harmful coping strategy to get through life.

[1]If you would like a copy of the Coping Strategy Flow Chart to assist you, one can be downloaded from the CEDRIC Centre Web site at; www.cedriccentre.com/worksheets.

8

The Diet Mentality

From reading the previous chapters, you are now aware of any re-sistance that may be alive in you which might thwart your attempts at change. You are also aware of the needs you have which lead you to use food to cope and, at least to some extent, where those needs came from. You are able to acknowledge some of the experiences in your life which are unresolved and that make up your own private mountain of unfinished business. And you know that your mountain ultimately leads you to feel overwhelmed more rapidly in day-to-day situations, hence your use of food to cope. You are also tuned in to the fact that you have other coping strategies: the Drill Sgt. with his all-or-nothing thinking; the PLA; and perhaps some procrastination, avoidance or isolation, to name just a few!

Well, you have waited long enough. It is time to talk about the Diet Mentality and explore in detail what it looks like; the thoughts, feelings, and behaviours which accompany it; and how to begin to shift your primary focus from the Diet Mentality to Natural Eating.

I have a list of criteria that we share with clients at the CEDRIC Centre to assist in determining in what ways and to what extent the Diet Mentality is alive in them. This is key information, because you must know the ways in which something impacts you in order to recognize it when it surfaces. You can then acknowledge it for what it is—just a coping strategy. Then look beneath the thought, feeling, or behaviour which was triggered in that moment to the need it created. We will fully explore each of these Diet Mentality criteria in a moment. Before we do this, let's clearly define the Diet Mentality.

The Diet Mentality, ingrained in you by key people in your life, is a detrimental approach to thinking and feeling about food and your body. As a child, your primary caregivers, siblings, peers, teachers, coaches, and the media are responsible for contributing to your sense of what is acceptable and what is expected of you in society. Later in life, your significant other and co-workers take on a prominent role in your sense of how you should look, feel and be. The key message of the Diet Mentality is that as long as the outside looks together, all will be well. Your soul, your spirit, and your Authentic Self take a back seat to how you look when the Diet Mentality is your belief system. There is no room for self-acceptance, no room for peace and contentment, and certainly no room for self-compassion. From the Diet Mentality perspective, you will accept yourself, feel peaceful and content, and have compassion for yourself when you get there. Only, there is no *there*.

Those of you who have actually reached the "goal," or were once at a weight or size that you thought was the goal, can attest to the fact that even then you did not feel good enough. You may have felt better about yourself to some extent, but your thighs were too this or your stomach too that. This is the ultimate sense of hopelessness and despair: to have worked so hard and obsessed constantly to attain your goal, only to discover that you are still not acceptable to yourself and that you still feel insecure and unworthy.

When you believed so fully in the Diet Mentality and that being a different weight or size would be the answer, or at least make things a hell of a lot better, and you arrive, but things aren't all that different after all, it is devastating because you believed this *was* the answer. Furthermore, you don't know what else to do to feel better about yourself or more secure in your world. So you say, "What's the point?" And you begin to revert to old ways of self-nurturing, and soon you are having a hard time maintaining this new shape and size. You see it slipping away. You feel even greater despair: but despair is now mixed with humiliation because everyone who commented on your new size is now witnessing the reversion. And while you are not hearing any derogatory comments, you are certain everyone is noticing but just not vocalizing their thoughts. You are equally certain they are thinking that it wouldn't last. And as long as you are convinced that everyone is noticing and thinking this, they may as well be, even if they are not.

I can't tell you how many clients I have had—and this is also true of myself in my days of coping with food—who were just devastated with a one- or two-pound weight gain. They were certain it showed, that everyone was noticing, and they felt like the fattest, grossest person on the planet. Conversely, those same clients would feel much more confident and secure if they were down one or two pounds. One or two pounds! Not a big deal in the grand scheme of things. Truly, not even noticeable to anyone, but to someone who believes that their entire worth is dependent on external approval and who believes that external approval will only come when they look like a super model, one or two pounds is truly devastating.

The Diet Mentality takes us out of our Authentic Selves: out of what we are feeling, thinking and needing. Instead, it puts the power in the hands of the weight loss centre, latest diet book author, our friends, family or media. We are blown about by the wind, constantly trying the next fad that comes along in an attempt to achieve that elusive goal of the "right" weight and thereby achieving happiness at long last. Recall that the definition of a coping strategy is: *any thought, feeling or behaviour that allows you to remain in an uncomfortable situation without being aware of how uncomfortable you are*. So the Diet Mentality, when you initially bought into it, was a coping strategy that you believed would meet your needs for acceptance and security. Also, it would support you to feel good about yourself and meet your esteem needs. It is a cure-all! It is going to kill three big birds with one stone, and you never have to look beneath your surface; you can be comfortable and safe in your disconnection from your insecurity, pain and trauma. Well, who wouldn't sign up? You get the results you want, and you don't have to acknowledge or change a thing about the inner you and your needs.

The problem, of course, is that it is you and your inner needs that triggered feelings of insecurity, unacceptability, and low self-regard in the first place. Therefore, if your Authentic Self is not acknowledged and her needs are unmet, you will continue to revert to those old coping strategies to distance yourself from your inner reality—regardless of what you weigh. In fact, once you begin to give any energy and credibility to the Diet Mentality, you have begun a vicious cycle of unmet needs and escalating, negative coping strategy thoughts, feelings, and behaviours. The Diet Mentality, as you are well aware, becomes the creator of unmet needs itself, forcing you to develop further coping strategies to cope with the behaviours, thoughts, and feelings which are triggered by the use of the Diet Mentality.

Recall those studies of folks who were restricted certain foods, or quantities, and quickly became obsessed with food and began to binge at the first opportunity. This is the natural outcome of the Diet Mentality: restriction, in an attempt to be acceptable on the outside while still feeling quite unacceptable on the inside, leads to an increasingly strong sense of separation and a battle of two aspects of yourself—the Drill Sgt. and the Authentic You. This battle leads you to forced restriction sometimes and at other times to have a free-for-all, depending on who is winning the fight in that moment. The Drill Sgt., in his attempts to stop you from spiraling out of control, tightens his grip on your relationship with food and further deepens his resolve to "help" you reach that weight, regardless of the cost. This prompts the Authentic You to rebel and resist this restriction every chance you get! Welcome to Disordered Eating. This is where restriction, overeating, or purging emerge to assist you in dealing with the distress you feel at being so out of control and unable to make yourself do what you believe you must do in order to be happy—lose weight.

It is shocking that so few of us, as we are spiraling down the hole of the Diet Mentality and into Disordered Eating, ever hear a message which offers us another way of seeing the dilemma we are living. We are rarely blessed with the gift of hearing a friend, relative, or media person say, "Just work on your relationship within yourself. Trust your worth. Stop trying to change the inside by changing the outside. It is the inside that created the outside, and you must attend to the creator before you can experience lasting change with the creation." Depending on how far along you are when and if you hear a message like this, you may feel great resistance to receiving it. You may mistrust the messenger: "That is my sister. She is always competing with me and just wants me to stay fatter than her." Or, "I can't possibly stop now. It would mean that all the years I have spent trying to achieve this goal are wasted, and I can't have that." Or perhaps, "My mom and I have always dieted together. If I stopped, what would happen to our relationship?" Resistance to change. It is all resistance to change. Some need feels threatened and invokes the Drill Sgt.'s coping strategy of resistance and disregard for new ideas. Clearly, something *must* change. If diets truly did offer a solution to what is going on for you, wouldn't you be free of it by now? Haven't you tried long and hard enough? I think so.

As I share each Diet Mentality criterion, just make a mental note of the ones you now use or have used in the recent past. Or, if you are one of those book marker-uppers, make a mark beside the ones that resonate with you. The more you invite yourself to consciously examine how and where these patterns are alive in you, the easier it will be for you to catch them in your day-to-day life. This means you can acknowledge them as coping strategies more readily and begin the healing process by identifying the need which lies beneath. Also, a short version of the Diet Mentality handout is available on our Web site www.cedriccentre.com/worksheets. This can be a very helpful tool to keep on hand or put on the fridge!

Now, let's look at the ways in which you may still carry the Diet Mentality.

1. You restrict the amount of food that you are "allowed".

Regardless of what you would really like to have or how hungry you are, you permit yourself to have only a certain amount of food because that is what the diet, plan, or Drill Sgt. says is allowable at that time.

2. You label foods as good or bad—legal or illegal.

I am certainly not trying to say that a chocolate bar is as healthful for you as an apple, let's say, but I am making the point that the chocolate bar is not "bad". It is just a chocolate bar. It may not be a choice that will support your goal if you make it too many times in a short period of time. I believe the concept of "everything in moderation" is a very important aid to overcoming the Diet Mentality. And the more negative energy you have around a food while you are eating it, the more damage you do psychologically. There is research which shows that, on a physiological level, food is received and processed more effectively by our bodies when we feel positive or neutral about it than when we have judgement of the food or of ourselves for its consumption.

3. Your thoughts about having certain foods lead to negative self-thoughts and judgements.

Certain foods, which you have labeled as "bad," become loaded with energy and judgement. This judgement is passed on to you for eating these foods or for even thinking about eating them. While you gnaw on a carrot, you may judge or envy others for eating certain foods that are on your "restricted" list. You may feel as though everyone is watching you, watching what you order, or noticing the more-than-ample portion. Eating in restaurants can be torture for someone who has rampant Diet Mentality. Their worth is completely wrapped up in their body and their relationship with food, and they believe that everyone else thinks the same of them. Therefore, everyone must be watching what they have ordered and judging it in the same way they are judging themselves. This is not so.

No one really cares what you do with food, unless they have rampant Diet Mentality themselves and are equally obsessed. Trust me! A combination of my own recovery experience and 13 years specializing in this field have proven this point time and time again. The only people who care what you do with food are those who are struggling with their own obsession. Those with a natural relationship with food will not even notice or care. The public eating thing, and all the judgements we carry about it, often leads us to order something which we judge as an "acceptable" choice, although it may not be what we really wanted. This then leads us to eat something which feels like an "unacceptable" choice, when we are alone and no one is watching. You may have noticed that when you are eating with friends or family, you can't even really be present, pay attention to what they are saying, or really enjoy their company because you are so focused on food and your body. This is just a coping strategy, trying to draw your attention to the unmet needs for security and acceptance in that moment, which your Diet Mentality only serves to exacerbate.

4. You restrict eating to certain times of day—whether you are hungry or not.

There are two sides to this point. On one side, you are hungry, but it is not an acceptable mealtime from the Drill Sgt.'s Diet Mentality perspective, so you are not allowed to satisfy your hunger. It might be an hour before lunch, so you will just have to wait! Or, it might be 10:00 at night and *you are not allowed to eat after 8:00.* The point is that you do not allow yourself to respond to the body's natural signals of hunger. This only serves to make you feel a greater sense of frustration with your body (that it's feeling hungry when it's not "supposed" to), and you attempt to distance yourself further from it. This leads to a greater sense of mistrust of its cues and a disconnection from your body, and it often leads to overeating when you next allow yourself food.

The Drill Sgt. and his Diet Mentality will always tell you that you really should not be eating, unless it is a socially prescribed mealtime. It doesn't matter how little you may have eaten beforehand or how many activities you have performed that require the energy and sustenance which food provides, he operates from the outside in, and every good Diet Mentality follower knows that you only eat at certain times, and certainly not just before bed! So restriction continues to be enforced, even if just in the mind and not the behaviour. And if this is the case and you choose to override the Drill Sgt. and eat anyway, unless you do this from a place of deservedness and knowing that it is okay to take care of your body, you are going to feel as though you are doing something dishonest. You will feel as if you are being bad and lack integrity simply because you chose to nourish your body when you were hungry.

The other side of this point is the one which most overeaters enjoy: legal binging! This means you are not at all hungry but, hey, it's lunch time! Yeah! The Drill Sgt. can't complain about you eating, because it is legally mealtime. As long as you make what the Drill Sgt. considers a half-decent choice, you do not have to hear much criticism at all from within. Also, no one on the outside will think anything of you eating at lunch time. This, of course, works equally as well for breakfast, coffee break, afternoon snack and dinner—even an after-dinner snack! It is all legal, as long as other people are doing it! The problem is that, once again, you are not eating in response to your body's natural cues of hunger and fullness. You are responding to external cues about when you "should" be hungry or when it is "socially acceptable" to be hungry. There is a definite sense of freedom that we feel when the Drill Sgt. has no leg to stand on and we can "get away" with eating, even when we are not hungry. Aren't we sneaky? Mind you, the only person we are really impacting with our cleverness is ourselves. And every time we choose to eat when we are not hungry just because we can, or we choose not to eat because it is not "the right time," we are only playing further into the Diet Mentality and driving ourselves farther away from our true selves.

5. You engage in all-or-nothing thinking.

I could write a separate book just on the discussion of all-or-nothing thinking, and I probably will, one day. It has already been mentioned a handful of times in this book, and you will hear much more about it as we go along. If you use food to cope, it is everywhere within. I guarantee it. It is one of the main reasons why you initially turned to food to cope. That sense of all-encompassing despair and a total belief in your unacceptability turned you away from your feelings and needs within, and it gave you the all-or-nothing message that you could "never" be happy unless you looked a certain way or had a certain person's approval. That thought took root because there was no sense of connection or groundedness; no consciousness within to hear the thought and say, "Wait a sec. That sounds a little extreme."

No, what happened then, and what happens countless times a day within yourself now, is that you have a need for security or love, and you don't know how to meet it because you have not had anyone model this for you. If all-or-nothing thinking is a pattern for you, your process may look something like this: you know something isn't feeling right; you may even be able to identify what it is that isn't working and the need that you have. For example, someone seems angry with you, and you have a need for reassurance/acceptance and security in the relationship. You then have the immediate and barely conscious thought that you don't know how to meet this need. This thought triggers a sense of overwhelm and despair, which in turn triggers the all-or-nothing thought that you are *never* going to be able to meet this need. (Just because you don't know how to meet that need in that moment does not mean that you can't learn how or that you will "never" be able to meet it.) This all-or-nothing thought triggers a greater sense of despair and hopelessness, and you turn to a behaviour such as food, isolation, avoidance, or procrastination to help you cope with this despair, never knowing that what you are really trying to cope with, what is really going on, is that unmet need.

In this circumstance you are now so far removed from your initial, triggering need that you would be hard pressed to say what it was. You are probably only conscious of the PLA, if you look for it, and of the times when you are overeating or performing some behaviour that you have judgement of, for example, eating or procrastinating. The Drill Sgt. and his all-or-nothing thinking have become such constant companions that, for the most part, you don't even notice when they are there, shutting down any possibility of growth and change, and driving your old coping behaviours.

A great way to start tuning in to the all-or-nothing thinking in you is to just stop and observe yourself every once in a while. I guarantee that, if you are feeling frustrated, rushed, pressured, annoyed, irritated, overwhelmed, hopeless, depressed, anxious or desperate, you are telling yourself that something must be a certain way—that *something should* be different, or that *you* should be different. Just ask this question of yourself: "What *is* it that I am telling myself must be or go a certain way?" Self-imposed deadlines and expectations are the most common example of this. You will find, as you check in, that you are rushing about like mad, feeling annoyed and resentful of others because you have told yourself that something must be done in such a way by a certain time. Does it really? Really? No, not really. You would like it if it were. But that is very different from the story which had you rushing about and feeling annoyed with others (especially those who were not rushing about as you were).

Your story was that it was *imperative*. You *must* get that thing done by that time or... or what? What is the need that would be unmet? Most likely, it was the need for approval. In some cases, perhaps it even seemed as if the need for safety and security would be unmet if you didn't get that thing done by your self-imposed or even some externally-imposed time line. Now *that* is a different story.

Imagine this. Let's say your house is a pig sty, and someone is coming to visit. You have a need for approval, even for cleanliness and order, maybe for peace and relaxation, all of which depend on your tidying up the house, or so it seems. Your Drill Sgt. will zero in on those needs and tell you the house must be spotless from top to bottom, ready for the white glove inspection before they arrive and before you can even think about relaxing. These Drill Sgt., all-or-nothing thoughts trigger you to feel pressured, rushed, stressed, anxious, annoyed and frustrated with the mess *and* the people who created it. And if you live on your own and the mess was your creation, you will be annoyed at the people who are coming over, even though they never asked or expected you to clean like a mad woman. If you were to stop and check in, notice the pressure sensation or the PLA, and ask what it is that you are being all-or-nothing about right now, you would soon discover that you are telling yourself the house must be spotless in one hour or else!

You realize this is your Drill Sgt. and his all-or-nothing thinking, and you say: "That's just a coping strategy." "What are the needs I have that triggered me to use my all-or-nothing thinking?" You identify the needs for approval, order and peace, and ask yourself: "Is there any other way which isn't all-or-nothing that could meet my needs?" Guess what? There are many. For starters, you could offer yourself some approval unrelated to the state of your house; just general approval and acceptance for all the things you are. Then you could allow yourself to pick a few key areas which you would like to tidy and get started, giving yourself permission to have some areas which will be unattended. No doubt, as you are cleaning, you would rather be peaceful and relaxed than have your peace depend on what your guests think of the state of your home!

All-or-nothing thinking also manifests itself in the focus you place on food and weight. Can you remember the despair you have felt over a weight gain of one or two pounds? It is not the one or two pounds that did it—they are nothing really—it is the all-or-nothing story you told yourself about what those one or two pounds mean that has you so depressed. Stories such as: "You will always be fat." "You will always be unhappy with your body." "You will never be able to stick to a diet." "You have absolutely no willpower." "You are lazy." "Your weight is going up and up, so you may as well just give in and get really fat." "They will never really accept you until you weigh X." Who does that sound like? Your Drill Sgt., perhaps? There is definitely some all-or-nothing coping strategy going on here.

You have yourself over a barrel with this train of thought. From this perspective, any time you set a goal for yourself and you don't meet it exactly when and how you believe you should, you are going to hear about it from the Drill Sgt. You are doomed to experience the feelings of depression, anxiety, and hopelessness that accompany his all-or-nothing prophecies. It's sad to realize those Drill Sgt. thoughts really are your own creation based on your interpretation of the behaviours of key adults and peers when you were a child. Your interpretation of events at that time was fundamentally skewed for two key reasons:

1. You were a child and had no frame of reference for other people's behaviour, except in relation to you. Meaning, as a child, everything, at least in our minds, revolved around us.

2. Your frontal lobes, the areas of our brain which are responsible for rational thought, were not fully developed. In fact, we are typically into our twenties before that part of our brain is complete. So your ability to understand and make clear sense of what was happening around you was limited by your biology.

But no one tells us this when we are children. And no one sits us down early in our twenties, when we could really understand it better, and says, "By the way, all those things that happened when you were a kid—all those things that you think had anything to do with you being lovable or worthwhile—had nothing to do with you. It was just that your brain could only make sense of things in relation to you, so it became about *you* somehow, but you can let that go now, and know that it was *not* about you and that you are worthwhile! You are lovable! Now go forth with this thought and let the old one go."

You can imagine the relief and freedom we would experience if we really allowed ourselves to receive this thought; if we let ourselves trust it; if we witnessed that person's behaviour now, modeling their statement that we are lovable, we are worthwhile. What a shift this would produce in our sense of Self. This is because, externally, our needs for love, acceptance, and belongingness would finally be met. We could then focus, from a place of security and love, on our own esteem and on reaching our full potential. Instead, most of the time, the people whose behaviour has brought us to the place of feeling "less than" and doubting our acceptability are not aware that they are responsible. Their behaviour was perfectly acceptable to them, and they aren't even thinking it may have hurt us, or, if they are, they lack the self-esteem and ego strength to take responsibility. Instead, they go on treating us just the same, which only serves to reinforce our Drill Sgt.'s belief that we truly are unlovable or unacceptable; that something about us must change before anyone will truly love us and we can justly feel "secure".

All-or-nothing thinking is very harmful on every level. As soon as you have told yourself that something has to be a certain way, you have shut yourself down to any other possibilities or outcomes, and this makes you extremely vulnerable to life and all the twists and turns it naturally takes. There is much more on the all-or-nothing thinking in the chapters to come, so if this resonates with you at all, stay tuned.

6. Future Focus

The Diet Mentality is all about the future. The Drill Sgt. is only interested in what you have done that wasn't good enough and what you are going to do to make it better—to redeem yourself, so to speak. So your goal setting and your thoughts about life in general will be centered around what you are going to do in the minutes, hours, days and months to come that will finally make you an acceptable human being, bringing you all that you desire and deserve. As we discussed when we looked at The Matrix, the only place where you can truly effect change in your behaviour, thoughts, and feelings is in the present. If you are not conscious of what you are doing, thinking, and feeling, the moment will pass you by, and it will become another of those past experiences for which you are criticized by the Drill Sgt. In the Diet Mentality, you are all about that future fantasy of what you are going to do; how you are going to feel; how you are going to look; what life will be like when... The obvious problem is that, if you are out there fantasizing about the future, there is no one home to actually take action in the moment and change the patterns that keep you from realizing those goals.

Some of that future focus exists in you because it is just too painful right now to be in the present moment. You have the Drill Sgt. on your case constantly; you have memories of past pain and hurt that have yet to be healed and moved through; you also have the day-to-day chores and responsibilities of life with their own trials and tribulations that, on top of the mountain of unfinished business, make the present moment a bit of a drag to say the least. Who wants to hang out here? Clearly, some part of you does. Some part of you knows, on a gut level, that gently challenging yourself to be present and identifying what is really going on for you is the only way which will enable you to really change those old thoughts, feelings, and behaviors that keep you stuck. And some part of you believes that *you can*, or you would not have picked up this book. By gently challenging your Drill Sgt., with his all-or-nothing thinking, and encouraging him to support your attempts to create lasting change (to focus on the things you are doing differently), you will make it safer every day to be in the present moment, and you will begin to see how truly capable and powerful you are to create the life you desire.

For now, it is a great start to check in every so often, and, in addition to the PLA and all-or-nothing thinking that you are looking for, see if your thoughts were in the past, the present or the future. Then, just tenderly invite yourself to be in the present moment and to take whatever action you can to meet whatever needs are currently unmet. You won't have to work hard to find the PLA, all-or-nothing thinking, and future focus. They are ever-present at the start of this process; they go hand in hand, so typically, if one is there, they are all there. This makes them much easier to find and let go, because you don't have to work on three separate pieces. You just notice that they are there, and ask yourself this: "What is the need I have which triggered me to use those coping strategies right now?" Now you are in the present and are in problem-solving mode, not problem-enhancing mode! You are in the driver's seat, and you will feel the difference energetically.

At the CEDRIC Centre I frequently notice that our clients rapidly discover their own strength and ability to change old patterns and then spend a considerable amount of time resisting actually doing it! They try a tool once, and it works like a hot damn. They freak themselves out with their power and their competency. It flies directly in the face of their deep-seated core beliefs that they are stupid, incapable, undeserving, unacceptable and not good enough. So, for a period of time, while they wrestle with the part of them which thinks that these beliefs keep them safe, they resist using the new tools they know will work to bring them into the present, feeling confident and secure. I have found that the length of time a person spends resisting their newfound awareness of their own strength and efficacy is directly proportional to their level of self-esteem at the time they begin this process. It depends on how deeply that individual has bought into the harmful core beliefs of their childhood, and on how long they have been living as if those beliefs will directly impact the length of their recovery process. This is why it is so wonderful for me to work with a client who is fed up with their life as it is. They don't care if they have to turn into a pumpkin, they just want the old mindset and behaviours gone! I love working with these clients, because that degree of frustration produces a person at the action stage of readiness for change, and this is when things really get moving.

For those of you who are wondering whether your process may be slowed exponentially by your own fear of letting go of those old beliefs, let me say this: the time difference in a recovery process for someone who is so fed up that they are ready to do anything (they actively do use the tools), versus someone who isn't quite there yet and frightens themselves a bit with the ease of some of these processes, is typically a matter of months. It is not a big chunk of time in the grand scheme of things or considering how long they have been engaging in this behavior. So don't worry. Let go of the all-or-nothing thinking which just crept in. Tell your Drill Sgt. to relax; you will be fine. You will get there. Acknowledge the mixture of needs for security, for acceptance, for esteem and maybe even self-actualization which were stirred up just a moment ago. Just allow yourself to have that all-or-nothing thought, "I'll never get this." Or perhaps, "Well, she said a couple of months, so I should have this down pat by Christmas!" Let it go, let it go, let it go. Relax. Breathe. Yes, breathe. Just stop and breathe deeply for a moment. Notice the sensations in your body that were created by that little sojourn into all-or-nothing thinking and its nasty big brother, intrusive ideation (worst-case-scenario thinking). Just calm down! Don't be in such a rush. You can't live in the future.

The present moment is where your life is being lived, whether you are conscious of it or not. So, just tune in to your tummy. What do you notice there? Any PLA? If so, ask yourself what need you have which may have triggered this coping strategy. There's no need for any action right now; you are just seeking information. How challenging is it for you to keep yourself in this moment? How split are your thoughts? How many of those encroaching thoughts are all-or-nothing? Is there any of that pressure sensation or any of the emotions of anxiety, depression, despair, hopelessness or resentment? If so, all-or-nothing thinking is present. It is not essential that you figure out what triggered the all-or-nothing thinking. You can just acknowledge that you are using a coping strategy and ask what needs are foremost right now. Sometimes, though, the need has been created by the all-or-nothing thought and does not exist in reality at all. If, as you go about your day, you notice the sensations of all-or-nothing thinking, it can be helpful at this stage in your healing to identify the thoughts themselves, and expose them for the bunk that they are. This really needs to be done on paper or on the computer. Currently, you will not be able to do this successfully in your head. The Drill Sgt. is too insidious and too sly; he will convince you that the thought is not all-or-nothing thinking, it is fact! So write down the thought you just had or are currently having when you notice the future focus and sensations of distress and PLA, and you will immediately see the all-or-nothing thinking in them. Then you can challenge this simply by saying, "What are some other possibilities?" And you will immediately feel a lessening of the tension and pressure you have been carrying.

7. Your weight is the central focus of your life.

In the Diet Mentality you base decisions about what you can have/do/be on how much weight you have lost or gained. This approach to life has only two sides: all or nothing. On one side, if you have gained a bit, your Drill Sgt. says you deserve to be punished, and you will attempt to restrict or isolate yourself. On the other side, if you have lost weight, you feel more deserving and feel more positive self-regard. Oh, and if you have stayed the same, as far as the Drill Sgt. is concerned, you may as well have gained weight because you did not make progress toward your goal. The Catch-22 here is that when you are criticized by the Drill Sgt. for not making progress because you have either maintained or gained weight, you will feel that your needs for acceptance and love are unmet, and you will turn to your primary coping strategy to deal with the thoughts and feelings which that unmet need triggers. And your primary coping strategy is food! So the threats and criticisms of the Drill Sgt. about fluctuations in your weight actually drive you to use your coping strategy, which leads to more obsessive focus on food and body image and eventually, in one form or another, to a binge.

Your weight is external. It is not your Inner Self but simply a by-product of your natural shape and size, coupled with self-esteem and self-care. It is painful to be so exposed to others. It seems unfair that our primary coping strategy should be one which leads us to experience obvious physical characteristics, when there are those who primarily cope with alcohol, pot, or even shopping, and their symptoms of this coping strategy are very subtle in many cases, unless you live with the person, that is! Then they become quite obvious and damaging to the relationship. If you are feeling insecure in your body because you believe that others are judging you, the reality is that it's not about your weight. It's about your old, unmet need for a deep, core sense of security and the need for love and acceptance. If you were to notice you were having a bad body thought and then to ask yourself what need is unmet, **unrelated to your body**, you would discover that something from your list of unfinished business was triggered, and/or you were feeling overwhelmed with all-or-nothing thoughts. Yes, if you took five minutes to write out everything you could think of which was possibly impacting you—thoughts, feelings, behaviours, past, present, future—in that moment and independent of your body shape and size, you would find that your needs for security and acceptance are feeling unmet in many places. I absolutely assure you that, if you took action to meet just one of those needs in just one of those situations, your negative body thoughts would diminish because, regardless of what you weigh and what you look like to yourself and to others, those bad body thoughts are triggered by unmet needs unrelated to your body. The sooner you get the hang of reminding yourself of this, the sooner you will be freed from many bad body thoughts, and the sooner you will be feeling confident and secure in all areas. You are witnessing yourself taking action and showing how competent and capable you are of keeping yourself safe and meeting your needs for acceptance and love.

Now, your Drill Sgt. may have just chimed in loud and urgent with, "But that's not true! You *are* overweight! You aren't perfect, yet! You have to do something. If you don't focus on your body this way, you are in denial and you will lose your motivation"! He's freaking out. His all-or-nothing thinking is over the top because the safety and security needs that he believes currently (kind of, sort of) are met by having the rigid Diet Mentality as your base are falling apart. When you have a bad body thought, ask yourself honestly how frequently does it have anything to do with your health concerns. Really. Isn't it usually much more about what you might look like to others or about the possibility that you may lose their approval if you don't look a certain way? Isn't it true that most of your bad body thoughts are all about everyone else accepting you? In your current state of mind, you most likely believe that you are unacceptable to nearly everyone out there until you accept yourself.

If you have developed true health concerns, such as, Diabetes, Fibromyalgia, food allergies, or intestinal problems, you may be saying, "But it *is* about my body. I must do something for my health!" I agree. You must do something about your relationship with food if you are currently making choices which aren't honouring of your health concerns or simply of where you want to be in life. Right now, the reality is that you aren't. You aren't making those honouring choices now because you are more focused on meeting your needs for safety and security, and for love, acceptance, and belongingness than you are on meeting your needs for esteem. This is where self-care and honouring choices come into the picture. This is reality. This is your truth. And the sooner you accept this and lighten your focus on food while you heal those underlying needs which trigger you to use food to cope, the sooner you will be able to make lasting changes to your relationship with food that feel like honouring and pleasurable choices and not like punishment and restriction. The only thing that your current focus on food and body image does for you is to lead you to want to numb out with your coping strategy even more. This will cause you to feel more frustrated, more out of control, and on and on and on.

8. The Diet-Binge-Guilt Cycle

The dynamic I have just described above is what is known as the diet-binge-guilt cycle. This is when you either actively restrict yourself from having what you want or what your body needs, or you think about eating a certain food, then tell yourself you should be restricted. Those thoughts and behaviours are followed, sooner or later, by a binge. This is quickly followed by thoughts of self-judgement and feelings of guilt which trigger you to commit to even more restriction, and so it goes.

Figure 3: The Diet-Binge-Guilt Cycle

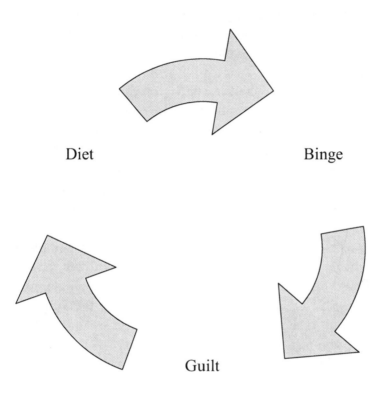

Diet   Binge

Guilt

A binge, according to the current medical/psychiatric model, is when someone eats more than twice what a "normal" person would eat in one sitting. Well, I disagree with this definition. In my personal and professional experience, a binge can be: two boxes of Kraft Dinner; a container of ice cream; two hot dogs; one hot dog; two crackers; an apple; a bite of chocolate bar or the whole damn box of chocolate bars! It doesn't matter how much it is, in terms of quantity. What matters is how your Drill Sgt. perceives it. The same amount of ice cream that was perfectly acceptable on Monday can be completely unacceptable on Tuesday for a variety of bogus Drill Sgt. reasons, such as:

- You had some yesterday, and you can't have some every day. (All-or-nothing, because you have had ice cream two days in a row, now you are having some every day for the rest of your life!)
- You were hungry when you had it on Monday, so it was okay, but you are not hungry today. (Instead of asking why you are using food to cope—eating when you are not hungry—the Drill Sgt. just berates you.)
- You ate it at a socially-acceptable mealtime yesterday and now that it's bedtime, you want some! (More all-or-nothing thinking. "There is a right and a wrong time to have ice-cream.")
- You ate it with others yesterday, so it was okay because others were doing it too. Today you are on your own, so it is just about you, and you don't deserve it because you are not at your goal weight yet. (More all-or-nothing thinking. "Until you have reached your 'goal weight,' you are undeserving of what you want.")
- You gained ½ a pound yesterday—it must have been the ice cream—so you can't have any ice cream until you reach your goal! (And even more all-or-nothing thinking.)

I could go on and on. The point is that it really doesn't matter how much you eat in regard to whether or not that eating constitutes a binge, it matters how your Drill Sgt. internalizes it. This will determine whether that bowl or pint of ice cream, or those few crackers and cheese, get labeled a binge. If they do, you feel guilt, a need to restrict (diet), and ultimately to binge some more. When they get labeled as just ice cream or crackers and cheese, they offer no additional energy; therefore, there is no need to tune out with more binging or other coping behaviours.

By now you are probably getting the message loud and clear, not just in your head but also on a gut level, that the judgement you place on yourself around food and weight only serves to drive your need of this coping strategy through the roof.

Any goals we set for ourselves around food and for our body arc doomed to fail in the long run, because:

    a) our motivation is skewed (we are trying to meet needs for acceptance and security through our appearance);

    b) we don't regard ourselves highly enough or believe we are deserving of that acceptance and security independent of how we look; and

    c) because we need to and *will* use food and body-image focus to cope until we learn to meet our needs for security and acceptance in other ways.

One more point needs to be made. You do not have to be on a "diet," in the standard sense of the word, in order to have the diet-binge-guilt-cycle alive and well in you. A standard, externally imposed diet isn't really all that different from your Drill Sgt. telling you that a certain food is "good" and another is "bad," or that *you* are good or bad depending on what you eat. So don't allow your denial to kick in. I have had many clients who insist that they have never dieted, so the Diet Mentality doesn't apply to them. These clients discovered, after reading the Diet Mentality criteria, that they had been engaging in Diet Mentality thoughts and behaviours for many years—all the while thinking they aren't dieting! It's okay. It's very subtle and insidious in our society, and we are essentially raised in this mentality. Of course, it seems so natural or second-nature that we truly don't believe it is even there. Just like the Drill Sgt., many of us are so accustomed to the internal chatter and criticism that we deem it normal. It is who we are. In fact, many times I have had clients say, "What if I get rid of my Drill Sgt. and there is nothing there? I don't think I can handle the silence. It might be worse than the criticism. At least that's something!" Are you getting savvy? Did you notice the all-or-nothing thinking? Even in thoughts of letting go of the Drill Sgt., he gets in there and gives you his all-or-nothing play-by-play of what terrible things will happen if you let him go. And right now, if you let those thoughts happen in your head without tuning in to the PLA or pressure sensation they create, they will shut you down. In a matter of seconds you have entertained thoughts of a life without the Drill Sgt. Then because the Drill Sgt. himself said it wasn't a good idea, you tell yourself you shouldn't do this, and you close that door. If there isn't someone there (either yourself witnessing this on paper or a counsellor who sees you doing this and calls you on it) to point out that you just allowed the Drill Sgt.'s all-or-nothing thinking to shut you down, you can easily find yourself committing to a life with the Drill Sgt. as your constant companion. Just because you had one split-second thought of a life without him, and he said it might not work out so well, you believed him and shut this new thought process down because his voice is so powerful right now. It won't always be so, but he does have the rule of the roost right now. This is the reason that any time you really want to effect change in your Inner Self and your coping strategies, you should write down the thoughts you are having, or tell someone else who can help you challenge them.

9. Exercise

You know you have a Diet Mentality perspective on exercise if either of the following scenarios fit for you:

1. You feel great resistance to exercise but judge yourself as lazy, lacking willpower or worthless for not exercising. These judgements make you feel intense negativity and disgust toward yourself/your body.

2. If you do exercise, it often feels good, but you then place your focus not on the fact that you are exercising and that that is a step in the direction of self-care and self-esteem, but on the fact that you don't go more often. You are not burning enough calories. You can only do 10 reps, and you are supposed to do 12, and so on. Or you set unrealistic expectations and rigid standards of how often you will go and what you will do when you begin exercising. This can sound something like, "I'll go Monday, Wednesday and Friday for 1½

hours first thing in the morning, and then I'll find some time on the weekend to do one more workout."

This is all well and good, if this is a realistic amount of time for you from a scheduling and a physical fitness perspective (you may be better off starting with 20 minutes at home). Also, what if morning isn't a good time for you? You are just not a morning person and are setting yourself up to fail by expecting yourself to suddenly be one. And what if you don't like the gym? What if you loathe it? What if going to the gym, the pool, or wherever is not a place you enjoy, resulting in an aversion to it? What if you are not feeling well one day or are just low on energy for a variety of valid reasons? Are you going to cut yourself some slack and either let it be all right if you don't go, or let it be okay to do a lighter workout? What if... what if... what if?

Someone who is exercising for self-esteem needs and self-care (more than anything else) would be able to say that exercise does not feel like work or a hardship because it is pleasurable. They would also be able to say they are flexible with themselves about when they go and what they do. This is because they know that they want to feel pleasure and enjoyment and not punishment or pressure. Someone who exercises from a place of positive self-regard does only as much as is reasonable for their current state of health and trusts that, as their health and endurance improves, they will naturally choose to do more because they want to feel as strong and healthy as they can in their body. There is no need to pressure, cajole, threaten or berate themselves before, during or after exercising to ensure they "keep it up". This is all old Drill Sgt. stuff.

This is all coming from the belief that you can not be trusted to do what is best for you, so you must be beaten into submission—for your own good, of course! If you allow yourself to approach your physical fitness from a place of self-love and wanting to be the best you can be, you will find that you have a variety of activities which you enjoy, and you allow yourself to choose from this variety the one which you feel like doing at that time. Your focus from this approach is not on calories, or even the amount of time spent on that activ-

ity, but on how you feel in your body as you engage in that activity.
How is your energy level? How do your muscles feel? What is your
breathing like? This approach to exercise is about how you want to
feel in your body—not about how you want your body to look. That
comes later, naturally. Invite yourself to explore exercise from the
perspective of creating an integrated whole which easily sustains the
goals and desires you have for every aspect of your life.

The CEDRIC Centre staff believes so strongly in this self-esteem approach to exercise that we do not offer our clients fitness
programs based on the standard model of weight-loss and toning
as our goal. Rather, our approach, which our clients experience
through the skillful tutelage of our two medical exercise specialists,
is all about being in connection with your body as you exercise. Your
body is not a tool that you use to meet your needs for acceptance
and esteem. It is the symptom or the manifestation of your current
level of self-regard. Therefore, the more you engage in exercising
your body from a place of how those movements feel and how they
enhance your sense of connection and trust in yourself, the more you
are naturally deepening your sense of security and trust in yourself
and meeting your own needs for approval, love and esteem. Any
other approach to fitness is doomed to be short-lived and filled with
Drill Sgt. pressure and criticism.

10. Social engagements

Social engagements, when you live in the Diet Mentality, are always first and foremost about how you will look at the event, whose
approval you seek and what you must look like or wear in order to
get this approval. At some point, after you have exhausted yourself
planning how you are going to achieve this miraculous weight loss
or toning in the few short days, weeks or months you have before the
big event, you may actually find yourself asking if you really want
to go. I don't mean the you that is frightened of not getting this approval. I mean *you*! The Authentic You. Do you really want to go?
Why? What do you think will be so special that makes you want to
be there (separate from all that physical appearance stuff and seek-

ing approval outside yourself)? What would happen if you allowed yourself to come from that Authentic Self and make the decision to attend or not to attend based solely on what truly feels right for you?

Making decisions to attend or not attend social events based predominantly on how you look or how you expect others will judge your physical appearance is total and complete Diet Mentality. It is buying hook, line and sinker into the story that you are nothing more than a body, and your appearance is what gives you value. This may be exactly what you believe right now; so imagining yourself going to a function and not feeling insecure feels far fetched and as if you are dreaming. That's okay; I've been there. So have most of my clients. Ultimately, we all get to that place where, either by conscious choice or by believing we have no choice at all, we let go of our belief that we need external approval or validation, and we allow ourselves to risk experimenting with validating and approving of ourselves. It is a radical concept to one who is deeply imbedded with the Diet Mentality. But it is freedom, and it is the only way to say good-bye once and for all to any of the Diet Mentality patterns which are alive in you. In the next section of this book, we are going to be speaking in great detail about your relationship with yourself. You will develop a deeper understanding of how this relationship came to be, as it is today, and you will start to experience the feeling of coming from internal validation rather than external validation. But first, one more key piece of the Diet Mentality: clothing!

11. Clothes!

Some of you have a Drill Sgt. who at the very thought of discussing clothes is saying, "No way. You are not buying any new clothes until you lose weight!" Well, check in. Any all-or-nothing thinking going on? Yes, for sure. That's okay. Just invite the Drill Sgt. to read on and let him know that you are not going to do anything which doesn't feel right to you, regardless of what Michelle says.

The issue of clothing is huge. It is one of the key methods of punishing ourselves for not looking or being the way the Drill Sgt. says we should be. It is also one of the primary reasons you have so many nasty thoughts about your body and consequently use food to cope more and more. From the Diet Mentality perspective, you do not permit yourself to buy any new clothes that would be comfortable and fit your body as it is now, because:

a) you are going to be losing weight soon, and you don't want to buy anything that won't fit you in a few weeks (how long have you been telling yourself this?);

b) you are disgusted and ashamed of your body, and you don't want to see yourself in the mirror let alone have a salesclerk see you or what size you take;

c) you know what size you are, and you don't want to take that size, so you are not going to allow yourself to buy anything unless you can fit into something smaller;

d) you allow yourself only to buy things that you can *almost* fit into, as an incentive, you tell yourself. As a result, you have a closet full of clothes you have seldom or never worn but can't get rid of because you *will* fit them one day; and

e) your Drill Sgt. believes that you would become complacent and lose your motivation to change if you allowed yourself to buy clothes which fit you comfortably. How's that for all-or-nothing thinking? Well, let me ask this: How motivating is it to feel your clothes chafing against your skin or to feel your stomach ache because it is crammed into your outfit? How motivating is this? Or does it just make you feel awful and want to numb out with food?

Ask yourself this question: "If I took everything from my closet(s) that doesn't fit me comfortably right now (and out of the garbage bags downstairs and out from under the bed), what would remain?" This is reality. This is truth. This is where you are and what you are dealing with, and the sooner you allow yourself to be as comfortable as you can physically be in your body, the sooner you will be able to shift your mental energy from criticism and contempt to compassion and successful forward motion.

The Diet Mentality will always lead to Disordered Eating. There is no way that it can't. Many studies have been conducted where men and women, who have a natural relationship with food (they eat when they are hungry, stop when they are full and don't think about it otherwise), are put on a strict diet. The outcome is always the same. The men and women begin to obsess about food. The longer the restrictive behaviour or mindset exists, the stronger and more prominent the obsessive thoughts and behaviours about food become. Inevitably, without exception, when those men and women are "freed" from their restrictions, they binge. And they binge big time! In those studies, the whole process I just described typically lasts from one week to one month. One week! One week, and those natural eaters are now binge eaters—at least for the first while following the study. There is no follow-up research that I know of to show how long it takes for those participants to return to Natural Eating.

The point is, if you subject a Natural Eater to a brief period of restriction around food, they become obsessed—not only with their bodies but also with food. They binge the first chance they get. Now imagine this process being alive in someone over a period of a year? Five years? Ten Years? Twenty? Now add messages and modeling from friends, family and media about this person's body needing to look different from how it looks now. And to make it really challenging, add some unmet needs for security and approval from the past, and what do you get?

You get someone who is so tuned out to their own body that they don't even know what hunger feels like—if they have even allowed themselves to experience it in the past five years. You get someone who loathes their body: someone who sees their body as the bane of their existence. They believe it is the cause of all their pain and suffering and that the only way to change their body, and thus change their suffering, is to restrict and make their body conform to what they believe it should be based on those external messages. You get someone who has bought so fully into the Diet Mentality that they can't see that every single restrictive thought or action takes them further from themselves—further from the peace and self-acceptance they are so desperately seeking.

You get someone who:

a) feels compelled to eat when they are not hungry;
b) may start eating out of physical hunger but eats past the point of comfortable fullness; or
c) does not allow themselves to eat when they are legitimately hungry (their tummy is growling or other signs of hunger are clearly present).

In other words, you get someone with a disordered relationship with food. They are so far removed from knowing and trusting the natural signals of hunger and fullness in their body that they don't know what to do. So they persist in focusing outside themselves on the next diet, the next exercise plan, and so forth, as a means of finding this elusive control.

They try harder and harder at the very behaviour which brought them to this dysfunction in the first place. What else can they do? They don't know that it is their underlying needs for security and approval which are triggering them to feel unacceptable. They don't know that there are other ways (which actually work!) to feel secure and grounded in themselves and in the world. They keep trying the old Diet Mentality and spin around and around in the diet-binge-guilt cycle until they come across a message or method for achieving a solid sense of security and trust in themselves that enhances their self-respect and dignity, leading them to a higher place. And here you are allowing yourself to hear a new message that flies in the face of all your Diet Mentality training because you know there must be something more. Just keep reminding yourself of the points that were predominant for you during this discussion on the Diet Mentality, and, in the weeks to come, you will no doubt prove to yourself that there is another and better way, and you will never do the diet thing again—even in your head!

9

Post-Traumatic Stress Disorder

You may be asking yourself why we are suddenly talking about post traumatic stress disorder (PTSD). Isn't this book about letting go of food-coping strategies? Well, it is. *And* one of the things I have discovered in working with distressed clients for so many years is that the use of food as a coping strategy goes hand in hand with the use of thoughts, feelings, and behaviours which are associated with the diagnosis of post traumatic stress disorder. In my experience, PTSD is just a grouping of symptoms which describe a certain overall state of being. As a professional, treating those who use food to cope, I find that the key diagnostic symptoms of PTSD are almost always present in people with eating disorders. This makes good sense, because the basic definition of a trauma is: *any experience of a threat, real or perceived, to a person's body or psychological state, or the body or psychological state of someone close to this person.*

Most of us who use food to cope have experienced some degree of trauma in our lives, typically, in childhood. News-worthy traumas, such as: war, natural catastrophes, assault, rape, or serious accidents are clearly traumas by anyone's definition. Everyday traumas are so frequent in our society and individual life experience that we frequently discount and dismiss them. These everyday traumas, such as, death of a loved one, divorce, and juvenile bullying are real losses to both our emotional and physical sense of security as adults and even more so as children.

Verbal and physical abuses are traumas. Most everyone has experienced the humiliation and damaging effects of verbal abuse. If our ego strength and our sense of esteem are solid when these events occur, we can slough it off or work through it with some help. If we are already feeling a lack of security and acceptance in our world, every experience of verbal abuse, for example: judgements, name calling, put downs, and yelling will constitute a trauma. Physical abuse, slapping, hitting, spanking, and outright beatings, regardless of their purpose in the eyes of the punisher, are traumatic events. Neglect is trauma. The act of having your needs and your Self ignored or devalued is traumatic.

Those who use food to cope have no doubt experienced some form of trauma which triggered the development of and dependence on a series of coping strategies. These coping strategies come together to form the characteristics of post traumatic stress disorder. You may be reflecting on your past right now and thinking of events that were clearly traumas, by my above definition, but that you have learned to discount. You may also have told yourself that everyone has similar experiences and that it's no big deal.

I had a client in my office some time ago who lived as a child in a war-torn country. When I proposed to her that perhaps some of her use of food to cope arose out of needs for security from the trauma of war, she said, "Well everyone there experienced that. This would mean that millions of people have been traumatized!" And I said, "Yes, that is exactly what it means!"

People seem to think that trauma happens only to a few unfortunate victims. This point of view has allowed much trauma and abuse to be overlooked. The truth is that most people will experience some significant trauma in their lives. We can gauge this from the rampant use of powerful coping strategies, such as: food use, alcoholism, shopping, gambling, drug and sexual addiction. In this past decade, major changes to the Child Welfare Act occurred because there is a profound realization that yelling, slinging insults, blaming, hitting of any kind, isolating, and any form of inappropriate touching are detrimental to the mental and emotional state of the little being who experiences them.

Mom gets drunk and starts yelling. The old perception was that it's just how Mom was. The new perception is that it's abuse, and no child should have to experience this. What can we do to protect that child? Social Services steps in with some counselling, intervention, and possibly foster home placement so the child does not have to endure the dysfunction and trauma of Mom's drinking and verbal abuse.

Mom and Dad go out for the night, leaving the children, who are all under ten years of age, at home to fend for themselves. In the past, their behaviour would be seen by some as a poor parenting choice. Others would have dismissed it as normal. It is now seen as the neglect that it is.

A high-school teacher fondles a student's breasts when she stays after school for some assistance. It happens just once. The old perspective would have had the child discounting the experience due to shame or fear of judgement. If she told her family, they likely would have done nothing but suggest that she not spend time alone with the teacher. The responsibility and therefore judgement of blame would be placed on the child. In recent years it is more likely that a teen will tell someone. And if she does, it is very likely that the police will become involved. The teacher will be charged, lose his job, and possibly go to jail. The child would receive counseling at a sexual assault centre or through a program directed at teens. The message would be clear: this is trauma, this is not okay, this is not your fault, you have a right to feel angry.

There are many examples of situations or behaviours which most of us experienced as children that were truly undermining of our sense of significance, safety, and love in the world. These are now clearly understood, by those in the field of counselling and child welfare, as abuse. They were abusive then. They were traumatic then. Just because the energy at the time was *Oh, that's just how it is* doesn't mean that we didn't feel traumatized or that our sense of safety in the world was not seriously undermined by those experiences. It was common then to here such comments as: "We don't talk about those things." "That's just the way it is." "Well, my dad used to give it to me worse, so you have nothing to complain about." It is irrational thinking; however, it was the climate in which most of us were raised so we bought into it, just like the Diet Mentality.

We are willing to continue to discount and dismiss our experiences of trauma because we tell ourselves that that kind of thing happened to everyone. Well, you are right to some extent. That kind of thing did happen to most everyone. So the reality is that most everyone experienced some form of trauma as a child which had the potential to severely undermine their sense of security in the world and their sense of trust in others. Furthermore, it is not the severity of the trauma or stressor that dictates whether or in what way a person will manifest symptoms of PTSD. *The key factor is the meaning or significance which a person attaches to the stressful situation.* How you made sense of it and what your physical and psychological state was before you experienced the trauma are key factors in whether you will develop PTSD.

If we were not yet grounded in ourselves at a level of esteem needs at the time we experienced some form of abuse, neglect or other trauma, we would have interpreted that event as potentially threatening to our existence. In some cases it truly was. In many cases it was the emotional and psychological impact of those abuse experiences which impacted us most severely. So, while we may not have been physically on the verge of death, the experience undermined our sense of security on a deeper psychological and emotional level. Our sense of who we are in the world—our worth and deservedness of respectful treatment and of dignity—was undermined deeply in many of these situations. This was traumatizing, without a doubt! Yet most of us were either told directly or indirectly to ignore or discount our natural and appropriate responses to that trauma. And that interpretation led us to develop a number of coping strategies to deal with our natural and appropriate responses. We developed coping strategies, such as: anger, fear, sadness, depression, aversion to certain places and people. These coping strategies, plus a few others we will discuss in a moment, form the criteria for a diagnosis of post traumatic stress disorder.

Thus, in my opinion, the traits which comprise a diagnosis of post traumatic stress disorder don't imply illness or dysfunction. They are actually natural and appropriate human responses to the experience of trauma. Arguing that what happened to you wasn't as bad as what happened to someone else misses the point entirely. The point is it was traumatic to you. And if that trauma wasn't acknowledged and attended to in a way that felt safe, respectful and dignified, you would most likely develop many ongoing coping strategies to deal with the deep sense of a lack of security and trust in the world which the trauma elicited in you.

The following examples of post traumatic stress disorder are also known as coping strategies.

THOUGHT-LEVEL PTSD SYMPTOMS (coping strategies)
1. **Suicidal Ideation**
    Thoughts of killing yourself by your own hand, or passively, by being in a car accident or getting hit by a bus.
2. **Intrusive Ideation**
    You engage in worst-case-scenario thinking. What starts as a perfectly safe and innocuous thought can take you down the path of imagining terrible things happening to yourself or those you love, for example: *Your partner is ten minutes late. He's never late. Soon you imagine an automobile accident where Bob is killed, and your thoughts escalate to wondering how you and the children will manage without him. You will be forced to sell your home and move away from friends and family...* I could go on, but you get the picture.
3. **Carrying a belief that you won't live long**
    You believe you will be short-lived, and therefore you live your life as though this were true. You take risks with your body, for example: through sexual promiscuity, extreme

sports, or walking down a dark alley at midnight. Conversely, you become a hypochondriac, fearing that every ache and pain is a symptom of the fatal illness you knew would strike you one day. You don't plan for the future in terms of relationships or money, which frequently creates great stress and frustration and can lead you to use the coping strategy of suicidal ideation.

4. **Self-blame**

It's entirely your fault! Everything! Everything people feel and experience. Somehow, you should have known what they would need, think, feel and do. You should have done something to prevent it or make it better.

5. **Paranoid Ideation**

You may be thinking that everyone is watching you; people are out to get you; you can't trust anyone; everyone is a child molester. Most of my clients carry at least one of these thoughts and absolutely believe it to be true. Just think of how many people you share your Authentic Self with? Not too many if even one. How did you feel the last time you went out for dinner? Were people watching you, thinking about you?

FEELING-LEVEL PTSD SYMPTOMS (coping strategies)

1. **Depression**

You're just blah. Things seem grey. Unless you must do them, you don't have much interest in many things, and, even then, you are motivated more by pressure than pleasure.

2. **Anxiety**

You feel nervous and anxious, frequently if not all the time. This is your P.L.A. which arises out of the mountain of unfinished business.

3. **Irritability and Impatience**

You have plenty of both. Everything has the capacity to irritate and annoy you—the needs of others, most specifically. You may come across as relaxed and patient on the outside:

others may perceive you as easygoing, but inside you are feeling increasingly frustrated. Resentment is building and you are about to blow. You may do this outwardly, and/or you may take this frustration out on yourself in the form of verbal abuse from your Drill Sgt., or perhaps even physical abuse in the form of overeating, substance abuse, over-exercising, cutting, or hitting yourself.

4. **Alexithymia**

    This is a disconnection from feelings and an inability to identify what you are feeling or to know how to express it.

Behavioural-level PTSD Symptoms (coping strategies)

1. **Sleep disturbances**

    They may manifest themselves in the form of bad dreams, or with difficulty getting to or staying asleep.

2. **Angry outbursts**

    You may not direct these at anyone in particular, although it is possible your partner or your children (if you have them) bear the brunt of this coping strategy. Even if you are not directing your anger at any one individual when you let loose your wounded energy and others are nearby, it takes a pretty strong and grounded individual to not feel assaulted and impacted. And someone *that* strong or grounded, unless they were your therapist, would probably remove themselves from the situation until it was rectified.

3. **Hypervigilance**

    You are tuned in to everything and everyone. This is why you are the one who remembers all the little details of pretty much everything that anyone ever said or did. The intention here is to be on the lookout for any potential harm coming down the pike and be well ahead of it. This pattern goes hand in hand with the catastrophizing of the intrusive ideation-coping strategy. The underlying motivation here? If I am hyper-aware of everything that's going on around me and feed this information to my brain, it can make contingency plans for anything that could possibly happen. I can then rest because I know that I can handle it even if the worst happens! Of course, all that worse-case-scenario thinking and hyper-vigilance or "preparedness" only serves to increase your state of anxiety and your belief that something bad is going to happen: *It's just a matter of time.* Who can live happily when they are imagining some traumatic event is just around the next bend?

4. **Jumpy Jumpy**
   Have you ever been startled when someone came into the room and you weren't expecting them? Or you didn't hear someone come from behind and you practically leapt out of your skin? These situations will happen to all of us, to some extent, if we are surprised. But those of us who have an exaggerated fight or flight response will be seen by others as jumpy, and we will have a harder time calming down after a fright. We might find ourselves getting very angry at having been surprised, when others would just laugh and let it go.

5. **Food, Drugs, Alcohol, Shopping, Gambling, Sexual Addiction, TV, Video Games**.
   All behavioural-level coping strategies are ways of distancing ourselves from the present moment.

Remember that a coping strategy allows us to remain in an uncomfortable situation without being aware of how uncomfortable we are. Well, what if the uncomfortable situation is now within us? It is years after our trauma, and we have turned against ourselves because of years of feeling the anxiety and distress of that trauma. These were perfectly appropriate responses at the time, but no one ever validated or acknowledged them. We are tired of feeling anxious and constantly insecure. Nothing we try seems to make a difference. Even medications for depression and anxiety don't take it all away. Our P.L.A. and our 24/7 self-blame, in the form of our Drill Sgt., are driving us nuts. We must get *away from* ourselves because we can't seem to find a way to *live with* ourselves. Bring on the behaviours. Bring on the big guns. Take my mind off the feelings and thoughts that keep me stressed and preoccupied. It can be a relationship, so I can now focus on the other person and project my feelings of anxiety and frustration onto them. It can be food or drugs, so I can numb out. Whatever! Just get me out of myself!

Food has become a deeply-ingrained way of coping with the natural and appropriate responses to the trauma you experienced. Yet, because you are unaware that your anxiety and other thoughts and feelings are natural responses, you judge rather than seek to understand and heal them. You turn away from yourself and your pain, and you focus your energies on certain behaviours which make you feel better in the moment or, at the very least, keep you occupied and give you something on which to focus. Sometimes, we may obsess about food and body image, among other things, because we like to have something to which we can attach our anxiety and distress. It seems scary to just be feeling anxious and not have it be about something obvious. Furthermore, since we are tuned out to our past experiences of trauma, we feel the need to create something in the present to justify that feeling of anxiety. This is how many of us come to find ourselves obsessed with and enmeshed in substances, in other people's lives, and in food. It's something obvious in the present to which we can attach this distress. Maybe even something we have some power over.

You actually have a truckload of power over your anxiety and distress, once you figure out where it originated and give yourself the validation and acknowledgement you did not get when the trauma(s) occurred. In essence, your power resides in your ability to meet your own safety and security, love, acceptance, and belongingness needs.

Let's talk for a minute about alexithymia and intrusive ideation. I have previously mentioned both a few times, yet it is likely you have not heard of either before. They are fundamental contributors to your use of food to cope. They are also symptoms of PTSD, so they definitely deserve a closer look.

Alexithymia

Now bear with me here. I am going to take you on a bit of a journey in order to explain a very important part of your recovery process. If you were sitting in my office, I would be leaning over and beginning to draw a diagram on my whiteboard to illustrate this piece of information, and you would be laughing at my poor artistic ability. However, since we are not face-to-face right now and the computer won't draw what I would like it to, I am going to do my best to explain it; therefore, I ask for your patience.

A study was conducted by psychologists in 2000 which looked at childhood experiences of trauma (physical abuse, sexual abuse, emotional and verbal abuse, and neglect) and the later development of disordered eating behaviours. They were looking to determine the mitigating factors which would lead someone with a childhood trauma experience to later develop an eating disorder. And what they discovered was that there were two factors which went hand in hand. One was a condition called alexithymia (a-lex-**i**-thy-mi-a). The other was a condition we are all familiar with—depression. It is my opinion that alexithymia leads to depression, which results in the ultimate shut down of our senses.

Alexithymia is characterized by:
1. Difficulty identifying and describing feelings in yourself or other people.
2. Difficulty distinguishing between feelings and the bodily sensations associated with emotional arousal.
3. Restricted imaginative processes. This means your imagination is skewed to the negative. You have few positive dreams or fantasies and can have frequent intrusive ideation.
4. Thinking which is concrete and reality-based. This is your all-or-nothing Drill Sgt. in the flesh!

In other words, alexithymia makes it difficult for us to know what we are feeling or even *if* we are having a feeling. It makes it difficult for us to tell whether the sensation we think we are having is physical or emotional. It makes it difficult for us to dream or imagine positive fun things. Moreover, we get stuck in very concrete, "logical" thinking which can make us rigid—most often with ourselves.

The good news is that you can learn to distinguish what you are feeling and move through this feeling very quickly. Even better news is that, in order to be able to let go of what you are feeling, it's not essential to know where the feeling originated.

Since you have very likely been distanced from a true connection with your feelings since childhood, you may feel some resistance to connecting with them again. You may begin to fear that there will be a considerable backlog of feelings which will sweep in and overpower you if you were to open the door. This is just your Drill Sgt. trying to maintain the status quo because his task is to keep you safe, and this is new and different and therefore, by his standards, unsafe. As you begin to connect with your authentic feelings in the moment and learn how to effectively release them, you are going to become more powerful and competent at taking care of yourself than the Drill Sgt. has ever been. And the ways that your Nurturing Parent will learn to take care of you will lead to greater self-esteem and peace.

If you have lived your life disconnected from your feelings for the most part, you are very likely wondering what the value of being connected to them would be. In fact, your Drill Sgt. may be saying something such as: "Feelings make you weak." "Other people won't respect you if you let your feelings show." "You're just a cry baby if you can't control your feelings." Check in with yourself for a moment and ask where in the past you may have either heard these very words spoken, or if you witnessed significant people in your life modeling the behaviour of hiding, discounting, or denying their feelings?

Your use of the coping strategy of alexithymia is actually what leads you to discount and deny your life experience now. Have you ever had the experience of suddenly feeling totally overwhelmed? You are certain you are overreacting because you don't know where all this emotion came from, and maybe others around you aren't reacting as strongly or aren't so demonstrative. In addition to feeling emotional, you are compounding your pain by judging and berating yourself for this feeling. You are certain there is nothing going on in your life to justify your strong reaction in that moment. Does this experience sound familiar?

I assure you that, if you were sitting in my office recounting a recent similar experience, we would be able to identify the underlying trigger(s) within moments, and it would not be I who was spoon-feeding you or forcing those thoughts. No, you are the one who would be able to quite clearly list for me all the things which are currently going on in your life. Issues with food and body image (no doubt both at the top of the list), work, home, relationship with others, and money would all appear from within and be up on my fabulous whiteboard, highlighted for you to see. At this point, you would look at me and say, "Wow, I guess I do have a lot going on. No wonder I feel so overwhelmed!"

And I (having brilliantly left enough space at the side and at the bottom of my whiteboard) begin to draw the following... Okay, bear with me, I'm drawing a mountain. Just trust me on this. You are looking at your list of things which are going on in your life, and you are also seeing a mountain off to the right. This is what I call your "mountain of unfinished business". You will recall that this is the accumulation of all your past experiences which feel unresolved; all the feelings which have been left unexpressed and all the stored trauma and pain of your life. To whatever extent it exists, it is there. At the beginning of the recovery process, most people (unless they have done a fair amount of therapy or self-work already) have a pretty big mountain of unfinished business. I say this not to worry you but to validate that you have a reason for doing what you do and for feeling what you feel. Once you begin the recovery process, your mountain of unfinished business will erode quite quickly into a molehill, and ultimately you will be up to date and living your life in such a way that things get attended to as they arise: no unfinished business exists or can exist.

Back to my office and the whiteboard... So, now we have your list of stressors (things that may be impacting you right now) and a drawing of the mountain of unfinished business. Now to that, I add the stress threshold scale.

The stress threshold scale (STS) looks like this:

1   5   10

A state of 1 on the STS reflects a state of inner peace and tranquility. You feel relaxed and calm. A state of 3 through 9 on the STS is a state of PLA. You feel increasingly agitated and can't quite relax as you move from 3 through 9. Something isn't quite right, and, until it is attended to, you won't be able to let go and unwind—that is, not without the help of one of your behavioural coping strategies. The longer that thing, whatever it is, goes unattended or unresolved, the higher your level of stress. A state of 10 on the STS represents overwhelm mode. You are maxed out. You are knee-deep in every coping strategy you can get your hands on and still not feeling the numbness or relaxation which you seek. You are feeling irritable, anxious, even panicked: suicidal ideation would be kicking in here for sure, if you use this coping strategy, as would intrusive ideation (actually intrusive ideation would likely have kicked in at about 5 and may have played a hand in the increasing stress threshold level today, if you didn't catch it early on). All-or-nothing thinking is rampant at 10, and you are just generally overwhelmed.

Now let's say you are a lucky guy or gal and experienced minimal trauma as a child. You were taught to have clear and strong boundaries, good self-esteem and you deal with things as they come up; moreover, you have little or no unfinished business in your life (I think there are five people like this on the planet). If this is you, you are able, without having gone through therapy or taken medication, to wake up each morning with a stress level from everyday demands and life events of about 2 (probably higher in our society, but let's think the best).

So, if 10 is the point on the stress scale where you are pushed into harming yourself with some unhealthful coping strategy, some pretty big events would have to happen all on the same day to max you out. Because of your moderate to high self-esteem, you have the self-care skills to attend to yourself prior to reaching 10, and barring major ecological disaster; therefore, you are not at all likely to see a 10 or even an 8 on the scale, and your overall state of being is pretty confident and relaxed.

But let's say you are you and have a mountain of unfinished biz. This means you start the day, before you are even out of bed, with lots of the PLA and a stress level of a 5 (and I'm being generous here—for some of you it may be more realistic to say you are start-ing the day at an 8). You wake up to a feeling of anxiety in the pit of your stomach.

And you know what your self-esteem is like and how quickly you rush to take responsibility for everything, including others' needs and feelings. Just stepping out your front door is a big deal some days when you are feeling focused on your body in a negative way. And certainly a sideways glance, whether truly directed at you or not, is enough to add a few more points to your stress level. An issue or two with the kids, or work, or the car, or money, or your partner, or friend, or parent, and where are you? You are at about 25 on the scale of 1 to 10. And you didn't even realize that you were feeling anything until you suddenly break down crying, develop a killer migraine, begin to get very short and tense with everyone, find that you have just eaten an entire box of cookies, or all of the above. Even then, the alexithymia would make it hard for you to appreciate that you had any "good" reason for doing what you have done. Your Drill Sgt. will go to town, informing you that you are overreacting and just too sensitive, by saying, "It's not that big a deal. What's your problem?" This only adds to your stress level, and, before you know it, you are eating again or having terrible thoughts about your body—all of which seem to be appearing from nowhere. Are you starting to understand why you have been so wedded to the belief that your issues with food and body really *are* about food and body? Can you see now that they are not?

You have been tuned out to your feelings and are unable to ap-preciate that they are valid and have good reason to be there. You may be unaware of anything until you reach an 8 or higher on the stress threshold scale and find yourself eating or berating your body. Of *course*, you think it is about what you are doing with food or about your body. It is the only thing you are conscious of in that moment, so this must be what is impacting you, right? No, not right. Just because it is all you are conscious of does not mean it is all there is. It just means that you are adept at tuning out to your feelings and needs. The Diet Mentality is just the tip of the iceberg. In actual fact, it's the feelings and needs and experiences which have lain beneath your conscious awareness that have driven you to use food to cope and to feel so overwhelmed in that moment. Not food itself. And this is a key distinction.

Hopefully, you have now started to experiment with some of the new concepts you have learned and have gained a sense of what your mountain of unfinished business might contain, at least some of it. If so, you have begun to prove to yourself that even when you don't think there is a good reason for what you are doing with food, believe me, there is. When you notice your use of food to cope, even one experience of asking yourself what might be impacting you now (past, present, future, thoughts, feelings, and behaviours) will often be enough to prove to your Drill Sgt. that you are not a wimp, a baby, or a weakling who can't cut it when everyone else can.

I assure you that, when you allow yourself to see in writing all the crap (figuratively speaking) that's on your plate, you will have no choice but to cut yourself some slack. So the unfinished business, as well as the disconnection from your feelings which comes from alexithymia, set you up for overload day after day. Until you begin to acknowledge and validate how much you have going on and begin to develop some strategies for lightening your load (past and present), you will continue to rely on food to cope. In whatever way you use it currently, it will remain, because it is the only way you find release.

You may have read this and thought that you weren't *abused*; that what happened to you wasn't *that bad;* or that your parents did the best they could and you just have to get over it. Yes, your parents absolutely did the best they could—we all do. I am not about blaming them. From my perspective, assigning responsibility to parents or caregivers for the appropriate and healthful care of a child is not blame. It is the appropriate assignment of responsibility. It becomes blame if you believe that they must do something now to make it better for you. The only reason I attend to this time in your life is not to blame your primary caregivers but to support your awareness that there are good reasons for your negative thoughts and behaviour, and that is the best way to get your Drill Sgt. to ease up on you. This is necessary for you to no longer tune out to your Authentic Self or use food as a coping strategy. Once he is on side, allowing for the possibility that you have a fine reason for doing what you do, you can set about the life-enhancing task of building a loving and compassionate relationship with yourself, which you greatly deserve.

The study I mentioned, which determined that alexithymia and depression were the mitigating factors between the experience of abuse and the later onset of eating disorders, also led to the discovery of something which is significant, and this we see continuously proven in our work at the Centre. The discovery was that the form of abuse which impacted children the most was not physical or sexual, although those forms of abuse did undeniably have a profound impact on one's Locus of Control and self-esteem. No, it was actually the emotional abuse and neglect which had the most dramatic and lingering impact. These forms of abuse were "the silent treatment," or withdrawal of love and affection as punishment, which truly are torture to a child and very significantly undermine their sense of safety and security in the family and in the world. In Section IV, when we address your relationship with others, I will provide you with more information on this piece.

Intrusive Ideation

Intrusive ideation is a coping strategy thought pattern. It is borne out of trauma and is a key component of post traumatic stress disorder.

An example of intrusive ideation is when your partner goes fishing, and, before you know it, you picture him falling out of the boat

and drowning. You feel the sensations of pain and suffering, his panic, your loss and grief. You imagine how you are told and how you
feel when you hear the news. You imagine calling his family to no-
tify them—whom first and how to tell them—the funeral and what
you will wear, say and do; the bills; your children; and how you
will ultimately cope. Your partner is having a great time, but you are
traumatized and feeling panicked. You have just lived his death very
vividly. But if you are not aware that you have just done a little number on yourself in the form of intrusive ideation, and that you have
just told yourself a story which has traumatized you, then you will
feel as if your current state of anxiety has just come out of nowhere.
As a result of your story and not because of anything your partner
actually did, you may even begin to have feelings of annoyance or
resentment towards him, without realizing that you are experiencing
those feelings because of your own intrusive ideation.

And depending on where you are in your recovery process, you
probably have these experiences countless times a day. In actual
fact, everything is just fine, but you are taking yourself on a journey
to hell with these intrusive fantasies about death, abuse and suffering. The worst-case-scenario of every event you and your loved ones
experience gets played out before you—you feel it; you live it—and
this certainly adds to your stress level. Each experience of intrusive
ideation is traumatizing, or re-traumatizing, if you are imagining
old abuse or trauma experiences. You are living it; it may as well
actually be happening, because you are experiencing it as though it
were.

Studies have been conducted on the nervous system and brain
patterns of humans when they imagine certain scenarios. Without
exception, when people are asked to imagine or to watch traumatic
situations, even if they are happening to people they don't know,
they experience physiological responses which are strikingly similar
in intensity to the responses one would experience if they were actually, physically experiencing that trauma. In terms of physiological
reaction, there is little difference between the scenes which are completely imaginary and the scenes which are actually viewed. That's

how powerful our brain is. This is why, even when life seems to be just fine, you are feeling anxious and distressed. In various ways throughout the day, you continuously traumatize yourself with intrusive ideations. Those ideations trigger the adrenal system in your body to produce the chemicals associated with the "fight or flight" response. This leads to a state of heightened awareness and anxiety—the PLA. It also leads to a need to numb out or find a sense of control through your behavioural coping strategies.

Just ask yourself how often you come to consciousness, as though from a dream, feeling anxious and icky? And how many times, if you were to ask yourself what you were just thinking, would it be either a recollection of some past painful experience, or the projection of a trauma which might happen in the future to you or someone you know? Probably, very often.

The coping strategy of intrusive ideation is borne from a misdirected attempt to be in control and prepared for any eventuality. It often appears from a time in our lives when, for our physical, psychological, or emotional safety, we truly needed to be on "the ball" and have many contingency plans to keep ourselves safe. Unfortunately, what really happens now when we use this coping strategy is that we take ourselves out of the present moment, where we are truly safe and in control, because we are sitting at our kitchen table or at the office and everything really is okay. Through the creation of a nasty fantasy, we bring into that safe and okay situation feelings of panic, trauma, and powerlessness. Even if the present situation is truly stressful and traumatic in and of itself, invoking worst-case-scenario thinking does nothing to help you think clearly and rationally.

We originally began to use this coping strategy because it helped us as children to feel more powerful and somewhat soothed by the belief that we would be able to protect ourselves if whatever traumatized us were to happen again. This was truly the best we could do for ourselves then. Continuing to use this coping strategy as an adult, when we have the physical power to protect ourselves in a variety of life-enhancing ways, is only an unnecessary continuation of the torture and abuse of our past. And it has the nasty little side effect of triggering our P.L.A. and our need for food to cope. It keeps the alexithmyia and depression alive because it is too painful to be present. In order for you to reach a nice stable 2 or less on the stress threshold, which is where you deserve to be, the intrusive ideation must go.

The thing is, what triggers your intrusive ideation now is any sense of insecurity or the potential lack of security. Yes, I know this is pretty much a 24/7 experience for you right now, hence the frequency of intrusive ideation you likely experience and why you feel so anxious and overwhelmed much of the time. You see, all of these coping strategies that we are discussing feed into each other. They will continue to do so until you address the present items or issues which create the underlying feeling of insecurity or a lack of safety that is alive in you. Are you beginning to see how everything comes back to those unmet needs for security and acceptance?

What can you do currently to begin to meet your needs for security and to diminish the amount of intrusive ideation you experience?

1. Start inviting yourself to be conscious of when you are telling yourself an intrusive ideation story. (Initially, you will likely be more conscious of your PLA than of the story itself, so look for this or any of your behavioural-coping strategies.)
2. Once you are tuned in and notice that you are harming yourself with intrusive ideation, the next step is to acknowledge that you are using this coping strategy. This means you have a need for safety. Simply say to yourself, "I'm doing the intrusive ideation thing."
3. Then ask yourself what just happened. Prior to the intrusive ideation, what were you thinking about that made you feel unsafe or insecure? You will figure it out. You will prove that that nasty story was triggered by feeling insecure in the moment because of something else: often some all-or-nothing thinking.
4. Whatever the reason for the intrusive ideation and the underlying insecurity which triggered it, once you have identified what you were doing, ask yourself these questions: "What is

going on right now? "What is my reality in this moment?" In so doing, you have brought yourself out of the old story and into the present.

5. Now, reset yourself emotionally by asking the simple question, "How would I like to feel right now?"

6. You will then notice something amazing. The tight stomach and the icky feelings of the intrusive ideation will lighten and often completely disappear because, yet again, you have just taken yourself from a place of feeling powerless and stuck to a place of enlightenment, and you have put yourself in a position to find a solution to this problem. This is a very powerful place to be—a place where insecurity and intrusive ideation cannot exist.

As soon as you notice the intrusive ideation surfacing, don't spin your wheels berating yourself for it, and certainly don't keep following that path of traumatic thought. Just acknowledge it as a coping strategy, and look for the real-life, present situation which feels as if it is somehow compromising your need for safety and security. Most of the time this will be in relationship with someone else, and most of the time it will be your old core beliefs which triggered you to feel insecure which, in turn, triggered the intrusive ideation. Again, the key is to continue to both acknowledge the coping strategies when you notice them and to work on building a strong and healthful relationship with yourself. With self-dignity and self-respect, you will be able to handle any situation that life presents.

Keep coming back to how you would like to feel in this moment. Whenever you notice your intrusive ideation or any of your other coping strategies, just ask yourself how you would like to be feeling right now. Bring your attention to what you *do* want to experience in your life and away from what you *don't*.

Your consciousness of when you are using your intrusive ideation coping strategy will lead you to be much more tuned in to your PLA and to catch yourself heading down that nasty thinking path immediately—long before it triggers you to feel traumatized and needing food to cope. Ultimately, your conscious attention to this pattern, and to the underlying needs for security which triggered it, will lead you to no longer rely on this harmful way of coping with life. The less we engage in intrusive ideation, the more life becomes peaceful and relaxing.

10

Natural Eating

We have thoroughly explored the primary coping strategies of the Diet Mentality and post traumatic stress disorder. Now that you have a greater level of awareness of the thoughts, feelings, and behaviours that you have been using to cope with life's stressors, it is time to take a detailed look at where you are headed—Natural Eating.

Natural Eating is a term which describes a simple and easy relationship with food. You eat when you are hungry, and stop when you are full. It's that simple. This is the basis for a natural relationship with food. Anyone that you know who has a natural relationship with food will likely have very little energy around what they eat. Most natural eaters feel drawn to make honouring choices—choices that are in alignment with their overall life goals and passions. But whatever they choose to eat, natural eaters do not think about it much at all. They certainly do not carry guilt and shame, nor do they fear the judgement of others around what they have eaten or what they would like to eat.

Natural eaters also seem to maintain the same weight year round without any effort. They may exercise. They may not. The issues of food and body image just don't have the same charge or distress attached to them that they do for those of us who were schooled in the Diet Mentality. Sometimes, when you are in the throws of your Diet Mentality/diet-binge-guilt cycle, and you have a meal with a natural eater, this experience can leave you feeling very frustrated or just downright amazed. How on earth can they leave that half piece of chocolate cake? How do they even know they are full, and why wouldn't they eat it anyway? And what do you mean they ate a late lunch? Who cares if they aren't hungry? It's dinner time and this means legal eating. Why aren't they filling their plate?

We are so busy fretting and worrying over what to eat and how much, and letting those decisions be dictated by external forces, that it really is amazing to us to see someone who knows within themselves when they're hungry and when they have had enough. More amazing is the fact that they naturally respect those cues, and with so little energy! They are creatures from another planet, surely! Could we possibly learn to be like them? Rather, can we unlearn to be like we are now? Yes, we can! We can learn to tune in to the signals from our body about its level of hunger and fullness. We can come to a place of truly respecting ourselves so well that we won't eat a lot of foods which make us feel sluggish, bloated, or headachy. Through the reading and the exploration of yourself that you have done in the previous chapters, you have already begun the transition. Now let's support you to get really clear on what it is that you are transitioning to.

Before I begin, I must acknowledge Marie Cochrane. Marie was my counsellor years ago when I first began to explore the possibility that there was something more going on for me than a lack of willpower or just plain laziness. Week after week I showed up at her office seeking answers and information, and truly just desperate for someone to listen to me and support me through my pain and struggles with food. I was certain that, at any moment, Marie was going to produce some diet plan. Any time now, all the stuff about eating what you want, when you want, would begin to be curtailed by some "guidelines" or "rules" about what I "should" and "should not" be eating. In other words, I feared very much that this situation would turn into all the others I had experienced, where I knew I needed something else, but all I was presented with was a diet. After all, this is what my doctors had suggested despite statements that I thought I had a problem with food and could not stop eating.

Thus, I was somewhat reserved in my trust of Marie, but, at the same time, I could not stop myself from sharing with her. I had seen two counsellors prior to this: the first at the age of 13, when my parents separated. I had one session with her and was in no way ready or interested in sharing my pain, so I said everything was fine, and she never asked to see me again. Four years later I saw a second counsellor. That session was a disaster. I was feeling quite stuck. I had already been living on my own for two years and I think, upon reflection, I was just really sad about that. I was seeing the counsellor to work on my food issues, and the woman was very large. It was clear to me that she must also use food to cope, so before the session began I had a sense that she couldn't help me because she didn't "have it" herself. Then she made some very derogatory comments about my home town and what kind of people lived there. I didn't need to hear that judgement, I needed support and healing. So I left that session feeling even more hopeless. My all-or-nothing thinking was way up: "I had tried. There is no one who can help me. I am doomed to a life of food and body obsession."

Five years later, I responded to a brochure I noticed at the gym about using food to cope. I was fully expecting a diet of some sort—but this time, one that worked. I also fully expected to be in and out in a few weeks. I had no clue. I had no clue that my food issues were triggered by the abuse I experienced as a child. I had no clue at that time that my lack of friends was due to a need for isolation, my passive-aggressive behaviour, lying, and a general lack of integrity.

Within the first session I learned something momentous. Not everyone is sexually abused by their father. Really? I didn't know that. I had spent so many years discounting and dismissing that experience as something which everyone, or at least most people, experienced. I had talked myself into believing that it was a non-issue and didn't have anything at all to do with my being unable to stop eating. Well, Marie had a very different perspective. She asserted that my sexual-abuse experience was the root of my dissatisfaction with my body and my low self-esteem. This led me to use food to cope. This was a complete and total perspective shift, but, at the same time, I felt the truth of it. I didn't have to talk myself into believing that thought: it was true, and I knew it! I left that first session with no diet and a life-changing perspective. Wow! Double Wow!!

I worked with Marie every week, sometimes a few times a week, for six months, stopping only because I moved away to attend university. Before our work began, I was unable to offer myself any compassion or empathy and bring a halt to the 24/7 thoughts of food. I still had a long way to go in my healing, but, during those six months, I had gone from being completely tuned out to my body and what was going on for me and why, to being able to feel when I had a feeling, name it and respond to it. I learned that I was only obsessing about food and body image when I was overwhelmed—which wasn't all the time anymore. In fact, at that point, I could go days without binging. I wasn't dieting! And I wasn't gaining weight!

Marie was my shining light. A few years later, when I made the decision to work in this field, she was willing to be my mentor. She gave me a ton of support which ultimately allowed me to gain the skills and confidence needed to start the CEDRIC Centre. The reason I choose to acknowledge her in this chapter on Natural Eating is because I'm about to share the Model of Natural Eating. I have made some modifications over the years—added and expanded on a few points—but the basic model is the same one that Marie gave me all those years ago and which she has given me permission to share with you. Thank you, Marie.

As you read through this list of ideal thoughts, feelings, and behaviours around food, remember that this is your ultimate goal. It is not where you are expected to be now. Remind the Drill Sgt. that it takes time to shift a perspective, for example, the Diet Mentality, which has become a way of life. Invite yourself to pick one or two points from the Natural Eating list to focus your efforts on over the next little while. These points, coupled with the few from the Diet Mentality which you also chose to focus on, will give you a great framework. You will be more conscious of the old patterns which you would like to change, and you will also be able to offer yourself some new thoughts, feelings, and behaviours to replace them with.

PRINCIPLES OF NATURAL EATING

1. **Determine if your hunger is physical or emotional.**

    This means that, when you are thinking of eating or about to eat, stop and ask yourself, "Am I physically hungry right now?" Typically, if you have to guess or you can't tell, you are not. Also, you may get a response from within that sounds something like, "Who cares whether I'm hungry or not, just give me the food!" If so, you are definitely eating out of emotional need, that is, you are using food to cope. The most important thing that you can do right now is to let it be okay to use food to cope if you want to. It must be safe for you to check in, or you won't do it. If you even suspect for an instant that you are checking in with the intention of restricting yourself in that moment, whether you need food to cope or not, you will begin to create great resistance within to being conscious around food and then you are right back where you started. If this is your intention, you may as well return this book to the store. Right now, there must be a willingness within to allow yourself to use food to cope if you feel a need. So many people sabotage their process by turning Natural Eating into another diet. They make it so rigid and all-or-nothing that they have great resistance to checking in and becoming conscious about their relationship with food. This only serves to make their healing more difficult.

So, if you notice you are thinking about eating and: (a) are not obviously physically hungry; (b) are feeling hungry and are not allowing yourself to eat; (c) have already eaten or are full and wanting more, do the following:

2. **Acknowledge** that you are using your primary coping strategy and that that means you have needs which are unmet (unrelated to food and your body). You really need some

comfort and nurturing right now. Ask yourself if you can identify your present emotion. Remember, the desire to eat or restrict is not really about the food itself or even about your body, it is about those underlying needs for security and acceptance, and if the only way you believe you can get those needs met is through your body, you are in denial. You are also putting your energies into a remedy that hasn't worked yet and isn't about to start now! Acknowledge your underlying need that is triggering you to want to use food to cope. Acknowledge your need for nurturing and comfort, and ask yourself if you can identify your feeling. Begin to look beneath the behaviour to the feelings that triggered it, then at the thoughts which triggered the feelings, and ultimately at the needs that started it all. This is a process of working backwards, and right now it is best if you let yourself go through all the steps (behaviour, feelings, thoughts and needs). In a little while you will be able to go straight from your awareness of a coping behaviour to the identification of your underlying need. At the start of the checking-in process, when you notice the behaviour of wanting to use food to cope, it is easier to offer yourself a limited number of choices of feelings. For now, use the four basic human emotions: mad, glad, sad and scared.

3. **Validate.** Once you have acknowledged your desire to use food to cope and your underlying needs and feelings associated with it (which takes but a few seconds, once you have done it a handful of times), you are ready for validation. Your feelings are valid. Your feelings are appropriate, natural cues which arise in your body to signal you and let you know when something requires attention. They are always perfectly appropriate for the circumstance, because the circumstance, as you experience it, is not what is happening for someone else or outside of yourself. It is what is happening in *your* head—what you are telling yourself is going on. As we have discussed in previous chapters, sometimes our Drill Sgt. can

skew the story somewhat, and we see things very differently from others or from what really happened. The harmful beliefs you are carrying about yourself shade your perception of events. Everything gets filtered through the belief system of "I am bad," "I am wrong," "I am not good enough," and so on. The way out of this harmful pattern is to remind yourself of the Drill Sgt.'s tendency to reinforce bogus old beliefs, and stay with the feeling until you determine the reason for feeling this way. Begin to ask yourself what you would need to do in order to lessen or entirely relieve this feeling by asking this question: "In order for me to be completely peaceful right now, what would have to happen?" Remember this question, and your answer should not be about what needs to change with food or body. If this is the case, you are allowing yourself to stay on the surface, and you will not get to the root of what has triggered the coping strategy.

4. **Do not restrict yourself.**

   I know I have said it before, but it is so important that it bears repetition. *Do not restrict yourself.* If you feel the need to use food to cope while you are doing this piece of work about checking in, or after you have checked in, just tell yourself that you need your coping strategy right now, and it's okay. Restriction is punishment, and it creates negative feelings and a desire to binge. You will not always need food to cope, but for now you do. Most importantly, you are working to determine what you really need and how to give that to yourself. Make it as easy as you possibly can to engage in being conscious and in looking beneath your use of food to cope. Sometimes, this will mean allowing yourself to eat, restrict or purge, depending on the way you primarily use food to cope. Take the shame and guilt out of it. You do not need to be punished just because you are feeling overwhelmed and need to cope. The more you consistently demonstrate to yourself and the Drill Sgt. that you are actively working on a new way of being in relationship with food, the less guilt and shame the Drill Sgt. will dump on you when you find yourself using the old coping strategies. This is valuable because it is often the Drill Sgt.'s contempt and criticism that leads you to eat and keep eating, or conversely, to not allow yourself to eat when you are physically hungry.

5. **Remember, there are no good or bad foods.**

   Despite your Diet Mentality training and what it has told you, everything is fine, in moderation. If you catch yourself thinking of foods as legal or illegal, remind yourself that this is Diet Mentality and will only keep you mired in Compulsive Eating. Certainly there are choices that are more honouring of your goals for health and wellness. Yes, this is true. And the reality is that these foods aren't "bad". Labelling foods this way only leads *you* to feel bad when you make the choice to eat one. And until you are authentically at a place of regarding yourself highly enough that you freely choose to have more of those honouring choices in your repertoire, any pressure to choose anything, other than what you are wanting in that moment, will be seen as restriction and just more of the old Diet Mentality. So relax, lighten up, and focus on what's really important—*why* you are using food to cope. Heal this, and the rest takes care of itself.

6. **Eat what you want, when you want**.

   Yes, you read correctly. Assuming you're physically hungry there is no need to have a major battle in your head about what to eat. And if you are not physically hungry, you still don't need to have a battle. Just gently check in and identify the underlying triggers. Challenge yourself to let your food choices come from what you truly want to eat in that moment and not what you think you *should* have. Allow yourself to break the mould. Don't be afraid to have pancakes for dinner or pizza for breakfast, if that's what will satisfy you. Many times we have bought so fully into the social convention of what is a breakfast food and what is a dinner food (what you can't have before noon) that we don't even allow ourselves to have what we truly want when we want it. This is just more of the old Diet Mentality and creates a sense of restriction. Instead of just letting yourself have those pancakes for dinner, you might find yourself overeating a variety of things in an attempt to acquire the feeling and sensation you were seeking with the pancakes. Likewise, if you are partially through preparing spaghetti for dinner but discovered that you would really rather have something different, let it be okay to have that something else. Don't be so rigid that you force yourself to have something you don't want. As I said a moment ago, this will truly only lead to more overeating and a greater sense of mistrust within yourself.

7. **Stop when you feel physically satisfied.**

Try not to wait until you feel that over-stuffed feeling before you stop eating. Check in with yourself throughout your eating experience, and be honest about how full you feel. If you want to continue eating despite feelings of fullness, remind yourself that you are using food to cope and that it's okay. As I have outlined in the previous few pages, be conscious of this, and ask yourself, "What's up?" You may need to do this a few times during some meals, but it takes just a second and will relieve the guilt and anxiety so that you can just relax and be present. If you have any reason to suspect that by checking in while eating you won't allow yourself to eat if you still feel the need, then you just won't do it. A great mantra or thought that you can repeat to yourself right now to create a greater likelihood of feeling safe checking in is this: *It's okay if I feel the need to use food to cope now. I can do that without guilt, without distress, if I check in about why I need to use food to cope. I am not going to restrict myself.*

Also, be aware that many processed foods have special preservatives added to them which trigger an addictive response. Many fast foods, junk foods, high sugar, and trans-fat foods have been engineered to create a chemical reaction in your body which switches off your natural fullness signaling system. This is why there are some food stuffs that you are hard pressed to eat just one of. If you notice that there are certain fast foods, junk foods, or foods with lots of preservatives that you find yourself drawn to and eating the entire package in one breath, you can bet that these foods contain the substances that the manufacturers know will make you eat it all and want more.

A way around this is to visit your local health food store and purchase the healthful version of whatever junk food or treat you find yourself drawn to overeat. If it is bread, pick up some organic whole grain bread. If it is chips, pick up some great potato chips that contain simply potatoes, oil, and salt and taste fabulous. If you are drawn to sweets, pick up some organic chocolate almonds or some great organic dark chocolate. You just won't feel drawn to binge on those foods. You'll enjoy them more and have much less chatter from the Drill Sgt. during and after your eating.

8. **Remind yourself frequently that you can always have more, later.**

    This is such a key point. I frequently receive feedback from clients who, when they remind themselves of this point and truly trust themselves to follow through, note the urgency to overeat in that moment completely disappears. Promise yourself that you will not restrict anymore. If you promise that you won't restrict yourself, you can relieve any fear you may have about stopping to check in should you identify that you are using food to cope. You can make it safe to not eat everything right now, if you know that you will let yourself have **more** of that food **later** when you want it. Affix this note to your refrigerator or pantry: I CAN ALWAYS HAVE MORE, LATER! And mean it. When you next want it, let yourself have whatever it is. No Drill Sgt. No Diet Mentality. You can always have more, later.

9. **Eat as often as you feel the need, regardless of the time.**
    Let go of scheduled mealtime eating. If you are not hungry at dinner, wait until you are hungry and have your meal then. Likewise, if you become hungry in the afternoon, don't force

yourself to wait until dinnertime to respond to your body's signals. This process is as much about tuning in to the underlying triggering needs as it is about relearning to honour the natural signals of hunger and fullness from your body. Give yourself the gift of challenging the concept of "mealtimes". Begin to experiment with allowing yourself to eat when you are hungry, regardless of the time. Many people who use food to cope have a tough time with this key step because they are so concerned about the approval of others. They don't want to be the only one eating or not eating at a certain time. It will call attention to their relationship with food, and that is the last thing they want. If this fits for you, just ask yourself if you would rather have a free and easy relationship with food or have that person's approval? Either choice is fine. If the approval is paramount to you, just acknowledge that you are seeking to meet that need right now, and you are using your Diet Mentality coping strategy to do it. Then ask yourself if there might be some way for you to meet your own need for approval right now? Give yourself the opportunity to meet this need yourself. You might do this by saying, "I'm hungry and need food right now, and I deserve to take care of myself." Yes, that would work. You might also tell the key people in your life that you are experimenting with reconnecting with your hunger and fullness cues; therefore, you are going to allow yourself to eat when you are hungry, and this might mean eating at a different time. Ask them for their understanding and support. This works very well with spouses and co-workers because it takes away any energy we are carrying about potentially not having their approval or not meeting their needs for connection and shared mealtimes. You can still sit with the person while they eat and vice versa.

10. **Do not feel guilt.**

Last, but definitely not least, we come to the issue of guilt. Guilt is a throwback from the Diet Mentality. It is a coping strategy from the Drill Sgt. It is his way of manipulating you to do what he thinks you need to do. Whenever you catch yourself feeling some guilt about what you have eaten or what you want to eat, remind yourself that **to restrict yourself is punishment**. The more you restrict yourself in terms of when and what you eat, the more you will reinforce the message that you are undeserving, and you will continue to be plagued by bad thoughts about yourself. Restriction and guilt serve only to keep you focused on food and body image while you are spinning your wheels on the surface. They keep you from acknowledging that you have a legitimate need which is driving you to: (a) want a particular food; (b) eat when you are not hungry; or (c) eat more than the Drill Sgt. thinks you should. The guilt must go. And the more you remind yourself that food is just a coping strategy and seek to understand what is triggering you in this moment, the less guilt you will feel and the more you will be truly free to achieve the goals you have for health, wellness and life in general.

As you begin to experiment with Natural Eating over the next few weeks, keep in mind that it would be normal if you were unaware that you have used food to cope, or if you didn't remember any of your new tools until after the fact. It could be moments, hours or days until you realize that was a coping strategy. It doesn't matter. *It is absolutely 100% never too late to check in about what was up.* Don't kid yourself that you won't remember what triggered you. You will be able to figure it out, if you use the list-of-stressors tool, regardless of what length of time has passed.

Ah, yes, the list of stressors. Let's take a look at this now, because it is the tool which you are going to employ when you notice yourself using your food coping strategy to help determine what the underlying need/trigger is. The list of stressors puts you in the driver's seat because it supports you to be conscious of why you are doing what you are doing with your coping strategies. And it proves to you, in short order, that *there is always a good reason for why you do what you do.* It also supports you to attend to the unmet need which triggered the desire for this coping strategy in the first place, and this is a place of true power.

The List of Stressors

The list of stressors provides you with concrete and simple steps to aid in becoming aware of times when you have used a coping strategy and to identify the need which was triggered. You can then find solutions to meet your needs in life-enhancing ways. Below, I will speak about how the list of stressors specifically pertains to food, but please keep in mind that this tool will work exactly the same for any of your coping strategies. When you notice them, you can use the list of stressors to resolve some of these detrimental devices, such as: Avoidance; Procrastination; Co-Dependency; the P.L.A.; Depression; Alexithymia; Anger; Blaming; Drill Sgt. Criticism and Bad Body Thoughts; All-or-Nothing Thinking, and Intrusive Ideation.

One more point: the list of stressors will work, without a doubt, but you must use it! You can't just think about it. So those of you in the contemplation or determination stage of change should read this over and get a stronger sense of how it might work; but only through action will it actually effect change for you.

If you are feeling resistant to writing and giving yourself the gift of empathy and information, check and see if there is any resistance to change coming up or any all-or-nothing thinking going on. Is the Drill Sgt. telling you this won't work, or is there a part of you that isn't quite sure you are ready to stop using food to cope? If this hits home, it's because you have gone into all-or-nothing thinking and are telling yourself that, if you do this piece of self-awareness and personal growth, you will be unable to use food to cope if need be. This is untrue. There is nothing stopping you or me from overeating, restricting, or purging whenever we want to. Let's face it, if our Drill Sgt., with his threats, can't get us to stop when we really want to, doesn't it stand to reason that anytime we really need to use food, we will be able to? Yes.

Also, let it be okay to throw your writing away when you are done. By all means, you can keep it; even have a lovely journal that you enjoy writing in. But if you are resistant to writing and getting your inner thoughts, feelings, and needs out on paper because you fear that others will read what you have written, you may be able to get over this hurdle by letting it be okay to immediately erase or discard what you have written *once you have read it over.*

Now let's start using the list of stressors in relation to your food-coping strategy. To make the best use of the list of stressors and consequently effect significant change in your use of food to cope, make a commitment to yourself (on a daily basis) to be on the lookout for any of the following experiences:

a) whenever you notice you are thinking about eating and you are not hungry;

b) whenever you notice that you are eating and you are not hungry, or conversely, you know you are hungry and you are not allowing yourself to eat; and

c) whenever you notice that you started eating out of true physical hunger, yet now you are full and you are still eating.

When you do notice that you are engaged in one of the above situations with food, do the following:

1. Stop and take a deep breath. Really. Stop... Breathe... You might notice the PLA. In that moment of stopping and being present, you have already stepped out of the behaviour and into a more refined state of conscious awareness.

2. Invite yourself to be aware of what your thoughts are. Do not get carried away by them—just notice them. What thought-level coping strategy is dominant right now?

3. Notice what you are feeling in your body—any emotions you can identify (mad, glad, sad and scared)—and also any physical sensations, for example, tension in your shoulders or nervous tummy. If it had gone unnoticed before, you will likely tune in at this time to the permeating level of anxiety.

4. Then ask yourself, "What just happened? What might I have just experienced or thought of from the past, present or future which could have impacted me and led to feeling the need to use food to cope?"

Cover all the bases—anything you can think of: past, present and future, and any thoughts feelings or behaviours you may have about those past, present and future things. Write out your responses to these questions. Don't do this part in your head until you are very familiar with this process on paper; that is, very familiar with the inner workings of your Drill Sgt. and underlying needs. The Drill Sgt. is too slippery, and he will sabotage your process if you retain those thoughts. He will have you buying in to an all-or-nothing thought so fully and quickly that you will come away from this process feeling stuck and hopeless. In fact, if you do come away from this process feeling this way, I can guarantee your Drill Sgt. has had the last word and is telling you a nasty all-or-nothing story. So even if you feel some resistance, are just feeling too tired, or don't have the time, it is important to write down your experiences at this point. Remember, you can always throw them away as soon as you are done if privacy is a concern.

Remember and reinforce to yourself that it doesn't matter if your Drill Sgt. thinks these particular events are too small and insignificant to be impacting you, write down anything you can think of which could have had an impact on you just now, however small and unlikely the Drill Sgt. thinks it is. On the surface, a triggering event can truly be as simple as your favourite bakery not having your favourite muffin, or someone giving you a strange look on the street. This process is about looking beneath these seemingly "small," (at least from the Drill Sgt.'s perspective) surface events to the underlying and fundamental needs that were triggered in those situations. Recall that your alexithymia (the disconnection from feelings) makes it hard to know that anything is up for you until you are already maxed out on your stress threshold. So it will seem at first that you are "overreacting" to whatever the trigger was in the moment. But remember that your response was not only in relation to this immediate trigger but also to all the unfinished business you have within you right now. You will prove to yourself very quickly with this method that, if you are behaving in any of the three key ways around food, as outlined above, you are using food to cope, and this means you have a need which is unmet. Letting the Drill Sgt. shut you down or criticize you for being weak or too sensitive will only compromise your recovery by either slowing or shutting it down all together. And we definitely don't want that!

5. Once you have made your list of stressors which may be impacting you, look it over. One or more items will jump off the page and you will feel an emotional reaction to seeing that written down. The emotional reaction may be an increase in your P.L.A. It may be a feeling of resistance or a feeling of sadness, fear, anger—perhaps, even joy. It might be a feeling of deep knowing and acknowledgment as you connect with the reality that this particular event is significant to you in ways you hadn't previously acknowledged. Any or all of the above may occur as you create a list of stressors. The key is to acknowledge the feelings that you are aware of from these events. Next to the item(s) on your list which have really struck you in your review, make note of the feelings which come up as you think of them. Ask the Drill Sgt. to relax here, and just let the feeling come; reassure him that this is part of a process which will culminate in a much-desired solution and that you are not going to get stuck in the feeling.

6. For each item or *the* item that really struck you from your list of stressors, ask yourself: "What need do I have (safety and security, love/acceptance/belongingness, esteem) around this issue which are unmet in the way I am addressing it/have addressed it/plan to address it?" Write those answers down.

7. Ask yourself: "What is one thing I could do for that item which would allow me to feel that I was taking a step toward meeting my need?" Let go of your all-or-nothing thinking

here! Write down any possible solutions you can think of,
however far-out and unlikely. One will surface as feeling
"right". Another way of asking that question which may fit
better for you is: "What needs to happen in regards to that
item on my list in order for me to feel peaceful right now?"

It doesn't have to be a perfect solution or attend to the issue completely. Rather, the key piece here is to prove to yourself that your
true intention is to respect and honour your needs, and then begin to
do whatever you can to meet them. This is how you will build your
inner sense of security and integrity and heal yourself completely,
not only from the use of food as a coping strategy but also from
any of your other harmful coping strategies, such as, all-or-nothing
thinking, bad body thoughts, alexithymia and co-dependent behaviours. It can be very helpful to bounce these ideas off someone. This
is where a good counsellor is indispensable; someone who can hear
the plans you are making for meeting your needs, and someone who
can point out any subtle all-or-nothing thinking, co-dependency, or
passive-aggressive behaviour. A friend who is a few steps ahead on
their healing journey (someone who is stepping clear of their own
harmful coping strategies) can also be an invaluable resource at a
time like this.

If you are feeling a little concerned at the moment upon reading
this for the first time and thinking it might be a challenge to figure
out how best to meet your needs, let this concern go as best you can.
We each have an innate sense of what we truly need and also of how
we can best meet this need. The only reason you may be doubtful is
that you have had some key people in your life (and your Drill Sgt.)
telling you frequently that, for whatever reason, you are not allowed
to do this, or it just won't work. As we proceed in our work together,
you are going to learn many ways of meeting your needs in specific
situations.

A key note: above, I said that one of your brainstormed solutions
to meeting your need(s) would just feel "right". If you have this feeling and it is immediately followed by a sinking feeling, a sense of

frustration or hopelessness or despair, or by the desire to eat or engage in your primary coping strategy, this is good news! This is your Drill Sgt. and your Authentic Self feeling triggered by the thought of doing something new. Your Drill Sgt. is responding by going into all-or-nothing thinking and intrusive ideation. Your Authentic Self is responding by going into resistance because it thinks you are going to create a greater need for security by acting in this new way. The reality is, unless you do respond in this new way, you will continue to feel fragmented and unsafe: you will continue to look outside of yourself for validation and acceptance instead of feeling grounded and secure in your regard for yourself and in your ability to keep yourself safe. Therefore, if you notice that a sinking or stuck feeling accompanies your identification of your unmet needs and your solution to meet them, this is normal behaviour at first. It is to be expected, because you have yet to prove to either the Drill Sgt. or your inner little being that you are capable of handling things in a different way and that it will be so much better for you to do so. Don't just let the Drill Sgt. or the fears of your Authentic Self shut you down.

Another way to look at this last piece is to imagine yourself in a relationship with someone. Let's say that you are married to a man. In this relationship with your husband, you consistently make promises you don't keep and renege on your commitments. You ignore his feelings or criticize him for having them. You consistently place him in situations which create a lack of security for him, and then you judge or ignore him when he expresses his concern about this. When he responds to all this hurt, rejection, frustration, and lack of security in the relationship with you by turning to food to cope, you judge him for that and express your disgust at his weakness. Ouch! What state do you think your relationship with him would be in at the point you awoke to your behaviour? How much trust and safety would there be between the two of you? Might he have cause to mistrust you? Might he have cause to feel resistant to anything new you are trying in the relationship because of your past pattern of fits and starts? I think he is very wise to be mistrustful and to question your integrity and ability to come through.

If you use food to cope, you can guarantee that this verbal assault and mistrustful relationship is what takes place within you every day and probably has for years. The only solution is to be consistent in your reassurance and in your new ways of behaviour. And when you aren't, because sometimes you will forget or it will seem too hard at first, you must find the courage within to take responsibility for your behaviour. A simple *I'm sorry, I forgot all about this new way of doing things* will do. Ask for forgiveness from within, and ask your Authentic Self what you could do now to demonstrate your trustworthiness and enhance your sense of inner security. Action is the key here—words will not be enough. Intention is good, but it must be followed by action. If not, there is no integrity, and trust can not be built.

Above all, remember that you have previously had to tune out to your inner knowing because it wasn't safe to be aware of the dysfunction around you. You have had to compromise your integrity to survive. You no longer have to do this. You can acknowledge and validate your authentic feelings and needs. In so doing, you will prove how capable you are and how safe it is to be conscious; in fact, you will prove how incredibly unsafe it is to be unconscious. You will begin to enjoy the feeling of confidence and empowerment that comes from knowing what is and isn't working in your life, and from knowing that you have the skills to do something productive and life-enhancing about every single situation that comes up.

I highly encourage you to use the list-of-stressors tool on a daily basis for a few weeks. You will soon see clear patterns emerging in terms of the situations which trigger you to use your coping strategies. This information will be put to great use as we progress with our work on your relationship with yourself and your relationship with others. After the first few weeks of regular self-exploration in this way, you will have proven to yourself that: (a) there is always a reason for doing what you do; (b) it is safe to be conscious of your feelings and need(s); and, (c) you can always find a solution to every problem. In essence, each time you use the list-of-stressors tool, you are not only meeting your needs for security and acceptance but also for self-esteem.

SECTION III

YOUR RELATIONSHIP WITH YOURSELF

Now it's time to talk about your relationship with yourself. We have had some conversation about what your current relationship with Self looks like and how this impacts you, when we spoke about the Drill Sgt. and his way of motivating through criticism. And chances are, those of you in the action stage of change have already had an experience of having a new type of conversation with him that was much more helpful to you and brought you closer to feeling integrated and adult, if only momentarily. If you are still in the contemplation or determination stages of readiness for change, continue to allow yourself to just read and gather information. Make mental notes of the pieces that you really identify with, and you will come back to them when you are ready to take action. It's all good!

In this section we are going to look at current patterns of thoughts, feelings, and behaviours that are primarily to do with your relationship with you. Yes, you have one! Even if it has not received a great deal of attention and you would rather not acknowledge it, it is there. You are there. It is key to establish a solid, constant connection with yourself as a part of supporting you to continue on your path to integration and no longer using food to cope. To this end, we will be exploring all the coping strategies which you may currently be using to maintain or numb out to your old harmful stories and beliefs about yourself.

This piece of work on relationship with Self is very exciting. It allows you to free yourself from the old, stifling perspective you have of yourself in relation to the world and everything in it. This radical shift in perspective gives you the freedom to live your life in a way which is truly honourable and gratifying.

11

External Versus
Internal Locus of Control

As we explore your relationship with yourself, we will continue to return to the concept of ensuring that you are doing your best. Doing your best simply means doing what is reasonable for you based on your ability and within the framework of a life that is balanced and honouring of you. The Drill Sgt.'s current perspective of "best" means perfection at all costs. And unfortunately he doesn't determine what is "perfect" for you based on the concept of who you really are, because he believes that the real you is unacceptable. Therefore, all of your authentic needs and feelings are immediately discounted in favor of what someone outside of you says is right to feel, think and do. This keeps us stuck in a fragmented state. When we are focused predominantly on what other people think or do as an indication of how we should be, we are unable to bring our Authentic Selves to any relationship. We must remain in one of our personae as a ruse to gain approval and reduce the potential for rejection.

The Drill Sgt. within you is constantly comparing you to everyone and everything. His intention is, at long last, to gain for you a sense of true security and approval in the world. His method only serves to keep you feeling insecure and fragmented. Comparing yourself to others keeps you stuck in a pattern of judgement of yourself and others.

How do you compare to this woman in terms of looks? Her thighs versus yours? Her nose? What is she wearing? What size does she take? What about intelligence? What was her test score versus yours? Did she just say something stupid, or did she blow you out of the water? How about finances? Well, at least *you* are more self-aware, right? Oh, damn. She's read *The Four Agreements*, also. Suddenly you are feeling diminished and insecure, as well as feeling animosity toward someone who is being just themselves.

The external comparison game that the Drill Sgt. plays, by way of assessing your acceptability and perfection, gives one the feeling of being jerked around from moment to moment. One moment you are feeling good because you have "one up" on someone, and the next moment you feel worthless because someone else is "better" at something than you. Then you must work harder and harder at everything else just to prove that you are acceptable.

Any time you are dependent on external feedback or on being better than someone else at anything for your sense of security and confidence, you are extremely vulnerable. And as long as your highest value is what you look like, you will remain a vulnerable, insecure, food- and body-image focused individual. You may object and declare that your highest value is *not* what you look like! You value honesty, compassion and similar traits. Well, this may be true. You *may* value those things. But what is it that absorbs your focus most of the day? What is it that you continue to assure yourself will make all the difference? Not honesty, compassion or authenticity. It's your appearance. Anyone who uses food to cope believes that, if they just managed to get their food and weight issues under control, their life would be different. Okay, that's true. But without healing the underlying triggers and past trauma, it would not be all that different. Certainly not different enough that it's worth spending most of your current thought energy obsessing about what you ate or what you are going to eat.

The concept of doing your best is not a new one. It is a great motto, but this concept must be approached from a very deliberate and conscious Nurturing Parent. Why? Because once your current "motivation through criticism" Drill Sgt. gets hold of it, look out! His definition of "best" is perfection. And perfection to him means that you are so amazing that you never do anything which isn't just right for everyone. You never upset people. You never have a contrary thought or opinion. In other words, you are the "perfect" co-dependent. You look a certain way, which satisfies everyone, but not so incredibly fabulous that you alienate people. You absolutely never, ever make a mistake, and you know everything (or at least you are very skilled in pretending you do!). As far as the Drill Sgt. is concerned, anything short of complete approval and acceptance outside of your Self is a failure on your part and unacceptable.

The Diet Mentality of our society says that the way to be externally acceptable is to have breast augmentation, liposuction, no noticeable body fat, and a million dollars. It is not only unrealistic and unnatural, but it is also unhealthful. Ah, but the Drill Sgt. in you doesn't really care, because the most important thing to him is meeting your needs for security and acceptance. And he believes that those needs must be met outside of yourself and can only be met when you have total acceptance and approval from everyone. He'll worry about your quality of life and your health and wellness later. Right! Any of you who have been playing the Diet Mentality game for long will know that "later" never comes. From the Drill Sgt.'s perspective, there is always something more that you need to change/do/be in order to secure your place in the world. The only way the Drill Sgt. knows how to do this is to continue to pressure you to look a certain way so that you will finally get the approval and sense of security in the world that you so desperately seek.

What we are talking about here is called the "External Locus of Control". The External Locus of Control (ELOC) simply means that the power over your life and what happens in it comes from outside of you. Let's consider the ELOC as something that you rate on a percentage scale. A very high ELOC means that 75 to 100% of what you do, think, and feel in your life is dictated by other people. If someone else thinks you should look a certain way or do a certain something, you immediately begin to question what you previously thought and felt was right for you. And it isn't just one or two people that you feel dominated by—it's everyone. When you have a high ELOC, you are constantly looking outside yourself for feedback about how to be, what you should do, and how acceptable you are. There are many problems with this, but it all boils down to the fact that your life is not in your hands. You are completely dependent on the moods and mental well-being of every individual you come into contact with. Therefore, you could never, not in a million years, feel secure. Your approach to meeting your needs for security and approval is consistently undermining your true potential to meet those needs now. Some obvious examples of how an External Locus of Control may play out in your life are:

- You are driving along, having a peaceful moment, when someone cuts you off and then honks and gives *you* the finger! A person with a strong ELOC will take this personally and feel upset that that person was mad at them. They might even begin to question what they may have done to upset the road rager, and they begin to feel insecure. In worst cases, they will believe it had something to do with how they looked. They may even be grateful that he didn't yell something about them being fat! Regardless, they will definitely begin to think about their body and about food.

- You show up at the office and someone who usually is quite friendly doesn't even acknowledge your "good morning". If you are a person with a high ELOC, you will immediately begin to wonder what you have done to upset this person and what you can do to make them happy with you. You won't be able to let it drop until you have had some positive interaction with this person. But you will also not likely be able to just ask them if they are upset with you. Your PLA goes up, and you are reaching for food to cope at coffee break if not before!

- You are walking down the street and you pass a group of people walking the other way. Just as you pass them, a great laugh erupts. Your ELOC will have you believing that there was something about you which they found funny. If you are particularly insecure about your body, you will assume they were judging your body size. You will immediately become depressed and wish you had worn something else or that you had chosen not to go out today. Regardless, you head for home as soon as you can, cocoon with your favorite comfort foods, and tell yourself you will do something about your body tomorrow.

These are just a few simple, everyday examples. And not one of them includes any interactions with key people in your life. Those are even more likely to have you coming from a high ELOC and feeling more overwhelmed. Remember, the key piece here is this: if you are at all inclined to believe that your sense of security and approval must come from outside of yourself, and that who you are naturally and authentically isn't enough to garner this approval, you will have a high ELOC and feel dominated easily by the moods and needs of others.

In any of the above and relatively benign examples of ELOC, you can see how quickly your state of being is impacted and overrun by the moods and behaviours of others. Your high level of ELOC is due to three key pieces within you that work together to completely undermine your self-esteem:

1. Your current **all-or-nothing thinking** makes you believe that there is a right and a wrong in every situation. In most cases, there truly is not. In most cases there is *your* truth and *their* truth, and both have merit once you understand them. There is room for both. The Drill Sgt. is desperate for concrete explanations—a clear sense of right and wrong. He believes that knowing something for certain means you have more security. Unfortunately, what this kind of all-or-nothing, concrete thinking does is bring you a false sense of security which is bound, at some point, to be undermined by

reality—reality being what *is* true and not what you would like the truth to be. There are very few absolute truths. The greatest sense of security in the world comes not from having the external world nailed down, but from being strongly grounded within by your values and principles, and by trusting in your self-worth.

2. Your current **belief that you lack security and approval** makes you desperate to fit in and be liked, even by people you don't particularly care for. This leads you to behave inauthentically and compromise yourself repeatedly in an effort to ensure that others will think well of you. This lack of integrity in relationships leads to further fragmentation within and a strong sense of insecurity which, sadly, you seek to resolve by trying harder to make others happy and like you.

3. Having assumed there is a problem and that it must have something to do with you, your Drill Sgt.'s willingness to discount your authentic feelings and needs makes you quick to assume **it is you who is "wrong"**. There is such a strong lack of trust in your perception of things that the Drill Sgt. automatically sides *against* you and *for* the other person. It doesn't matter who they are, whether they have the slightest clue what they are saying, or how competent you are on the subject, if someone is saying or doing something which doesn't feel right to you, but they seem confident or at least are acting confidently about their perspective, the automatic reaction of the Drill Sgt. is to encourage you to believe them and doubt yourself. How many times have you actively talked yourself out of your authentic feelings and thoughts on a situation because someone else seemed more certain, only to later receive information that validates what you were thinking and wanting to say? Far too many, I'm willing to bet.

The point here is that, if anyone outside of you appears anything less than blissfully happy or has a contrary opinion to you, you will take this on and make it about some failing on your part. You will buy in to your internal story or perhaps even their story that you have done something wrong or that your thinking is wrong. This leads to more external approval-seeking, more tuning out to what is true for you, and a reinforcement of the old belief that your authentic thoughts and feelings are unacceptable and should be kept well hidden.

And how does your External Locus of Control impact your use of food to cope? Having an elevated ELOC means that you have a very high level of insecurity and a strong need for external approval. You are willing to throw yourself over for anyone who appears more confident and sure of themselves than you. You don't trust your own feelings and perceptions of events, and this further undermines your sense of security in the world. And we know that the needs for security and approval are the two key needs which will drive you to use food to cope. Currently, those unmet needs for security and approval trigger your Drill Sgt. and the bad body thoughts and intrusive ideation which accompany him. These thoughts trigger you to feel sad and scared, or depressed and hopeless, and those feelings trigger you to use food to cope in a confused effort to both numb out and to make yourself more acceptable.

Now here's a thought... if the Drill Sgt., regardless of his positive intent, is so willing to throw you over and buy in to any negative feedback from others, while encouraging you to believe that everything that is going on for everyone is your fault and your responsibility, I'm here to tell you that he can't have it both ways. Either you are responsible for everything, or you are not. And if he wants to encourage you to buy in to the belief that you are so powerful that you are the cause of all the feelings and behaviours of everyone around you, including the lady at the office, the person in the car, and the folks passing by on the street, then I say you have to allow yourself to take responsibility for all the good things you see happening.

Each time someone is having a great day, gets that promotion or wins the lottery, congratulate yourself! You did it! It's your "fault"! Ridiculous! Right? Yes, it is. So, remember this. You are no more responsible for the needs, feelings and behaviours of others than you are for the weather. And freeing yourself from that old, bogus, double standard is truly as simple as making a commitment to no longer take responsibility for the feelings and needs of others (barring dependent children). (We will talk much more about this in our work on relationship with others.) Whenever the Drill Sgt. tries to tell you that your need for security or approval hangs in the balance because someone didn't smile at you, ask him this: "Are you willing to encourage me to take equal responsibility for the good things that happen around me? If not, I can't possibly be responsible for the bad!"

And that brings me exactly to where we need to be: the antithesis of the ELOC—the antidote for co-dependency. Enter the Internal Locus of Control (ILOC). No, we are not talking about vanity and selfishness. We are not talking about the all-or-nothing fear of complete self-absorption which the Drill Sgt. believes will happen if you allow yourself to listen *first* to yourself *then* to others. We are talking about a secure, trusting, peaceful, expansive and inclusive state of existence that comes from knowing what you feel and need, as well as from being committed to respecting this above all else. Again, remember, don't go all-or-nothing on me here. Trust me. Allow yourself to remain open to the possibility that *you can trust yourself to know what's right for you* and to have your needs met in ways which respect you and everyone you may come in contact with. It isn't all-or-nothing. There is more than enough room for you and all your feelings and needs in every relationship you have or ever will have, once you stop buying in to the belief that there is a right and a wrong, an either/or, a black and white.

An individual with a high ILOC is motivated predominantly by their own needs and feelings. On the extreme end, someone with an approach to life which is 100% ILOC is considered a narcissist or a sociopath: no concern or consideration is given to the needs of others. I am not encouraging you to completely tune out to what is going on in the world around you. I encourage my clients to go for a 75/25 split. That's 75% Internal Locus of Control to 25% External (just in case your Drill Sgt. was trying to convince you to turn the split the other way!) Why 75/25? Because we can't feel truly secure in the world when we permit ourselves to be controlled and manipulated by the feelings, thoughts, needs and behaviours of others. But we do live in a society. This means we are going to run into other humans from time to time, and we must have a way of interacting with them which both honours us and respects them as individuals. Being true to yourself first is clearly fundamental to your sense of groundedness, security, and eventually to your ability to realize your full potential. We must always return to what we truly think, feel and need, and then demonstrate our ability to take action to meet those needs in ways that are respectful and right for us. To clarify, I am not saying that 25% of the time you let others dictate your actions. What I'm saying is the 25% that is ELOC represents your consideration of others feelings and needs in determining not *if* you will meet your need but *how*.

Yes, that's right. We are not talking about letting others influence us out of taking care of ourselves and honouring what we need and feel. Rather, we are talking about allowing ourselves to consider how our behaviour may impact others, and how we can take steps in ways which acknowledge and respect the feelings and needs of others while simultaneously meeting our needs. In the end, you will always do what is right for you. You will just do it with consideration for others. And in case you are wondering, this doesn't mean going silent and underground so as not to ruffle feathers. This doesn't demonstrate respect or dignity to either party. What I am speaking to is learning how to have courageous conversations about your feelings and needs and trusting that, above all, you have the right to take care of yourself first. Yes, you do!

"How on earth do I get there?" you may be asking. Well, a solid 75/25 split requires you to challenge some of the old beliefs and stories you are carrying about your worth and deservedness. As long as you are clinging to the old beliefs that you are unworthy or unacceptable, for example, you will still lack trust in your right to have what you want and need. This lack of trust will continue to lead you to give more credence to what others think, feel and need than to your own needs. We are back at square one, feeling less than others and believing that you need their approval in order to be acceptable and loved. This, as you are very well aware, leads you to feel quite insecure and to rely on a variety of harmful coping strategies just to make it through the day.

If your goal is to have a life which is free from the 24/7 focus on food and body image that you currently experience, then your goal is also to create a life experience that epitomizes the 75/25 split of Internal versus External Locus of Control. All of the pieces we have talked about so far will be helpful in creating that life-enhancing balance. And remember to actively challenge the double standard of the Drill Sgt., when you notice him blaming you for the bad or stressful things which are going on around you. This will give you a great boost in your ability to deflect other people's moods and feelings.

Now let's explore another piece which will greatly influence your ability to step free from your current ELOC: Core Beliefs, also known as Your Personal Story.

12

Core Beliefs:
Your Personal Story

The entire concept of a relationship with yourself hinges on what you believe about your own worth and acceptability. If you are still buying in to the old story you learned as a child/young adult that you are: (a) undeserving of love; (b) unacceptable as you are; or (c) unsafe in the world, you will have a difficult time trying anything new which goes against that deeply-ingrained story. Thus, while you may truly desire to change your relationship with food and to feel better about yourself, the underlying belief that you carry will continuously undermine your efforts and ultimately bring you to a place of paralysis and procrastination. This only reinforces the old belief and leads you to feel more stuck and hopeless. You may question why you are bothering to try to change when you have never been successful and always return to the same old behaviour. You may also feel as though you should give up. This is not uncommon, but it is important for you to see it as the old all-or-nothing thinking that it is.

I believe that you won't stay in this defeated and doomed place for long, because something in you wants more. You want a life that is yours to live; one that inspires and fulfills you. And this desire motivates you to try again. Unfortunately, what you have been trying and re-trying is not likely to work. The restriction of the Diet Mentality and the "motivation through criticism" of the Drill Sgt. only serve to reinforce your old defeating beliefs. The simple act of tuning out to your body and listening to what someone or something outside of you says you *should* do is a gesture of disrespect and a true indignity to yourself.

As a child and/or young adult, you may have had to adopt an ELOC in order to survive in your family of origin or in other certain circles. You may have had to tune out to your authentic needs and feelings in order to remain in an uncomfortable situation, without being aware of how uncomfortable you were. As an adult, you are capable of creating relationships which support you to be the best that you can be. But as long as you are buying in to the old story about your worth and deservedness, you will continue to create relationships and life situations which mirror this old harmful perspective of yourself.

Brain Development and the Formation of Beliefs

Because we are very vulnerable as children and teens, we are highly sensitive to the feelings and behaviours of people around us, and we know it. We need these people to take care of us.

A key point is that we also have an undeveloped brain until we reach the age of about 19 to 21, as mentioned in Chapter 8 (the Diet Mentality). The last parts of our brain to fully develop are our frontal lobes. These lobes house our capacity for rational thinking, allowing us a broader perspective on the world. Prior to 21, we are predominantly driven by our old brain, which is totally immersed in concrete, all-or-nothing thinking. The old brain's prime directive is to assess situations for any threat and then give you two choices: fight or flight.

When we experience situations as children, for example: rejection; punishment; lack of praise; lack of interest; being left out; or verbal, physical, emotional and sexual abuse, our old brain tells us we are in danger, and we go into fight or flight mode. However, since we can't very well fight (until we are older) or leave the situation as dependent children, we must find a way to deal with it that best meets our fundamental needs for security and approval. This happens in two significant ways, and both are thanks predominantly to the old brain and its all-or-nothing thinking.

1. We make it about *us*. The dominant old brain can only interpret things in relation to us. From this naturally-childish perspective, everything which happens in the world has something to do with us. We are particularly attentive to any person or situation which may undermine our sense of security in any way. The child's brain is incapable of coming up with this thought: "This has nothing to do with me. Dad just had a bad day." It only knows that something is threatening your emotional or physical security, and this triggers the fight or flight response. Again, since you can't leave and aren't likely to be successful in a fight, your choice is to find some way to ensure the harmful situation is not repeated. Making it about us means that we can then potentially control the situation, even if just in our minds. If you caused it, you can do something to ensure it does not happen again, right? This is the old brain's way of thinking. While it helps the little person in that situation to feel safer for the moment, it has the harmful side effect of making you a highly skilled co-dependent.

2. In addition to making everything about us in order to feel some degree of control and safety in our environment, we also use the coping strategy of going within. We begin to withdraw our Authentic Selves from the situation, and, more and more, we interact through our fragmented personae. We work hard at being who we think the other person wants or expects us to be rather than who we truly are, and we do

this because we have incorrectly interpreted the situation as being about *us*; therefore, *there must be something wrong with us,* if we are being neglected or mistreated. As we have previously discussed, the process of fragmentation leads to a scared, little Authentic Self surrounded by a fairly large and dominant Drill Sgt. The Drill Sgt. is simply the internalization of the models you had for nurturing and support, and he is doing his best to acquire the security and approval that you need. He's going about doing this based on the erroneous, old brain belief that you are responsible for all those painful events; therefore, you must be flawed and unacceptable as you are.

The pattern of making it about *you* and then withdrawing into yourself means there is no one left to challenge those old thoughts and stories you have told yourself about what was really happening in those situations. That's it. You're done. Your old brain told you a story to make sense of the situation the best it could, and now, many years later, you are still living as though this story were true—as though you deserved to be treated this way because you truly were "bad" or "fat" or "ugly" or "stupid" or just plain "not good enough."

Your Old Core Beliefs

Let's take a good solid look at that old story of yours and what you are still telling yourself about your role in the situation. First, let's explore the old core beliefs that are influencing you on a daily basis.

1. What does your Drill Sgt. say about you when you are being self-critical?
2. What names does the Drill Sgt. call you when you are angry and frustrated?
3. What were the words people in your life used to describe you when they were angry or disappointed in you?

4. What messages about yourself did you receive from your parents, other family members, and/or peers (these can be verbal and non-verbal)?

Consider the above information. If you could capture the essence of your doubts about yourself in a single sentence: I am _____ _____, what would it be?

You may actually come up with a few sentences. Some common and very debilitating old beliefs which you may be carrying are: I am ugly; I am fat; I am stupid; I am worthless; I am undeserving; I am not good enough; I am not enough; I am unacceptable; I am unlovable; I am a burden.

If you take a look at your core belief statements and then ask yourself what's important about..., as we did for the Drill Sgt. piece earlier. For example, if you carry the belief that you are not good enough, you would ask yourself, "What's important about being good enough?" You would keep asking, "What's important about that?" until you felt that you had reached the bottom and the core answer. This will lead you to discover that each of your core belief statements boils down to wanting approval or security. Remember, those are the two fundamental needs we have as children—after our physiological needs for food, air and water, of course.

Allow yourself to be completely honest right now about what you truly believe at your core. Those old beliefs are only a child's confused interpretation of the events going on around them. They were not true then, and they aren't true now, regardless of how much evidence you could show me to the contrary. We will prove this together in a few minutes.

Now think about your earliest recollection when you thought and felt this way about yourself. What was going on? Who was it that gave you this message verbally or non-verbally? What do you now know, as an adult, about the situation which you couldn't have known, imagined, or understood as a child? What was going on for them? Have you since witnessed this person behaving similarly toward someone else, perhaps even toward themselves?

This process of stepping into a new sense of yourself can only work if you are willing to let go of your old story—a story I can absolutely assure you isn't true. I'm not saying that the actual physical events you experienced didn't happen or the words you heard weren't said. I am assuring you that your interpretation of those events—your story—is skewed and harming you unnecessarily.

If you find yourself feeling resistant to this exercise and to really looking at those old situations from a new perspective, take the time to ask yourself, "What do I think will happen if I allow myself to let that old story go? What benefit do I get from holding on to my old interpretation?"

Sometimes we resist seeing things in a new or different light, despite much supporting evidence, because we fear that we must say that those events didn't impact or harm us if we let go of our story. Trust me, this is not so. You were clearly impacted by those events or you wouldn't have had to implement the coping strategy of co-dependency and making it about *you*, as well as the Drill Sgt., alexithymia, food, and body-image focus. No one here is disputing that you were impacted. What I'm saying is that, instead of being impacted once for each incident, which is traumatic enough, the old core beliefs which you carry only serve to re-injure you daily. You don't deserve this and it doesn't benefit you in any way. It is my intention to support you to stop.

A Letter of Fact

A great exercise for shifting your old beliefs is writing a letter of fact. A letter of fact is a letter containing only the concrete details of a situation. There is no interpretation or assumption of what the other party was thinking, feeling or intending. Just the physical truth. In other words, if there were ten people in the room at the time of the event in question, they all would have to agree on what was physically said and done. Those are the facts; however, their interpretations of why it happened would differ. This is because their interpretation, through the lens of their own beliefs and perceptions of the world, creates a distortion, and the facts become skewed. They cease to focus on the reality of *what* happened, but focus instead on their assumption/interpretation of *why* it happened. This attaches particular emotions to an event, and the thought/feeling loop continues to solidify their perspective of the event as accurate.

This is particularly powerful in events which our psyches perceive as threatening to our physical, emotional or psychological safety. Recall our discussion on Post-Traumatic Stress Disorder when I stated that any threat, real or imagined, gets logged away in our brains with powerful feelings attached. The interpretation that was formed at the time of the event, through our distorted lens, becomes a solid, irrefutable fact from our perspective. And this "fact" directly impacts all of our interactions with ourselves, and with others, until such time as we begin to allow for the possibility that we may have misinterpreted the event. The willingness to challenge this old story requires courage. It means that you are feeling safe enough in yourself to step out of the pseudo-security of the old belief and be open to a new perspective. This requires enough self-love and self-respect to no longer be willing to harm yourself unnecessarily with a confused interpretation of someone else's actions.

If you are willing to be open to the possibility that your old brain has led you to confuse your interpretation with reality and that you may unnecessarily be harming yourself, give this next exercise a try. For those who are in the action stage of change, challenge yourself to write a letter of fact for just one of the events you can think of which led to your current perspective of yourself. Remember, it's just the facts, even if you are absolutely certain they were thinking and feeling a certain way. Challenge yourself to stick to the actual physical truth with no interpretation and assumption. Anyone who was there, or the proverbial fly on the wall, would be obligated to acknowledge what actually happened. It can be difficult to do this at first, because we have been telling ourselves such a story about these events that we believe our interpretation, or we fear that we will lose our sense of the truth if we don't add the assumptions we've made. The facts will stand scrutiny. Your interpretation only harms you.

My first experience of writing a letter of fact came years ago when I had to submit a report on behalf of a client for their court case against someone who had sexually assaulted them as a child. The lawyer said, "Just the facts". My first attempt was filled with "facts," or so I thought. The lawyer came back to me and gently said, "This is a great document. I wish we could use it, but we really just need the facts of the situation and not your interpretation. This would never stand up in court." So I had to go back to the drawing board and remove the parts which really meant something to me: my interpretation of the feelings and needs of that client and of the impact of the assault on their current life. I had to present a document that was dry and "factual". It was a great experience because, in so doing, I realized how invested I was in the story and how much attachment I had to a certain outcome. The facts still spoke volumes, and the client won their case. You can't argue with facts. They are what they are. But you can really confuse things when you try to assume what someone was thinking and feeling, or why they did what they did.

So give yourself the gift of putting down on paper your story of one event you remember which led you to the creation of your old core belief. Write it with no interpretation, and make it a document that could stand up in court. It is irrefutable because anyone there would have written the same report. Then step back and take a look at it. Without the old coping strategy of co-dependency and making everything about you, what remains? Now add to that some of the facts which you have uncovered in the years since that event about this person's life situation and what was going on for them at the time, or what you now know about their own level of self-esteem and their character. You will now have a story which doesn't implicate you in causing the event. Now you could let go of this belief, if you were willing. Just ask yourself, "Based on what I now understand about that old situation, is there any life-enhancing reason to hold on to this old story?"

And, if you are lacking facts about this person and what was going on for them, and you feel that you need these in order to trust what I am saying, ask yourself to track someone down: maybe even that particular person. Alternatively, you could ask someone who was older than you at the time of the event and who knew that person for their perspective. Chances are, you are capable of offering yourself the support and feedback you need in relation to this person and this event, if you are willing to allow yourself to step back and see how they behave(d) in life generally and how they treat(ed) others.

Remember, this is not about discounting or diminishing your experience. This is not about having to forgive the other person for their behaviour toward you, although you can if you want to. This is all about freeing yourself from old harmful beliefs which just aren't true and which undermine the quality of every interaction in your life. It is about taking those events, which you absolutely believed happened because of something wrong with you, and giving yourself the gift of seeing that it was all about the other person. Yes, you were impacted by their behaviour, but you were not the cause of it.

The Double Standard

Allow yourself, for a moment, to gently recall one of the events which created your old core belief(s). Now ask yourself if you would jump on the bandwagon and judge someone else if they had had that same experience. Would you continue on a daily basis to reinforce that hurtful message? Would you rub it in? Or might you offer them compassion and empathy and do whatever you could to show them the strengths and beauty that you see in them? Would it just go without saying that you would be immediately drawn to offer your reassurance and support, and maybe even to feel angry and hurt on their behalf?

Well? What do you think? Would you keep pouring salt in their wound? Not likely. That would be sadistic. You are far too kind and considerate for that, so why do you do it to yourself?

We have actually been here, through our work together, haven't we? The Drill Sgt., with his positive intent but confused and abusive ways, keeps throwing that hurtful comment or event in your face, because he wants to ensure nothing ever happens to make you feel hurt and humiliated again. However, the reality is you experience this hurt and humiliation daily because of what he says and how that old story leads you to interpret everything which happens around you through the lens of your old belief.

If your old belief boils down to believing that you lack security and approval, how exactly are you creating a sense of security and acceptance for yourself by consistently pointing out your "flaws"? Doesn't your life experience show that you have only grown to be more insecure and more willing to perceive yourself as being unacceptable as you are? Aren't you now more out of control than ever before? The old "motivation through criticism" doesn't work, folks. You can't create a solid, secure, loving relationship with anyone by berating them and only pointing out what you perceive as their flaws, or by withholding love and acceptance until they attain your Drill Sgt.'s idea of perfection. No one would stick around for that unless they felt so unworthy of anything good that they were willing to let you treat them as an inferior. And if they ever wanted to begin feeling worthy and more positive about themselves, one of the first things that would absolutely have to go is their relationship with you! It couldn't possibly remain as it was if they wanted to create a life that was filled with love and peace.

Let's turn this around and look in the mirror. Despite the Drill Sgt.'s positive intention that lies beneath all his criticism, you can't possibly create a loving and peaceful existence for yourself as long as you are willing to continue to beat yourself up with old beliefs formed as a young person that were untrue then and are untrue now. You will always find evidence to support what you believe. It is a human truth. This is why, in scientific experiments, the results are only considered valid if the experiment was conducted in such a way that the researcher did their best to *disprove* their theory. That's right, *disprove*!

We are so willing to interpret results to suit ourselves that we will overlook mounds of evidence to the contrary and focus on the one piece of evidence which can be manipulated to support what it is that we want to believe. Science has been aware of this for a long time. So, if a researcher gives it a really good go at disproving what they believe to be true, and it turns out at the end of the day that their original belief is still standing with a statistically-significant (better than chance) result, then, and only then, will they allow their original belief to be considered "true". And even then, it is always acknowledged in any report about the research that certain variables may have influenced the results; therefore, another study conducted at a different time with a different group of people may reach a different conclusion. Whew, how's that for allowing for any possibility that what you believe might not be true? Science must do this because science won't work if it is built on a false foundation, and because we know enough about life and human nature to know that "truth" can change. Things continue to look different the more we know about them.

Now to bring this back to you and your recovery process, let's just make this point crystal clear: your Drill Sgt., with the best of intentions, has been reinforcing your old beliefs on a daily basis. These beliefs were formed when you were too young to have a fully-developed, rational-thinking brain and when you lacked enough life experience to be able to interpret situations in any other way except as directly pertaining to and caused by you. Since that time, with the best of intentions to keep you safe and garner you as much approval as you can handle, the Drill Sgt. has been interpreting every single life situation through the distorted lens of that confused childhood perspective on the world. Those experiences which fit the belief are grasped as absolute proof that you are stupid, or unacceptable, or not good enough. Those that don't fit perfectly are adjusted and manipulated to fit. And those that don't fit at all are thrown out as just plain "weird". They are considered flukes and do not count. Have you ever heard yourself say, "That guy must be a loser if he likes me so much!" "I wonder what's wrong with him?" Or even, "It's just a matter of time before he finds out who I really am, then leaves."

With storytelling like this going on in your head, bent toward proving and reinforcing your old beliefs, how could you possibly see it if the guy was truly amazing and if you were truly amazing as well? And, if the relationship did end eventually, as many naturally do, your tendency to make it about your unworthiness or unlovableness would taint the entire relationship experience. This would leave you with nothing but grief and a deeper sense of despair, when it could leave you with gratitude and joy for the wonderful moments you shared. It's all a matter of the story or theory that you are pitching to yourself on a daily basis.

Just for one day, I challenge you to be a scientist. Make a commitment to yourself that you will only interpret events from the perspective that your old belief is untrue. Yes, that's right! Don't get caught up in the authenticity factor. You've been lying to yourself for decades. I'm giving you an invitation and an opportunity to free yourself from that old bogus story and to allow yourself to see what is true right now.

So for the next 24 hours, notice the things that happen to and around you, and, whatever your standard old story is, offer yourself exactly the opposite. Interpret everything in the reverse of how you typically would. For example, if you would normally make everyone's behaviour about you, challenge yourself on this day to make it about them, and see what happens when you don't take it on. If your belief is that you are not good enough, see what happens if you interpret events of the day through the lense of this belief: "I am great", or "I am deserving of good things."

If you feel some resistance to this exercise, allow for the possibility that perhaps a part of you knows that your old story is bogus, but it meets some need for you (or so you think). You may be clinging to the old harmful story because you don't know any way to meet those needs if you didn't have that story to drive you or to "help" you make sense of things. If you are resistant, just check in for a moment and ask yourself, "What do I think will happen if I allow myself to believe the opposite of this old story for just a day?" Whatever the answer, just keep asking *what's important about that* until you get to the end of the line.

Does it boil down to needs for safety and security, or needs for love, acceptance and belongingness? Or a bit of both? Then ask yourself, "How has holding on to this story of my experience helped me to feel safer and more loved?" "Is it possible that this old story just keeps me wounded, and any needs I might have could never be met as long as I am feeling insecure and unloved and am, therefore, responding to the world as though it is an unsafe place?" Would you be willing to experiment with this for one day, even one hour, if a day is too much right now? Step out of the false security that your old story provides, and allow yourself to feel the freedom of new possibilities.

Remember, this is just for one day. If you want to return to the old story after 24 hours, you most certainly can. And you can return to it as many times as you like, for as long as you like, while you are figuring out what is really true for you. Just remember, as long as you are only allowing for one possible explanation to your past experience, you are in all-or-nothing thinking and this will keep you stuck. There is nowhere to go. The "security" of "knowing" what happened in that old story way isn't any security at all if it consistently undermines the quality of your life, to which you can attest. When you can allow yourself to be open to new possibilities in the present and to new interpretations of that old story, the world becomes a completely new and wonderful place.

Ensure you make both mental and physical notes about what you noticed on this day. Give yourself the gift of seeing on paper the outcome of your experiences, thoughts, and feelings from challenging the validity of your old belief out there in the real world. You can even challenge your belief if you are alone in your house for a day. You know there will be situations which arise with machinery, or you may drop something. The old belief would have you feeling somehow wrong or unworthy, and anger would rise in you, mostly directed toward yourself, but you will also probably notice yourself blaming the person who made the "stupid thing". But, if you brought to this situation your new belief that it's not about you, or that you are more than enough, you wouldn't likely feel anything other than natural frustration at the machine. The same event has occurred. But with one thought, you feel angry and diminished. With another, you feel very little and go on about your day without the weight of this experience added to your already very heavy load.

The Freedom of Other Possibilities

To help you along in your experiment, take a few minutes and write out four other stories to explain the facts of the event you experienced. Let these new stories not be about you at all. Let them be about the person who did or said that painful thing. Create some stories about what may have been going on behind the scenes for them which could justify their behaviour.

Your original story might be: My grandmother hated me; she treated me terribly. All the other grandchildren were loved, but all she did to me was to tell me I was fat and ugly. There was something so wrong with me that even my own grandmother hated me!

The letter of fact would say: My grandmother told me I was fat and ugly. (This is the truth; everyone there would have to agree to it.)

Other stories might be:

1. My grandmother told me I was fat and ugly because she had serious body-image issues herself and couldn't handle any body which wasn't a toothpick.
2. My grandmother was an unhappy character and liked to make other people unhappy, pushing their buttons and verbally abusing them.
3. My grandmother grew up in an era where it was okay to critically comment on someone's weight and appearance. This was seen as a sign of love and caring.
4. My grandmother was talked to this way by her parents and believed it was okay; the other grandchildren were boys, and you didn't talk this way to boys.

You can keep going if you can come up with more than four alternative stories of that time. And keep in mind that telling yourself new stories or allowing yourself to challenge your old perspective doesn't mean you have to forgive this person, or in any way suggests approval of their behaviour. Not at all. Again, the facts of the case stand scrutiny. What we are working on here is separating you from your story which currently has some interpretation that harms you unnecessarily and that continues to impact the quality of your life today.

And, always keep in mind, what is "true" is not what you wish were true (I know that's frustrating to admit!) or what you think "should" be true. What is true is reality: what is actually, really happening. Remember the letter of fact? That's what's true. No interpretation and wishing and guessing and assuming and shoulding—just the facts.

Challenge yourself to do something radical: be open to the possibility that there truly is another way of seeing those experiences which is true: one that doesn't require you to harm yourself with self-defeating thoughts on a daily basis, if you believe it. Allow yourself to be open to any and all possibilities, particularly if the one you are about to settle on harms you in any word, thought or deed. You deserve to be happy, and peaceful, and loved. And, if your Drill Sgt. has something to say about that, ask him what his intention is and what's important about that?

Your Desired Belief

It is very freeing to step out of your all-or-nothing thinking and old core belief, and to allow for the possibility that what you have believed about yourself or about old situations isn't true. Stepping out of this old belief leaves a vacancy—a space that needs to be filled with a new thought or belief. If spiritual enlightenment is your ultimate goal, at some point you will find yourself in a place where you don't need to replace this old belief with anything: you just exist peacefully in the space that is left when it departs. For the rest of you, who either don't necessarily desire that or who are still on the path to enlightenment, there is the desired belief.

The desired belief is the new story, the new thought which you will offer yourself whenever you notice the triggering of that old belief. Your desired belief will ultimately become your automatic thought: your "default setting," as I call it. For now, it will require some consciousness on your part to reinforce the new belief, but it isn't hard to do.

First, let's figure out what your desired belief is. The best and simplest way to do this is to take a look at your current belief. Let's use *I am not good enough* as our example.

Your current belief is that you are not good enough. Now ask yourself: "What thought could I invite myself to think that is directly opposite to that old belief?"

I am good enough? Not quite, although that is exactly opposite. No, what we are looking for here is the desired belief that knocks your socks off—the thought that makes you feel as though you are doing something wrong or being a bad girl just to think it. That's the one we want. The one that freaks the crap out of you! How about: I am great! I am wonderful! I am perfect!

When you imagine inviting yourself to think any of these thoughts, how does it feel? Remember you are looking for the new belief statement that feels "wrong" to think. It will feel wrong because it directly flies in the face of what you currently believe. If it feels so-so or a little different, that's not it. That's too soft, and you are still giving in to the old belief. Let yourself be freaked out a little with your desired belief; then you'll know you've got it.

And don't worry. You are not suddenly going to become some egotistical individual who lives with her head in the clouds. Right now you are far, far, far to one end of the spectrum of self-judgement with your current belief. You have lots and lots and lots of room to come back the other way before you get anywhere near vanity. But right now, any thought which challenges that old belief will feel strange and, as such, will be judged by the Drill Sgt. as "wrong".

It's up to you to challenge the Drill Sgt. when this happens and, again, to just come back to, "What's important about me continuing to believe...?" Or, "What's important about that?" Any time you receive judgement or resistance from the Drill Sgt., keep coming back to that process of dialogue with him. Soon your Authentic Self will know and trust that the Drill Sgt. really is on your side, and the Drill

Sgt. will understand that he needs to radically alter his approach if he really wants to support you to be the best you can be.

So what is your old belief? And what is the desired belief that freaks the pants off of you? All right, let's move on.

Old Versus New

Now let's do a wee comparison of the impact of the old versus your desired core belief. Those of you in the action stage of change will be taking some time now, or when you are near a pen and paper/computer, to write out the answers to these questions and to fully explore what comes up for you as you compare old versus new thoughts of yourself. Those of you in the determination or contemplation stages of change will benefit greatly from reading over the questions and taking a moment to consider each one before moving on. Allow yourself to start exploring the impact of your thinking on your use of food to cope and the quality of your life on the whole.

Start by asking yourself:

- How does it impact me to continue to believe my old belief?
- What choices do I make because I believe that thought about myself?
- What things do I do or not do?
- What places do I go or not go?
- Whom do/don't I approach for friendship or partnership?
- What things do I not ask for?
- What needs go unmet?
- What kinds of experiences, expectations and behaviours do I put up with in others because I believe that about myself? Then invite yourself to consider the following set of questions:
- How would my life be if I allowed myself to live as though I believed my desired belief?
- What if I really did feel and think that way about myself?
- What would happen?
- Would I do anything different?

- What choices would I have made, or be making now, in relationships, career, self-care?
- Who/what would I want in my life that isn't there now, or at least not as much as they/it could be?
- Whom/what would I no longer have in my life?
- How would my behaviour toward myself change?
- Would my need for food to cope be any different?

Well, what do you think? Can you find any reason to keep thinking that old thought about yourself? Knowing that it came from that child's brain, was never true about the whole of who you are, and impacts you negatively each day, is there any reason to keep that belief alive? Any reason, aside from fear, that is?

If you feel fearful of letting it go, I urge you to review Chapter 1 (Readiness for Change) and just get clear on how that's playing out in you right now.

Aside from fear of the unknown, the obvious reason people choose to hang on to their old belief is that they still believe it! It still feels true on some deep level. And because the confused logic of the Drill Sgt. says that they need to carry this belief or they will be unsafe and unloved, they cling to that old painful, bogus story. They are fearful that, if they start to behave in accordance with their desired belief, they will be judged, criticized, and risk the limited security they currently experience in their world.

And yet, as we have discussed already, the old belief doesn't provide any real security or love at all: rather, it keeps you feeling constantly insecure and stuck in the belief that you need external approval in order to be okay.

Much of your life experience has been lived through the lens of your old core belief. Every interaction has been framed by that thought about yourself and interpreted as though it were true. Every choice you have made has had that story about yourself at its core. So, of course you still believe it on some level. You have come to see it as a part of you or who you really are. Deep down, in your gut, you are going to require some life experience to really shake it loose.

What we have done so far is provide you with the empathy and compassion for yourself to get the Drill Sgt. on your side with this process. With him on your side and his understanding of the falsity of your old story (or at least his willingness to allow for the possibility that it might be untrue!), you will be much more successful in actually living your life in the days to come from a new belief.

Putting It All Together

Now, let's quickly recap the main pieces we have discussed so far that will aid in freeing yourself from your current belief.

- We started out discussing a child's brain and their limited, self-focused perspective on the world.
- Recall that we talked about writing a letter of fact: just the concrete, physical realities of the experience which anyone in your place would support.
- Then we discussed the double standard and an experiment of one day in which you set out to "prove" whether your old belief is true, using the scientific method of disproving your old belief whenever possible.
- We also looked at what was going on inside and around that person at the time of the event.
- Then we challenged you to identify a desired belief which really felt "wrong" or scary to even think about let alone put into action.
- Lastly, we looked at how your old belief impacts your life versus how your desired belief likely would.

We have done a good piece of work here on really understanding where your beliefs came from, how they impact you, and getting clear on what you would like to do differently (your desired belief). Now it's time to challenge yourself to let go of the old belief.

You do this by first noticing when you have been triggered to slip into your old belief. Once you start to invite yourself to look for the cues, you will notice your core belief has been triggered quite easily.

Your cues for your old belief are: the PLA, insecurity, hopeless-ness, despair, depression, bad body thoughts, Drill Sgt. criticism, procrastination and all-or-nothing thinking, to name a few. In es-sence, your cues are any of the coping strategies which you have identified in our work together thus far: anything on your coping strategy flow chart. You see, you developed each of those coping strategies to help you cope with the pain of the unmet needs for security and approval that arose out of those initial traumatic experi-ences when your old core belief was first formed.

Because you now consistently reinforce the old belief and pret-ty much interpret every event through that lens, there is a constant sense of insecurity and disapproval within you. This is experienced by us as the PLA. Each time you reinforce the old belief, you tell yourself that your needs for security and/or approval are unmet, thus calling forth one of your old coping strategies to help you deal with the distress of that unmet need. Remember, this cycle currently hap-pens within you all day, every day, whether the story you are telling yourself is true or not. You could be perfectly safe and perfectly loved, and you would still feel insecure and have the PLA going on. You will continue to need food to cope with the distress of those harmful thoughts and feelings, as long as the old belief is running the show.

Now, even though you could use any of the coping strategies you have identified as indicators that you are buying in to your old belief, it's much easier to choose just one or two to start. It is probably safe to say that you are now able to identify when you are feeling anxious (the PLA) or having a bad body thought, so we will use these coping strategies as your primary focal point right now. In most cases, all you would have to do at any moment of any day is to stop and do a gut check, and you would find one if not both of those coping strate-gies. If you are willing to do so, I invite you to trust me that, when you are feeling the PLA or having a bad body thought, you are very likely reacting from an old core belief which is undermining your sense of security or approval in the moment.

Begin to check in with yourself regularly throughout the day, and ask yourself what you are feeling. Is your tummy feeling a little anxious? Do you feel some tightness in your chest? If you are feeling the PLA or are having a bad body thought, allow yourself to assume that you are being triggered by an old belief. Then run through your list of old core beliefs. Remember, you may have more than one; having three or so is quite common, although they may all boil down to one main belief. You will very likely find that one of your beliefs is at the core of what you are feeling in that moment. If you can, it's great to write this out the first few times you try it. Those of you in the action stage of change will be all over this, and it will benefit you greatly. Otherwise, stop what you are doing in that moment, and just be fully present with your thoughts. Let yourself get clear on the present "facts," or what is really going on by anyone's interpretation. Then ask how your old belief is getting in and making you feel anxious and insecure?

When you write this out a few times for greater awareness, your writing would look like this:

- I notice I am feeling the PLA. What just happened to trigger one of my core beliefs? (Here you would write out the thought or experience you just had which triggered the old belief.)
- What are the facts of the situation?
- What are the needs I had in this situation (or imagined having, if it were a future situation) which were unmet?
- What is one small step I could take toward meeting these needs?

This process is a great and speedy way to prove to yourself that, just like food, alexithymia, and intrusive ideation, your old core beliefs are merely coping strategies and are just indicators that you have unmet needs in that moment. The more you allow yourself to see the unmet needs for security and approval that lie beneath your old core beliefs, the easier it will be to avoid being seduced by destructive thoughts when they arise. This spares you the depressed and anxious feelings, and the use of food to cope that typically accompany these harmful, bogus thoughts. It also puts you in the powerful position of being able to identify unmet needs and to take steps to meet them.

Acting As-If

You are now fully aware and present with the situation that is triggering your old belief, and you can even see the facts versus your old belief interpretation. I am going to ask you to do something which will momentarily feel a little inauthentic. I want you to call forth your desired belief into your mind and then act *as-if* you believe it in that very moment. Yes, it will feel inauthentic—*because it is*. You don't really believe this about yourself just now; you are just faking it, and you know it. I know it. But no one else does! And frankly, what you currently believe about yourself is so bogus that you are allowed to be inauthentic in relation to that old story. So tell yourself, "I know that I don't really believe this about myself now, and how I'd like to feel about myself is: I am... (your desired belief). And I'm going to allow myself to act *as-if* I believe this, just for now."

If there is resistance to this, just remind yourself of the work you have done in getting clear on the origin and the validity of your old belief. It's not true now and wasn't true then, and you cannot continue to believe this about yourself and have the life you desire and deserve. Furthermore, you are *supposed* to feel as if you are doing something "wrong"; as if you are being a phony and will be caught at any moment. That's how you are supposed to feel the first few times that you challenge an old belief and challenge yourself to act *as-if* you believe the new one.

In order to feel more grounded and settled with this new thought, I have found it takes just a handful of times of offering yourself an invitation to act *as-if* you trust your new belief. Just a handful! It takes five times (often less) to reinforce your new, true statement until you start to really feel that it's okay to believe that new thought when you notice the old bogus one impacting you. That's not many times at all. Considering you have that old belief triggering you to feel anxious and insecure throughout the day, you are going to have enough experiences in one day alone, if you stay present, to be able to effectively challenge the old belief and to begin to feel more comfortable and deserving of the new one.

Feeling any resistance to giving this a go? If not, great! Move forward by challenging the old belief when you notice the feelings of PLA and insecurity or any bad body thoughts. Remind yourself you will feel weird, as if you are doing something you are not allowed to do, in holding this new belief about yourself. And remember that it's just a handful of times that you need to remind yourself of what's going on, and to reinforce this new thought, before you overcome the resistance and the anxiety about your new belief. It gets easier and easier to have this new thought arise and for you to trust that it is okay for you to think this way about yourself.

If you are feeling resistance, that's great! You are coming hard up against your old belief, and the Drill Sgt. isn't quite ready to let that go. Do the questioning exercise, and ask him: "What's important about me not letting go of this old thought, and what's important about that?" And when you get to the end of it all and it comes back to feeling secure and loved, just ask him: "How have the years of carrying this old belief supported me to feel loved and safe in my world? Hasn't the consistent reinforcement of that old story only undermined my sense of trust and safety in the world and in others?"

Then ask the Drill Sgt.: "Would you be willing to allow me to experiment with this exercise for one day? If after one day we find more evidence to support our old belief than our new one (which I absolutely assure you, you *will not* find), we can go on believing the old story, no harm done."

If you resist acting *as-if* because you are concerned about the reactions of others from your new state of being, hear this: *You are not going to change all that much outwardly from a handful of experiences where you no longer buy in to an old story. You will im-*

mediately begin to feel different on the inside, but it may take some time for those outside of you to really notice that anything about you has changed.

And let me assure you also that anyone in your life who truly loves and cares for you will absolutely support you and delight in your feeling more confident and secure. It will make your relationship with them a great deal better than it's ever been because you will be much more able to fully participate in the relationship, that is, to give love and to receive their love more fully.

If it is anyone's intention in their connection with you to have power over, control, or abuse you, they will be unhappy with the changes that take place when you begin to value yourself more highly and to trust that you deserve respect and dignity in your relationship with yourself and with others. It will be threatening to their need for power over you. So, if you begin to experience resistance from someone in your life as you act *as-if,* or truly begin to believe your desired belief, it is a sign that the relationship is one of control and harm, and it needs to be healed.

This healing can look like a series of courageous conversations, counselling sessions, or perhaps even taking a break from the connection while you both heal your issues of insecurity and mistrust. We will talk much more about this in the upcoming section on relationships. For now, just know that in order to truly heal your use of food to cope and to truly release your old belief, you must be willing to commit to growing to a place of having only life-enhancing relationships which honour both parties with love, respect and dignity. It is so do-able; you need only change the belief which just crept in and told you that it is unattainable. And now that you know how to go about doing this, it's up to you to give it a go.

Don't let your old belief and the Drill Sgt. have the last word. Challenge yourself to act *as-if,* and you will soon see that there is nothing wrong with loving and respecting yourself. It is right! It is your birthright!

NB: For a wonderful tool and great information on the concept
of truth versus what we wish were true, I highly recommend *Loving What Is* by Byron Katie. The CEDRIC Centre
has many copies in our library, and it's a wonderful way of
shaking off your old harmful stories and beliefs.

13

Building Self-Esteem

Everything we have discussed so far, and everything we will discuss in the chapters ahead, comes back to your core beliefs. We will be looking at numerous pieces and tools for healing you and your connection with others. I encourage you to continuously remind yourself that, currently, each of those pieces is the way it is because of what you believe. And those beliefs create limitations.

If you truly want to create change in those areas which feel unfulfilling or downright dreadful, you must be willing to acknowledge the impact of your *old* beliefs and to challenge yourself to consciously direct your attention and your behaviour to your *desired* beliefs.

You may recall that I said you need only to actively challenge an old belief five times, sometimes less, in order to begin to feel more grounded in your new belief and to start to naturally respond to situations this way. You will soon discover that it takes no effort at all to naturally default to your desired belief, following a less emotionally-charged situation.

In more emotionally-charged situations, you will need to approach them more consciously with: (a) the awareness that your old belief may get triggered, and (b) a clear sense of your desired belief. Make a commitment to remind yourself of your desired belief, should you be triggered and feel anxious or insecure in any situation. Assure yourself that it is okay to care for yourself in this way. And remind yourself of the concept of an ELOC versus the ILOC, and that you want to be coming first and foremost from a place of consideration and respect for your needs and feelings. Do this, and the only relationships you could possibly have will be those of love and respect.

For some of you, the discomfort of inviting yourself to risk and to challenge that old belief feels overwhelming; you would prefer to just look the other way and pretend the old belief wasn't triggered. Well, you can choose to do that. This is your process, after all. You can go into resistance and avoidance for as long as the need exists; so don't sweat it. Let yourself do what you need to do right now. When you are ready, gently challenge yourself to come back to this piece. If you are uncertain about moving forward or just want to know what to expect in terms of thoughts and feelings as you challenge your old belief and implement your desired one, the following discussion on discomfort and change may be helpful.

Discomfort = Change = Good Stuff!

When we actively begin the process of letting go of our old core beliefs, we frequently feel awkward, uncomfortable, phony, forced and inauthentic. I implore you: don't judge this as an indication that you are doing something wrong or that you are doomed to fail at this recovery process. These feelings of discomfort and unfamiliarity are not bad, wrong, or in any other way inappropriate. The thoughts and behaviours you are asking of yourself are simply so very different from your "norm," that is, from what you are accustomed to, that they naturally feel strange. And as human beings who have been schooled in all-or-nothing thinking, we have been trained to judge anything which differs from our regular experiences as wrong.

This is simply not accurate. If you continue allowing yourself to think this way, you run the risk of not witnessing and experiencing all the benefits of the change which are taking place. You are judging your experience in the moment as bad or wrong because it feels strange or different from what you are accustomed to. If you find yourself heading down this path, I encourage you to remember that you have begun this process of change because you want things to be different—because you recognize that you have a need for a change in your thoughts, feelings, and behaviours around certain things. This being the case, how much sense does it make to judge yourself as failing in your process because things are feeling different, when that is what you initially desired!?

You are expecting to have complete comfort and familiarity with a brand new way of thinking, being and feeling about yourself, your body, food and relationships. Does this make sense? Does this seem like a realistic expectation to have of yourself? Of anyone? Please tell me you said no!

After just a handful of experiences in which you remember to offer yourself your desired belief when the old bogus story kicks in, you will begin to really feel and know the difference between the old and the new ways of approaching any life situation because, although it is different, the new way does feel better. Much better. You will begin to feel freer and more connected to your true self than ever before. You will feel yourself detaching from the energy and co-dependency of others. This will create its own motivation for you to pursue the new ways of thinking, feeling, and behaving which you are learning, instead of those old, harmful coping strategies. In a relatively short period of time (typically, in a few months), the old way of coping with life's stressors begins to seem so foreign, so unnecessary, so draining and unproductive that you naturally and freely choose the new way.

With any behavioural change, this entire process is the same for each of us. If you were a hunt-and-peck typist and then learned to type "properly," you would go through this process of initially feeling forced and uncomfortable, to arriving at a place where the new is so much more peaceful, effective and life-enhancing. You will choose to use it exclusively, and it becomes second-nature to the point where hunting and pecking takes too long for it to even be considered an option. This is the exact process which you will experience with food, body image, substance abuse, co-dependency, anxiety, depression, post-traumatic stress and other common coping strategies of our society.

Do your best to welcome this new, strange, inauthentic feeling which accompanies your desired belief: know that it's a great sign. After all, if you feel exactly the same at the end of this process as you did in the beginning, I don't think you would be feeling successful! So prepare for some gentle discomfort; don't force yourself to be challenged to extremes. Be kind, and only ask of yourself what is doable for where you are right now. Change is what you seek. Simply because it is new, change feels a little unsteady and shaky, and it initially creates doubt and uncertainty. After all, you are stepping into the unknown, and you won't have complete trust in something new until you have experienced it. Just know that these changes will result in a very safe, secure, trusting and peaceful state of being which you will carry with you everywhere and at all times. That is worth a little conscious effort.

Trust in me as best you can. Trust in this process. Trust that feeling different and unnatural is a very good thing right now, providing you are not doing anything life-threatening!

Trust in Yourself

Frequently, you will find that you resist being conscious about what you feel and think and need; yet, if you were just to check within, you would be able to identify quite clearly what is and isn't working for you in that moment. If you resist being conscious, it is likely because your Drill Sgt. tells you that, if you are conscious, you *must* attend to whatever is going on *now*.

So you are scaring yourself *out* of consciousness with the threat that you must then take immediate action regardless of what is going on or how you feel about it. The fear of having to take action, once you become conscious, typically comes from one of two beliefs:

1. You believe that you don't possess a tool which will work effectively, so it's better to be "semi-conscious". You can then pretend you didn't know what was going on. You are certain failure will come.

2. And/or you believe that taking action to honour yourself or meet your need(s) will create such stress and strife in your relationship(s) that it's just not worth it.

Now let me point out the obvious all-or-nothing thinking in these patterns.

a) "I am absolutely doomed to fail, so I am better off not to try." Not so. You *could* be successful. Or you could also, by doing something differently, begin to change the old harmful pattern on a small scale that will result in a large-scale change.

b) You are buying in to the all-or-nothing thought that taking care of yourself will create distress for someone else and possibly lead to the demise of the relationship. Not likely. In most cases, people want those with whom they are interacting to be direct about their needs and to take responsibility for them. It is much easier to have a relationship with that person; in this case, you! If someone resists your respectful and authentic sharing about your needs, it simply means that that person is more interested in controlling you or the situation than in truly loving or respecting you. This is very important information for you to possess. It is more proof that the actions and words of others are not about you.

c) You are buying in to the belief that, if you identify what is bothering you and leading you to use one of your primary coping strategies (the PLA or food, for example), you must take action. Not so. You can just notice it. Really! If you can invite the Drill Sgt. to let it be okay for you to be aware of what's going on and to not have to take action right away, the whole world opens up. Suddenly, it's safe to be conscious of everything you are thinking and feeling, and of all the subtle nuances you are picking up around you. There is nothing to fear if you trust yourself to not respond or take any action of any kind until you are feeling grounded and clear about what's up for you (which beliefs were triggered and what needs you had in that situation) and what feels like the most respectful and dignified way of attending to that situation for both parties. We will talk much more about this concept in our work on our relationship with others. For now, just begin to allow for the possibility that it is okay for you to be conscious of what you are thinking, feeling, doing and ultimately needing. It is safe for you to be aware because you really, truly don't need to do anything about it until you feel truly grounded and safe within yourself.

Making it Safe to be Conscious

When you live from the old pattern of buying in to those old all-or-nothing thoughts, then use the coping strategies of denial and unconsciousness, you compromise yourself. Please know that there is no benefit to judging yourself for this choice. Just recognize and support it as a choice. It's all right to say, "I know I'd really like to do..., but right now I just feel too scared or too overwhelmed at the thought of asserting this need, so I'm choosing to go along with Mary Jane." Speak it; name your choice. Be proud that you are making a conscious choice which best meets your needs at that time, and let it be all right to take care of yourself in this way. You can also add a piece that says, "I am working to get to a place where I can respond differently to this situation, and, for now, this choice feels as though it will best meet my needs." In other words, cut yourself some slack. And know that the part of you which is feeling anxious or frustrated with your choice is feeling that way because it has needs for respect and trust which were unmet by the choice you made. Then you can step into a wonderful dialogue with yourself that will lead to solid integration within and self-honouring behaviour without. I call it "Plan A, B and C." We'll discuss this in one moment, but before we do, here is a little bit more on supporting and loving yourself now.

When you find yourself behaving in such a way that your needs for respect and trust in yourself are unmet, it is key to remind yourself of this: at the moment of deciding how to respond to that situation, you truly believed your most fundamental needs for safety and security and/or love, acceptance and belongingness would be threatened if you were to make the choice you really wanted to make—the choice that would be most honouring of you. This makes sense, if you are still buying in to your old core belief and still feeling responsible for the needs and feelings of others. You made a choice that felt the safest and best at that time. Even if it feels as though you have compromised your integrity or didn't honour your esteem needs or your self-respect, you chose consciously as best you could.

It may seem as if I'm asking you to compromise yourself and love it. Not at all. What I'm inviting you to do is to love *yourself*. Consciously acknowledge what is true for you, and accept that that is the way it is right now. This is the quickest way I know for building an integrated sense of Self: you will become firmly grounded in who you are and what you want. You will be provided with the internal security and strength to act respectfully on this awareness. What more can you ask?

You could, if you wanted to, berate yourself after the fact for not coming from a place of esteem. But that will only compromise your self-regard further and diminish your self-esteem. If there is any part of you which resists being conscious of what you need or what you are feeling at any moment, check in and see if the Drill Sgt. is telling you that you can't handle the situation; your measly tool kit won't cut it; and by acting on your authentic needs, you will be creating a "situation". Just see if he is in there forecasting doom and assuming the worst with his all-or-nothing thinking. It is always your choice whether you want to continue to believe him and allow him to have the last word. You could simply acknowledge that while his intent is to protect and support you to meet your needs for security and love, he is actually diminishing your self-confidence and robbing you of opportunities to prove that *you are already safe and loved*.

And most importantly, when you realize either before, during, or after that you have chosen to compromise your esteem needs because you felt that your security or acceptance needs were threatened, do your very best to acknowledge that that is what you needed to do at the time. Then set your mind to the task of getting clear on what you would like to see yourself doing that would be different and how you might bring that awareness in to the next similar situation. Here is the concept of Plan A, B and C.

Plan A, B and C

Something which made an enormous difference in my recovery process was to challenge myself to offer compassion and care to *me*. It felt weird, even a little stupid at first, because I was far removed from really loving myself or seeing myself as worthy of loving and care; however, in my recovery process I found it extremely beneficial to ground myself by gently rubbing my tummy, just like you might gently caress a child who isn't feeling very well. Each time I did that, I was making a physical connection with my Authentic Self. In my thoughts I was also acknowledging the needs which were unmet for her and affirming that I was doing the best I could. If the situation was one which was likely to reoccur or wasn't yet complete, I would set about making a plan for how I would like to handle things in a way that would meet my needs. My adult Nurturing Parent, by listening intently to what my Authentic Self felt, would give her a sense of security and respect and trust. If I began at any time during that dialogue to feel pressured or fearful, that was my indication that the Drill Sgt. had stepped in and was *telling* us how it was going to be rather than *asking* us what we needed. If that happened and I was aware of it, I questioned the Drill Sgt.'s intention, thanked him, and reassured him that I had it under control.

I would then reassure my Authentic Self that I would take specific steps to meet her needs in the next similar situation (Plan A). We always had a backup plan (Plan B), just in case I wasn't as confident in that moment as I hoped to be. So I went into the next similar situation, having checked in with my Authentic Self (often I did this in the car on the way to an event), and reminded myself of how I'd like to behave (Plan A) and what would be an acceptable second or Plan B. Plan C would be defaulting to the old belief and behaviour, while offering myself empathy and compassion for that choice. The old behaviour without compassion was not an option.

Let's say the situation is this: I have a friend who calls me in the evenings and talks for hours about her problems. In the past, my needs for acceptance have led me to compromise myself and listen to her when I really didn't want to and had other things which I needed to do for my own self-care. When I screen her call and don't answer, I am scared and have feelings of guilt, as though I am doing something wrong and being a bad friend. That's my old belief: *I'm not allowed to meet my own needs if someone else has a different need.* That's my good old co-dependent training kicking in. So I commit myself to changing this pattern because it causes me distress and doesn't meet my needs for trust and self-respect (also known as my esteem needs). I dialogue with my Authentic Self and we come up with our plans. The Drill Sgt. is welcome to take part, as long as we all understand that we are not committing to any plan unless it feels honouring and respectful of us.

Plan A would be to answer the phone and immediately state that I have some things to take care of this evening, so I can talk for only 15 minutes. This might sound like, "Hi Georgette, it's nice to hear your voice. And I must let you know that I have to get going in 15 minutes." And stick to it! After 15 minutes, it's up to me to say, "Georgette, I am interested in what you are saying, but I must get going. Can we talk another night?" In the next call you would also set the same time boundary. Soon Georgette gets the point that you are there to talk with her, but she can't go on for hours. She begins to respect that you have needs too, and soon she's asking you if you have time to talk, not just assuming you do, and getting to the point because she knows she's got a limited amount of time. Respect for yourself grows because you are valuing your time and the things you have in your life.

Plan B would be to answer the phone, begin the conversation and then have someone else in the house interrupt you and say you have to go. Alternatively, you invent something which must be attended to or somewhere you have to be. This is not the best choice because you are not being authentic. However, if having the direct boundary-setting conversation is too challenging for where you are with your sense of deservedness right now, this is better than being on the phone all night. You won't like the feeling of being dishonest, so you will very shortly go to Plan A.

Plan C is to do the old thing (be on the phone for hours because you are not quite ready to set any boundaries, real or manufactured), adding compassion and empathy to the mix by saying, "I understand that I chose to stay on the phone with Georgette because I didn't feel worthy of asking for what I needed and was afraid to set a boundary with her. I am working on getting to a place where I can trust myself to put *me* first, and, until I'm there, the best I can do is to love myself for doing the best I can in each moment."

In my own process, I was surprised at how many times I was able to pull Plan A out of the bag, successfully, amazingly. And each time I did, I enhanced my self-esteem, and both my Authentic Self *and* the Drill Sgt. trusted me to handle things more and more. You see, when you are clear on how you want to respond in a situation to enhance your self-esteem and confidence, and you are aware of how you will feel if you respond in the old way, it soon becomes a non-issue. You will do what is truly best for you from a place of esteem and ILOC. Once you are aware of how it impacts you and that there is a viable alternative, it is too uncomfortable to repeat that old harmful behaviour. The old approach will only add to your mountain of unfinished business and lead you to use food to cope, usually as soon as you get home or when you are next alone.

Using the Plan A, B and C concept, it wasn't long before I had gained enough confidence and trust in myself that I began to feel fully integrated. I was no longer three separate people (my Drill Sgt., my Authentic Self and Nurturing Parent). I was one whole person who was strong and able to trust myself to take good care of all of me. This is integrity. This is being whole. You won't have to ask me if you are there. You will know it. Many clients describe this experience of acquiring integrity as all the pieces of the puzzle suddenly clicking into place. Remember the Cha-Ching?

This is your payoff for staying tuned to what you want and need. Right now, the Drill Sgt. will tell you there is no payoff, only pain, suffering and ostracism. Pooh on that! You are already suffering, aren't you? Can you question your strength and your self-esteem more than you do now? Can you possibly compromise yourself for others more than you already are? It's doubtful. The Drill Sgt. wants you to be paralyzed by fear of the worst-case scenario when the truth is, you are already living it!

Once you allow yourself to grasp this reality, there is no reason to tune out to your needs or the feelings which will alert you to them. And the more you listen to your Authentic Self telling you what she needs and feels, the more you will be in a position to respond in ways that enhance your self-esteem and create a strong, solid foundation for all your interactions.

Again, tune in. Do your best to honour yourself, and, if you should choose to compromise your esteem needs at any time, let go of the judgement by reminding yourself that you needed to do that because your needs for security and acceptance felt threatened—and they take precedence. Then set about making a Plan A and B, in the event a similar situation occurs.

It is also very important to congratulate yourself whenever you move through the judgement to the problem-solving stage, and to give yourself a big round of applause whenever you enact a Plan A or B. Considering the old beliefs you are currently carrying, it is truly a great achievement to be able to behave in a self-honouring way in any situation. If we were in the same room and you shared your experience of using a Plan to change your behaviour, I would absolutely be expressing my joy at your courage and strength. Since we can't be together, find someone to celebrate that with, or, at the very least, acknowledge it for yourself. Allow yourself to bask in the pleasure which your new, honouring behaviour created. Really feel the difference in your thoughts and in your body for having taken action which took care of *you* first. You deserve it. And remember, anyone who says otherwise is simply more interested in controlling you than creating a healthful and mutually respectful relationship.

The Power of Doing

I'd like to take this moment to reinforce a key message that is inherent in our work so far: if you want to change any behavioural pattern or old belief, it really doesn't matter what you do or how you do it. What matters is that you *do something*—take some action. Don't just default into the old patterns of behaviour that have you mired in feeling powerless and dependent on the approval of others. This is why I say that, at the very least, add some compassion and empathy for yourself to this behaviour if you choose Plan C. Take some action that is different from the old pattern, and you will immediately begin to experience a very positive affect on your self-esteem and thus on your life overall.

Your action does not need to be absolutely right or orchestrated perfectly. It just has to be some action that is different from the old action. Creating positive self-regard is that simple. Do something different. Take some new action. Challenge yourself to step out of the old familiar, comfy, stifling, suffocating, abusive box in which you have been living.

Sometimes, the things you try will work really well; sometimes, they won't work at all. It doesn't matter. You have still increased your self-esteem because you showed that you had the courage and the respect for yourself to try something new and different.

The only thing that keeps you resisting the concept of doing something new is your all-or-nothing thinking, as we discussed earlier. Allow yourself to imagine, even for a moment, that there really is no universal right or wrong. There is no perfect choice. What is truly right for you in the moment is all that matters. Can you hear this? Can you allow yourself to stop and offer this thought to yourself?

Notice if there is any fear or resistance stirred up by this concept. If so, could you ask the Drill Sgt. what's scary about allowing for the possibility that there is no *one* way—no *right* way? Based on the cues from your Authentic Self, does it have anything to do with the Drill Sgt.'s lack of trust in you to determine what is truly best in that moment? Well, that's okay. It makes sense that he wouldn't be feeling completely confident and relaxed with the idea of you beginning to take your cues from within and just go with what feels right to you. It's likely that he has never seen you do that before. He's also a throwback from the time when you had to focus outside of yourself on the needs and feelings of others in order to get by. So it may take a little time for him to relax and trust that you are able to figure out what's right for you and that it's okay for you to do this.

So his resistance to your taking action that is contrary to the "security" and "approval" of the co-dependent mindset is understandable. I encourage you to keep coming from the Nurturing Parent and offering him the reassurance and feedback that you don't exactly know what you are doing either, but *that's okay*. As long as you commit to taking no action until you feel grounded and peaceful about what is truly right for you, there is nothing for the Drill Sgt. to fear. It is safe for him to let go and allow your Nurturing Self and Authentic Self to work together to identify what is truly right for you in each separate moment.

Soon you will begin to notice a beautiful pattern emerging. You will begin to be more and more conscious of the people and situations that trigger your PLA and even your use of food to cope. You will be able to check in and ask your Authentic Self what she is feeling and needing in that moment. You will be able to discern what is really, truly, factually happening in that moment versus what the old beliefs you have been carrying are telling you is going on. Then you will be able to offer yourself compassion and nurturing, and you will be able to come up with an honouring way of responding to the situation—*if* a response is truly warranted. You will begin to witness yourself taking action outwardly to honour yourself, when that is required. And if no response is warranted because it was all in your head from your old beliefs, you will be able to relax and let this go. And either way, you will be feeling more and more grounded and trusting in your feelings and in the validity of your needs. Self-love and self-compassion begin to flow in you, and you draw more and more loving and compassion to you from others. It is a beautiful cycle, and you are on the path to living this yourself—each day of your life.

We have a few more pieces to explore before you will be able to feel as if you have all the information and ammunition you need to make the above statement a reality.

Now let's delve a little deeper into two key concepts of your relationship with yourself—self-compassion and the respectful ac-knowledgment of your authentic feelings. Then we will explore your Authentic Self a little more closely and learn how to dialogue with her and with the Drill Sgt. more easily and naturally.

14

Self-Compassion and the
Respectful Acknowledgement of Feeling

The psychic energy it takes to maintain the Drill Sgt. and to resist his harmful messages is enormous. It is energy enough to send a rocket to Mars and back. Once you get started, the psychic energy it takes to honour and respect yourself is miniscule. In fact, loving and respecting yourself *gives* you energy; it fulfills and sustains you in and of itself. Self-compassion gives you a sense of strength, courage, deservedness and inner peace which cannot be attained any other way.

This is the reason self-compassion is so very important. From understanding why you do what you do with food, to dialoguing respectfully with the Drill Sgt., to cutting yourself some slack if you choose a Plan C and not a Plan A, to allowing yourself to buy clothes which fit you comfortably now: it's all about demonstrating self-respect and self-compassion.

Each of these new ways of thinking and behaving toward yourself is leading you in the direction of self-compassion, which will bring peace and strength. You may be thinking, "I don't care about that, I just want to stop using food to cope!" Well, if you haven't put it together for yourself already, consider this: if you are feeling strong and secure in yourself and offering compassion and respect throughout each day to yourself, how likely are you to cross over your stress threshold and need to use food to cope? Ever? Not likely. This truly is the quickest, easiest, most life-enhancing and freeing way to overcome your use of food to cope. And it has the beautiful side-effect of creating a much stronger and more grounded you than anything the old Diet Mentality and Drill Sgt.'s "motivation through criticism" approach could ever offer.

I mentioned earlier, when we discussed core beliefs, that as children and often as adults, we believe that others know what is good for us, and we trust that they have our best interests at heart. Check in about yourself now and your behaviour around others. Would you agree it is true that often in relationship with the people you care about, you have their best interests at heart? Is it also true that sometimes in the past you have made jokes, exaggerated, ridiculed, laid on a guilt trip, or judged someone you are close to in order to get what you want? Even once? This doesn't make you a bad person. It only makes you human; a human who has a need and who knows no other way to meet it—just as the people in your past did: the ones who have given you some negative beliefs about yourself.

There is no point judging yourself for your behaviour toward others or toward yourself in the past. You could not have done anything different. You were not aware of your motivation and you did not possess the tools to change your behaviour and make it more supportive or appropriate. You are still responsible for how you behaved, but you must forgive yourself. You truly knew not what you were doing!

Most of us have harmed ourselves far more than we have ever harmed anyone else; therefore, the first place to start making a change to your limiting beliefs and your behaviour is within. Feeling and expressing genuine compassion toward ourselves is one of the most challenging parts of this process, because we are carrying a belief that we are undeserving of love and care. When I work with a client and we begin to explore the notion of offering compassion toward ourselves, I always meet with strong resistance. This is natural, and I felt this resistance at the start of my process, too.

Stop and check in briefly. What do you feel when I suggest you offer yourself some compassion about your past behaviours and treatment toward yourself? What arguments do you find yourself offering to avoid being compassionate?

The Story of Emily

In one of our first sessions, I suggested to Emily that the process of recovery would require her to forgive herself for her past behaviours, and to offer herself compassion and understanding for why she behaved as she had, and why she continues to do what she does around food, relationships, and every aspect of her life. She stared at me blankly, nodding but not committing. A sceptical *Uh-huh* escaped her mouth, and I could tell she was already envisioning failure with thoughts such as: "Another attempt at recovery down the tubes. Back to the diet centre. . ."

At the thought of offering herself some compassion and understanding, Emily was ready to give up on the whole process of recovery. I asked her what was going on for her in that moment and she said, "I feel as though it would be copping out to be compassionate with myself; as if I would be letting myself off the hook, and I am worried that, if I weren't on my case all the time, I'd never do anything about my problem. I just can't imagine accepting myself as I am, and I think I need to do that if I'm going to be compassionate with myself, so. . . I can't imagine being compassionate. What have I done to deserve compassion? I'm constantly letting myself down and not doing what I say I will."

Emily was struggling with some faulty reasoning. She believed her problem was lack of willpower, and, if she only tried hard enough, she would be able to stop overeating. If she could just stop overeating, she would lose weight and everything would be great. Emily still believed that her problems had appeared because of being overweight and of her lack of willpower around food. While I agreed with Emily that effort is required to make a change in one's behaviour, I did not agree with the way she was going about it. Berating and pressuring herself through ultimatums and guilt was doing nothing to create a strong connection within. If anything, it was pushing Emily even farther away from her feelings.

A good example of this is a story which Emily shared with me about a typical but poignant evening. Emily had agreed to meet a friend for a drink one Saturday night. As she was preparing to go out, she began by showering. She noticed, with sadness and disgust, the rolls around her waist and the size of her thighs. She had weighed herself earlier that day and hadn't lost an ounce since the day before (she was still dieting). As she stood naked in front of her closet, stuffed full of clothes, and began to look for something to wear, her self-talk went something like this: Nope, too small, too tight. I look too fat in that. That shows my rolls. That colour doesn't suit me. That's out of style, and so on. She finally settled on something which she wears so frequently she has jokingly and embarrassedly begun to call it her "uniform"—a baggy T-shirt and the only pair of pants she can still wear. She is frustrated that, when she does want to look stylish, she has nothing good to wear. In keeping with the theme of withholding compassion, she won't buy herself anything that fits well and looks good.

She looks at me and says, "Nothing looks good on my body as it is now, so why bother? Also, don't forget that I'm trying to lose weight, so why would I "waste" money on new clothes?" Instead, she stands in front of her mirror, criticizing herself for being fat, and criticizing her body for its curves and rolls. It is time for her to leave to meet her friend, and Emily is so frustrated and so uncomfortable in her body that she wants to cry. She certainly doesn't want to go out in public the way she is feeling about herself. She picks up the phone and prays silently that her friend will answer. "Hi, Janet," she croaks into the phone, "I'm sorry for the late notice, but I think I'm coming down with something. I'm going to have to cancel our drink tonight." She hangs up the phone, feeling relieved to have avoided the public viewing but feeling guilt and anger with herself for lying to her friend: she is isolated once more.

She knows she is going to binge now; there is no way she wouldn't binge after the way she has been feeling about and talking to herself. Now that she has the night to herself, there is nothing to stop her. She works her way out of the pants and breathes a sigh of relief as she slips on her big flannel nightie. She finds herself in the kitchen, rooting through the cupboards. She knows she isn't physically hungry, but there is a gnawing, topsy-turvy feeling in her stomach, and she thinks some sort of food will help. She grabs a bag of nachos, some salsa, a bag of cookies, a big glass of pop and heads for the TV. An hour later, she comes to. The nachos, cookies and pop are gone. She knows she ate them but doesn't really remember tasting any of it. She is conscious of feeling very full; kind of sick, really, and that topsy-turvy feeling is still there. She feels sad and scared that food couldn't take it away. She wonders if it will ever go away. And feeling very heavy and tired, she thinks that it probably will not.

Another evening is spent using the coping strategies of isolation, food, negative self-talk, and feelings of disgust, frustration, resentment, guilt and shame. If you use food to cope, you can resonate with Emily's evening. You have spent many like this in some way, shape and form. At any point in that evening, Emily had the power to turn the whole situation around, if she had only been willing to offer herself some compassion from a Nurturing Self point of view by saying: "Yes, it is frustrating that my body is so out of shape and that I have used food to cope so frequently that I weigh more than is healthy or normal. And the only thing which is going to change *that* is to figure out *why* I am using food to cope, and take care of that."

In this case, if Emily had offered herself the reassurance that there most certainly was a reason for her to use food to cope that night, and it wasn't because she was fat or lacked willpower, she could have turned the whole evening around, even if she ultimately chose to stay in. She could have identified that she had too many things going on that day, and she just didn't have the energy to go out. If only she could have let it be okay to take care of herself and to offer support to staying in rather than feeling guilt and shame as though she were copping out or that she was only staying in because of how her body looked, Emily would have felt little or no guilt and likely even empowered.

When she and I took a look at the day she had had leading up to that moment, it was clear that her day had been stressful and she felt the need to be "on" all day. She really needed to stay in because she felt so tired and overwhelmed; moreover, she did not have the energy to "put on the façade". But her Drill Sgt. wasn't willing to let that be enough of a reason. So she had to work herself into a self-hating tizzy and then numb herself with food to prove how unacceptable she really was.

These patterns, repeated daily in some way, shape and form, serve only to reinforce the old beliefs and deepen our current belief that the Drill Sgt.'s way of doing things is the only way. Again, if Emily had only been able to come from her Nurturing Self at any point in this evening and say, "This is a coping strategy, Em, what's really going on?" things would have been immeasurably different for that night and the next day, too. We all know how these evenings linger and lead us to beat ourselves up the day after and beyond.

If Emily had been willing, in that moment, to sit down with her nachos and write out a list of stressors, she would immediately have seen what was going on for her: she had a good reason for feeling overwhelmed, and she really needed a quiet night at home. Her co-dependency and low self-esteem made it very difficult for her to ask directly for what she needed and to just say she was too pooped to go out. Instead, she had to create such personal distress and then lie to her friend and say she was sick, just to meet her need for rest and peace. Thankfully, Emily was very tired of feeling so disgusted with herself that she was willing to try anything! Even the concept of self-compassion seemed like something worth trying, regardless of how the Drill Sgt. judged it.

Self-Compassion and Clothing

You will recall we talked briefly about comfortable clothing when we discussed the Diet Mentality earlier. It is a key point in recovery and the clearest indicator you will ever have as a compulsive eater that you are beginning to allow compassion for yourself. If you feel negatively about your body and each day, when you are getting dressed, you find that you have nothing to wear that fits you comfortably, it is absolutely not a waste of time or money to buy yourself a few new articles of clothing. If money is a concern, there is usually a good second-hand clothing store nearby that will have quality clothing in near-new condition.

There simply is no reason for you to not have comfortable and stylish clothing in this day and age except, of course, because you are depriving yourself. If this is you, you are punishing your body for being as it is. As hard as it might be to accept this, you must understand that your body is how it is because of your need for comfort from food. It did not get to where it is on its own. In order to be where you are today, you had to be there, stuffing your feelings with food which you were not physically hungry for. Again, this is not a failure on your part. In fact, allowing yourself to use food for comfort is likely the one and only act of compassion you do permit. When you begin to trust the messages your body is sending about hunger and fullness, and you can change your behaviour around food, your body will shift to a natural and healthful weight. Until then, every act of punishment or deprivation will send you looking to food for comfort. So be aware that the message you are sending yourself each time you wear those too-tight pants is that you are un-deserving of comfort and of feeling good about your body.

Is this the message you want to send? If it is, how do you think that treating yourself this way will help? Are you, like Emily, think-ing that restricting yourself will provide motivation? If so, consider this: in the behavioural school of psychology, it is called negative reinforcement when you take away or withhold a stimulus. Negative reinforcement teaches new behaviours only through fear of punish-ment, and once the threat of punishment is removed, the behaviour is destined to revert to its original pattern. Therefore, when you with-hold food, a new outfit, or compassion for yourself as a means of motivating an end to binging, you are really only delaying a binge. We must eat. It is a fact of life—a very frustrating fact for compulsive eaters who believe that avoiding food altogether would solve their problems in one fell swoop. Each time you punish yourself through restriction as a means of motivation, you are missing the point of the word "motivation". It is supposed to be about inspiration and encouragement.

For example, you may hear yourself having a conversation like this in your head: *You can have that new dress you want, but I'm not buying it in anything larger than a size 12 even if you are a size 18 now. You will just have to lose weight.* The dress hangs in the closet for months upon months, year after year—a bitter reminder of how you are "supposed" to be. It does not motivate you; it depresses you. It is a reminder of your "failure" and your "lack of will power". Nothing will maintain a need of food for comfort better than a consistent reminder of the fact that you are not what you think you should be.

If you use food predominantly from a restrictive perspective, you are likely under your natural weight; therefore, this concept works for you in reverse. For the same reasons as the person who may overeat, you are fearful of allowing yourself to eat what you want, when you want, and to buy clothes which fit comfortably. Instead of seeing your weight naturally decrease as you allow yourself to explore Natural Eating, you are likely to see your weight increase. This is not because you are doing something wrong or getting fat. It is because, until now, you have been forcing your body to maintain a weight which is lower than what is natural or healthy. This is why as soon as you relax your restrictive patterns, you gain weight. It is not a bad thing. Your body is sending the most obvious message that your patterns of restriction are neither normal nor healthful. It's your body working as hard as it can to reach its maximum potential. And in order to do that, it must be at its optimum weight (regardless of what you believe), which is clearly more than what you have been trying to achieve or maintain.

When you stop using food to cope on either end of the spectrum, the only possible result is that your body finds its natural weight— the weight which you won't even have to think about to maintain.

Year in, year out, that's what you weigh. If you must work hard to stay there, you are either using food to cope in an overeating way, or you are fighting to maintain a weight which is too low for your body. If you are a restrictor and want to stop, you must be prepared to allow yourself to buy clothes which are a bit larger than the ones you are now wearing. I encourage you to see this as a healthful, honouring step and not a failure. The Drill Sgt. and the Diet Mentality will lead you to believe you are doing something wrong. Remember the concept: Different = Change = Good Stuff. As Emily was, you must be so willing to no longer be controlled and ruled by food that you are prepared to challenge your former mindset and the Drill Sgt.'s old way of doing things. You will then be able to allow yourself to go within and to really listen to what your Authentic Self is asking of you at any given moment.

The Closet Exercise

With the utmost love and respect for you and your process, I am issuing you a challenge which will make a world of difference in your recovery. I invite you, some day in the next week, to go through your closet and drawers and take out everything which is uncomfortable to wear. Yup, that's everything. You are not going to throw or give them away; you are going to store them in boxes or bags and place them anywhere where you won't be seeing them each day.

Here's what you will place in the bags:

- Undies that are too tight.
- Bras that dig in.
- Pants that cut off your circulation or ride up.
- Blouses, sweaters, T-shirts, and so on, which you do not wear because they are too tight or you just feel uncomfortable in them.
- Dresses, skirts, everything which feels uncomfortable because they constrict you or make you self-conscious with the way they accentuate certain areas.

When I invite clients to do this, the main objections I hear are:

1. I won't have anything in my closet!

2. I can't afford any new clothes!
3. I'll never find anything which looks good on me!
4. I hate shopping for clothes!
5. If I get rid of those clothes and allow myself to buy new ones, I'll just keep getting fatter and grow out of those. I'm better off to stick to the tight ones, then I've got some incentive!

You have now had enough experience with me to have a sense of the all-or-nothing thinking inherent in those statements—to see the Drill Sgt.'s "motivation through criticism" shining through. And although you can probably even guess what I might have to say about these objections, I'll say it anyway, just to ensure the Drill Sgt. hears it loud and clear.

1. "I won't have anything left in my closet!" The truth is, if you were to take everything out of your closet that is uncomfortable now and you truly had nothing left, then you really didn't have anything in your closet to begin with, no matter how jam-packed it might be. The reality is, you don't have anything to wear, and you can't continue to harm yourself by withholding comfort in a misguided effort to motivate weight loss or to maintain a weight that is too low for you naturally.

2. "I can't afford any new clothes!" This may be true. Would you rather have an empty closet or two pairs of pants and three shirts at best, or would you rather allow yourself to visit the second-hand clothing store and pick up a few pairs of pants and some shirts to tide you over until you feel more comfortable with your weight and can afford new clothes. You can choose either. One choice will keep you feeling crappy and hating your body every time you dress. The other will make getting dressed less of a painful issue. It will give you the emotional energy and consciousness to attend to what is really going on and leading you to use food to cope.

3. "I'll never find anything that looks good on me!" This depends on you and what you are expecting of your body. I encourage you to allow yourself to go for comfort! Comfort

first, then style, just for now. If you don't have the socially-acceptable, perfect 10 body, there will always be something in any store which doesn't look great on you. Most clothes are made for people who don't exist. Sizing these days is absolutely nuts! Following my recovery from my compulsive eating, I usually took a size 10 and often a size 12. My weight has remained the same for nearly ten years since I found my natural weight. But for some reason, I now take a size 6! What's with that? Manufacturers are changing their sizes to meld with society's fixation of wearing the smallest size possible. I mean, since when has there been a size 1? Just the past few years, as far as I'm aware—and only then because of "downsizing" of sizes. Now strangely enough, I have to buy large underwear! No one would call me a large person, and yet the sizing for underwear is such that I must buy large, or it won't fit. How confusing might this be for the person who is still looking outside herself for validation of her "okay-ness" physically, only to see her pant size decreasing but having to buy larger lingerie? Anyway, the point is we can't be looking at sizes to determine how deserving we are of being comfortable and of looking as good as we can. It may be true that the shape of your body at this time is such that certain styles just won't work. It will also be true that you will find something that fits you well, is comfortable, and that you like. I have supported hundreds of clients through this experience and always, without exception—even if they hate the thought of going shopping for their current body—they find something which they like, and they are so very glad to have something comfortable and more than one choice in their closet! Never, ever, does having comfy clothes lead a person to use food to cope more than before. *Never.*

4. "I hate shopping for clothes!" See above! You don't have to love it or even like it. The point is not to be enjoying the experience. Let's be realistic. If you hate your body, you won't love staring at it in the mirror, regardless of your intention

in doing so. The point of this exercise is to provide you with more choices in comfortable clothing of all kinds. You can then take your current negative focus off your body and put your energy into creating an understanding of and change in the underlying triggers which lead you to use food to cope. This is what will make the difference to your body's shape and size.

5. "If I get rid of those clothes and allow myself to buy new ones, I'll just keep getting fatter and grow out of those. I'm better off to stick to the tight ones because then I've got some incentive!" Well, how has this worked so far? Doesn't the restriction of those clothes you currently have in your closet only lead you to feel yucky and sad and depressed? Doesn't that old "motivation through criticism" lead you to feel worse about your body, use food to cope, numb out? How inspired do you feel to move your body and make honouring choices around food when you are stuffed into a pair of pants and hating your body?

Your Beliefs About Compassion

Earlier, we spoke about the Nurturing Parent. It's time for you to actively begin developing your ability to support and care for yourself. Many of us have a hard time with the concept of offering ourselves compassion. It could be because we never received compassion growing up, or we had no positive role model for compassion. It could be that no matter how troubled our past, we feel that we are undeserving or wasting our time being compassionate toward ourselves: others have had it worse. There are many other reasons why we may resist compassion toward ourselves. Some of us may view self-compassion as a pity party and see it as a sure path to wallowing, depression, and complete powerlessness and victim-hood. Some of us may feel that we can only be motivated by criticism and pressure. Being compassionate and supportive toward ourselves is as though we are admitting defeat or inviting complacency.

The truth is, if pressure or criticism worked for you as a motivational tactic, you would have achieved your goal ten times over by now. As someone who uses food as a coping strategy, when you criticize yourself for eating or not having the body you believe you "should", or for not doing or saying what you feel you "should," **you are only reinforcing your need for food for nurturing and comfort**.

If a large part of your use of food for coping comes in response to feelings of self-judgement or loathing, it then makes sense that, if you were to offer yourself compassion instead of criticism, your need for food for comfort would be greatly diminished. So why do we feel such great resistance to the idea of offering ourselves compassion? Let's explore your reasons.

Take a minute to answer the following questions. Exploring these issues will help you to understand what your beliefs about compassion are and how they influence you. Those of you in the action stage of change will want to take some time and write out your answers. Those of you in the determination and contemplation stages will want to stop and invite yourself to consider what is true for you in response to each question. You may want to establish the intent within yourself to return to this in the future and to explore this more fully, depending on what you notice happening in your ability to understand the value of self-compassion and to actually begin offering this to yourself.

1. What does the word compassion mean to you?
2. What do you feel/think when you imagine being compassionate toward yourself?
3. What do you feel/think when you imagine being compassionate toward others?
4. Under what circumstances does it feel okay to offer compassion to yourself?
5. Under what circumstances does it feel okay to offer compassion to others?
6. Who was a model for compassion for you in the past? In what way did they model compassion?

7. What did they teach you about caring for yourself/for others?
8. Do you feel deserving of good things and good feelings?
    a) If so, why might you resist the notion of offering yourself compassion and support?
    b) If not, what has led you to feel undeserving?
9. Considering your answers to the above questions, what stands in the way of your ability to offer yourself compassion and support?

It is important that you invite yourself to reflect on your answers to these questions, particularly to number nine, when you are trying to develop the skill of self-nurturing. It is all too easy to berate ourselves for not doing what we think we should. How does it help to get down on yourself for not being more compassionate? It doesn't. Remember that you have a tendency to all–or–nothing thinking and that you are working toward change.

Whatever you are doing now or at any time, it is truly the best you can do. If you would like your thoughts, feelings, or behaviours to be different, you must learn to see them simply as coping strategies which are there to guide you to an awareness of unmet needs you have in that moment. They are really just signposts. And once you see the sign in yourself in any moment, the solution is *not* to judge or berate yourself for the fact that the sign is there, but to acknowledge the meaning of the sign and to identify the need which has been triggered and how best to meet it. Judgement and self-ridicule will keep you stuck in your focus on the signpost. There is no benefit in that for you or anyone else.

Allow yourself to feel as much self-compassion as you can. Just do your best. If you feel resistance to self-compassion, just allow the resistance. Remember, the point is not to force yourself to think or feel something which isn't authentic for you—that would be just doing what you have always done, and that's not compassion. In fact, it's the pattern of trying to force yourself to feel, think, be, and do something which isn't authentic for you that has brought you to where you are now. The solution lies in allowing whatever your truth is in this moment. This, in and of itself, is compassion. And the more you can invite yourself to just let your authentic feeling, thought, or need in the moment be okay, the more relaxed and peaceful you will become. You will have more energy to move forward in all areas of your life.

So, contrary to what your Drill Sgt. will tell you, compassion for yourself is not death to your motivation. It is what will ultimately free you of your self-imposed limitations. It will support you to overcome your self-judgements and rigid expectations. Do you remember the integrated self that I spoke of when I talked of the Drill Sgt. and the Nurturing Parent? Compassion for yourself forms the basis of the foundation for a strong integrated Self.

Explore your feelings and thoughts about self-compassion. Notice what resistance may be arising to this notion; just do your best to allow those feelings, while being aware of any resistance you may be experiencing. Let it be okay to feel what you feel. And as you are allowing the resistance and the feelings of fear and doubt, know that what you are really doing is being compassionate with yourself. This is the key to never again needing to use food to cope.

If there is any resistance in you to the thought of offering yourself compassion, ask what you did to deserve to be treated with such disregard and negativity. Whatever the answer, could you just allow yourself to feel as deserving of self-harm as you do? Just sit for a moment and allow yourself to feel as deserving of pain, suffering, and all the grim things you have in your life.

Now, could you allow yourself to let go of feeling as deserving of self-harm as you do? Just for now? Could you let it be okay to offer yourself compassion and love? Even for a moment?

Notice what surfaces in your physical body and your thoughts as you experiment with allowing yourself to feel deserving of harm versus deserving of compassion. Just notice the part of you which is ready to love and honour yourself, and notice the part of you which still believes that's not an option. It's okay; they can both be there. The truth is, they *are* both there whether you allow them to be or not.

So accept that, and know that the more you acknowledge the truths of the Drill Sgt. and of your Authentic Self, the more they will come to be aligned, and your integrated self will be onside with the value of self-compassion.

Now let's take a deeper look at feelings before we move on in our exploration of self-compassion.

Feelings

When it comes to talking about feelings as an indicator of their needs, I have heard many clients say that they don't know what they feel. This is both true and not true. You have honed the coping strategy of alexithymia so well that you can be using your food coping strategy and not even notice it until well after the fact. Clearly, you have an ability to tune out to your feelings. What you will discover, if you haven't already, is that you are able to identify certain feelings when you simply take the time to stop and be present with yourself and ask the question: *What am I feeling right now?*

To make it simple, give yourself just four choices: Mad, Glad, Sad and Scared.

These are the four basic human emotions. All the feelings you will ever experience can be boiled down to one or a combination of those four feelings. So for the next while, each time you check in to see what your Authentic Self is feeling, offer yourself just those four basic choices. You will find that what you are feeling will fit one or a few of these options.

What is important to really understand about feelings—yours and anyone else's—is that they are simply flags. Feelings are just indicators of what you need or want at any given moment. They also tell you what needs are being met, that is, when you are feeling peaceful, joyful, relaxed.

Feelings spontaneously arise from within, and we cannot stop them. At best, we can learn techniques to dull our awareness of them (such as, alexithymia and depression) or develop behavioural coping strategies, for example, food, TV and shopping, which help us numb out to our feelings. But we can't stop ourselves from having feelings. They are not good or bad, right or wrong; they just are. They are fundamentally important to your overall health and wellbeing. Feelings are your Authentic Self trying to tell you something important about what you need. When you know and trust this piece of information, you begin to cease judging yourself for having certain emotions. You realize that every emotion you have is just a signpost on the road telling you that you need to take a certain action, change course, or maintain the status quo. You begin to appreciate your ability to know what you feel—to respect and appreciate those signposts, because they prevent you from harm and distress when you allow yourself to listen to them.

Many of us have been given the impression by key people in our lives that any feeling other than happy is unacceptable. We have been taught that sadness and fear imply weakness and that anger is inappropriate. Is it any wonder we try as hard as we can to distance ourselves from our feelings when we have been given these messages? Is it any wonder that, rather than feeling grateful for the cue that we are feeling sad when we notice ourselves tearing up, we feel angry at ourselves and fearful of the judgement of others?

Learning to accept and embrace your feelings as an integral part of who you are is all part of being compassionate and loving toward yourself. Letting it be okay to be vulnerable and show your feelings to the outside world requires you to feel secure in yourself and trusting of your worth. Your feelings have something very important to tell you. Any time you choose to hide your feelings for fear of revealing some of yourself, you are in essence saying to your Authentic Self, "I care far more what this person thinks of me than for what you need right now."

It is impossible to build a strong, centred, confident *you,* who does not need food to cope in any way, as long as you are willing to continue to judge and dismiss your feelings.

Mad

Feelings of anger mean you are feeling threatened in some way. It could be a physical threat. More than likely, your anger will be triggered by some threat, real or perceived, to your sense of power and control in your world. So your anger could be coming from someone taking your job, cutting you off in traffic, ending a relationship with you or showing up late. These are examples of a need for control (also known as security) which does not feel met in that moment.

A great way of perceiving anger, which helps to shift it almost instantly, is to get in the habit of reminding yourself that when you feel even the slightest bit perturbed, anger is just the surface emotion. What is beneath anger is always the same: feelings of sadness *and* feelings of fear.

Knowing this, you can immediately diffuse your anger by acknowledging the sadness and fear that lie beneath it. Try it. As soon as you allow yourself to look for what might be making you feel sad and scared in a situation which has triggered anger, you will notice the anger dissipates, and you feel the sadness. This may not sound all that great to you now, but it is wonderful. The feeling of sadness is the true feeling underneath the protective cloak of anger. You may be angry and not really know why. As soon as you invite yourself to look beneath your anger to the sadness and ask yourself what might be making you sad right now, you are immediately transported to your Authentic Self, and you are aware of a deeper sense of connection which is much softer and gentler than your anger; you will be able to not only identify why you are sad but also what is required to heal that pain. If you allow yourself to stay in your anger, the best you can do is to blame and judge others and yourself because you are tuned out to what is really going on for you.

I see anger as flailing in the dark. It is healthful and appropriate if you feel that something is there but you can not see it, and you need to protect yourself as best you can. However, it isn't likely to solve anything. The reason is you often don't know what it is you really need to resolve when you are angry. If you are flailing in the dark, the idea is to get to the light switch. Illuminate the situation and identify what *is* there. This means taking a moment to notice your feelings of anger and to ask what is making you sad and scared. Now you are aware of what is really going on for you, and you cannot respond unconsciously. Most arguments we have with others will immediately fall apart at this point. This doesn't mean you won't get what you want or need in the situation. It means you are no longer arguing and angry. You are feeling your deeper feelings, and you are able to communicate those feelings and the needs that triggered them without the defensiveness or judgement which accompanies our anger. This makes it much easier for the other person to hear you, to share back, and to take their piece of the responsibility.

It may not have been safe for you to express your anger in your family of origin or in past relationships. You may have been judged, ridiculed, or even physically harmed for expressing your natural and appropriate angry response to a situation. Just as your old core beliefs around your worth and deservedness were never true, the story that anger is bad and that you are bad for feeling it—let alone expressing it—is just not true. You see, your authentic expression of anger forces others to see and to take responsibility for their behaviour toward you.

If you had people around you in your past who were uncomfortable with seeing what their words or actions were doing to you, they would have done whatever they could to prevent you from your authentic reactions. This means they might get louder or more aggressive to create such fear in you that you wouldn't show them any emotion at all. This also means they might ridicule you for having such strong emotions and leave you feeling as though you are bad or wrong. It is painful to be ridiculed and judged for our authentic, natural expression. It really hurts to be shut down when some part of us knows that what we feel is valid. But, if there is no one around us at that time with the consciousness and maturity to be able to see the validity in our feelings and to allow us to express them authentically, we will come away from that situation feeling judged and also judging ourselves.

This is so unfortunate because what we really need to do in these moments is to understand that the other person has limitations around their comfort and consciousness of feelings. If they are averse to or judging of our feelings, it isn't about us. It's about them. But often these lessons are learned when we are very young and are incapable of understanding that the other's response is not about us. We take it on. We internalize this message, and we begin to judge our own feelings. We turn on ourselves and begin to fragment and disconnect from our Authentic Selves. It is the only way we can be in that situation without feeling the pain so consciously.

Anger is a natural, healthful response to a threat. Remember this. And remember that, if you are feeling angry, it is really because you are feeling sad and scared inside. As you begin to experiment with this new way of seeing anger, you will prove to yourself that there is always a legitimate reason for you to feel as you do. You will also see that the simple act of looking for the sadness and fear beneath your anger shifts you immediately into a deeper connection with yourself and a stronger sense of groundedness within.

Glad

If we were to label feelings as good or bad, everyone would say that "glad" is a good one, right? Well, sort of. Yes, on any given day we would rather feel glad than sad. But glad has its issues, also.

Many of us have been taught that "you shouldn't be too happy". The expectations which many of us picked up from our society, peers, and caregivers are confusing at best: you are supposed to be light and joyful; you are not supposed to have any problems or needs; you are not supposed to be proud of yourself; you are not supposed to be more successful or happier than those around you, and on and on it goes.

So we are meant to be light and gay and happy, but not too happy and not too light. By whose standards? Where is the "happy scale" which tells us how happy we can be and where and with whom? And how do we know when it is okay to not be quite as happy? Is it okay to be less happy sometimes? My goodness, the fears and doubts surrounding the simple act of feeling joyful are overwhelming.

If someone around you is sad or upset, why on earth should you be sad and upset with them? How does that help? Why should you feel as though you must take on each others feelings? Can't you both just feel what you feel and respect that? Yes, but not if you were raised in a co-dependent environment where the people around you believed that you were supposed to make them feel better or at least not make them feel worse, or if those around you believed that sadness, fear, and anger were bad and that they had to do something if you felt those feelings. You weren't allowed to let people feel what they felt and just be happy. And you weren't allowed to just feel your feelings and to see that great self-awareness and strength comes from this.

We've all heard the saying, "You can't make anyone feel anything." I agree with that. It is your story about what is going on, what the intention of the other person is or was, and what will happen that is harming you and "making" you feel that feeling. Now having said that, remember that our feelings are signals. They are spontaneously-occurring indicators of what we need and want. So, if a particular person frequently triggers feelings of sadness, fear and/or anger in me, I am best to distance myself from them. Even if it is my own story that brings on those feelings around this person, clearly I am not "in a place" which enables me to be with them and not have that story arise. So the self-respecting thing to do is to take some space from the relationship and heal that piece in myself. And if it isn't all my own story and this person is behaving abusively or disrespectfully to me, I must honour myself and set very clear boundaries with this person about what I will and won't accept from them (more on that in a bit).

Stop and check in with your Authentic Self. Does she truly feel free to be the best she can be? Does she feel as if it is okay for her to be happy just because she is happy? Or does she believe that she has to temper her feelings to match those of the people around her?

Invite yourself to consider the possibility that you could allow yourself to feel what you feel regardless of the emotions of those around you. There is no need to pretend to be happy if you are truly feeling down. And there's no need to squash your happiness if someone else is feeling down. Those are co-dependent behaviours. You are living your life to make someone else happy in those instances, and, any time you try to do that, neither of you will be happy for any length of time.

Sad

Sad is a great feeling. No, I'm not crazy. And if we were to meet, I'd bet you would say I was one of the happiest people you ever met. So my love of the feeling of sadness does not imply that I live there. I like sad as a feeling because it is true. Anger has a story attached to it that is often murky and more focused on others than on yourself. Sad can have a story which isn't all true, but it is far more about you. Sad is the feeling which brings you to your true self more than any other. I believe that is why so many people who use food to cope do pretty much anything they can to avoid feeling it.

As we discussed earlier, anger is a mask for sadness and fear. Many of us who use food to cope prefer to hang out in anger on the surface of our awareness, because we believe anger is a more powerful feeling and that we will be protected by it. Well, sometimes it is true that anger protects you. Most of the time though, anger actually harms you. It is just a defense mechanism, a coping strategy. It is the way of being in an uncomfortable situation without being aware of how uncomfortable you are. That's not so great. Not if your intention is to heal the past and take charge of your life.

Sadness is the feeling beneath your anger. It's the real goods. You may be sad because of a story you are telling yourself, but sadness is your authentic feeling about that story. The more you allow yourself to feel your sadness when it surfaces, the more love and compassion you will feel for yourself on the whole; the more connected to your Authentic Self you will be; the more control you will feel over your life and the happier you will be. Yes, the more you allow yourself to feel what you are authentically feeling (the sadness, the fear, the anger) in this moment, the happier you will be because those feelings will be able to move through you, and they will no longer be needed. Stuffing them with food or bad body thoughts only prevents you from healing the thought or experience which triggered those feelings. Feeling them lets you move through them to a higher place of peace, joy and freedom.

Now let's explore two key ways that your authentic feelings of sadness may trigger you to feel uncomfortable in relation to others, and how to change that old harmful pattern!

Crying in public

Frankly, one of the quickest and easiest methods for shedding a truck-load of co-dependency and ELOC is to allow yourself to cry in public. Any time you feel sad and feel those tears welling, let yourself cry. And don't apologize or even say anything about it except, "I am feeling very sad right now." No apologizing. No caretaking. No shame. You are feeling a natural, healthful, appropriate feeling. Honour it. Respect it. Love it. Let yourself feel it. Holding it in at that moment simply says, "My feelings are bad." It also implies that you do not trust the person you are with to respect your feelings. And it says to yourself that you do not trust in your right to express yourself authentically.

Your feelings are not good or bad. They just are. You must learn to trust yourself to respect your feelings and to express yourself authentically. It is the only way to feel truly grounded and secure. It is also the only way to build a deep and authentic relationship with others. And if you don't trust the other person to respect your sharing of feelings, ask yourself, "Have I given this person a chance to show me how they would respond if I let them know how I was truly feeling?" If you haven't done this and have simply made the assumption that they would judge you or not be able to offer support, be honest with yourself. Be aware that you may simply be continuing to carry those old bogus stories that you learned in childhood into your present relationships. Allow for the possibility that the person you are in friendship or partnership with now is different from those people from your past and is, therefore, possibly able to respond differently to your authentic sharing of feelings.

I can't tell you how many times clients have allowed themselves to challenge their old pattern of hiding their feelings and discovered that not only was it safe to share with others, but it also made their relationship deeper, stronger and healthier. Of course, it would. How could you have a strong and deep bond when you never let anyone see who you really are or how you really feel about things? Your authentic sharing of your emotions is a great gift which you can give to a relationship. If the other person judges you, shuts you down, or does not reciprocate, this merely indicates that they had the same training as you, and they have not healed. You can ask them if they would like to work on that with you. Or you can put your emotional energy into relationships with people who are already able to connect with and express their emotions. There are lots of them out there.

So the next time you feel like crying and there is someone there, go for it. No apology necessary. Don't belittle your emotions by apologizing for them. Own your feelings. Be proud of your feelings. They are the gateway to your soul, and that is a very special place.

Tears of joy

One more word on crying in public: tears of joy are a beautiful thing. Whether it is a movie, a song, a sunrise, a child smiling; whatever brings those tears of joy to your eyes, embrace it. Welcome it. Say a silent prayer of gratitude for that beautiful, heart-opening moment.

You may have been punished or harmed in the past for your authentic expression of emotion. As a form of punishment, perhaps people in your life would take away things which they knew you liked or enjoyed. They may have put you down and diminished your successes. That is awful. That is very painful, and it is important that you acknowledge the injustice of that treatment. It is also fundamentally important to your life now, in the present, that you allow yourself the full expression of your gratitude and joy when it arises from within.

Your thoughts create your reality. So if you are constantly pushing against feelings of pleasure and joy, you are, in essence, creating a reality which is devoid of those feelings. I know that this is not what you want. So let yourself feel those joyful feelings. For a while you may feel that your tears of joy are mixed with tears of sadness.

This would be natural. You have been through a lot. You have had to hold back and disguise a lot of your feelings and happiness for many years. There is grief in that, too. You have not been allowed to live fully for some time. There is grief in that. Let yourself feel the grief. Acknowledge it. It is real. And so is the joy. Let yourself feel that. Soon the grief will pass, and all that remains is the pleasure of life.

Just as with tears of sadness, make no apology for your tears of joy. Don't try to hide them. This sends yourself the message that there is something wrong with your authentic feelings. There isn't. That's just your old training. Invite yourself to remember where that old training came from and how it harms you to continue with it. Then invite yourself to let it be okay to just feel what you feel. You will be beautifully surprised by the freedom you feel and by the shifts that occur in your relationship with others.

Scared

We have talked a great deal about fear. We have talked about resistance to change; fear of rejection; old core beliefs triggering us to feel fear; the Permeating Level of Anxiety, and that nasty intrusive ideation which re-traumatizes us daily.

A great deal of the fear we feel on a daily basis is our own internal creation. Those old core beliefs that we continue to empower simply by believing in them create an underlying sense of insecurity within. We have the power to no longer believe those old bogus stories about ourselves. But until we really know and trust that, we continue to believe them and feel the fear and insecurity which those stories trigger. The same thing occurs with our intrusive ideation. Those nasty stories we create, those worst-case-scenarios we design in our minds with the intention of supporting us to feel prepared for anything, only serve to create an approach to life which is totally fear-based. We are on constant alert for attack of any kind.

The irony is, whatever it is you are looking for, you will find. Even if you have had 100 positive interactions with someone, the one interaction you have that is negative or feels threatening in some way will receive the greatest focus. It's as though your Drill Sgt.

has been lying in wait for this person to commit a minor infraction, such as, showing up late, forgetting the milk, or saying something thoughtless, at which point he will say, "Aha! I knew it was just a matter of time before you showed your true colours. I knew you couldn't be trusted!" So the insignificant act of forgetting the milk goes down as proof that your old belief was true. Those other 100 encounters don't count for anything.

Clearly, the key to not living in fear and mistrust any longer is to allow yourself to acknowledge the experiences which you do have that are positive or even neutral. You have potentially had countless experiences with this person that have been positive. There has been one which did not meet your needs for trust or reliability. This is not "proof" that the person is unreliable. When we talk about communication in relationships, we will talk about different ways to approach this issue within yourself and how to communicate your needs to others.

Your fear is a natural appropriate response to what you believe is happening in that moment. Do not judge it. It is just a signal of inner needs which do not feel met at that time. What I want you to do is begin noticing your fear and whether it is the PLA you are aware of, or stronger feelings of panic and anxiety. Notice these feelings, and ask yourself what the thought was which triggered these feelings. Then ask yourself if this thought has anything to do with one of your old core beliefs? Is it any all-or-nothing thinking? Any co-dependent thought? Any intrusive ideation? Bad body thoughts?

You are probably thinking to yourself, "Heck, if I ruled all those things out, I wouldn't have a thought in my head." Precisely! Any of those thought processes I just mentioned are simply old coping strategies. They are harmful and are borne out of past trauma and your old interpretation of those events as being about you. When you begin to challenge yourself not to buy in to any of those old coping strategies, you are opening the door for a life which is peaceful and free, and for a mind which is silent. The 24/7 chatter will be gone. What will remain is a sense of clarity and groundedness which becomes your natural state of being. In this state, any feelings of fear, anger, or sadness will be immediately felt, recognized, and released as you readily identify the trigger and a solution.

No more unfinished business, not even for a moment. And no more need for food to cope.

Compassion for All of You

As discussed earlier, many of us have a lot of energy focused on our bodies. We feel negatively about our physical selves as a result of how we have nurtured ourselves in the past. Just as it makes no sense to berate ourselves for not being more compassionate, it also makes no sense to put ourselves down for having nurtured ourselves with food. The same goes for having purged to release feelings of panic or overwhelm. Cutting, also, is just a coping strategy and a clear sign that you are overwhelmed and feeling unable to cope in any other way. Compromising yourself in relationship with others often feels like the only option to meet our needs for emotional security and acceptance. So how does feeling ashamed and berating yourself for choosing any of these methods of coping lessen your need to do that? Whatever your behaviour, it was the only way you knew to make it through your feelings and some very overwhelming and stressful experiences.

You may recall how alexithymia supports us to diminish and discount our experiences, leaving us open to the Drill Sgt.'s judgement of us as weak and wimpy when we "suddenly" feel sad, scared or angry. Often you are using alexithymia because you have assessed the present experience as too overwhelming, so you must detach from any conscious awareness of feelings. When you begin to offer yourself the trust that there is always, always, a reason for why you do what you do, even if you can't put your finger on it in that moment, you will be putting yourself in the position of coming from compassion. You will be able to seek to understand and heal what is triggering your feeling or behaviour rather than judge it and shut yourself down.

Choose from the following list any behaviours which you engage in, and for each point which resonates, give yourself the gift of making a list (on a separate piece of paper) of the advantages and disadvantages of engaging in this behaviour. It may be hard to identify any advantages, but there definitely are some, at least one, or you wouldn't do it. So check it out, and allow yourself to see, written down before you, what is motivating you to do what you do and what is creating the resistance to allowing that behaviour. What needs are you seeking to meet in invoking this behaviour, and what needs do you believe would be met if you were able to no longer engage in it?

Advantages and Disadvantages of:

- Overeating.
- Being overweight.
- Seeing my body as the problem.
- Seeing food as the problem.
- Purging.
- Restricting.
- Dieting.
- Over-Exercising.
- Co-Dependency.
- Sexual Promiscuity.
- Drinking or using Drugs.
- Engaging in this recovery process.
- Cutting.
- Lying.
- Shopping.
- Exaggerating.
- Resisting Compassion for myself.
- Resisting Compassion from others.

Once you are aware of the reasons you feel drawn to both engage in and resist a certain pattern of behaviour, you can consciously choose to either allow or disallow the behaviour. Regardless of whether you choose to let it be okay, or you choose to resist taking part in that pattern, if you can allow yourself to be truly accepting of your choice, you will experience the sense of freedom, compassion, and self-love that flow from honouring your needs. Either way, you will be in a state of acceptance, and only positive self-regard can exist. You won't harm yourself. Even if you chose to truly allow it, you won't really want to engage in that old harmful behaviour. You won't be fighting it. When you allow yourself to feel as you feel, there will be no energy, no discord around it.

Many clients have said, "Michelle, you've taken all the fun out of it! Why would I even bother overeating now?" They are usually laughing as they say it, because they are actually quite relieved that the old behaviour no longer has the same emotional charge and pull that it used to. They now understand why they were doing it, and they were truly able to let it be okay for themselves to use that coping strategy if need be. And after a very brief period of time of truly allowing it, they just didn't want to do it any more. There was no point.

If you are resistant to letting it be okay to do what you feel you need to do in the moment to cope, experiment with letting it be okay to be as resistant as you are. Just let it be okay to feel what you feel and need what you need. Honour and respect yourself. Be authentic and not what you think you *should* do or be. Do what is true for you. That is true self-compassion, and that is the key to never again using food to cope, or any other harmful coping strategy for that matter.

Now let's explore your Authentic Self more fully.

15

Your Authentic Self

Your Authentic Self

Consider your answers to the following questions:

- Who am I really?
- What is it that I really like; enjoy; feel passionate about?
- How do I know when I'm living authentically and when I'm compromising my integrity?
- What if I discover who I am authentically, and the people around me don't like me?
- Worse, what if I don't like who I am authentically?

Frequently, our answers to questions such as these lead us to this very dangerous all-or-nothing thought: *Maybe I'm better off just continuing to compromise myself and leave things as they are. At least I know what to expect. It's a little too scary to start opening that can of worms.*

I think we have all had this conversation with ourselves at some point. And for some reason, despite how frightened we are of change and/or rejection, we persevere and persist with delving deeper into self-discovery. There is something inside of you which has been awakened—something that has known all along that you have value, and you deserve love and respect from yourself and others. It will no longer rest quietly and permit you to continue sacrificing yourself for others. The days of unconsciousness are gone. Now you know too much about what you think and what you feel. If you have been allowing yourself to explore some of the tools we have covered, you will notice that your alexithymia is starting to give way to self-awareness. You are beginning to know all too well when something isn't feeling right to you

Perhaps you will sometimes continue to choose to compromise your esteem needs. You will choose Plan C. And you are willing to do this because you continue to believe that more fundamental needs, aside from your own esteem and self-respect, will be unmet if you do not. As we spoke about earlier when we discussed self-compassion, there is absolutely no benefit to berating yourself for choosing to compromise your self-esteem. None.

The benefit comes from seeing those experiences of compromise or inaction on your behalf as opportunities for learning. There is a reason that you chose not to assert yourself in that meeting; there is a reason that you went along with the choice of movie even though you would rather have seen something else. You can berate your-self for not taking action which would honour your esteem needs or (and I like this choice best), you can choose to set aside the judge-ment and blaming of yourself and seek to understand what led you to make that choice. Your Authentic Self is what it is. Judging and blaming yourself for behaving or feeling or even thinking a certain way will not change your authentic response in that moment.

Consider this: if you were to commit yourself for the next week to just allowing yourself to feel, think and behave as you do without judging it as right or wrong, what do you think will happen? Take a moment and write down your responses to this question. Give your-self the gift of clarifying (in your mind and on paper) the beliefs you are carrying regarding allowing your authentic expression to just "be".

As people who use food to cope, we have successfully become numb to many situations, many feelings, many needs. Thus, many of us have developed a "persona" which is the face we show to the outside world. Typically, this face will be confident, competent, very sunny and gay, always giving of ourselves and our time to others. All those qualities are within you. You are this. And you are more. And some days the sunny persona just doesn't fit how you are truly feeling, and it takes a great deal of energy to maintain. The further we get into a disordered eating pattern with food, the more we enact the persona and the more draining it becomes just to step out our front door. Of course, in addition to draining ourselves on a daily basis to keep up the act of being happy and "together" (which in our Drill Sgt.'s mind = perfect!), we are making it impossible to develop close, authentic relationships with others. How can someone know who we are and be interacting with us when all we reveal is the actor? In my own experience and that of most of my clients, we created this persona because we believed that who we "really" were wasn't good enough, and, in order to be liked or accepted, we had to be a certain way. How can we possibly have truly intimate and deep connections with others when we are not showing them who we are? We are only showing them who we think they want us to be.

Here we are back at core beliefs. Where did you get the message that you weren't okay? What will it take for you to trust that you are okay just as you are? One result of continuing to carry that old, bogus belief is that you are draining much of your life energy every day by pretending to be someone you think others want or need you to be. And the longer you perform this act, the scarier it becomes to think about dropping it and letting your true self show through.

If you are married or have a partner, you may have established a relationship with this person based primarily on your persona or who you think they want you to be. This will create some distress for you, and possibly for them, when you begin to express yourself authentically. If this is the case and the relationship is one you care about and want to last through your transformation, take a deep breath, and give your partner the gift of knowing that you will be making some changes to how you present yourself to the world. You can say that, somewhere back in time, you made the choice to set aside your authentic expression and feelings and opted for what seemed like the safer route of being what others wanted you to be. You are now choosing to allow yourself to be in touch with what you really feel and want, because the cost of compromising yourself is too great. And don't forget to tell this person that you love them, and you very much want their love and support as you transition into a more authentic expression of yourself. It is your intention that the relationship thrive and flower into something even more beautiful.

As I have mentioned earlier, unless you are in an abusive relationship—one in which there are games of control and manipulation played—your partner will support you fully in becoming more aware of the Authentic You. They will be supportive of your learning to ask directly for what you need and asserting yourself clearly and respectfully. It will be a load off of them to be able to interact fully with you and to see that you are taking responsibility for your needs in a mature and healthful way. Your friends and co-workers will feel similarly—those who are healthy and desire the best for you, that is. Any friendships or other relationships which were built on one person controlling or having one up on the other will fail under this new way of being for you. It is not a loss. Rejoice that you no longer have to drain yourself for this person, and trust that the void will be replaced by new, deeply-fulfilling relationships.

Begin to use your newfound awareness of how you are truly feeling to cast off the persona and show your Authentic Self to the world. You are the one who pays the price for living as you do now. Conversely, you are the one who will reap the most benefit from honouring your true self.

If there is any fear in you about letting more of your Authentic Self shine through, make it less scary by trying out your authentic expression on people you feel close to and secure with, or even when you are alone. The important thing is for you to become as conscious as you can about what is truly going on inside you at any moment. What is your authentic expression, thought or feeling right now? Once you know this, you are truly in a position of power over your life. With this information you can consciously choose how to best honour your need. You can choose to express your thought or feeling, to ask for your need to be met, or you can choose to deal with it on your own. You can even choose to hold it in. The choice is yours—and the greatest gift you can give yourself in this regard is to let it be okay to choose whatever feels right to you.

Dialoguing with Your Authentic Self

We have talked a great deal about your Authentic Self in the previous chapters. We have talked about the fact that she exists. We have talked about how the Drill Sgt. does his best to support her but frequently ends up criticizing and stifling her authentic expression. We have discussed how your use of food to cope, and any other coping strategy, often stems from the unmet needs of your Authentic Self, which the Drill Sgt. seizes, judges, and shuts down. We have talked about how a true sense of security and acceptance in the world cannot exist within you until you become clear on what you really feel and need in any given moment. And you must be able to trust yourself to take whatever steps are necessary to honour the needs and feelings of your Authentic Self in that moment.

This is the path to complete recovery from food as a coping strategy; a path that is taken by every client at the CEDRIC Centre. These steps are absolutely necessary in order for you to be able to be conscious of what's triggering you in any moment, and to know what you can do about it to meet your needs in a respectful and dignified way for all concerned.

At the start of the process of exploring your Authentic Self and getting to know what makes her tick, it is helpful to engage in regular dialogues with her. These dialogues will start out on paper because it is imperative that you see her words and her needs written down. This is the only way for you to really begin to get a sense of the authenticity of her feelings and needs. If it remains in your head, your well-trained Drill Sgt. will squash her sharing and dump all over her needs for the sole purpose of maintaining his precarious balance of control and the pseudo-security and approval that he has managed to create.

The practice of dialoguing with your Authentic Self is what will bring you to a solid sense of inner integration. The fragmentation you are so accustomed to feeling, as well as the personae which you enact throughout your day, will fade to nothingness and be replaced by a sense of strength and wholeness that can never be undermined or removed. You know who you are! You know what you truly feel and need in any situation. And you know that you can trust yourself to respond to your feelings and needs with respect and compassion.

Set aside some time this week, or begin now if you are in a position to do so, and dialogue with your Authentic Self. As you dialogue, your intention is to always be coming from the Nurturing Parent. Sometimes the Drill Sgt. will elbow his way in. You will know this has happened because your Authentic Self has begun to feel pressured or will shut down. As soon as you begin to feel that sense of closing down or of fear, just check in and see if the Drill Sgt. hasn't joined in the dialogue and taken over for the Nurturing Parent who is still growing in strength. If you notice this, simply check in with the Drill Sgt. about his intention, and invite your adult Nurturing Parent to step forth again. Acknowledge the feelings of fear and pressure which your Authentic Self felt in that moment, and reassure her that it is safe now for her to share. She will be listened to and respected.

Start by simply calling forth the Nurturing Parent in you. If you find this challenging, imagine for a moment how you would comfort a child or a dear friend who is having a rough time. Let the compassion, caring and love that you would naturally bring to that situation come *through* you and be directed *within* to your Authentic Self.

Then take some time to consider what you would like to share or know about your Authentic Self. Consider that you are earnestly beginning the most significant relationship of your life; one that will be with you always—through thick or thin. The integration with your Authentic Self will enable you to realize your full potential and to live the life you were truly meant to live. So treat this relationship with the utmost respect. Don't make any commitments to your Authentic Self that you cannot keep. Do your best to honour and acknowledge her needs as she speaks them. Take responsibility *immediately* if you forget to follow through on a commitment or are prevented from doing so. Demonstrate your respect for her feelings and needs by checking in throughout the day whenever you notice your PLA is up: this is a good indication that your Authentic Self has just been squashed by your Drill Sgt. and that your Nurturing Parent is required to sort out the miscommunication within.

In case you are starting to feel a little overwhelmed with the magnitude of the responsibility for your Authentic Self, remember this: your Authentic Self is filled with love. She can be frightened and her trust can be compromised, but she is always willing to forgive and to trust again. If you begin to dialogue with her and then forget her for a time, there is no need to fear that you have ruined the relationship (that's just an all-or-nothing Drill Sgt. thought). You have only delayed your sense of integration and inner strength. And undoubtedly, you did that because something happened in your life which caused the Drill Sgt. to take over and impose his all-or-nothing thinking: this left no room for the needs and feelings of your Authentic Self.

Remember, there is always a reason for why you do what you do, and it has nothing to do with you being lazy, lacking willpower, ability or trying to deliberately harm yourself. The more you can remember this throughout this process, the more you will seek to understand what triggered your Drill Sgt. to kick in and take over. The willingness to trust and understand that your motivation is always positive is what will lead to your growth and ultimate integration.

It is best to practice being in connection with your Authentic Self when you are alone. Take a few minutes each day, more if you can, and just sit down and write from your Nurturing Parent to the Authentic Self. Ask her how she's feeling. Ask her what she needs. Ask her how she felt during a certain situation that happened earlier that day. And ask her if she has any questions of you. Remember, you are building a loving, trusting connection, and this must be a two-way street in terms of sharing and listening.

You can spend as long as you like at this exercise each day— 10 to 15 minutes is a good start. This should not feel arduous and forced. It should feel exciting and enjoyable. You are opening a treasure box, and the treasure within has the potential to make your life a heaven on earth. Invite yourself to practice this check-in daily, if possible, for a period of one month. If you forget this process, just pick up where you left off when you next remember. Also, remember that you can check in with your Authentic Self any time, any place. And the more you have practiced with your written dialogues on your own, the easier it will be to maintain connection with your Authentic Self at all times, regardless of what is taking place around you.

As you are dialoguing, whether in the beginning on paper or in your head, and you become more comfortable and familiar with your inner connection, remember to keep checking in to see how the Nurturing Parent (that's you!) and your Authentic Self are feeling. If there's tightness, constriction or pressure, it's a good sign that the Drill Sgt. is getting in there and trying to control the dialogue or to squash the expression of your Authentic Self. If you notice this, just ask the Drill Sgt. what his intention is. What is he trying to achieve in controlling the dialogue this way, and what's important about that? Then, connected to and speaking from your Nurturing Parent, assure the Drill Sgt. that it is imperative that your Authentic Self have a voice and that the Drill Sgt. can trust you to ensure she doesn't get carried away.

Once you have a strong sense of your Authentic Self—how she communicates, how she feels, and what she needs—you will begin to easily remain conscious of and connected to her when you are out and about in the world. The less emotionally charged the situation, the easier it will be for you to remain connected to your Authentic Self. For example, an issue over the pricing of an item at the grocery store will likely feel safe enough for you to remain connected to your Authentic Self while talking with the clerk. An argument with your spouse or a co-worker may be too emotionally charged for you to be able to stop and check in with your Authentic Self about what she needs in that moment. You will likely default for now to some old patterns of relating and coping in those more stressful circumstances. That's okay. Expect that. It's only natural at first that, when the stress is high, you will return to your tried and true methods of coping. You are doing a great job of building rapport as long as your Nurturing Parent touches base with your Authentic Self when you are feeling more grounded and relaxed, and gives her an opportunity to tell you how she was feeling, what she needed, and what if anything she needs from you now. This is also a perfect opportunity to set about making a Plan A, B and C. Being aware of what would have felt best to your Authentic Self in that moment allows you the gift of creating a plan and an intention for how you will honour yourself the next time a similar situation occurs.

This is how you build strength, integration and trust within—by taking the time to really listen to what you need in any situation, acknowledging these needs, and creating a solution to meet them. Begin with a few minutes each day, and you will soon see your consciousness in each moment blossoming. Your awareness of the real you, what you like, and what you are feeling and needing will grow to the point where you automatically, comfortably, and respectfully express your feelings and needs in every situation.

If you take the time to think about the men and women in your life whom you admire and respect, you will see that they all have one thing in common. It's not that they have the most money or nicest clothes or even the best marriage. It's that they are strong and grounded in themselves. They are clear in what they feel and need, and they are not afraid to ask directly for their needs to be met. These are the people you most admire; the people with whom you undoubtedly most enjoy spending time and feel safest. This is the type of person you are growing to become as you take steps to integrate the three key aspects of yourself. The sense of freedom and peace that these respected people most experience as a part of their daily existence will be *your* payoff for your conscious effort in attending to the needs and feelings of your Authentic Self, just as they do each day.

Now let's explore one more tool which will support you as a framework and guide for your work with your Authentic Self and in your recovery from the coping strategies that currently undermine your quality of life—your personal Mission Statement.

What is a Mission Statement and Why Do I Want One?

The simplest method I have discovered to create a personal Mission Statement comes from a workbook by Jack Canfield (author of *Chicken Soup for the Soul*) and Janet Switzer titled *The Success Principles*.

I am going to share their method with you now, and you will have soon created a Mission Statement that is simple, concise, and speaks directly to your values and what you believe your purpose in life is. Even if you don't know in this moment what your purpose might be, you will in a few minutes! Very exciting!

Jack Canfield defines a Mission Statement as a declaration of your purpose in life, and he goes on to say: "Purpose is the reason you create the goals you create and pursue the activities you do." So without a clear sense of our purpose in life, we have little motivation to create goals and follow through in achieving them. We need something that is going to be sufficiently meaningful (beyond that family wedding or school reunion) to motivate us to challenge those old patterns of coping. A personal Mission Statement is just that tool.

How Do I Create One?

Take ten minutes to answer the following questions and create your personal Mission Statement. Again, this exercise is taken directly from *The Success Principles* by Jack Canfield and Janet Switzer, who borrowed this exercise from Arnold M. Patent. Arnold is a gifted spiritual coach and can be reached at www.arnoldpatent.com.

1. List two of your unique personal qualities, such as, *enthusiasm* and *creativity*.

2. List one or two ways you enjoy expressing those qualities when interacting with others, such as, being *supportive* and *inspiring*.

3. Assume the world is perfect right now. What does this world look like? How is everyone interacting with everyone else? What does it feel like? This is a statement, in present tense, describing the ultimate condition, the perfect world as you see and feel it. Remember, a perfect world is a fun place to be. For example: *everyone is freely expressing their own unique talents. Everyone is working in harmony. Everyone is expressing love.*

4. Combine the three prior subdivisions of this paragraph into a single statement.

Example: *My purpose is to use my creativity and enthusiasm to support and inspire others to freely express their talents in a harmonious and loving way.*

Wasn't that amazing? Read it over a few times. Get a feel for it. Does any part require a little tweaking, or does it feel right? I love the simplicity of this exercise, even if it's hard to fully grasp and appreciate the meaning of your statement right now. You have just captured the essence of yourself, your passion, your vision for the world and your role in it. That's a very powerful statement. The power of intention is limitless. When you create a Mission Statement from your values, principles and passion, and you allow yourself to have the intention of letting it guide you in your goal setting and action planning, you have a foundation for your life that is more powerful than anything you have experienced before. And you created it!

My Mission Statement, created with this exercise, is as follows:

My purpose is to use my optimism and intellect to educate, support and inspire others to honour and love themselves and create happy and fulfilling lives.

It's so simple and concise. It provides me with a strong foundation. My Mission Statement grounds me in my purpose. What is my intention? Why am I doing what I do? One look at my Mission Statement and the answer is clear to me.

The most amazing thing about this process of defining my purpose in life so succinctly is that rather than feeling limited or confined by the preciseness of my Mission Statement, I feel freed by it. I no longer have to wonder, worry or have any uncertainty about the validity of whatever task I am engaged in. If it supports my Mission Statement, I do it. If it doesn't, I don't.

And if you are stuck in the pattern of putting others' needs and feelings above your own, calling your attention to your Mission Statement will help to ground you and give you a sense of entitlement to honouring your needs. Think of it as a permission slip from the universe to care for yourself first. This creates immense freedom in your personal and professional life, allowing more time to spend on the things that really matter to you.

It's your own personal compass. If you start to feel a little out of balance (for example, using your coping strategy more than you were last week, or noticing that you are more abrupt and short of patience), simply checking in with your Mission Statement and reminding yourself of your purpose will clarify what is required for you to instantly return to balance.

Now What Do I Do With It?

The best use of your Mission Statement is to reference it regularly. Post your Mission Statement in a few key spots on the walls of your home and office. Make a small one and laminate it for your wallet. Do whatever you can over the next while to remind yourself of the message that is your Mission Statement. You may wish to start your day by reading it over and centering yourself around its message.

Give yourself the gift of referring to your Mission Statement at least once a day for the next week. Make note of what you feel when you check it over versus how you felt before reading it. Make note also of any changes in your behaviour and your focus, your effectiveness, and your state of mind over the next week. Purpose is powerful. You may need to have a discussion with your Authentic Self and your Drill Sgt. about this in order to get everyone's support for making use of this tool. Allow yourself the time to do this and for each piece to be heard. You will find that even if there is some resistance to grounding yourself in your Mission Statement, once you give both your Authentic Self and your Drill Sgt. an opportunity to share their concerns and needs, you will feel free and supported to proceed.

Now that you have a clearer sense of who you are authentically (at your core) and how to establish and maintain a strong connection with your Authentic Self and with your Drill Sgt., you are well on your way to achieving a true sense of inner strength and integration. Let's take a look at another fundamental piece in your relationship with yourself that will make all the difference in your ability to no longer use food to cope and to truly love and respect yourself.

16

Taking the Pressure Out of Goal Setting

In the next chapter we will be exploring the concept of self-care. But first I need to take you on a little detour. In order for you to be able to fully embrace the concept of self-care, you not only need to be able to offer yourself understanding and compassion, which you now know very well how to do, but you also need to be able to feel safe—even excited—and open to the concept of establishing realistic goals. Let's begin our exploration of the concept of self-care from the perspective of compassionate goal setting. This is an innovative way of approaching goal setting, and it will help greatly to quell the pressure of the Drill Sgt.'s all-or-nothing thinking and to ease the fear of the Authentic Self in engaging in something new.

Some Background on Your Resistance to Goals

If there is any part of you which feels resistant to the concept of goal setting, it won't be your Drill Sgt. He loves setting goals. He loves creating rigid guidelines and ridiculous expectations to "support" you to achieve your needs for security, acceptance and esteem. No, any part of you that feels resistant to fully engaging in this discussion on goal setting would be your Authentic Self. She is deathly afraid of schedules and structure. You see, your Authentic Self is accustomed to the Drill Sgt.'s high-pressure tactics and "motivation through criticism". She is understandably very reluctant to set herself up for any potential failure which is bound to be the outcome of the old method of goal setting. To your Authentic Self, having a clearly established goal right now is like walking into the lion's den. It is to be avoided at all costs.

Your Authentic Self's reason for all this resistance is quite understandable. It is directly related to the perfectionist, all-or-nothing thinking of the Drill Sgt. As we discussed in the section on core beliefs, we have received the message from key people in our lives that we are not acceptable as we are. Many of us have been carrying this belief since we were small children. And, in our efforts to distance ourselves from this painful thought, we strove to be the best—better than anyone else, ever. In fact, I have heard many clients say that if they can't be the best, why bother? They have talked themselves out of pursuing their passions before they even begin.

Thanks to our old beliefs and those of our Drill Sgt. (who reinforces them on a daily basis), when we take on an idea or a goal, we don't just do it, we really, really, really do it. And still, we think we are *less* than others, *lazier* than others, and *must do more* than others. It is confusing to us to hear others speak of our accomplishments or of how thorough or intricate our handiwork is. We are sure they are just being nice because, after all, we are nothing special and anyone could do better.

Maybe your thoughts about yourself aren't quite that strong. Maybe they are. I'll bet the above paragraph resonates with you on some level. Those of us who have turned to food as our coping strategy have a common need to prove our value and our right to exist.

In our culture, nothing receives more acknowledgment than what someone does. We are all about results, production and outcome. We are so very externally focused that many people live their whole lives entirely disconnected from their emotional selves and are only marginally aware of their authentic thoughts. Hence, in a misguided effort to prove our value, we strive to do more, be more, produce more. . . We repeatedly compromise our esteem needs to gain that elusive and coveted external approval. In so doing, we become increasingly fragmented and detached from our Authentic Self—our only indicator of what we feel and need at any moment. The consequences of disconnecting from the authentic, thinking, and feeling part of yourself are disastrous. You are living some of them now in your use of food to cope, your frustration in relationships, and your stifled creativity and passion.

You may recall, when we talked about alexithymia, that we discussed the stress threshold and how we are so often unconsciously on the verge of maxing out that it truly only takes something which is, on the surface, very minor to send us running for our coping strategy.

The learned skill of distancing from your feelings and needs has led you to a pattern of repeatedly engaging in situations where you feel overwhelmed, powerless, unable to cope, and out of control. You will recall the definition of a coping strategy: a*ny thought, feeling or behaviour that allows you to remain in an uncomfortable situation without being aware of how uncomfortable you are.* The coping strategy of alexithymia creates a state of low-grade distress (the PLA) without your being able to put your finger on the reason. This can be very unsettling. Our minds run amok very easily on worst-case scenarios and intrusive ideation, when there truly may not be anything wrong.

When we come from the perfectionism/need to prove our value, our Drill Sgt. is continuously bombarding us with stories of how we must *be* in order to be acceptable. His all-or-nothing thinking, his constant messages that we are so far from acceptable now, lead us to feel more overwhelmed and less capable; more frightened to take any step in any direction lest we fail and receive more criticism. This results in more intense feelings of hopelessness and immobility. This is where we turn to the coping strategy of procrastination. It is a tool we use to avoid having to experience the failure that we are certain is imminent. After all, we have tried and failed so many times. The unrealistic expectations and complete lack of empathy and compas sion of the Drill Sgt. create the certainty that we can

Traditional Goal Setting: The Cycle of Pressure and Procrastination

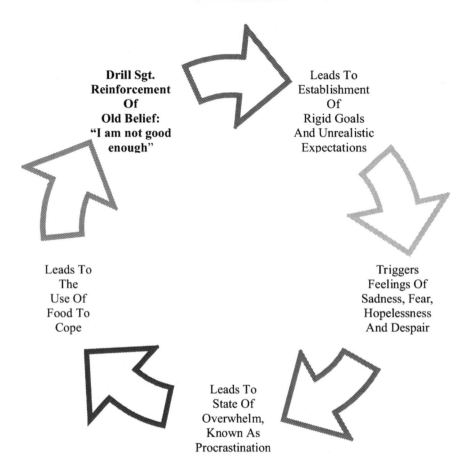

Drill Sgt. Reinforcement Of Old Belief: "I am not good enough"

Leads To Establishment Of Rigid Goals And Unrealistic Expectations

Triggers Feelings Of Sadness, Fear, Hopelessness And Despair

Leads To The Use Of Food To Cope

Leads To State Of Overwhelm, Known As Procrastination

never attain our goals, so our Authentic Self responds with, "Why bother?"

We continue to perpetuate the cycle of the Drill Sgt.'s bogus beliefs and unrealistic expectations. This triggers strong emotions which lead to feelings of being overwhelmed and, consequently, can cause procrastination toward our goal. The feelings of despair and hopelessness, along with the fear of the Drill Sgt.'s criticism, paralyze us, and we turn to food to help us numb out and distance ourselves from the intense feelings we are experiencing.

You know this cycle. I'll wager you have lived it every day for at least a decade—maybe two or three or more. Your goals in the past may have been food-related, body-related, relationship- or work-related, financial, and so on. But consider this: if your usual internal motivation tactic is pressure and threats of punishment upon failure, how enticing is that? How enjoyable and encouraging and rewarding will it be to work toward this goal? How long can you remain focused on the task? And what is the cost of not following through? Can you allow for the possibility that it is possible to create and follow through on countless goals for all the different aspects of your life without feeling pressure and fear?

Invite yourself to fully receive this next statement: **Any goal that you ask of yourself that is not established from a place of self-respect and dignity and an acknowledgement of what is truly doable for you at that time is doomed to fail.** It cannot succeed. Not for long, anyway. Sooner or later you will feel overwhelmed by the pressure of those expectations and will begin to procrastinate and ultimately use food to cope yet again.

Keep in mind this vicious cycle is of your own creation. It is only your Drill Sgt. and his all-or-nothing thinking that keeps you stuck in this cycle of self-harm, constantly diminishing your self-esteem. There is no legitimate reason for you to be forced to do what the Drill Sgt. says you must do, in the way he says it, and in the time frame which he has created. This cycle is created and maintained by all-or-nothing thinking, and, at any point when you realize you are stuck in this cycle, you can step outside of it simply by asking yourself to identify the all-or-nothing thinking you are engaged in, and then asking yourself what some other possibilities might be. You can also shake your all-or-nothing thinking loose by asking, "Is that true?" Once you become conscious that you are in the cycle, you have the power to choose to continue to take part in it, or you can choose to invite your Nurturing Parent and your Authentic Self to collaborate on what they would like to achieve. Then you, as a unified entity, can go about making that a reality in a way that is truly respectful of you and which allows for the ups and downs and unexpected bits and pieces that are a part of everyday life.

Resistance to Goals and the Diet Mentality

One of the things which brought you to this recovery process is that your ability to restrict and pressure yourself around food (as a means of weight control and of being acceptable) has abandoned you. Thank goodness! But I know that, when your primary coping strategy stops being effective, it's a very scary thing, especially if we don't have a viable alternative. We will often dig in our heels and try harder to make that old coping strategy work, certain that it is we who are a failure and not the coping strategy.

You have had years of experience setting goals around food and weight loss. You have come to believe in the message (reinforced by the diet and fashion industry, in part) that you just have to try harder next time, and then you will be successful. Even though any positive body image, acceptance of your body, and comfortable relationship with food has been fleeting and hard to maintain, you have experienced it, either personally or vicariously through advertisements, for example, just enough for you to be certain that it's possible.

The diet industry nets billions of dollars each year, convincing you that those goals are attainable through a program of restriction and tuning out to your body's natural signals of hunger and fullness. And those goals may be attainable, but the methods through which they are attained are certainly not sustainable. It is this truth that leads to what is commonly called in our society, "falling off the wagon" or "being bad". The judgement of our inability to "stick to the plan" leads to the establishment of more unrealistic goals which, in turn, leads to more and more experiences with disappointment and failure.

Remember the cycle of pressure and procrastination above? Peppered with lots of commentary from your Drill Sgt., this cycle is painful and feels unfair to your Authentic Self. It is understandable that your Authentic Self is resistant to committing to anything which may not succeed perfectly and speedily. There is no acknowledgement of her needs and feelings; no acknowledgment of any external event or experience which may have made it difficult for her to "stick to the plan"; no acknowledgement, whatsoever, that the "plan" doesn't meet her needs and is completely unrealistic, given you use food to cope! And there is absolutely no room in that old Diet Mentality for you to consider the needs of your body.

Even if it's not a diet- and body image-related goal, your Authentic Self will be exceptionally reluctant to make a commitment which she may not be able to keep. As a result, major procrastination ensues, for how can anyone be certain they will be successful or what that success will look like when they are trying something entirely new? You certainly wouldn't expect perfection from anyone else trying something for the first time? Why persist in expecting it of yourself with this process? It is because the Drill Sgt. is full of all-or-nothing thinking and old core beliefs, and he is absolutely convinced that, if you can't get it right the first time, you are doomed to perpetual failure. The solution is not to try harder. It is to try something else. And the something else is not just some thinly-veiled, alternate version of restriction and pressure. The something else is *empathy* and *compassion.*

The Goal Setting Solution

All this is to say that your Authentic Self has very good reason to resist the goal setting process as you have previously attempted it, particularly if it has anything remotely to do with food and body image. She's terrified of "failure" and receives more verbal abuse from the Drill Sgt. She's already hanging on by a thread, but the great news is the solution is easier than you might imagine.

It's time for you to practice your inner mediator skills. The Nurturing Parent will have a great opportunity to grow and prove to both the Drill Sgt. and your Authentic Self that she can handle things and meet everyone's needs. Each time you approach goal setting of any kind this way, you will actually see your all-or-nothing thinking falling away and your self-compassion and self-empathy growing.

Again, I strongly urge you to perform this process in writing or on the computer the first few times. It is essential in these early stages of changing old, deeply-ingrained patterns of behaviour to see your thought processes written down. You become more conscious of the slippery Drill Sgt. and of the strength of your needs and feelings. It also gives you much more opportunity to brainstorm other possibilities and to catch yourself slipping out of your Nurturing Parent and into Drill-Sgt. mode. There are six steps to this process.

Step 1
State your intention: What is your goal or desired achievement?

Step 2
Establish the intention within yourself that you will not move forward in any way with this goal until you feel completely peaceful and grounded with the method which you have chosen for its achievement. This is stepping you right out of any all-or-nothing, Drill Sgt. dictatorship and into a sense of integration and respect for all the aspects of your being and the various needs that may be triggered for you in establishing this or any goal.

You may say something like: "This goal is very important to me; however, my connection with myself is more important. I commit to not moving forward in any way on this goal until I feel truly united and peaceful about my approach to reaching it."

Any pressure, any anxiety, any resistance or procrastination means your Drill Sgt. and his all-or-nothing thinking have taken over, and you are once again caught up in the cycle of Pressure and Procrastination. If you notice this, just name it and start over. No big deal. It will happen. The exciting piece of this process is that you will begin to notice yourself slipping into the old cycle sooner and sooner each time and naturally pulling yourself out and moving forward. Ultimately, you will get to the place where an inkling of all-or-nothing thinking gets noticed immediately, and you attend to it easily from within—in seconds—and with no escalation to feeling-level coping strategies and/or need for food to cope.

Step 3

Now that you have identified your goal and established your intention to find a method which every part of you feels good about, the next step is to dialogue with your Authentic Self. Let her be heard. Give her a forum to express her fears and concerns about the goal, as well as any feelings of excitement and eagerness which she may be experiencing about its attainment. Remember, in order for her to converse openly with you, you will need to ensure that you are consciously coming from the Nurturing Parent and not from the Drill Sgt. The best way to know for sure where you are coming from is to speak out loud, from time to time, throughout this process. Listen closely to the tone in your voice as you invite her to tell you, the Nurturing Parent, what it is she needs in order to feel safe committing to a specific goal or to the goal setting process in general.

If your tone is terse, critical or even impatient, you are coming from the Drill Sgt., and your Authentic Self will not feel safe sharing openly; therefore, you will get only the surface information if anything at all. If you notice this happening, just take a breath and invite yourself to connect with the mature, compassionate part of you which you would draw from when supporting someone else. Let this part of you ask your Authentic Self what her concerns are in relation to following through on setting or attaining the goal. And hold the space for her to respond. This means waiting—openly and willingly. When she does share, make sure you are clear on what her needs are and which needs are unmet when she considers going ahead with creating a goal or with the goal as it is set now.

Then, just as you would with a friend or child, acknowledge and validate her feelings and needs. Let her know you will consider what she's said and that you won't move forward until you have come back to her and developed a plan which works for all aspects of your being.

Step 4

The next step is to go within and ask the Drill Sgt. what his needs are in relation to this goal. What is important to him about setting and attaining that goal? Get really clear on this. For both the Authentic Self and the Drill Sgt., you, the Nurturing Parent, want to have a clear concept of what their needs are in relation to this goal and what needs are currently unmet.

Acknowledge the needs and intention of the Drill Sgt. as best you can, and offer him the same assurance—you won't proceed with a plan until it feels like a fit for all of you.

Step 5

Take some time to consider how you might meet the needs of both your Authentic Self and the Drill Sgt. Often you will find that, although they express themselves very differently, when it comes right down to it, their needs are remarkably similar. My experience has been that often the only difference is the sense of urgency and immediacy of the Drill Sgt. versus the desire for freedom and autonomy of your Authentic Self. The Drill Sgt. wants you to be doing it all, perfectly, starting at 6:00 a.m. tomorrow morning. Your Authentic Self wants time and space to work up to consistently following through on the goal. She wants the reassurance that, if she commits to the goal overall, she will not be berated when she is struggling, or when life experiences intercede and make it difficult or impossible for her to follow through at that moment.

The Drill Sgt. really does have your best interests at heart, and I have found, without exception, that if he sees you consistently making strides toward the achievement of your goal, he pretty much shuts up and leaves you alone. Your day-to-day inner dialogue (in relation to your goal) should be fairly friendly and quiet if the goal is one that your Authentic Self can live with comfortably and without fear, and the Drill Sgt. sees you making daily progress toward it.

Step 6

Once you have a sense of how you might proceed with a goal in a way which honours the needs of all parties, you will feel your resistance melt away; you will feel strengthened, enhanced and united in your pursuit of your goal. At any point in the future should you find your motivation waning in regard to that same goal, just revisit both your Authentic Self and your Drill Sgt., and ask what needs they have which are unmet. Likely, you just need a little tweaking. Often you will find that you have just forgotten to attend to a particular need and the Drill Sgt. has taken over again. He just needs a gentle reminder that you are in charge. You can handle it, and he will relax.

So, if you get clear on a method of attaining a goal which feels good and peaceful, and you begin to see yourself making headway, you will likely not hear much if anything from the Drill Sgt. about it. If you begin to hear from the Drill Sgt. or notice yourself procrastinating on following through with the goal, this is your cue to step into your Nurturing Parent self and have an inner dialogue. You will soon identify the all-or-nothing thinking which has crept in. Just repeat steps 1 through 5 again; you will feel your peace and energy for the goal returning.

A Compassionate Goal Setting Example

A number of years ago I decided to begin exercising again. I had completely sworn off exercise during my early recovery days (how's that for all-or-nothing?) because I had used over-exercising to cope. I couldn't do anything remotely physical without feeling immediately sucked into focusing on the size of my stomach and thighs and how many calories I had burned. I went instantly into the old Diet Mentality whenever I was even thinking of exercise. In fact, many times, the mere thought of exercising would trigger a need to binge all night; first, from the pressure and fear of not doing enough; second, from the guilt and shame of not going; then from the frustration and overwhelm I felt for having overeaten yet again! Vicious cycle, that one!

I didn't know much about all-or-nothing thinking early in my recovery: it was so much a part of me that I couldn't even see it. I had no clue what moderation was. I had no idea that it was my Drill Sgt. and his all-or-nothing approach which was triggering me to resist doing something that, in moderation, was very good for me and actually a very significant part of the healing process (more on that later).

My approach to my exercise trigger was to avoid it altogether. No exercise for me! I went for a few years with absolutely no formal exercise. I really enjoyed it, actually! It was quite a change from the Drill Sgt.'s constant pressure and focus on pounds and calories. But all along I knew it wasn't quite the right solution. It was temporary. And at some point I was going to want to move my body. I wanted to feel as though I was caring for myself. I also wanted to feel healthier and more connected with my body.

Now, I'm not advocating giving up exercise. What I'm saying is that my all-or-nothing thinking at the time could only come up with that solution. The possibility that I could negotiate with myself and that there actually was a solution which would work for all of me was never a consideration. And by the way, because I was practicing Natural Eating—eating when hungry, stopping when full—my weight did not increase at all during this time. In fact, without exercising at all, I started losing weight and came to the natural weight I am today.

After a few years of my total exercise ban, I began to want that sense of truly caring for and being in connection with my body; however, at the mere thought of exercise, I could feel my Authentic Self becoming fearful as she recalled the Drill Sgt.'s all-or-nothing pressure. She could feel the noose of calorie counting and rigid expectations tightening, and she was balking at just the thought of going anywhere near a gym!

It was clear I was going to have to do some serious listening and negotiating. So I first asked my Authentic Self what she needed in order to feel safe experimenting with exercise again. Her reply was that she needed to be able to go as frequently or infrequently for as long as she wanted, even if it was just five minutes. She also needed to be assured that we would explore many forms of movement and exercise, and not just the gym—ideally, not the gym at all! She asked if we could experiment with doing exercise that was fun first, exercise second. When I asked her what activities she had in mind, she said she wanted to play tennis, swim—but not laps—learn to rollerblade and go for bike rides. Her idea was that, when I felt as if I needed to move my body, we would choose one of the fun activities and not be focused on weight loss or calories burned. In fact, she was pretty adamant that, if my main focus was on the weight and calories thing, she was having no part of it.

The Drill Sgt. put up a bit of a fuss at first, because his all-or-nothing approach said that, if we didn't go to the gym four or more days a week for an hour each time, we'd get nowhere; it wasn't safe to let the Authentic Self decide anything because she was too soft!; we wouldn't be happy until we reached our "goal," so the faster the better! He hadn't really learned a whole lot in three years, but that's because I had no other information to give—until I learned this little gem of inner negotiation and of not committing to anything until I felt peaceful and grounded with it.

Once the Drill Sgt. heard my Nurturing Parent say that our intention was to be consistent and to be as healthy and as happy as possible, he relaxed his all-or-nothing thinking and gave me the reins with the understanding that he would take over if it looked as though we were not following through.

The plan was that we would start out by doing one of our fun, fitness-oriented activities. Ideally, this would be one day a week but, most importantly, only when we felt like it. We would stop whenever we were no longer having fun, or at any moment we began to feel pressured or a focus on weight and calories kicking in. In the beginning, this meant absolutely no expectations of what days and times, frequency, or length of time we would do anything. Our goal was that, within six months, we would be naturally, happily, effortlessly engaging in some form of physical activity at least three times a week.

I don't know what this sounds like to you. Perhaps the thought of taking six months to get to a place of exercising for who-knows-how long for three times a week sounds like nothing. If so, that would be your Drill Sgt. speaking to you. Consider this: How often do you actually exercise each week now? How consistently? How much do you actually enjoy, look forward to, or eagerly anticipate it? How much do you currently pressure, cajole, or threaten yourself to do any form of exercise? How frequently do you end up using food to cope before, after, or instead of exercising?

As I mentioned above, at the time of establishing this goal I had gone three years without exercising—just Natural Eating. During that time I noticed my body freely finding its natural weight, so I was no longer "buying in" to the belief that I had to exercise to maintain or lose weight. I knew that for me, the gym and the machines only enticed me to focus on pounds and calories.

I also knew that I wanted to approach exercise from the perspective of what truly felt good to my body. This meant being in touch with my energy level (and ability) and *not* with the number on the screen or on my watch. I had to be willing to do what felt like fun, because I knew that I wanted to approach exercise from a place of respect for myself and not from a place of punishment or of not being good enough. Getting to a place of actually wanting to exercise three or more times a week felt like a great place to be because I hadn't really exercised for three years.

As I began to experiment with fun exercise and only for as long as I wanted, my Authentic Self really tested the limits. She would go for a bike ride around the block. She'd play tennis for ten minutes against the backboard and then say she was done. I think we actually exercised four or five times that first month. She was checking to see whether I really meant it when I said that we would only participate when she felt good about it, and we would stop when she was tired or not having fun any more. Soon, she began to trust that I meant what I said. During this time I had a few chats with the Drill Sgt. to reassure him that six months was a ways off and to relax and trust that we would get there.

It was amazing! As soon as I began to really trust that I wasn't going to force myself to do anything I didn't want to, I began to get excited about exercise. I began to find ways to move my body that were new and pleasurable. I'd walk because I enjoyed walking. I would take the long route on my bike because I wanted to explore and not because it meant five more minutes of exercise. I did lots of dancing, even in my living room, and I surprised myself by beginning to enjoy running (one of my favorite forms of fun exercise these days). I just let it be okay to do what I wanted for as long as I wanted, and I trusted that my intention wasn't to "get away with anything" as the Drill Sgt. had believed for so long. My intention was to be the best that I could be. I just never responded well to "motivation through criticism". Take away the criticism and the all-or-nothing thinking, and I'm in like a dirty shirt—just as you will be.

This process worked equally well for me with my yoga and meditation practice, with beginning to take vitamin supplements, and with eating well. It worked with any goals I wanted to attain for work and personal growth, for relationships, and any hobbies or interests I wanted to pursue, such as, playing the guitar.

In fact, once I wrapped my head around the concept of inner consensus and moderation, the world was my oyster, as it will be yours. I just had to be willing to let it take some time. And when I reminded myself that the old method had never led to any consistency or longevity with any of my previous goals, it was easy to step back and let myself set a broader, long-term goal.

Just keep coming back to the reality of what you have truly achieved with your "motivation through criticism" method of goal setting. How happy are you, really? How peaceful, content, and in control of your life do you feel each day? If your ultimate goal is to be healthy and happy, can you allow for the possibility that your current method of attaining this goal isn't working all too well?

Choose something which feels small but significant to you, and allow yourself to approach the attainment of that goal from this perspective: know that if you feel paralyzed or find yourself procrastinating in the attainment of your goal, it's because the Drill Sgt., with his all-or-nothing thinking, has taken over. Just repeat steps 1 through 5 and you will be back on track. No harm done, just more learning experience; more conscious awareness on your part, and that's always good.

Now let's explore the concept of self-care and how to go about making self-care your top priority while still having a life!

17

Self-Care

Self-care is fundamental to your ability to no longer need food as a coping strategy. If there is any part of you which, in picking up this book as a recovery tool, was hoping to just stop the food thing and not deal with yourself, your body, your emotions, or your needs, you are no doubt already feeling sorely disappointed, perhaps even a little overwhelmed. This chapter will strengthen your awareness of yourself and your needs. As best you can, trust me that this is truly a gift that will lead to a life which is rich, fulfilled and content.

Whenever you feel resistant to the concept of self-care, or even to reading further, you will notice the PLA is there. And the only reason you would be feeling any PLA regarding the concept of self-care is if you have gone into all-or-nothing thinking, and your Drill Sgt. is telling you that you have to do it all, perfectly, now! Not so, not so. Any such thoughts which are allowed to go unchecked will only serve to undermine what is truly a fundamental step in your complete recovery from food as a coping strategy.

As we explore this piece and any others in this section, you may notice the PLA or some resistance to staying present. In that case, just come from the Nurturing Parent in you, and invite the Drill Sgt. to share his all-or-nothing thinking. Then refer to the previous chapter on compassionate goal setting and, as you learned to do earlier, dialogue with your Authentic Self and your Drill Sgt., and come up with a solution or goal which truly makes all aspects of your Self feel peaceful.

The principle elements of self-care used to create and maintain a balanced life can be divided into two key sections:

1. **Self-Care In Relationship With Others.**

    This includes: boundaries, values and principles in relation to co-workers, family, friends, and general interactions with the public.

2. **Self-Care In Relationship With Yourself.**

    This includes: the physical (exercise, nutrition, rest/sleep, body awareness and health care); spiritual (meditation, prayer, community service); and emotional aspects of yourself (awareness of and respect for your feelings and needs, hobbies and interests).

In the next section we will be exploring self-honouring ways to be in relationship with others. For now, let's focus on self-care in relationship with your Self, and acquire a nice solid understanding and foundation for this. There is plenty of time to attend to our relationship with others.

We said that self-care is comprised of three key pieces: physical, spiritual and emotional. We will explore each one of these pieces separately, including ways to establish your own balance of self-care in each of these areas, as well as any resistance or objections which the Drill Sgt., in his all-or-nothing thinking, might be tossing around.

Physical Self-Care

Physical self-care includes your level of physical fitness, your daily nutritional intake, the amount of rest and sleep you get each day, your awareness of physical sensations and needs in your body, and overall health care. All of these areas require some attention each day, even if it's just a little mental acknowledgement of each one.

It's good to have a daily inner checklist conducted by the Nurturing Parent—not the Drill Sgt. The checklist will speak to your goals in each of these key areas of physical self-care. The Nurturing Parent will gently invite you to keep them in mind as you go about your day.

Remember, any goals you established are going to be goals that feel respectful and reasonable to all of your Self, so there is no fear in remembering them or in allowing yourself to attain them. In fact, when you are fully on board with a goal, the attainment of it is practically effortless. This is very new and different from your old method of goal setting and of approaching change around your physical self. As you begin to identify areas of self-care that you want attended to, it's natural at first to find yourself stuck a few times in the old all-or-nothing thinking and the pressure and procrastination cycle.

Physical Fitness

Chances are you are reading this section with one eye closed and a cringe on your face. We often feel incredible resistance to looking at our stop-and-start approach to physical fitness (whether we over-exercise to cope or do the all-or-nothing thing just to appease the Drill Sgt.). Regardless of how you have approached fitness in the past, it's all been coming from the old Diet Mentality. Your whole approach needs to be tweaked (or overhauled) in order for you to find lasting success and enjoyment with exercise.

Your resistance to looking at your current approach to exercise is just more of the Drill Sgt.'s all-or-nothing approach to life. You likely fear that, if you allow yourself to approach this exercise thing "compassionately," you will "get soft". That's just the Drill Sgt. who still believes that his "motivation through criticism" approach is the only one that works. And all you have to do with that is come from your Nurturing Parent and remind him how well his approach has worked so far. Have you really achieved any lasting happiness and peace with his approach? Is it ever "enough"? Nope.

You are reading this book because some part of you understood the title immediately. You know from your own experience that food is not the problem. You know that in order for you to be free from food as a coping strategy (and any of your other coping strategies), you must be willing to take a look at what is *really* going on for you. Exercise is the same. It doesn't matter whether you cope with exercise by resisting it, or use it as a form of control or self-punishment. What matters is your current approach of investing energy into focusing on something that is only a coping strategy.

Being able to identify when exercise is becoming a harmful coping strategy versus a life enhancing piece of self-care is an important part of creating a sense of openness and safety to the concept of physical fitness.

If you are feeling resistant, forced, or preoccupied with exercise, you are using it as a harmful coping strategy. It has become a method of taking you out of the present, where something isn't feeling good or safe, and putting your focus on something which you feel you can control. Any bad body thoughts and criticisms of your current shape or weight are also indicators that you are using a harmful coping strategy.

As we have discussed in earlier chapters, the solution here is not to work harder to make your body "perfect". It is to: (a) identify that you are using a coping strategy and then seek to understand the underlying cause(s); and (b) to discover what needs you have which are being triggered and leading you to feel overwhelmed, thus leading you to resort to your body image- and exercise-coping strategy. Look for needs that are independent of body image and physical fitness, as well as needs around health and wellness. Make a list of stressors when you notice the old coping strategy arising (focus on food and body image), and you will soon prove to yourself that not only is there always something more going on for you, but there is also always a gentler and more compassionate way to approach issues of health and self-care.

So, armed with the ability to know when you are using exercise as a harmful coping strategy and with the tools to figure out what is really going on, you are ready to explore your personal goals for self-care regarding physical fitness.

Let's talk about why we need to exercise at all. Simply put, you live longer, healthier, and happier when you are physically fit. You are more relaxed and handle life's ups and downs more readily when you are in good physical health. Also, you feel more confident and secure in life when you know you are physically well and strong.

No doubt you have an idea in your head of what a natural size and shape for your body would be. Notice I don't talk about weight here? That's because your weight is truly irrelevant. The number on the scale tells you absolutely nothing about your level of fitness, health and wellness. It doesn't represent anything at all about how your body is functioning on the whole, or how well you are caring for it.

The two greatest indicators of physical fitness are cardiovascular health and level of energy. That's it! Regardless of your weight or even your size, if you have good cardiovascular health and your energy level is high, you can consider yourself to be healthier than the average Joe or Jane, as the case may be. Many studies have been conducted on these subjects, and the results of these studies have been used to produce television documentaries. The results showed that people with good cardiovascular health are healthier overall than those with less stamina, regardless of what they weigh. Moreover, one study looked specifically at men and women who, by today's standards, were labeled by their doctors as obese. This study showed that many of those men and women exercised regularly and were much healthier overall than slimmer men and women who did not exercise regularly. I could go on, but suffice it to say: what you weigh is insignificant to anyone and anything when it comes to self-care and true health. The only people who care about the number on the scale are those who are stuck in the Diet Mentality and who still believe that their worth comes from a number.

How you feel in your clothes and how light and free you feel when you move your body, as well as how much energy you have overall, are the best indicators of your level of fitness. So think for a moment about what would feel comfortable to you as a short-term goal around physical fitness based on those criteria. Would you like to be able to walk around the block without feeling fatigued? To walk a mile? To run a short distance? To play with your children for a half hour and still have some energy? Come up with something small but still a challenge from where you are now.

Guard against having a goal such as climbing stairs without feeling winded. It's not doable, even for the fittest of the fit. You can certainly climb stairs and feel *less* winded than you do now, but the nature of stair climbing (not the Stairmaster at the gym but actual stairs) is that it requires an immediate, short burst of energy from your body, and that always makes us huff and puff, as does sprinting. It's natural, it's healthful, and it's not an indicator of your physical fitness. So if you have been waiting to be able to climb those stairs at the office without feeling winded, you will be waiting a long time. You will always be a bit breathless at the top; however, the more your cardiovascular health improves, the less winded you will become.

Have you a short-term goal in mind? Something challenging but not overly so? Keep in mind we are approaching the concept of self-care from a long-term perspective. This is your life. By gently and naturally taking steps to establish and maintain a sense of balance within, you will be enhancing your ability to love and care for yourself for the remainder of your life. Wouldn't it be worth taking the time to achieve a goal that is sustainable, enjoyable, and will bring you enhanced self-esteem, even though it may take six months to achieve? When compared to the old all-or-nothing approach, this one doesn't just promise results, it delivers. And that's because you are coming from a place of respect and caring for yourself—from an ILOC (remember the Internal Locus of Control)—and not from the dysfunction of the ELOC.

I have mentioned the time period of six months for the attainment of your goal, and I do so for a few key reasons:

1. It's long enough to work out any bugs associated with the needs of the Authentic Self versus the Drill Sgt.

2. It allows for any of life's ups and downs and unexpected twists and turns: for example, you get the flu, have an important deadline, or unexpected company arrives from out of town.
3. It gives you the space to step out of your all-or-nothing thinking.
4. It is long enough that you will actually see yourself consistently following through on your goal—freely and happily—by the time your goal of six months arrives.

If you feel compelled to advance your goal date, don't. Not now. Let yourself experiment with this time frame. If you complete your goal earlier and are consistently following through within, let's say, three or four months, by all means establish another goal in the same fashion, or just acknowledge the achievement of that one and keep it up. The only reason you may feel compelled to shorten your time frame is if you have some ELOC or need for approval kicking in: a wedding or family reunion, for example. If you are consistently following through on your steps toward your goal, you will feel so much better about yourself that what you weigh or what size you are at the time won't be an issue.

What feels like a reasonable goal for you? Take some time and dialogue about that goal with your Authentic Self and your Drill Sgt. Get everyone on board and feeling peaceful. If you are feeling any pressure or fear, you are still in all-or-nothing-thinking mode and need to ease up on the parameters of the goal some more. Trust yourself to follow through. If once you have begun working toward your goal and you notice yourself feeling stuck or beginning to feel pressured or paralyzed, have a chat with the Drill Sgt. and determine what's triggering his all-or-nothing thinking. Return to the goal setting exercise and renegotiate. The key to any success with self-care is to approach it purely from a place of compassion and health and not from needing external acceptance.

The results of many studies on Disordered Eating now show that exercise is a key component to a speedy and lasting recovery. This does not speak to exercise done from the Drill Sgt.'s high-pressure, all-or-nothing approach. This is exercise done from a place of being in connection with your body and having an awareness of its cues of fatigue and strength. At the CEDRIC Centre we have two medical exercise specialists whose approach to fitness is not from the perspective of weight and body fat but from a place of: *How does your body feel when you move it? Where do you notice tension or pain? What do you wish your body to feel like when you move it?* With these thoughts in mind, they then establish individual exercise plans which are geared around your answers and your goals, and each exercise is one in body awareness as well as a means of increasing physical fitness.

We have found that clients who take part in this self-awareness and self-honouring way of creating an exercise plan are still using their plans and enjoying them over a year later versus the old all-or-nothing, get-to-the-gym approach which typically lasts three months at most.

So let yourself set a reasonable goal, and give yourself the time and space to follow through and integrate this behaviour in your day-to-day life. Be gentle, and focus on how you want to *feel* in your body rather than on how you want your body to *look*. Internal and not External Locus of Control is required for lasting success in any aspect of self-care.

Nutrition

You are probably reading this section with *both* eyes closed and your fingers forming a cross in front of the book! Not to worry. Anyone who knows me knows that I don't go within a hundred miles of anything that looks or smells like a diet. So it's safe to read on.

The reason for exploring the concept of nutrition is that it is key to self-care. On some level, you have always known this. Part of the guilt and shame you felt in the past came from eating something with lots of sugar or high trans-fat content. It's not just the all-or-nothing thinking of the Drill Sgt. and his Diet Mentality, it's that on some level you know that that choice isn't the most honouring one for you and where you want to be in terms of health and wellness.

Everything in moderation is the key to nutritional success. Unless you are allergic to some type of food, there is no need to cut anything completely out of your diet. And I know from my years of experience in this field that, when you consistently make choices about what, when, and how to eat, and from the place of what your body needs in that moment, you will no longer hear from the Drill Sgt. about food—even if you are having chocolate cake or my favorite: a grande ½ sweet soy mocha with double whipped cream!!!

Do your best. This means choosing foods which have the least amount of preservatives and additives. The quality of the food you eat is equally as important as what you eat. Look for "certified organic" labels when shopping. If you are going to buy potato chips, buy the fabulous organic ones that are natural and actually taste like potatoes! Buy natural yogurt and mayo. Use extra-virgin olive oil. If it's a choice between full sugar or fat content or something with artificial sweeteners, go for the full fat! Not only does it taste better, but it is also much better for you, and you will feel fuller, faster. That's the thing about natural fat. It's good stuff. We need it in our diets. In fact, foods which are high in naturally-occurring fat content signal certain hormones in our body which tell us we are full. These hormones do not get triggered by low-fat or highly processed foods; therefore we can easily end up eating much more of something filled with chemicals and still not feel full, than if we went for the full Häagen-Dazs experience!

Let me be clear: I am not a nutritionist. I support the viewpoint that you should talk with your doctor before you begin to make any changes to your diet or to your nutritional intake. I have, however, read and researched the area of nutrition for both my personal and professional needs for almost 20 years.

Every book on nutrition essentially comes down to the same thing:

1. Eat a diet filled predominantly with organic foods.

2. Eat very few processed foods or foods with white flour and white sugar.
3. Eat some good quality protein every 2 or 3 hours to fuel metabolism, even if it's just a handful of almonds or a boiled egg or two.

The more healthful the food you eat, the healthier you will be overall. Go ahead and have that cinnamon bun; invite yourself to get it from the organic bakery. It truly will taste much better, and you'll hear much less from the Drill Sgt., regardless of the caloric content. Oh, and invite yourself to stop checking the fat and caloric content on labels. Keep in mind that low-fat doesn't have anything to do with "healthier". In fact, often it is just the opposite. If you feel some resistance to letting yourself choose the healthful option regardless of what the fat or caloric content is, you are still buying in to the Diet Mentality. Trust that eating in response to your body's signals of hunger and fullness will bring you to a natural weight for your body.

The reason we choose not to have our clients work with a nutritionist at the beginning stages of their recovery process at the Centre is twofold:

1. You must have a good grasp on your Drill Sgt. and your Diet Mentality before you can begin to change your nutrition and avoid having it become some new form of restriction or punishment—this takes some time.
2. I know from my own experience that people who use food to cope know pretty much all there is to know about nutrition. You know what you are "supposed" to be eating for the betterment of your health and wellness; however, should you feel that you need guidance in this area, by all means, seek the advice of a nutritionist. We recommend holistic nutritionists and clinical herbalists. If you would like a referral to the ladies we confidently refer to, please e-mail me @ mmorand@islandnet.com.

The reality is: the combination of your use of food to cope, the Drill Sgt.'s all-or-nothing thinking, and the Diet Mentality have you so confused about what you really want versus what you are "supposed" to have that you can't make heads or tails of all the nutritional information. You focus on reading labels and zeroing in on the caloric and fat content, when they tell you nothing about the quality of the food or what it will do in and to your body.

Frequently, clients will look at me with total shock and surprise—even some guilt—as they say, "You know, yesterday I went out for lunch with some friends and I actually, truly wanted to have the salad!" That doesn't surprise me, unless they hated veggies! We are naturally drawn to foods which are honouring of our bodies and their nutritional needs. The reason these men and women are so surprised is that they have always thought of salad as a "diet food". They aren't sure whether they chose the salad because they really wanted it, or because it's some unconscious attempt at control from the Drill Sgt. to make them think they really wanted salad when they really wanted the burger and fries.

To that I say, "Did you feel any sense of restriction before, during, or after the meal?" "Did you notice yourself turning to food to cope soon after the meal?" If the answer to either of these questions is yes, it's likely you were playing a bit of a game with yourself and denying what you really wanted. That's okay; just take a moment and dialogue with your Authentic Self and the Drill Sgt. Find out what would need to happen for both of them to be onside and support your choice of burger and fries.

If the answer to my questions is no, then you were just naturally and freely wanting that salad. No big deal. Don't get attached to it. Next time, you might naturally and freely want the burger, and that's all right. If you start to get attached to wanting salads or believing that you *should* want them because you wanted that *one* salad, you will soon find yourself back in restrictionland and then binging or purging to cope with this sense of restriction. If this happens, just go back to the basics: Am I hungry? What would I really like? Everything in moderation.

As you explore Natural Eating, you will undoubtedly find that there are times when you freely and joyfully choose to eat foods which previously you had to force down your throat because they were part of the dreaded Diet Mentality. When we begin to explore Natural Eating, we sometimes believe that we are meant to have a free-for-all and choose only those foods which were previously off limits. That's just more all-or-nothing thinking. The concept of Natural Eating isn't to swear off salads and fruits! It's to eat what you want when you want; start when you are hungry, and stop when you are full. The impetus to choose those old forbidden foods is coming from the Authentic Self who thinks this is just another hair-brained, Drill Sgt. scheme to control your food and weight: she wants to get all the "good" stuff while she can.

The simple fact that she perceives foods as good or bad, and feels pressured to get all the ones she fears will soon be restricted, is a good indicator that the Diet Mentality is still ruling. In that case, just remind yourself this isn't a diet. This isn't a food plan. This is a lifestyle which is simply geared around *what* you feel hungry for, when you *do* feel hungry. End of story. It will help you choose what you truly want to eat at each meal and have much less energy around it. In time, your food choices will have no energy around them whatsoever; they will simply be about what you feel like eating at that time. You will naturally stop when you are full, and you won't think about what you ate or about food again until you are hungry.

Just do your best to let go of the need to judge what you are eating, and keep coming back to the concept of Natural Eating:

- Eating when you are hungry and stopping when you are full.
- Everything in moderation.
- You can always have more, later.
- No good or bad foods.
- No guilt.

Notice any emotional needs which are being met through food, and use the list of stressors to sort those out. You will soon find that you are tuned in enough to your body to notice which foods make you feel good and light, and which ones make you feel tired or bloated. You can still choose to eat the ones which make you feel tired and bloated, of course. Just choose consciously, being aware that you may not feel very energized after that meal, and let this choice be okay.

One more key word on nutrition: *Water*. One of the most important things you can do for your health and wellness is to drink lots of water. Everything inside of your body needs water to function properly. Your energy level will diminish greatly if you don't have enough water in your system. Your liver will not be able to flush toxins from your body. You may get headaches and joint problems, for example, if you are not drinking enough water on a daily basis.

Many clients, both men and women, have an aversion to water. I also struggled with this. It was as if drinking water were a symbol of self-care. There was no other reason to drink water. It had no taste or seemingly met any need. And I, like many clients at the early stage of healing, wasn't ready to do anything just because it was good self-care. I still felt far too unworthy of care to do that. Instead, I'd order soda pop or, on a "good" day, juice. I'd feel a little pang of guilt, knowing I wasn't making the most honouring choice for me but still not feeling worthy. I was still coming from an all-or-nothing mindset and believed that I had to have that pop *now* because I might not allow myself to have it later.

I invoked a goal setting exercise around drinking water. I invited myself to let it take six months for me to get up to naturally, freely and easily drinking eight or more glasses of water a day. It worked! The first month, I resisted. After that, I felt great whenever I drank water. I really felt as though I was taking care of myself, and this made me feel even better and more worthy of care in other areas. The beauty of self-care is that it seeps into every aspect of our lives, so it doesn't matter where you start, soon you will be doing it everywhere, all the time, naturally.

There are many great books available, to be explored when you are ready, on nutrition and what your body requires to function optimally. My favorite is Sam Graci's book *The Path to Phenomenal Health*.

I encourage you to let yourself experiment for a time (six months to a year) with Natural Eating, and with this recovery process on the whole, before attempting any structured change with your nutritional intake. I am certain that, during this time, you will naturally find what foods really work for your body and which ones don't. You don't need an outside influence to tell you this. Eat when you are hungry, stop when you are full. If you have this piece down, everything else falls into place. If you don't have this piece down, any attempt to fiddle with your nutritional intake is only going to be received within yourself as restriction and a continuation of the Diet Mentality, which is where you came in!

Rest and Sleep

Just as we often feel an intense resistance to the gesture of self-care of hydrating our bodies, we also frequently resist resting it adequately. Many of us who use food to cope resist going to bed at a decent hour and force ourselves to stay up, yawning and exhausted. We frequently eat at these times, often because we are tired. This only adds to our emotional and physical fatigue.

Sometimes we stay up late because we are desperate for some time for ourselves. If we have partners and/or children at home, roommates, and so forth, we will find it challenging to have space to ourselves to just *be*. If late at night is the only time available for just us, we will covet that time and be very reluctant to give that up, even to the concept of self-care and sleep. If this sounds like you, clearly there is a lack of balance between the social you and the independent you. You are stuck in "giving" mode, and it is imperative that you begin to carve out some time each day that is just for you. You'd be surprised what 20 minutes of uninterrupted *you* time can do. It doesn't have to be hours. Have you caught your Drill Sgt. kicking in with all sorts of reasons why you can't have time just for you each day? If so, take a moment now and write out the all-or-nothing thinking that kicked in. See it. Name it. Don't let it go unchecked.

Personally, I find the best moment to have time for myself is first thing in the morning. These first 15 minutes or half-hour when no one else is up (it's just me with my cup of tea) are the most tranquil and enjoyable of the day. I can use this time for meditation, self-reflection (journaling), yoga, or engaging in one of my hobbies: anything that is just for me and feels life-enhancing. It's a great way to start the day and really ground myself in my body, my goals, and intentions for my life overall. I find that my morning routine also flows much more smoothly when I have started with this quiet time. *When* you take time during the day for yourself is not important, the fact that you *do* is what matters.

Many books speak to the importance of enough quality sleep on your overall health. In fact, sleep deprivation is a common cause of depression and anger management concerns. It is hard to have the energy to be grounded and patient, to practice good self-care, and to interact well with others when we haven't had enough sleep. Imagine years of sleep deprivation and how this might be impacting the overall quality of your health and your state of mind.

The human body functions best when we fall asleep between 9:00 and 10:00 at night. The rule of thumb is a minimum of 8 hours solid sleep. Anywhere from 8 to 10 hours is considered good. The majority of us get less than this most nights, which means we are sleep-deprived. Just check and see. Do you wake up feeling refreshed and energized, ready to go? If so, you probably get the right amount of sleep. If not, you are either not getting enough sleep, or the sleep that you are getting is disturbed and not deep enough to provide you with the rest and healing which your body requires on a daily basis.

If your sleep is disturbed, some common reasons for this can be: emotional stress; physical aches and pains; disturbances from family members, including pets; or a mattress that isn't right for your body.

It is a good idea to do some gentle stretching and relaxing of your body before you get into bed. Just a few minutes will make a big difference to your physical and mental state of readiness for sleep. You will fall asleep faster and sleep more soundly. And if you practice this behaviour for a few weeks, you will find that the simple act of beginning to stretch at night brings you feelings of restfulness because your body knows that it is time to go to sleep.

If you feel you are not getting enough sleep, ask yourself if you would be willing to experiment with getting more sleep, and see what if any impact this has on your overall state of being, your stress threshold, and ultimately your use of food to cope. If you are a person who considers themselves a night owl or one who has a difficult time getting to bed early, it's time to practice some goal setting. If your ultimate goal is to be asleep by 10:00 p.m. and you usually go to bed at 11:00 or even later, begin by establishing your six-month goal of more often than not getting to sleep by 10:00. Dialogue with the Drill Sgt. and with your Authentic Self, and see if perhaps fifteen-minute increments might feel doable. Always remember to start small with any change; you can always increase the increments. This will enable you to see what, if any, resistance or obstacles you encounter. They are easier to deal with on a small scale. Your short-term goal could be that for three nights a week, you will go to bed 15 minutes earlier, with the ultimate six-month goal of most nights going to bed by 10:00 p.m.

Do you notice anything surfacing within you? Any resistance? Any all-or-nothing thinking? If so, just process it. What's the story that the Drill Sgt. is telling you? Is it true? What are some other possibilities? Could one of those be more likely than his story? Or perhaps you notice the sense of peace and relaxation which comes from imagining yourself taking some time to implement these changes. Do you feel the openness and flexibility that comes from establishing your intention without the rigidity of the old goal setting mentality?

And one more thing about rest... allowing yourself to rest throughout the day is imperative to your state of balance and overall health. Many societies still embrace the concept of "siesta" or afternoon nap. You may have noticed that you have a lag in your energy level around 2:00. This is standard operating procedure for the human body. I often wish I could go back to pre-school days and have my afternoon nap! Our North American society does not permit a full siesta, but we can always find 10 to 20 minutes for meditation, or a few moments just to close our eyes and breathe deeply. (We will explore the value of meditation when we talk about Spiritual self-care, but earmark it now as something which will make a dramatic difference in your energy level throughout the day and your sense of balance and peace within.) If you want to experiment with some rest in the afternoon, apply the same goal setting approach, and invite yourself to perhaps start with two days a week when you will take 5 to 10 minutes in the afternoon to practice some breath work or mindfulness. Your ultimate goal may be 10 to 20 minutes most days. Give yourself a window of six months or more to obtain this goal. Remember, think long-term, lasting change. We are not going for a quick, all-or-nothing fix when it comes to self-care.

Earlier, when we looked at coping strategies, did you identify "busywork" as one of your primary coping strategies? The term "busywork" means keeping yourself busy around the house or office in a meaningless or inconsequential way. If you have a belief that you are not good enough or not acceptable as you are, you may feel the need to prove your worth by always doing something. You may have a very, very difficult time sitting still and resting while others are working or active around you. That's just your old belief kicking up, and you know how to challenge that now. If you have forgotten, flip back to Chapter 12 on core beliefs, and nip that old bogus belief in the bud!

Body Awareness

There are many ways to explore awareness of your body. Mindfulness practice and breath work are two key facets, and we will explore them shortly when we talk about your spiritual self-care.

For now, let's talk about two key methods for being more present in your body and being tuned in to its signals of hunger, fullness, fatigue, pain, joy, pleasure, and more: Hatha Yoga and Pilates.

Hatha Yoga

At one time, yoga would invoke images of a man in a loin cloth sitting crosslegged under a tree. Then it became about the "yoga body"; that perfectly flexible, not-one-ounce-of-fat body that looked hot in a leotard. Thankfully, yoga is beginning to return to its roots. The word yoga means "union". The practice of yoga is meant to bring each of us into a greater sense of union with ourselves and with the bigger picture of life. If you engage in a traditional form of yoga, for example, Hatha Yoga, you will see instantly what is meant by yoga as union. Hatha Yoga focuses on the purification of the physical as leading to the purification of the mind and vital energy. It is what most people associate with the word "Yoga" and is the main style of Yoga practiced outside of India for mental health, physical health, and vitality. Hatha Yoga is a very gentle practice of stretching your muscles and moving your body in rhythm with your breathing. The very practice of Hatha Yoga brings you into connection with your body and to a state of mindfulness and peace within. You are fully present in your body, but unlike traditional exercise which causes you to focus on your size and shape and what *isn't* right with your body, Hatha Yoga brings you to an awareness of your body from the sense of gracefulness which is inherent. It brings your attention to your strength and to the union that exists between your mind and body, and you naturally begin to feel a loving sense of connection with something greater than yourself.

Hatha Yoga is the form of yoga which is most frequently practiced as a preparation for mediation because it brings to you a state of peaceful awareness and connection with your body.

Those of you who have used bad body thoughts as a coping strategy will find that Hatha Yoga is a beautiful way to start being in your body more comfortably and consciously. Studies have shown that just a few weeks of practicing Hatha Yoga lead to a dramatic improvement in self-esteem and body image. Your flexibility and tone improve, and each time you practice, even for 10 to 20 minutes, you feel more grounded, peaceful, and integrated in your body.

There are many wonderful videos on Hatha Yoga, and most towns will have a registered professional yoga instructor who offers traditional Hatha Yoga classes. Once you have a sense of a 15- to 20-minute routine, you can do it on your own any time, any where. I find myself practicing Yoga while my son plays at the park; sometimes other mothers join in and we have an impromptu yoga class! I'll use it in my office between clients to ground myself, and before or after a run. If you step out of the all-or-nothing thinking, you will realize that pretty much anything goes! If your intention is to care for your body, you will find time here and there. It may be for only five minutes one day; however, you will be happy for the time you do get rather than feeling as if there's no point because you can't devote more time. Any time is better than no time. Any effort you make toward loving and caring for yourself will be received as just that—a gesture of love and care. And you can never have too much of that.

Pilates

Pilates is a form of exercise and strengthening which focuses on core stability and awareness. The "core," as it relates to Pilates, is the trunk of your body. Pilates is a wonderful form of exercise because it teaches you how to become aware of and connected to your body as you move. It is impossible to practice Pilates for a few weeks without noticing that you have begun to carry yourself differently in your day-to-day life. Not only does your posture improve, but your awareness of your body also blossoms. Soon you walk and feel as though you were a graceful dancer, even if you have never danced a day in your life.

What I love about Pilates is that the focus in traditional Pilates is not on weight loss or what you look like, but on core strength and feeling connected to and integrated with your body.

The goal in physical self-care is to truly honour and respect the needs of your body. In order to do this, you must to be connected enough with your body to know how to read the signals it is sending. Pilates and Hatha Yoga are two excellent methods you can employ to create that connection.

As with Yoga, there are many new branches of Pilates which are more focused on weight loss and looks rather than on form and inner groundedness. Just snoop around at your local video store (or go on line), and look for videos or classes which are offered in traditional Pilates and Hatha Yoga. You will know from how resistant or how open you feel whether a particular form of body awareness is right for you. If it's called *Pilates for Abs*, it's probably not a good call right now. Likewise, *Yoga for Weight Loss* is probably not coming from a place of being truly centred in your Self first.

And whichever form of movement you choose (if you even choose one at this time), approach it with the same goal setting approach we spoke of earlier. Let it be enough right now to commit 20 minutes once or twice a week. You decide; but let that decision be an integrated and peaceful one.

Health Care

General health care encompasses any minor aches and pains, little rashes and miscellaneous who-knows-what, the ever-popular Pap smear, chronic headaches, tummy upsets, P.M.S., Peri-menopause and all sorts of other ailments and concerns which you may be experiencing.

Self-care means taking care of *all* of you: your emotional self, psychological self, spiritual self and physical self. If one of these areas is being ignored or set on the back burner, all others will suffer.

If you have an ailment that you have been putting up with and have allowed yourself to be satisfied with treating only its symptoms, you can trust that your overall state of emotional, psychological and spiritual awareness is suffering as well. It's hard to feel safe being aware of your body when you are in pain. And if your Drill Sgt., with his intrusive ideation, has gotten in there, you may have convinced yourself that you have some life-threatening illness, and it is better not to know. Also, many of us who use food to cope, whether we restrict or binge or purge, are certain it shows. The doctor may take one look at us and know what shameful beings we are. Many of us may have had the experience of a doctor offering us "support" that feels a lot more like criticism. The following comments were given by well-meaning doctors to some of our clients: "You are obese." "You look like a skeleton." They have your best interest at heart, but motivation through fear tactics and criticism (sound familiar?) is not the way to go. They often hand us a diet plan and/or prescription for the latest anti-depressant. We know this isn't the answer. We've been there before. When the professional doesn't know what to do, we feel overwhelmed and more depressed.

Two years ago, staff at the CEDRIC Centre conducted an on-line study. They asked participants about their experiences with their GP's around the identification and treatment of their eating disorder. Over 90% of respondents said that not only did their GP offer them a diet and a prescription for an anti-depressant upon diagnosing their eating disorder, but they also usually did not recommend counsel-ling. Following their appointment, those same respondents said that they immediately used food to cope, and most did not follow through with their doctor's recommendations.

The reason I mention that doctors did not suggest counselling in most cases is not because I am an outraged or biased counsellor. It is because all current research on recovery from Disordered Eating points to a three-pronged approach as being the most successful for a complete and lasting recovery: (1) counselling; (2) gentle exer-cise and body awareness (as described earlier); and (3) mindfulness practice. It's very exciting to see the research reflecting what we and other like centres in North America have known for years from our practical experience—mind, body, spirit. All three must receive at-tention and care in order for deep and lasting change to occur.

I know from my personal and professional experience that, in most cases, if you advised your GP that you use food to cope but are taking steps to attend to this isssue and would like a physical to identify any other concerns which may be impacting your coping strategy, almost all doctors would willingly comply, and it is highly unlikely that any would mention your weight again.

It is my understanding that the average GP gets less than one hour of training in diagnosing and treating Disordered Eating throughout their entire medical education. Also, let's not forget GP's are people! They have grown up in the same society as you. And if you think of the high percentage of people who have bought into the Diet Mentality, there will be some who are physicians. So, we can't find fault with your doctor if they continue to buy in to a flawed medical model of treatment exclusively with drugs and/or the old Freudian psychiatry. General practitioners can not be up on current research for the treatment of every possible ailment. It may also be that many doctors are stuck in their own use of food to cope or, at the very least, are followers of the Diet Mentality.

It is essential that every one who experiences Disordered Eating finds a sympathetic GP. The key is to allow your GP to participate in your self-care. If they are unaware or confused about food as a coping strategy or how it may be impacting you, educate them. Share this book with them. Invite them to visit our Web site. Again, in most cases, simply letting your doctor know that you have identified your coping strategy and are taking steps to heal it will be enough reassurance for them to support you in your endeavour. If you know your GP may be negative about your weight or diet plan, you most likely will not feel safe and more open to consulting them for general health concerns. This is important because, as I said earlier, the other key areas of your life will suffer if you are not physically well.

There are so many ways you can begin to demonstrate self-care for your physical Self. Just choose one that really fits for you right now and get started. By "get started," I mean first with compassionate goal setting and then with the actual attainment of the goal.

Now let's explore the *spiritual* and *emotional* aspects of self-care.

Spiritual Self-Care

When I speak of spiritual self-care, I am speaking to consistent practice of whatever philosophy, belief system, and/or religious orientation you may currently practice or feel drawn to. There are many spiritual philosophies, and you need not follow or subscribe to any one religion in particular to consider yourself a spiritual person. In essence, spirituality is simply allowing for the possibility that there is something more than the physical reality. If you are a spiritual person, you believe that there is something bigger or greater than yourself—some greater plan or purpose or supreme conductor of all things. You may feel drawn to call this essence God. Some may call it Spirit; the Divine One; the Earth Mother; the Universe; Buddha; Krishna; Shiva; Allah or one of many others. The key isn't how you refer to your concept of spirituality. The key is that you refer to it at all; that you allow for the possibility that the physical reality may not be all there is to see and know.

Spirituality is a very tender and personal thing. It is not my need or intention to have you believe anything which does not authentically come from within and feel right for the person that you are. I simply invite you to explore the concept of spirituality, if it is not already a part of your daily life.

There are two primary ways of exploring your spiritual self: meditation/prayer and service to others.

Meditation and prayer can be done any which way. There is no one method that works for everyone. The key to knowing whether the form of prayer or meditation that you are using is right for you is how easy it feels to do. It *should* be easy. Your spiritual Self should just flow and feel effortless in its connection with that something greater. If you are expending too much energy, it is likely you either have your Drill Sgt. and his all-or-nothing thinking in there, telling you how it should be and/or what you should be experiencing, or it's just not the right form of practice for you.

The purpose of exploring our Spiritual Selves is that the more we connect with that sense of something greater, the more we feel increasingly peaceful, grounded, loved, accepted and full within ourselves. This doesn't lead us to selfishness and an aversion to connection with others. Rather, it has the beautiful effect of making us stronger and more complete in ourselves, thus giving us so much more love, passion, and compassion to bring to all of our connections with others. From the beggar on the street to the annoying co-worker, to your ex-husband/wife, you have so much more space within you to be filled with compassion, while still being strong and grounded in yourself and in your connection with something greater.

I am not going to propose any one form of meditation or prayer. As I said, your spiritual Self is a unique and very personal thing, and I encourage you to step out and explore the possibilities (that is, if you don't already have a concept of Spirit that works for you). It has been my experience that, inevitably, if we are left to ourselves in this area, we will find ourselves in exactly the right place. I invite you to begin to explore a daily practice of meditation or prayer. It is absolutely the best way to feel instantly reinforced, strengthened and held.

In addition to whatever spiritual practice you feel drawn to, Staff at the Centre invite our clients to practice mindfulness, which, although it originates from the Buddhist school, is truly non-denominational. It is simply watching your thoughts; watching your breathing; being present in the moment.

It is the best tool for noticing the Drill Sgt. and not reacting to him or getting drawn in to his all-or-nothing thinking, intrusive ideation, or your old core beliefs. It makes implementing any of the changes you have learned much easier. It is very simple, and soon you will start to notice how much more relaxed and peaceful you feel overall, and how much space and time you have between your experience of events and your reaction to them. It is this space which is key, because the space allows you to notice what is happening, notice your immediate reaction or natural response, then reflect on that response and actually choose whether or not you want to go with your immediate response or whether you want to respond differently, or perhaps not at all.

This is true freedom: to be able to consciously choose your reaction to situations as they arise. You are conscious and present, and you just know that you can trust yourself to respond with respect and dignity to any situation because you have the peace and groundedness within yourself which slows things down and gives you time to think before reacting.

Now, if you are new to the concept of self-care and spirituality (and now I'm talking about mindfulness practice), you may be feeling a little overwhelmed. If so, just stop and check in with the Drill Sgt. Identify the all-or-nothing thinking which is present in him at that moment, and ask him if he can be certain that that is true. Explore other possibilities.

I remember years ago, before I had begun to learn about and to practice meditation and mindfulness, I was speaking with a counsellor friend and I said, "You know, I just feel as though my life is happening so fast; I just need to find some way to slow it down and be able to breathe for a moment." And she said, "You know, the best tool I've found for slowing things down and feeling grounded is meditation." Well, at that time I was knee deep in some major life issues: separation from my son's father and all the emotional and other bits and pieces that go with that; completing a master's degree; a baby under a year old; the new CEDRIC Centre; various other interpersonal relationships that needed healing; oh, and did I mention bankruptcy! To say my life was a bit messy is an understatement. It was a time of great change and healing for me, but it was certainly bumpy! So when my friend said "meditation," I just about laughed, cried and died all at once. It felt so passive, so simple. Too simple, certainly, for my big life crises! Wasn't it?

Well, I ignored her advice and fumbled my way through life for about a year more. Then the invitation to meditation came to me through the back door. I was reading Deepak Chopra's *Grow Younger, Live Longer,* and he spoke about meditation as the key to balance and overall health and wellness. I was in a different place then—not so acute with my stress, having healed many old wounds, and able to imagine some benefit from sitting with myself in mediation. I already had years of experience of sitting with myself and doing a list of stressors, and I no longer used food to cope, so I knew the value of stopping and being with what was going on inside me. I took a class in meditation, and I must say that many pieces just fell in to place. For me, the experience of peace was profound, and it truly felt as if the pace of my life slowed down. I was accomplishing more than ever before and feeling so much more balanced and grounded in all areas; everything felt slower, as though it had more flow—not so bumpy. It was absolutely wonderful!

At that same time, a great deal of research was appearing about the benefits of mindfulness practice in healing from Disordered Eating, and about other successful and well-known programs for treating chronic pain and mental illness which had mindfulness practice at their core. I began to explore the use of meditation and mindfulness practice with our clients; it just so happened that all of my colleagues at the Centre were already practicing meditation or mindfulness. They were just patiently waiting for me to get on board. Bless them!

Without exception, the clients that practiced mindfulness for a few minutes each day moved through their recovery process more rapidly and felt a greater sense of inner strength and self-love than those who did not. Their ability to be aware of what they were feeling and needing at any moment grew quickly, and they were feeling more balanced and peaceful in their day-to-day existence, therefore able to respond more gently and respectfully to situations as they arose. No more unfinished business to push them over their stress threshold on a daily basis.

The Centre now includes mindfulness training and practice as a part of every healing plan, and all our group and individual work contains some aspect of mindfulness practice which is specific to that client and their needs. I encourage you to take a class, purchase/ borrow a CD or book on mindfulness, and explore the possibilities. Five minutes a day will make a world of difference. And mindfulness practice can be done any time, any where, even while you are waiting at the doctor's office for your physical!

Service to Others

Another aspect of your spiritual self-care involves the concept of service to others or giving back. I won't take long on this, but it does need to be said that we benefit most from giving and not from receiving. When we allow ourselves to set aside some time each week or month for some community service or helping someone in need, expecting nothing in return, we are actually receiving a great deal. Whenever we have the opportunity to improve someone's day or their overall quality of life, we are actually giving a gift to the world; that person will impact others in a different way because of our care and attention. And our actions will cause a ripple effect, touching many, even if we attended only to one.

There are many ways to be of service to others. It doesn't have to be a structured commitment; in fact, it may be best right now if it is not structured. Just look for little ways in which you can do something for someone. Each of us has gifts to offer or skills that we can bring to bear. Opportunities will present themselves. Just be clear with yourself that this is just one aspect of self-care and that *your* emotional and physical self-care need to be attended to equally. This will prevent you from getting caught up in all-or-nothing thinking at the expense of the overall balance you are working to create.

Emotional Self-Care

Essentially, everything we have done in our work together speaks to emotional self-care. Learning to love and respect yourself; to offer yourself compassion not criticism; acknowledging and validating your feelings, while attending to the underlying needs which triggered them: these are all pieces of emotional self-care. In addition to these ways of taking great care of yourself emotionally, there is one other piece that I want to invite you to consider: your hobbies and/or interests.

Your hobbies and interests are the things that you love to do; the things that make you feel alive and passionate and have nothing to do with anyone else. You may do them with a friend or partner, but you don't do those things for that person; you do them because you are drawn to those activities. Pottery, calligraphy, bird-watching, kayaking, hiking, knitting, crocheting, paper toile, photography, genealogy, even triathlons! It doesn't matter what you do for a hobby, but it should be something which evokes passion and happiness.

If you can't think of anything which you currently have in your life that fits the bill, ask yourself to consider your past and what kinds of things really jazzed you up then. Or are there any activities or interests which you always said you would like to try "when you have the time"? Is it possible you could find some time now to do something which you really love that is just for you, even if for only a few hours once a week?

Your relationship with yourself is truly the most important relationship you will have, and, if there is something that you would love to try or to have in your life on a regular basis, I am certain that there is a way to make this a reality. Whenever a client has shared a desire or interest with me, we have never failed to find a way to realize it. Sometimes it requires some education. Sometimes it requires saving up some money. But regardless of the steps you must take to get there, if you know what your goal is; if you stay tuned to why you are taking those steps, it's all part of the excitement of fulfilling your passion. Even a calculus class can be fun if approached from the perspective of a key step on the path to living your passion! Just keep the Drill Sgt. out of the motivation process, and let your Authentic Self tune in to what she really wants to explore.

Often the act of identifying and beginning to pursue one's passion is enough for them to see a dramatic decrease in their use of food to cope—even if their final goal is a few years away!

So give some thought to the pieces of self-care which you would like to embrace at this time, and let yourself begin. I like to invite clients to think of this as a one- to two-year project of lifestyle change, so consider it this way. Invite yourself to contemplate which pieces you would like to have as a part of your daily or weekly self-care, and what time frame you would like to establish for the realization of these goals, independently and as a whole.

For example, let's say you want to see yourself exercising three to four times a week on average; meditating and doing yoga daily for about half an hour all together; and making honouring choices around food more often than not. You would also like to see yourself taking strides a few hours a week toward the fulfillment of your passion. And you are willing to give yourself one year to get to this place? I would say that's reasonable. So, where do you begin?

Start with the compassionate goal setting tool for each of those pieces, as outlined in Chapter 16. Start with just one, then a month or two down the road when you are feeling as though that one is coming along, bring another one on board, and so on, until you see yourself creating a balance of self-care in those key areas. All the while, you will be attending to your emotional self-care by working on compassion and core beliefs, and by using the list of stressors whenever you find yourself turning to any of your old coping strategies. Here you have a great recipe for an even greater life.

Now let's explore the third piece in your recovery: your relationship with others.

SECTION IV

YOUR RELATIONSHIP WITH OTHERS

Now that you have a clear sense of how your relationship with yourself impacts your use of food to cope and your current life situation, you are in a place to begin to change your behaviours in relationship with others.

First, let's explore different types of relationships and how they may impact you. Then we will take that knowledge, coupled with your newfound clarity on your old stories and your new perspective on yourself, and we will discuss ways in which you can begin to actively change the way you relate to others in relationships. This is where all your hard work comes together. The concepts of Self-respect, Dignity and Natural Eating are no longer just new thoughts; they are a whole new way of approaching life that will lead to one filled with loving, healthful, and respectful connections on all levels. You have a right to this. You *do* deserve this. And you can create this for yourself.

Keep in mind that our goal in this piece of work is to create for you the most healthful, life-enhancing relationship with everyone you come into contact with. We are simultaneously working on your relationship with yourself because, as you interact with others, it will be your old stories and patterns which interfere and trigger old coping strategies. And it will be you who will be inviting yourself to view the situation from your new perspective and to respond to it in a new way. That's why relationships with others are such a gift, even the most challenging ones, because they drive us to be the best we can be within ourselves so that we can bring the most respectful and dignified us to each situation. And all of this is significant to you. Not just because, overall, life becomes much more fun, exciting and fulfilling, but because you will cease to need or want to use food to cope.

18

Family Styles: What's Normal?

I subtitled this chapter *What's Normal?* because most of us don't know what a healthful relationship should look like. You may think you are capable of having one now. You may even think you have one. And I'm betting that a few bells went off as we talked about codependency throughout our work together. This doesn't mean your current relationships must end. But it does mean that your recovery from the use of your old coping strategies will get you only so far, as long as you allow any unhealthful relationship you may have to remain as is.

By now, I trust that you are starting to "get" on a gut level that "it" isn't about the food. You know now that some of your old beliefs, as well as the fragmentation that exists within you, continuously come together to undermine your ability to respond to day-to-day situations with respect and dignity for yourself and the others involved. I am certain that, if you have tried any of the exercises we discussed previously, you are beginning to have experiences that prove food is not the root cause of your suffering but only a symptom—a coping strategy and indicator of unmet needs. If this is so, then thoughts, feelings, and behaviours about food and body image beg the questions: "What's up?" "What needs do I have that are unmet right now?" And, even if your alexithymia is alive and well and you have difficulty connecting with your feelings, chances are you will have an answer to this question if you just ask it. Your Drill Sgt. may discount the answer which you authentically provide, when you ask yourself, "What just happened to trigger me to need my coping strategy?" Then it's up to the adult *you* to step in and really listen to your Authentic Self and respond in a way which validates and meets those needs that caused you to use your old coping strategy.

It's All About Balance

You know this stuff. I've said it before, but I'm saying it again because it's possible that it hasn't quite sunk in. It's possible that you are hearing yourself say things about your relationship(s) which are clear indicators of unmet needs, yet you are still discounting those needs and/or judging yourself for having them; therefore, you are still feeling unbalanced and using food to cope.

I promise that as long as any aspect of your life remains unbalanced or your needs are unmet in certain areas, you will use your coping strategies. For those of us who have a disordered relationship with food, I look at food as the trump of coping strategies. And, if we are using food or body-image focus, it means that all our other coping strategies are overwhelmed, and we are pulling out the big guns.

Depending on how actively you are working through this material, you may have already discovered that your relationship with food is changing, and your dependence on its numbing effect lessening. Still, there are those times when you are very aware of your use of food as a coping strategy. These times are very frustrating to the Drill Sgt. who thinks you should be "done" by now. Don't be fooled or caught up in the judgement. Remember, judgement and self-criticism are just other forms of coping strategies, as is the use of food when you are not hungry or not allowing yourself to eat when you are. If you notice your Drill Sgt. judging your thoughts, feelings, or behaviours, invite yourself to check in with him by asking:

a) What is his intention in saying that?

b) What is he trying to achieve?

c) What is important about that?

Prove to yourself, as frequently as you can right now, that his intention is positive, his delivery pathetic. The more you prove and *know* this at your core, the less his judgement will impact you, and the more your Nurturing Parent will be present to offer you more gentle and constructive feedback and to identify the unmet needs which triggered your dear old Drill Sgt.

I trust that our work together has brought you to the place of being willing to allow for the possibility that you have an unmet need when you are reaching for your food-coping strategy. If so, could you also allow for the possibility that, as long as this need remains unmet, you will feel unbalanced and continue to use food as a coping strategy? And, could you allow for the possibility that it doesn't take an all-or-nothing solution to meet your need? You don't have to end a relationship for this need to be met (providing the relationship is not abusive, in which case, your need for security can never be met there). You will find a way to determine which need is unmet, seek a solution, and take action. We have talked about how to do this in relationship with your Self. In the next few chapters we are going discuss how to do this in relationship with others. Just as the exercises we have covered in earlier chapters have been helping you to identify certain beliefs and behaviours in relationship with yourself that may be impacting your need for food for coping, the next few chapters will continue to support you to identify beliefs and behaviours in relationship with others which you may not previously have explored. You may not have identified these patterns as being harmful because they have always been a part of your life and what you thought a "normal," "healthful" relationship looks like. Or, perhaps you have just bought into the belief that that's the best you can do. Not so.

It will be much easier to look at these pieces if you check your all-or-nothing thinking at the door. So, be on the alert for any of the pressure sensation and concrete thinking which indicates you have been tricked in to seeing only two possible solutions. If you notice it, just remind yourself that there are always more possibilities than we imagine, and invite yourself to remain open to any of them.

In What Kind of Family Did You Grow Up?

Now let's explore relationships from the perspective of parenting styles and how they impacted your view of what relationships and love "should" be. We have explored messages and behaviours from our primary caregivers which we received as children, and the impact of those messages in the form of old core beliefs. Now we are going to look at three distinctly different parenting styles that will allow you to identify much about yourself. This is one more opportunity for the Drill Sgt. to gain some empathy for you and your life experience.

The title of these three parenting styles (and the list of traits of each) comes from author and parent educator Barbara Coloroso. She can be reached at www.kidsareworthit.com. I strongly urge all our clients to read her book titled *Kid's are Worth It.* We have many copies in our library at the Centre. It is an important read, in my perspective, whether or not you have children, because it is very enlightening regarding the patterns of relating—patterns that you witnessed and learned in your family of origin—and how these patterns might be impacting you today. It is a great, great book, and your Drill Sgt. can't help but let up when you read just the first few chapters! Barbara also has another wonderful book on building integrity called, *Just Because It's Not Wrong Doesn't Make It Right.* I recommend it highly.

So, without further ado, let's look at these three distinctly different styles of parenting à la Barbara Coloroso: the Backbone Family, the Brick Wall Family, and the Jellyfish Family.

The Backbone Family

This is the ideal family structure. Lots of respect; the family is a democracy. No verbal abuse, put downs, mini-lectures and certainly no physical abuse or neglect. The core characteristics of this style of parenting and this kind of family are as follows:

- Parents develop for their children a network of support through six critical life messages given each day:
  1. I believe in you.
  2. I trust you.
  3. I know you can handle life situations.
  4. You are listened to.
  5. You are cared for.
  6. You are very important to me.
- Democracy is learned through experience.
- An environment is created which is conducive to creative, constructive, and responsible activity.
- Rules are simply and clearly stated.
- Consequences for irresponsible behaviour are either natural or reasonable.
- Discipline is handled with authority, which gives life to children's learning.
- Children are motivated to be all that they can be.
- Children receive lots of smiles, hugs and humour.
- Children get second opportunities.
- Children learn to accept their own feelings and to act responsibly on those feelings through a strong sense of self-awareness.
- Competency and cooperation are modeled and encouraged.
- Love is unconditional.
- Children are taught how to think.
- Children are buffered from sexual promiscuity, drug abuse and suicide by the daily reinforcement of the messages which foster self-esteem, such as: I like myself. I can think for myself. There is no problem so great that it can't be solved.
- The family is willing to seek help.

Man, doesn't that sound great? I read that list for the first time when I was pregnant with my son Ben, and I remember thinking that I wish I'd had that! I also remember thinking that's what a "normal" family should look like. I was grateful to be discovering what healthful parenting looks like on the eve of becoming a parent my-self. And it was enlightening, because I realized that my Authentic Self, who had always felt confused and resistant to the behaviour of my childhood caregivers, had known what she was talking about and needing all along. She wasn't too wimpy or oversensitive. She was healthy! The situation was not.

Take a moment now to identify behaviours of the backbone family which you currently bring to any of your relationships with others, and then give yourself a big pat on the back. You deserve to feel proud of yourself for those things. And remember, you deserve to have those things in your relationship with yourself, too!

Now read on and see what resonates for you from the other two styles of parenting.

Brick Wall Family

This is the style of family/parenting where there is no room for anyone's opinion but the head honcho. And if you disagree with him/her, nasty things occur. It is impossible to leave this style of family with your self-esteem intact and without a very confused perspective on relationships. The good news is that both your self-esteem and your behaviour in relationships can be healed. The core characteristics of this style of parenting and this kind of family are as follows:

- Hierarchy of control.
- Litany of strict rules.
- Punctuality, cleanliness and order.
- Rigid enforcement of rules by means of actual, threatened, or imagined violence.
- Attempt to break the child's will and spirit with fear and punishment.
- Rigid rituals and rote learning.
- Use of humiliation.
- Extensive use of threats and bribes.
- Heavy reliance on competition.
- Learning takes place in an atmosphere of fear.

- Love is highly conditional.
- Separate, strictly enforced rules (boys versus girls; eldest versus youngest).
- Teach what to think, not how to think.
- Risk of sexual promiscuity, drug abuse and suicide.
- Refuses to acknowledge the need to get help.

Okay, that's my Dad! Do you recognize any behaviours by your caregivers from your "caregiving" past? Are any of these behaviours things which you may currently do in relationship with your children or significant other, colleagues or other family members? How many of these behaviours do you catch your Drill Sgt. doing under the guise of good intent? Make sure that the Nurturing Parent in you gently points out to the Drill Sgt. that these behaviours actually diminish self-esteem and lead to the use of harmful coping behaviours and dysfunctional relationships.

Jellyfish Family

This is the style of family where one or both parents permit the kids to rule. Then every now and then, overwhelmed with the chaos, they might turn into brick-wall parents for a moment. The children in these homes don't know which way is up and which is down. There is no room for kids to be individuals and to learn respect for themselves because they are either being completely neglected, or their parents are so desperate for their *children's* approval and to be seen as "cool" that they copy and mimic everything the kids do. This forces the children to rebel or to engage in behaviours which are more "out there," just to feel as though there is something that is just their own. Kids in these families may either be "super mature" and take over responsibility for the cleaning, groceries, cooking, and care of the parents, or they may run away or turn to drugs, sex, or even suicide to feel a sense of separation and individuation. The core characteristics of this style of parenting and this kind of family are as follows:

- Anarchy and chaos in the physical and emotional environment.
- No recognizable structure or guidelines.
- Arbitrary and instant punishments and rewards.
- Mini-lectures and putdowns are tools of the trade.
- Second chances are arbitrarily given (depending on the mood of the parent).
- Threats and bribes are commonplace.
- Everything takes place in an environment of chaos.
- Emotions rule the behaviour of parents and children.
- Children are taught that love is highly conditional.
- Children are easily led by their peers.
- Risk of sexual promiscuity, drug abuse and suicide.
- Parents are oblivious to major family problems and fail to recognize the need to seek help.

Does this style of parenting resonate with you at all? Did you experience this pattern in your family of origin? Are any of the above behaviours those which you currently do in your relationship with others? Are they behaviours which you permit others to do in your current relationships? Again, check in and give some thought to how many of these behaviours you catch your Drill Sgt. doing under the guise of good intent?

Coming from the Nurturing Parent in you, gently point out to the Drill Sgt. that these behaviours only serve to diminish your self-esteem and lead you to feel the need for harmful coping strategies.

Often, families have one brick wall parent and one jellyfish; this can be very confusing for the children. There is no sense of safety and security in these environments, and the child's need for love and acceptance is unmet because the environment is unstable or the love conditional. Often the parents in these types of families are so self-absorbed and so full of their own all-or-nothing thinking that there is very little consideration given to the individual needs of the children. Children are seen as appendages of the adults and not separate beings deserving of respect and dignity. And that's what we, as children of these families, bring to our adult relationships: the belief that we do not have needs or rights independent of others and that, when we are in a relationship with someone else, their needs take precedence. We believe that we are not deserving of respect and dignity from others, so we are drawn to people who treat us that way. This only serves to reinforce this belief and is seen as "proof" that we are unworthy of true love and respect, if we even know what that looks like!

Now you *know* what it looks like. It looks like Barbara Coloroso's backbone family. What we have been doing in our work, in essence, is endeavouring to create a backbone family within your Self. It is so very important for you to love and respect yourself; for you to treat yourself with dignity; and for you to know that your feelings, needs and opinions have merit and are worthy of respect and sharing. That's all backbone! The Drill Sgt. is clearly Mr. Brick Wall. And your Authentic Self is all about jellyfish right now, because she's been taught that her worth is minimal and that she must compromise herself and be likeable in order to be safe. By now, you are sure to be seeing the holes in this theory and perspective on yourself.

The Brick Wall and the Jellyfish in my Family

I've mentioned my father quite a few times in our work together. He truly was the Drill Sgt. personified and the epitome of a brick wall parent. My brother and I lived in fear of his anger, which would manifest itself as yelling and putdowns or physical harm. In contrast to my father, my mother was a gentle lamb. She was kind and considerate, rarely raised her voice and never hit us or put us down. Unfortunately, she also did nothing to stop my father from harming my brother and me. It wasn't that she condoned my father's abusive parenting style, in fact, she felt the pain and hurt as much as we did, I'm sure. What led my mother to choose to stand by and not protect my brother and me was her own childhood experience of abuse and her subsequent low self-esteem. She didn't feel strong enough to stand against my father and wasn't able to put my brother and me first.

My mother was a happy, bubbly, bright child, and my grandmother will vouch for this fact. Although her mother and father both were hard-working, kind, gentle people, it was uncommon for my mom to experience any pleasurable physical contact from her parents. There was little or no communication or meaningful dialogue among each family member, and one did not discuss dicey or personal issues with *anyone* back then. My grandparents were raised in an era when one did not talk about S-E-X, and this approach was passed on to my mother. As an example, I remember Mom telling me that she had started to menstruate at the age of 12 (Christmas morning) and was traumatized when she noticed the blood. It was her older sister who came to her aid and explained what was happening.

As a child, my mom was repeatedly sexually abused by her older brother who also made many hurtful comments in front of my mom's friends. He physically abused her as well, throwing rocks at her legs and feet to make her "dance". He would lie in wait, nude, at the top of the stairs and jump out at her as she walked to her bedroom. Mom's coping strategy as a young child was to stay in her room, where she would read for hours. Of course, she couldn't tell her mom about the abuse; one just didn't talk about those things back then. She also coped by excelling at school sports. This gave her an excuse to leave the house early and remain after school for practices, avoiding the imminent abuse by her brother.

It is common knowledge that most people form their understanding of the opposite sex and sexuality in general at puberty. Because my grandfather would seclude himself in his den for hours after dinner, my mom had limited contact with her father and no warm and loving physical contact with any males. In addition, the assaults by her brother left her feeling used and broken, unwanted, unlovable, and powerless. She made sense of her abuse with the coping strategies of self-blame and harmful core beliefs, telling herself that she was somehow responsible or should have done something to stop him: she was now "tainted". Mom began early on to step into co-dependent friendships where she did the bulk of the work and the compromising. Some of her "friends" were disrespectful and treated her appallingly. It would be an understatement to say that her self-esteem was very low.

At the age of 16, she fell "in love" with her first boyfriend (my father). He was very intelligent, seemed so worldly and confident, and was good looking to boot. And he liked her! Wow! Mom felt such pressure to make this relationship work—to make him happy—because she believed so fully in her perception of herself as damaged goods that she was certain if he didn't marry her, no one would.

They married in 1966 and moved to a small community (this was the first time my mom had lived anywhere other than at home, and was in a sense an immature child herself). This is where my mother, father, brother and I lived until my parent's separation in 1983. For 17 years my Mom endured sexual, verbal, psychological and physical abuse by my Dad, all the while "keeping up appearances". She believed that what other people thought of you is more important than what *you* think or feel, so you must always look good and as though you've got it all together. Anyone on the outside looking in would have thought we were the "perfect" family.

Because Mom was the middle child in her family and therefore the "people pleaser," she had learned a variety of coping strategies. She believed in being as kind and loving to us children as possible, to counteract the abuse by my father. I am certain that my resilient and cheerful nature comes from the strong core in my mother that was able to endure all that she did and keep on going. And, though I appreciated her ability to love, hug and cuddle my brother and me, what I really needed as a child was an adult to step in and say that what was transpiring was not right or normal, and the way we were being treated by my father was abusive and unacceptable. I had a right to feel angry and scared in this environment, and I needed to have that right acknowledged and validated. My mother didn't believe that she could get by without my father. She had no place to go (this was long before women's shelters), no money, and had been taught that you worked hard to make a marriage a success. If, for some reason it failed, then you did not try hard enough, did not have sex enough, did not fix your hair appropriately, did not prepare the perfect meal, and so on. I longed for her to say, "Let's get the hell out of here"! But I didn't hear that from her. Instead, what I heard was her encouragement of my brother and me to find ways for making our dad happy, perhaps avoiding being harmed by him that day. While her intention was to protect us, her message only served to make my brother and me feel responsible for my dad's abuse. My brother and I became consummate co-dependents.

I was quick to place a lot of blame on Mom for my sexual abuse. As a child, I was certain that she knew what was going on, and, as with the verbal and physical abuse, was turning a blind eye. In fairness, Mom was never present when my physical abuse took place, and I never told her. I can now see that she truly was unaware of the sexual abuse, also. When Mom *did* learn about it (two months following my parent's separation), she was absolutely mortified and offered to support me in my healing in any way she could.

My mother had made the assumption that she and I were close enough that she could trust me to come to her with any problem. From my child's mind, I couldn't trust my mother to be there for me because for years she had been allowing my father to treat my brother and me abusively. What reason did I have as a little girl to imagine that my mother would do anything about this?

I had also bought in to the story that somehow I was responsible, or would be seen as responsible, for the sexual abuse, just as my mother had done as a little girl. Therefore, it felt safer not to say anything and just deal with it. My method of dealing with it was to focus on pleasing people in an attempt to prevent others from being upset with me. Sound familiar?

My mother couldn't have done anything different: she did not have the skills, awareness, or the self-esteem to know that she could assert herself and protect her children. Her own childhood experience left her without a language to express her feelings and needs (alexithymia). It also left her believing that she was bad and unworthy of love and affection. As much as she knew my dad's behaviour was abusive toward her and us children, she felt paralyzed to do anything to stop it. I've been there as an adult: knowing someone's behaviour was abusive but not having a clue what to do to stop it or even feeling of deserving of asserting my needs for respect and security. Perhaps you have been there too.

For many years I carried much resentment toward my mother and held her responsible for my experience. The truth is she *was* responsible, as my parent, for ensuring I was safe and loved. And, she did the best she could at the time.

My mother's trauma with her brother led her to create a story of her worth that was faulty. But no one ever told her that she was worthy of love and respect, so she found herself in a relationship with a man who was so insecure himself that he had to harm his wife and children in order to feel powerful. My mother's beliefs about her responsibility for other people's behaviours and feelings transferred to my brother and me, as we witnessed her behaviour around my father and heard her advice for us to just try harder not to upset him.

To this day, Mom shrinks at raised voices or derisive comments, and is overly concerned that others perceive her as intelligent, having been told many times during her marriage that she was "stupid". I believe my dad has a very high IQ and became easily frustrated with *anyone* who did not "get it" instantly, whether it was explaining the finer points of a fuel dragster's engine or math to my brother. I can tell you, my mom is a very intelligent, talented, remarkable woman, but she often has difficulty believing it. This is a testament to the damage that old core beliefs and hurtful and degrading remarks can wreak.

I tell this story, with my mom's permission, so that perhaps you will learn from it and talk to your parent(s) or anyone who has your trust, if you have experienced trauma of any sort as a child and have not dealt with it. It is likely that one or both of your primary caregiver's also experienced some form of abuse or trauma as children which led them to behave as they did. This doesn't mean that they weren't responsible for what they did or for what happened to you. It does mean that they had a reason for what they did, however convoluted or dysfunctional. The more you give yourself the chance to understand why these key people in your life made the choices they did, the freer you will be, because you won't make the mistake of *making it about you.*

If there is any part of you carrying judgement of yourself or blame for your childhood experience, I encourage you to take some time to gather information on the life experience of those who harmed you. You will prove to yourself that you are not at fault and that you were in no way deserving of being treated in that manner.

Having one brick wall and one jellyfish parent makes for a great deal of confusion for the children in those environments. We must become exceptionally savvy at reading the emotional states of the adults around us. We become chameleons, behaving one way with one parent and another way with the other. We are truly fragmented, and often this fragmentation is encouraged either through actual verbal reinforcement or through the behaviour we see modeled by the jellyfish parent toward the brick wall parent.

Now What?
Whether you have just uncovered some brick wall or jellyfish behaviours in yourself or in those with whom you currently have a relationship, in order for you to meet your goal of a life free from food and body-image focus, things must change. Do you remember the balance we talked about earlier and that, as long as there is a sense of a lack of balance in your life in any area, you will require your primary coping strategy?

If any of these behaviours, and those of the brick wall variety, are alive in your current relationships, they will assuredly upset your emotional balance. Why? Because these behaviours are either coming from your unmet needs, or they will trigger you to have unmet needs. To make it easy on yourself to challenge these patterns, post these lists on your refrigerator so you have a daily check-in with the three different styles of being in relationship. Then invite yourself to pick one thing from these lists to begin working on. Whenever you recognize any brick wall or jellyfish behaviours in yourself, reinforce the backbone behaviour which you would like to add to your repertoire, and gently nudge yourself toward a more honouring way of being.

Do you recall that in our work on compassionate goal setting we talked about stepping out of our all-or-nothing approach to change and embracing a long-term, lasting approach? Apply this concept here. You may have identified a number of behaviours that you would like to modify or let go completely. Note if you feel resistant to noticing these things in yourself or feel overwhelmed because your Drill Sgt. says you need to change them all, today, so as to no longer harm or be harmed. Consider this a part of your self-care and long-term change. This means that, as long as you get clear on which piece from each list you would like to be enhancing or letting go, and you see yourself taking strides each day in your interactions with yourself and with others to reach this goal, you don't have to be perfect today. You just need to show yourself that you are committed to making this change and that you are working on it. Then, as with every other goal and self-care piece we spoke of, you will hear very, very little from your Drill Sgt. about any of these things because you are making headway and demonstrating your commitment to change, and that's what's important.

So please remind yourself as often as possible that the ultimate key to forever being free from food as a coping strategy is "COMPASSION". Compassion for your Self and for others is the key. Anything else is all-or-nothing thinking. Letting go of judging yourself and others is the quickest and surest route to personal peace and balance. As a result of our work together, you now possess some tools to aid you in this. Make sure that you pick one or two tools for self-compassion that really fit for you, and give yourself at least a few minutes each day, for one month, for active practice.

While you are exploring how these three different styles of parenting and relating may currently be impacting your relationship with others, please remember to ask yourself how they may also be impacting your relationship with yourself. As I mentioned earlier, my Authentic Self—my gut instinct—knew all along that the type of parenting which I received was not right. It wasn't how one human should treat another, and I railed at the injustice of it, even as a child. Then my Drill Sgt. started to kick in with his well-intentioned support, which he learned how to deliver from my brick wall parent, and told me to suck it up and stop being so sensitive. My Drill Sgt. worked tirelessly for many years at talking me out of my instinctive feelings and innate needs for safety, love and acceptance.

The only way to cope with this situation was to become fragmented. I had to disconnect from certain aspects of myself that had an inherent sense of right and wrong. My sanity depended on it. I started to discount and tune out the Authentic Me in favor of the External Locus of Control provided by my Drill Sgt.'s perspective and by my father. Being authentic and fully present in my feelings at that time was just too painful and too confusing. That fragmentation—the isolation of certain parts of my Self—was so confusing and dishonouring of my Authentic Self that it took me years to overcome, partly because of the experiences which led me to fragment initially, and partly because of the things I allowed to happen to me while I was so tuned out to my true Self.

Before I could even begin the healing process, I had to first realize and be willing to admit that I had some healing to do. I then had to find a safe place to begin. If you have come this far in this process, you too recognize you have some healing to do, and you have no doubt begun to create a life for yourself which provides you with some space to heal—even if it's the few minutes each day that you have had to read this book.

Congratulations to you! That really is a great achievement. And is your Drill Sgt. telling you your situation wasn't as bad as mine or someone else's, and that you shouldn't feel as you do? Furthermore, did he say that there is something wrong with or weak in you which has led you to become fragmented? If so, check in about his intent in saying this to you. What is he trying to achieve in discounting your experience? What is important about you believing you were not impacted by your experience or that is was less significant than that of others? Let the nurturing adult have a little conversation with him; "seek to understand," and you will be amazed at what you discover.

Let's now take a look at stages of development in relationships, and identify where your key relationships are at now, how this impacts you, and what you can do to shift these patterns. Ready?

19

Developmental Stages

Now that we have explored the different styles of families and parenting, let's explore the developmental stages in relationship with other humans that each of us will ideally go through on our journey through life. The benefit in exploring this, much like the value in exploring family styles, is that you will come to see what "normal" looks like versus what you may have experienced. This is helpful information if you are seeking to uncover any harmful patterns of behaviour and thought that came from unmet developmental needs in your childhood and are still impacting you today. Once you become conscious of what you needed as a normal, healthy, natural human child, you can begin to see more clearly the harmful patterns which developed as a result of your best attempts to meet those needs. This understanding and awareness allows you to actively try new ways of meeting your needs that will be life-enhancing and far more effective.

Remember, the keys to any true change are empathy and compassion. Once you truly understand that there is a legitimate reason for why you think, feel and act as you do, you cannot help but feel compassion for yourself. And out of compassion, true change can occur. You are no longer just the Drill Sgt. trying to approach your problems with yet another rigid and critical plan. You are a nurturing, caring parent who respects and honours the needs of her Authentic Self above all else. Life truly is your own creation. And with empathy and compassion, you can begin to create whatever you desire.

So let's explore the way things are meant to be. Then we will take a look at how they truly often are. We will then focus our efforts on getting you back on track.

The Three Developmental Stages

There are three basic developmental stages that we are meant to traverse in our relationships with others. They are dependence, independence and interdependence. Put succinctly, we all start out as infants, completely dependent on others. If we are blessed to be supported consistently and are *gently* encouraged to develop as individuals, we continuously develop from our very first step as a toddler to complete independence in our twenties and beyond. Feeling secure and grounded as individuals, we are able to form healthful, respectful bonds with others that honour their individuality without compromising our own. Together, we create a relationship which, overall, is equal in terms of give and take. That's the plan. Sometimes the plan goes awry, as we will soon discuss in more detail.

Let's explore each of the stages mentioned above, and give you an opportunity to begin to consider your life experience thus far and how these stages apply to you specifically.

Stage 1: Dependence

As children, we are naturally and appropriately dependent upon our caregivers and community to support us, love us, provide us with healthful modeling, and essentially be responsible for all of our needs. If we are permitted by our caregivers to be dependent on them, turn to them for guidance and comfort, and trust that they will be there if and when we need them, we feel safe to begin to step out on our own. We are then able to develop into secure, independent beings that can, when they need or desire to, allow others to care for them, be there for them, and support them without feeling as if their independence and sense of Self is in jeopardy.

The passage from dependence to independence is not meant to happen in one fell swoop. Ideally, it begins as we take our first steps as toddlers and culminates in our leaving home as young adults, ready to be entirely responsible for our financial, physical and emotional care. Psychologist John Bowlby was interested in the process of our development, particularly as children, and the impact that the relationship with our primary caregiver(s) had on our ability to develop healthful relationships as adults. After numerous studies on this topic, Bowlby developed a concept called "Attachment Theory" which, in brief, states:

"Our primary motivation in life is to be connected with other people, because it is the only security we ever have. Maintaining closeness is a bona fide survival need. Through the consistent and reliable responsiveness of a close adult, infants, particularly in the second six months of life, begin to trust that the world is a good place and come to believe they have some value in it. The deep sense of security that develops fosters in the infant enough confidence to begin exploring the surrounding world, making excursions into it, and developing relationship with others. The infant may race back to mom, be held by her and perhaps even cling to her whenever feeling threatened. In secure attachment lie the seeds for self-esteem, initiative and eventual independence. We explore the world from a secure base."

Think about that for a moment. Having caregivers who are loving and consistent in their care and their presence in our lives gives us the messages as children that we are of value: we have worth. Recall that, as children, we are completely self-absorbed; we are meant to be. We have no other frame of reference, and our frontal lobes are not developed enough to have this rational thought: *That's not about me; Mom's just having a bad day.* We are sponges, and we naturally absorb and internalize everything that we see and experience, including the emotional state of others. As children, if we have a solid foundation in the consistency and love we feel from the key people in our lives, we have no reason to even entertain the thought that we are not good enough or unworthy of love and affection.

You have no doubt met that rare breed who did grow up in an environment which provided a secure sense of attachment. They are both enviable and frustrating to behold for someone who questions their self-worth. These grounded folks just do their thing. They live their lives. They have an air of confidence and self-assurance which is so natural and potent that you can just tell that they are whole beings—not fragmented, fearful ones. Early in my recovery, these people would drive me bananas. From my place of self-loathing and fear, there were times I felt hatred for them. It seemed so unfair that they were free and confident in themselves while I had to struggle to feel okay smiling at someone! It also seemed to me at that time, in my own limited awareness and development, that they were superficial and inexperienced in life.

I believed that as they didn't have my experience in life, they were younger than I was—more juvenile—however, the truth is they weren't superficial or juvenile at all. They were the most amazing creatures: normal! They were thinking and doing the things that ordinary people between the ages of fifteen and thirty were meant to do, if they hadn't been encumbered by other people's baggage and co-dependent patterns. They were free! What a shift in perspective this was. My judgement and envy of these folks disappeared the moment I realized they were healthy, normal human beings. And I could learn a great deal from these people.

And I learned fairly quickly that my problem wasn't with them at all; it was with my own judgement of myself as lacking or tainted—broken. As I began to understand more of where my own behaviours and beliefs came from, I actually came to really love these "normal" people and to feel grateful that they modeled that sense of assurance and groundedness in Self that I had never before seen. Instead of distancing myself from them, I began to gravitate toward them, and I found my relationship with others getting easier and easier. I was connecting with healthier people, and I was growing healthier myself.

Bowlby also says that, "Connection with others is the only security we ever have." I believe this is true, especially as children when we are truly dependent on others for our next meal and a roof over our heads. But I do believe the distinction needs to be made that you can create a great deal of security and a very solid inner foundation as an adult—independent of anyone else. This is important for you to know because you must trust that, regardless of what kind of home you grew up in or what kind of security your caregivers provided, you can absolutely create for yourself, now, as an adult, a strong foundation within yourself of security and trust. In fact, this inner sense of security and trust is the only true, lasting security you will ever have. People come and go from our lives as their needs change, or as ours do, or as their time comes to pass. We most certainly can feel security and trust in our connections with others; moreover, any relationship that doesn't have that feel to it is either an acquaintanceship or a harmful relationship and should be left behind. The concept we are speaking of is that you not feel dependent on another human being for your sense of security and trust in the world. This sense of security needs to come from within—from trusting your worth and deservedness.

Bowlby does make the key point clearly that if our care and love was inconsistent as children, it will have a direct impact on the kinds of relationships we will have as adults. He goes on to say that secure attachment is necessary to develop self-esteem and solid independence. Remember when we talked about the brick wall or jellyfish families, and I said it's impossible to make it out of that kind of home with your self-esteem intact? Well, the concept of attachment theory helps to illustrate this further. You must feel safe physically, emotionally, and psychologically in your environment. That is a fundamental human need. And as we have discussed throughout our work together, if your need is unmet, you will find all sorts of ways to have it met, even if that means turning on yourself, blaming yourself, or seeing yourself as faulty, flawed or unlovable. You will naturally do whatever you have to do to ease the anxiety and pain of this unmet need. This is normal.

The idea is to have some solutions which honour you and enhance your self-esteem, not diminish it. In the brick wall family there is no safety and no respect. You will either turn against yourself to cope, or act out and harm others. In the jellyfish family, there is no consistency; no adult setting boundaries and guiding your path. It is overwhelming and scary to be a child and feel as if there is no one supporting you to make decisions and figure things out. Either way, your self-esteem is deeply compromised by the sense you make of this situation as a child.

Ideally, we have a solid secure base from which to launch ourselves as individuals. And that "launching" is permitted to take some years as we grow from infant to adolescent and beyond. Our caregivers hold the space for us to step out and step back as we feel the need, and they do not judge or criticize us for wanting or needing independence. They are not in a hurry to offload us or so desperate to be needed or depended on that they stifle our natural growth and exploration of ourselves and our world. If we are blessed to have this experience as children, we naturally flow into the second stage of development: independence. If not, we take a different, circuitous and damaging route called co-dependence, which we will discuss in a moment.

Stage 2: Independence

Whether we arrive here via co-dependence or are fortunate enough to come from a safe and secure environment where we were permitted to be dependent until we were ready to let go, once we enter the stage of independence, our task is to get to know ourselves intimately and to love and respect this being that is us. Learning who we are, what we need, and then taking steps to meet these needs in ways that demonstrate love and respect for ourselves is what it means to be an individual. Up to this point in our work together, you have been developing your inner awareness of Self and enhancing your skills in caring for you as an individual.

Each of us needs a certain period of time as an individual, independent of others (parents/significant others), to come to truly know ourselves and to develop a sense of ourselves as a unique and valuable person in the world. If you are in a committed relationship which has some co-dependent tendencies, it will be important to establish firm boundaries about: (a) time for yourself, (b) deepening your sense of security and awareness as an individual, and (c) no longer taking responsibility for the emotional needs of your partner. We will talk more on how to go about this when we explore boundaries in detail.

In our work on self-care, each of the key pieces we spoke about (physical, spiritual and emotional) was addressed, because they enhance your sense of who you are and what you need, augmenting your respect for yourself as well as your desire and ability to seek life-enhancing coping strategies and healthier relationship with others. I have spoken frequently about the importance of setting aside time each day for your relationship with yourself, both through general self-care and through the acknowledgment and validation of your feelings and needs. Independence from any substance, harmful coping strategy, person, establishment, or organization is dependent on a strong and healthful relationship with your Self. Use the tools you have gained in the section on *Your Relationship with Your Self* to step into yourself fully as an independent being.

When you respect yourself as an individual and take the time to truly know and honour who you are and what feels good to you, life gets easy. It just flows. You are not pushing against or compromising yourself in any way. You have no need of any harmful coping strategies. That 24/7 inner chatter that you are accustomed to hearing is gone, and you experience peace—perhaps for the first time in your conscious life.

You absolutely owe it to yourself and to everyone in your life to be the very best you can be. You see, when you rise to your highest Self, you are providing the modeling and opportunity for those around you to rise to this level also. And it just gets better and better.

Stage 3: Interdependence

You can successfully engage in intimate relationships with others only when you have developed a keen sense of who you are, and you trust yourself to respect your feelings and needs first and foremost. And by the way, "intimate" does not mean sexual; it means emotional openness and closeness with someone. You can have intimacy with friends, family, and with your significant other. When you are interdependent, you engage in relationship with someone else without losing yourself to the relationship. You do not feel responsible for others' feelings and needs. You speak to what you want and need, and you allow others to do the same. If your needs differ, you discuss this and then work together to reach a solution which truly meets both your needs. No one feels as if they lost. No one feels resentful, overrun, or burdened by the other. Interdependence means you maintain an independent Self, even as you engage in building a life with someone else.

Balance and time for yourself are fundamental needs that are givens in an interdependent relationship, and room is made by both parties to allow the other the space and time they require to feel fulfilled and satisfied in their life. In interdependence, you do not become enmeshed and dependent on the other for your sense of esteem and security in the world. In an interdependent relationship, the individuality of the other is cherished and respected. There is a deep, strong connection borne out of like values and principles, and it is sustained by a commitment to honour these values and hold the vision that the two have created for their relationship.

There is a strong sense of trust and respect in an interdependent relationship. This allows you to approach all communications with this person from a win-win perspective and not an all-or-nothing one. This means you feel no sense of panic and urgency, which is common in disagreements, because you don't go to a place of: "Oh my gosh, you're disagreeing. That must mean it's over!" Or, "Well, she wants that, so I guess I'm not going to get what I want yet again!" Interdependence, by its very nature, means that you strive to support the other to be the best they can be: you don't take responsibility for them, but you do what you can to provide love, support and encouragement. You so respect yourself and the other as individuals that you come to understand that anything you do which undermines the sense of confidence or security of the other person is truly an act against yourself, because it diminishes the quality of the relationship and therefore impacts negatively on the quality of your life.

You begin to know, on a gut level, that the more conscious you are of your feelings and needs, and the more respect you feel for those aspects of yourself, the more clearly and confidently you state your needs to others. This means you have far fewer disagreements and misunderstandings. And when you do have confusion in a relationship, you know that the space is there for discussion and healing. You continually feel safer in sharing yourself with others, and deeper connections develop from mutual trust and respect. Interdependence is absolutely beautiful. And again, it must be built on a solid foundation of you as an individual coming into the connection. Interdependence means you know who you are and what you want and need. It is not up to the other to guess or to figure it out. If you can't articulate your needs, it is not the fault of the other. It is an indication of work to be done in your relationship with your Self. This works the other way, too. It isn't your fault if someone else doesn't clearly articulate what they need. It is their responsibility to identify what they need and to ask for it in a way that creates the greatest likelihood of getting that need met. If you have any doubt or confusion about these last few statements, it is time for you to explore the concept of co-dependence.

Co-dependence: Our Default Relationship Setting

Earlier in this chapter, I said that "ideally" we moved through the three stages of development in relationship as: dependence, independence and interdependence. In reality, the fact that you are reading this book confirms that you somehow "took a wrong turn at Albuquerque," as Bugs Bunny would say. You have found yourself in a place called co-dependency. Not a happy place, but a place you are no doubt all too familiar with and which, in its own painfully oppressive way, feels like home.

If your process of individuation was thwarted by your caregivers, either through their own resistance to allowing you to mature; through a death or divorce; through physical or sexual abuse; or through emotional abuse or neglect (guilt trips, manipulation, silent treatment, yelling, judging or labeling, as so on), your needs for dependence were unmet as a child, and you have come to engage in a self-defeating style of relationship called co-dependence. In co-dependence, you focus all your energy on meeting the other person's needs. Your happiness feels completely dependent on their happiness and, as such, you are very emotionally vulnerable and have no real sense of security or control in your life. If your partner is unhappy, you also become unhappy or engage in some emotional and psychological gymnastics in an attempt to determine and correct "what you did". It is unbelievable to you that someone's bad mood or frown doesn't have anything to do with you. The co-dependent perspective is that you are responsible for everything people think, feel and do.

Wow! That's a lot of responsibility. You can't relax until everyone is okay. And if anyone has a problem or may possibly have a problem with you relaxing or taking time for yourself, you won't do it. In co-dependency, you will choose to suffer any time, any day, before consciously doing anything which may incur someone's wrath because the need for external validation and approval is so great. It is no wonder you feel exhausted and have no time for yourself.

We talked a bit about this when we discussed Internal and External Locus of Control, and we discussed how important it is to your recovery process to begin to honour your needs first, which means stepping into independence. Put succinctly, the only way out of co-dependence is to learn who you are as an individual, and begin to live your life with a commitment to your dignity and self-respect first and foremost.

Why You Assume "It" Is About You

The term co-dependency means that you perceive yourself as responsible for the feelings and needs of others. Those of us who use food to cope have an abundance of co-dependent training, and that is why we need to use food to cope. It is overwhelming being so responsible, so at fault. Our food focus gives us something else to concentrate on, however harmful, and momentarily decreases our state of anxiety. It is exhausting to be consistently inundated with the belief that whatever other people are thinking, feeling, doing, and needing, it's all about us. Somehow, we did or didn't do something which created this thought, feeling, behaviour, or need in the other, and sooner or later we are going to be held responsible for this thing—whatever it is.

You may perceive yourself as being responsible for the feelings and needs of others, but this is just downright untrue. You are *not* responsible for what someone else thinks, feels and needs, or for their behaviour. You are not responsible for how someone else chooses to interpret their world or for how they choose to respond to their interpretations. No, you are not. Even if they say you are, this is only an indication of their own co-dependent belief system.

It is very likely that, if you are one of the "assume it's about me-er's," you experienced times in your life when you were held responsible for whatever wasn't working in someone else's life. You likely experienced a time when you were blindsided by someone's wrath or judgement of you, and you were blamed for something that happened to them. Regardless of the absurdity of this accusation, this experience has disastrous effects if it happens repeatedly or happens around a traumatic or highly-emotional event. And, you will recall that as a child, you have no ability to offer yourself the thought that it's their stuff and not your responsibility for how they feel. You will internalize the message that, even if you don't know what you did or how you did it, you are responsible for the pain of others, and you come to believe that you are responsible for eradicating this pain. In fact, in many cases, this experience happens in childhood with your primary caregiver(s), so your very basic needs for security and love seem to rest with your taking responsibility for the other's pain and making it better. It seems this is the only way to gain forgiveness and thus be assured of love once more.

If you are in relationship with a friend, colleague, or significant other who has difficulty taking responsibility for getting their needs met, you are likely to be blamed frequently for their dissatisfaction with life and with your relationship. You may hear this message frequently: If only you would... they wouldn't: get so angry; feel so stupid; feel so sad; do... Or "you make me so... "(fill in the blanks). We do **not** have the power to make anyone do or feel anything that they are not willing to do or feel, so don't take that one on.

This message can also be stated non-verbally by a person who acts angrily or dismissively of us until we press, cajole or sacrifice ourselves enough and take responsibility for their feelings and needs. It may sound something like this: (for the record, you are Person A.)

> Person A: "Is there something bothering you?"
> Person B: "Nope."
> Person A: "Have I done something to upset you?"
> Person B: Silence...
> Person A: "Are you upset because I came home ten minutes late?"

Here you have totally set yourself up. The person said nothing was wrong, and yet you continued, taking responsibility for feelings they may or may not have been having and that *they were ultimately responsible for expressing*. Now, whether they were annoyed with you or not for coming home late, you have laid your neck on the chopping block and given them carte blanche to blame you for their bad mood or behaviour, feelings, and needs. They have not learned to take responsibility for clearly articulating their feelings and needs. You have enabled them to do so, thus perpetuating the cycle of co-dependence in your relationship.

And as hard as it may be to believe, when you are steeped in the co-dependent mindset that their demeanor truly had nothing to do with you, it can be pretty annoying for Person B to be badgered for details if they don't want to talk about what's going on, or if nothing truly is bothering them and you won't accept that.

In mature and respectful adult communication, each of us is responsible for expressing our feelings and needs. If we have had the experience of being judged or ridiculed for the expression of our feelings and needs by significant people in our lives, we will feel exceptionally vulnerable doing this. If we have internalized these judgements and now have a Drill Sgt. reinforcing them, no one need ever say or do anything critical toward us for the rest of our lives, and we will still feel terrified and certain of rejection at the thought of directly asking for what we need.

Yet, to expect someone to guess what's bothering us, or read our minds, is just not appropriate. In essence, we are setting this person up as we were set up, that is, to assume that someone's mood or behaviour is our fault or responsibility in some way. You don't like feeling this way or appreciate the burden it places on you. Why would you perpetuate this or seek to create this pattern in your primary relationships? The only reason would be because you didn't know any better until now.

The trick to changing this assumptive pattern is to start by noticing when you are assuming that you have done something to upset someone or haven't sufficiently met their needs. Then just check in and ask yourself if they have adequately expressed their feelings of discontent. Have they been clear about what caused them injury or what need went unmet? Or are they being quiet, sullen, withdrawn, sarcastic, or maybe sighing heavily or slamming cupboard doors? These are passive-aggressive behaviours and not healthful or appropriate ways of asking for what you need.

If they haven't expressed anything to you directly, *don't assume it's about you.* In fact, assume it isn't! Remind yourself that it is up to this person to let you know if there is something they need from you—they shouldn't make you guess. Guessing only enables them to continue to keep you stuck in this awful co-dependent pattern, and it doesn't teach them anything about healthful communication or responsibility for their own needs. I encourage you to let it go.

If you absolutely can't let it go, try my ten-second rule: give yourself ten seconds to check in with yourself and ask if there is something that you are conscious of having done that was not respectful of this person. If you can't think of something within ten seconds, let it go. If you *can* identify something disrespectful which you have done, step up and acknowledge it. Once acknowledged, you don't need to pay any more. If the person continues in their mood or carries a grudge, then it is about them. You are free. Let it go.

If you have invoked the ten-second rule, still can't think of anything you have done to upset someone, and still can't let it go (old training dies hard), there is one more thing you can do. It should be your last resort and not your default setting. You can check in with the person about how they're doing and if they need anything from you. Approach this person from an *I can see you're troubled, and I'd like to help* perspective and not from a W*hat have I done wrong?* perspective. Assume that you are blame free.

Honour the response you get. If they say nothing's wrong, let it go. If they say they don't want to discuss it, let it go. If they give you the silent treatment, let it go. It is their responsibility to communicate their needs to you. It is not your responsibility to guess what they are thinking, feeling and needing.

To recap, the trick to no longer buying in to the responsibility for everyone's feelings and needs is being aware of the following:

1. Notice the assumptive thought that you have upset someone.
2. Did they clearly express their feelings and needs in relation to you?
3. If not, don't assume it's about you! Assume it isn't!
4. Let it go!
5. If you can't let it go, try the ten-second rule.

6. If you still can't let it go, ask if there's anything they need. You must approach this person from the mindset that you are not to blame for their behaviour.
7. Believe them if they say it's not about you.
8. If they say it is about you, remember you are only responsible for 50% of any relationship. Even if they want to dump 100% on your door, you don't have to accept it.

I challenge my clients with a homework assignment that goes like this: if you are going to harm yourself by making assumptions about what someone is thinking about you, or that you are responsible for their mood or experience, you have two choices:

1. Confirm your assumption. Ask them!
2. If you are unwilling to ask them, you must commit to letting the assumption go. Be willing to believe that "it" is not about you.

This is such a great exercise. I love the feedback clients bring from this. If clients choose option No. 2 because they don't want to ask someone to confirm or deny the assumption they are making, they let it go. Imagine their surprise when they realize that they actually did let it go and had a great time with this person. They felt so free and light that they begin to let go of any assumptions they notice themselves making. Relationships take on a whole new perspective and possibility in this new, non-assumptive state of being.

If clients choose option No. 1, it's just amazing how their life shifts. No. 2 is the slow train. No. 1 is the bullet train! Either one will get you there, but No. 1 makes it immediate and jacks it up a notch. The feedback from No. 1 is always the same: the other person wasn't thinking what my client assumed they were. Whatever was going on for this person had nothing at all to do with my client, and, in fact, they really like xyz about my client! And you need to try option No. 1 just two or three times in order to really prove "it's" not about you.

An example of option No. 1 in action would be a client of mine (let's call her Joy) who took me up on my challenge to check out her assumptions on the day of her staff Christmas party. Joy had a colleague whom she perceived as having the "perfect body". Joy always felt physically judged by and inferior to this woman. She was not looking forward to this event because she was feeling unhappy with her own body, didn't really enjoy group social functions, and to top it all off, this woman always seemed to end up speaking with Joy's husband and the two of them sharing a great laugh! Despite the "evidence" that this colleague clearly looked down on Joy, I encouraged her, for her own sake, to either check it out or drop it. She came to see me the next week and shared this story:

"I got to the party, not feeling very great about my body or very comfortable being there. But I did like my outfit! She (the colleague) was in a gorgeous dress and looked absolutely fabulous. I immediately started to feel insecure, as though I needed to hide myself behind a table or something. My stomach was churning. I stopped and asked myself why I was feeling so anxious. The answer? *Because* she *looks great and I look like shit.* So I asked my Drill Sgt., because that was clearly a Drill Sgt. comment, what his intention was in saying that. It all boiled down to his belief that she was judging me as fat and ugly and that I wasn't being approved of, which of course was all about him wanting me to be happy! So I realized I could sit there all night feeling awful and assuming she's thinking I look like crap, or I could just go and talk to her and find some way to find out what her perception of me really is. I went and stood next to her and joined the conversation. Soon enough, it was just the two of us chatting. I found myself naturally complimenting her on her dress; it *was* stunning. And do you know what happened then? I asked her—I actually asked her!—what she thought of my outfit and how I looked. It was so great! I was nervous, but I needed to ask. She said she noticed me as soon as I came in and loved my suit. Then she told me that she always loves what I wear and that I always look so together. Can you believe it!? We had such a great conversation after that, and I felt so light and free. I had the best time that night that I have ever had at a party."

Yes, I absolutely can believe it! Inevitably, "it" isn't about us. Our assumptions are almost always inaccurate. Remember, your assumptions are created by your core beliefs more than they are by anything that is really happening in your current existence. So, because she was willing to take me up on my challenge and was eager to be free of her co-dependency and assumptions, Joy learned that not only did this woman not judge her negatively for her appearance, but she also actually liked Joy's style and thought she had it all together! Of course Joy's working relationship with this woman improved, and Joy's feelings about her own sense of style and her appearance dramatically improved as well.

So when I say option No. 1 jacks it up a notch, I mean you don't just get to believe that "it's" not about you, you also come away with some piece of positive feedback, and you may have just had a deeper conversation than you have had in years! Perhaps you have even taken a key step toward a great friendship with this person.

One more piece about checking in and communication with others: in a little bit, we will be talking about abusive relationships and how to identify one. I will give you a preview because it is relevant to the pattern of assumptions and blame in relationships. If you ask someone how they are doing or if there is anything they need, and they: (a) yell at you; (b) start criticizing or blaming you; (c) threaten to you with harm; or (d) thwart you from having or doing things you enjoy, get out! Leave the conversation. There is no point in trying to talk rationally and resolve an issue when someone is in this state. They are not in a rational frame of mind and are only concerned with being right and having power over you. You don't have to say anything. Just go. Don't wait for their approval in order for you to take some space. In that moment they are not rational, remember? Trust your feelings, trust your needs, trust your worth, and remove yourself.

If later you choose to continue in this relationship, it is important to your overall healing that this pattern of communication be healed.

It can not be allowed to be repeated (we will explore this in a couple of different ways in the chapters to come). I want you to know and trust that regardless of what your life experience has been up to this very moment, you do not deserve to be yelled at or criticized by anyone. There is no place for disrespectful behaviour in a life of dignity and respect. It doesn't belong. If you doubt what I say, it is time to review the piece on core beliefs. Ask yourself what your belief is which leads you to deem that this is acceptable. Also, ask yourself what all-or-nothing thinking you may be having that makes you feel this is better than...?

The pattern of assuming it's about us typically goes back to our childhood, so it's been around a long time. It's going to feel strange and uncomfortable. At first, it may even be anxiety-producing to not take responsibility for others moods or needs. Remember our discussion about Discomfort=Change=Good Stuff? I guarantee that you will feel a lot of relief and freedom in the end if you are willing to feel a little discomfort up front.

Co-Dependency, All-Or-Nothing Thinking, And The Permeating Level Of Anxiety

Speaking of anxiety... I have been wanting to share a great piece of awareness with you—something that I trust will help make your checking-in (with yourself) easier and more profitable. It is this:

We have already said that, if you notice you are feeling the PLA at any time, any place, you can guarantee that you are in all-or-nothing thinking. Well, nine times out of ten you can *absolutely* guarantee that your all-or-nothing thinking in these moments is coming from a co-dependent thought. You are fearing someone's reaction; fearing their need; fearing rejection or judgement and feeling responsible for it. I guarantee it. If you notice you are feeling anxious or unsettled—that low level state of distress that I call the Permeating Level of Anxiety—it's because you are telling yourself that someone has a need that you must meet whether you want to or not, whether it works for you or not, because if you don't meet it, they will be _____! (fill in the blank). What's your story? You must do X because, if you don't, they will do/feel/think/be Y. This is assumption and all-or-nothing thinking. And it is all stemming from your co-dependent training.

Prove it to yourself right now. Stop and do a gut check. Any sense of the PLA there? If so, ask yourself what's going on in your world right now that you are telling yourself must be a certain way. Where's the all-or-nothing thinking? Then ask yourself, "Whom is this about?" "Whom am I trying to impress or pacify?" "Whose needs am I seeking to meet?"

You will find that, while it's true you are ultimately seeking to meet your own needs for approval and security, you are seeking to meet them through making someone else happy or making someone else approve of you. This path to meeting your needs for approval and security just doesn't work. It's too risky. You are completely dependent on the moods, emotional maturity, and consciousness of everyone around you.

I do hope you are getting a glimmer of how key this piece of information is. Now you have a direct line from your awareness of your PLA to your all-or-nothing thinking to your old co-dependent training. You can go instantly from *hey, I'm feeling a bit anxious here* to *in what way am I focusing on other people's needs or approval right now?*

This is key, because you will notice that your PLA shifts and often dissipates entirely with the second question: just naming it makes it go away. You will get the sense of shaking off the PLA and the co-dependent thought as well. Now, keep in mind, if you want to move through this pattern swiftly and let it go, you must commit to a few weeks of frequent gut checks and quickie conversations with yourself. I call this "resetting yourself".

You noticed you were getting off track because you felt the PLA, and you brought yourself back to centre by identifying the co-dependent thought and shaking it off with either the ten-second rule or checking it out or letting it go. You may find yourself needing to do this ten times a day for those few weeks (it takes only a minute each time), but then you will be a master at noticing the moment you begin heading down that old path, and you will reset yourself instantly.

Keep in mind that your efforts in this regard will benefit you in two ways: (1) by leading to less anxiety and less co-dependency in your relationship with others; (2) the more adept you become at noticing the PLA and identifying the co-dependent thought that triggered it, the less likely you are to escalate to the point of needing food to cope in any way.

Take some time and make a list of the key relationships you currently have in your life. Ask yourself where they fall in the spectrum of dependency, co-dependency, independence and interdependence.

Then, going back to your needs list, ask yourself which needs are consistently met in that relationship and what needs are consistently unmet. This is key information to have as we explore relationships in the next few chapters, so hang on to this. I'll show you what to do with your answers in order to turn any unmet needs you identify into an opportunity for empowerment and fulfillment.

In Closing

Consider this, whether you knew it or not, you have spent your life thus far mastering the skill of co-dependence. You have bought fully into the belief that, to some extent, you are somehow responsible for and have the power to control others' thoughts, feelings, and behaviours if you just do a certain something in a certain way. Co-dependency can only be healed by *doing*. It can not be changed by just thinking or talking about it. Your actions in relationship with others will make the difference to whether you continue to believe "it's" about you or not. And you will continue to believe this old story until you give yourself the gift of challenging these patterns and see that it is just a story. It is just a belief. It is not true.

When you release yourself from the bondage of this old harmful belief, you give yourself the opportunity to be fully and completely responsible for your life and to make of it what you desire. Then you become an independent being. And you are truly free and truly ready to be in a loving, healthful, interdependent connection with everyone in your life.

20

Abusive Patterns In Relationships

In this chapter we are continuing our exploration of relationship with others. We will discuss some traits of emotionally-abusive relationships and what to do if you discover that you have one or more of these relationships in your life. You will likely recall that I have previously stressed the point that as long as you have an unhealthful or abusive relationship in your life, you will have a very hard time letting go of your primary coping strategies. This is especially true when you are around this person or anticipating seeing them. This is because you will need these coping strategies (security, comfort, trust and reassurance, to name a few key ones) to deal with your naturally- and appropriately-occurring unmet needs.

This is a fact. These are the same needs that anyone would have if they were in an unhealthful relationship, and these needs are not going away on their own. So, let's add to the skills and awareness you have already acquired (skills such as, compassion/empathy/ awareness of your coping strategies and needs, and your awareness of your right to be taking care of yourself first) and learn how to identify the harmful connections in your life, and how to begin to make your world a safe and joyful place in which to exist.

There are four key types of abuse we may experience in our relationship with others: sexual abuse; physical abuse; emotional abuse; and neglect. We briefly spoke about each of these when we looked at post traumatic stress disorder, alexithymia, and intrusive ideation. I would like to revisit them in a bit more detail, focusing primarily on emotional abuse, which is the most common form of abuse and therefore the one most likely to be in your current relationships in some form.

Sexual Abuse

Many people consider the term "sexual abuse" to refer to the assault of a child. The reality is that sexual abuse can range from any unwanted verbal innuendo, gesture, or physical contact, to rape. Many people who use food and body-image focus to cope have had one of these experiences. *Many* do, not one-hundred percent, so don't rack your brain trying to recall an assault if you aren't already aware of this in your history. The most harmful byproduct of sexual abuse is that it turns us against our bodies. It undermines our sense of safety in our very being. In our attempt to create a sense of safety following an assault, we frequently engage in self-blaming behaviours. Studies have shown that it is human nature after a sexual abuse experience for the survivor to make statements to themselves and others (if they tell anyone at all about the assault) that remove the blame for the event from the perpetrator and place in onto themselves. Statements, such as: "I shouldn't have been there." "I should have said no." "I should have said no more forcefully." "I must have been doing something to give them the impression that I wanted that to happen." All sorts of statements such as these only serve to make us feel responsible for something that was not our fault.

I have had many clients say (and I once thought this myself) that they must have a certain look or a way of walking that makes people think they want to be treated this way, or that they *give off* some sort of sexual vibe whether they want to or not. That's just not so. What we're giving off, if anything at all, is a sense of innocence, trust and insecurity. After an initial sexual-abuse experience, if we don't heal the wound and the sense of a lack of security in our bodies that was created by this event, we go through the world feeling unsafe and as though anyone who is assertive/aggressive enough has a right to our body just because they want it.

The experience of being forced to be sexual in any way, when we didn't want to be or before we were developmentally prepared for it (psychologically as well as physically), can lead us to a place of sexualizing the world. From this perspective, everything has the potential of sexual innuendo. To be on the safe side, we perceive every gesture, every look, and every comment from a sexual perspective first. The truth is things are not always about sex. In fact, in many cases, it is our own sexual-abuse history which makes us respond to situations as though sex or some sort of sexual gesture is expected from us and that we must "put out". We come to see this as our role—our purpose in life. And, if we want to be approved of, we had better honour this role as best we can whether we want to or not. It is very important for you to begin to allow for the possibility that the world is not obsessed with sex in the way you think it may be. And also allow for the possibility that if someone does show interest in you, they are not saying that they expect to be sexual with you or that you are obliged to respond in any way at all.

If you have ever engaged in any sexual act which you did not want to partake in at that time or with that person, you will have a sense of compromised security in your body and in relationship with others. It is important for you to put energy into healing your relationship with yourself and to learning how to set boundaries with others about what you are comfortable with and what you are not. No one has a right to your body but you. You have the right to refuse access of any kind to your body, whether it is a hug, kiss, touch of the hand, or any other physical contact. You have the right to say, "I am not comfortable with that." If you feel any anxiety or distress about setting boundaries with others about physical contact, this is a big red flag. When it comes to your body, this indicates that you have confused beliefs about just who your body belongs to and what your rights are versus the rights of others.

Sexual abuse in any form turns us against our body, as I said earlier. It makes us mistrust any feelings or cues our body gives us about what we need or want. The pattern of self-blame perpetuates this distrust, which only serves to distance us more from our bodies and serves to truly make us less safe and more likely to experience another assault in some form. If we are sending ourselves the message that what we feel can't be trusted in order to look after ourselves and that our bodies are to blame for what happened to us, we will be far less likely to confront someone who is forcing unwanted contact or attention on us. Instead, we can find ourselves trying to talk ourselves into being okay with what is taking place, even when we are feeling terrified or repulsed inside. These feelings of detachment from our body, of anxiety and repulsion, come to be associated with our sexuality, and, just like old co-dependent patterns and old core beliefs, they come to feel normal, regardless of the discomfort they bring.

For the record, healthful sex feels good. It is pleasurable on all levels. Anxiety, fear, mistrust, doubt, sadness, anger, shame, and guilt have no place at all in a healthful sexual experience. In a wholesome sexual experience of any kind, you feel safe and respected. You know that you can trust yourself to do only what feels good to you, and your partner will respect any boundaries you set or requests you may make at any time during your encounter. If you have any confusion about whether your sexual relationships are healthful or harmful to you, there are many wonderful books on healthful sexuality in relationships which will help you to see what physical intimacy can be and what it absolutely should *not* be.

Those of us who have experienced some form of sexual abuse often turn to food to cope as a way of attempting to soothe ourselves, feel some form of control in our lives, and, most significantly, create a body that is least likely to attract any sexual attention. This could be a childlike body resulting from extreme restriction, especially if the sexual abuse took place just as your body was beginning to mature sexually. You may have internalized your experience as a belief that being a woman—being sexy and full-bodied—is not safe. This could also be an overweight, which we likewise believe would not attract sexual attention. Neither of these solutions works as you no doubt have discovered, if you've tried them. Someone will find you attractive. Someone will be drawn to you.

The goal in any sexual healing, regardless of your past experience, is to come to a place where you absolutely know that *you* own your body. Nothing happens to or around it that you aren't one-hundred percent comfortable with. That's that. When you know that you can trust yourself to be boundaried and clear with others about what you will and won't accept in the way of conversation, touch, or gestures pertaining to sex or your body, you have absolutely nothing to fear in being the most beautiful, confident, sexy, dynamic, passionate *you* that you can be. If any of this discussion on sexual abuse has hit home, let this be your goal: own your body. Know that you have a right to feel safe and respected at all times, and demand this of the people in your life and, most importantly, of yourself.

Physical Abuse

Any form of physical contact done with the intent to control or harm is physical abuse. On the receiving end of physical abuse, you will likely experience either the fight or the flight response to a threat. You will want to retaliate, or you may feel as if you just want to run away. Hitting, kicking, throwing things at someone, rapping someone on the head, pulling hair, intentionally bumping into someone or violating their space (getting in someone's face) are all forms of physical abuse.

A good rule of thumb in determining whether something is abusive or not in any form is to ask yourself: "How does this feel to me?" If it feels harmful, it is. End of story. No one in the whole world needs to validate this for you. You are not too sensitive! You feel what you feel. If you feel threatened and unsafe and feel pain, you are being harmed. Now, as I have said before, sometimes our thoughts have more to do with our old experience of things than what is really going on, but frankly, who cares!? If you are feeling harmed or unsafe, you must remove yourself from the situation immediately. Later, you can sort out what was your old story versus what was really happening.

In a healthful relationship there will be room for discussion and understanding afterward. In an abusive relationship there will only be judgement and criticism of you for taking care of yourself and endeavoring to feel safe. Remember, the key here is not to let anyone else tell you whether you are or aren't being abused. Let yourself hear what your Authentic Self is saying in that moment. She will let you know if she is feeling safe and respected or not. If the answer is not, remove yourself quickly.

If you find yourself wanting to physically harm someone, to throw something at them, hit them, bite, claw, kick, and so on, you are likely perceiving the situation as harmful and threatening to you somehow. It could be that you are feeling emotionally power-less and wanting to strike back and hurt the perpetrator as you have been hurt. It could be that you are being or have been physically threatened by this person, and you are responding this way in an attempt to either balance the power or to create a sense of safety for yourself. Either way, the relationship is toxic and very harmful for you.

The moment you notice your own desire to harm someone in this way, remove yourself immediately from the situation. You are not in your rational self. You are way, way, way over your stress threshold, and you need to cool down and feel safe in yourself before anything productive will be achieved with this other person. Always remember, your goal is to be living from a place of dignity and respect for yourself and for others—but yourself, first.

Emotional Abuse And Neglect

Emotional abuse is so common in our society that it is fright-ening. Just think back to the characteristics of the brick wall and jellyfish families that we explored earlier. Many of these character-istics are emotionally-abusive behaviours that are showered upon children by their parents. Most of these parents learned these styles of parenting from their own parents. In fact, if you were to ask a brick wall parent about his or her parenting style, they would most surely say that they are a softy compared to their own mother or father. We are all doing the best we can at any given time. As you've no doubt learned in our work thus far, we can work to change only those thoughts, feelings, and behaviours which we are conscious of and that we desire to change.

It is quite possible that your primary caregivers (or your significant other, friends, or colleagues) are unaware that what they are doing in their relationship with you is abusive. They may notice that they don't feel very good when they hurt you. They may notice that they aren't proud of this pattern of behaviour. They may notice that it harms your relationship with them. But, just as it was in your relationship with food, knowing that something isn't working doesn't necessarily mean that you know why it isn't working or what to change.

These folks that may be harming you with their abusive behaviour are one-hundred percent responsible for their actions, and they may not be conscious that there is anything at all wrong with their actions. This means, you are one-hundred percent responsible for caring for yourself in this relationship. You can't leave it up to the person who is abusing you to validate your feelings and experience of their abusive behaviour. They either aren't conscious of the fact that their behaviour is abusive because they have managed to justify it to themselves somehow, or they know it's abusive, and they do it anyway because it allows them to feel powerful and as though they have control over you. If your goal is to feel peaceful, happy, safe, and free from food as a coping strategy, you can't let your security and safety in any relationship be dependent on the whim of the other person—ever.

The following list comes from a great Web site hosted by Dr. Irene Matiatos. I encourage you to visit her site if any of your current relationships fit these criteria for an emotionally-abusive relationship. Dr. Matiatos is a licensed psychologist in private practice, and her Web site can be found at http://drirene.com

Signs Of An Emotionally Abusive Relationship

The following behaviours are indicative that you are in an emotionally-abusive relationship.

Does someone in your life:

- Ignore your feelings?
- Disrespect you?
- Ridicule or insult you, then tell you it's a joke or that you have no sense of humour?
- Ridicule your beliefs, religion, race, heritage or class?
- Withhold approval, appreciation or affection?
- Give you the silent treatment?
- Walk away without answering you?
- Criticize you, call you names, or yell at you?
- Humiliate you privately or in public?
- Roll their eyes when you talk?
- Give you a hard time about socializing with your friends or family?
- Make you socialize (and keep up appearances) even when you don't feel well?
- Seem to ensure that what you really want is exactly what you *won't* get?
- Tell you that you are too sensitive?
- Hurt you, *especially* when you are down?
- Seem energized by fighting, while fighting exhausts you?
- Have unpredictable mood swings, alternating from good to bad for no apparent reason?
- Present a wonderful face to the world and is well liked by outsiders?
- "Twist" your words, somehow turning what you said against you?
- Try to control decisions, money, even the way you style your hair or wear your clothes?
- Complain about how badly you treat him or her?
- Threaten to leave, or threaten to throw you out?

- Say things that make you feel good, but do things that make you feel bad?
- Ever left you stranded?
- Ever threaten to hurt you or your family?
- Ever hit or pushed you, even "accidentally"?
- Seem to stir up trouble just when you seem to be getting closer to each other?
- Threaten to harm, take away, or abuse something you love: a pet, a child, an object?
- Compliment you enough to keep you happy, yet criticize you enough to keep you insecure?
- Promise to never do something hurtful again? But does!
- Harass you about imagined affairs?
- Manipulate you with lies and contradictions?
- Destroy furniture, punch holes in walls, break appliances?
- Drive like a road-rage junkie?
- Act immature and selfish, yet accuse you of those behaviors?
- Question your every move and motive, somehow questioning your competence?
- Interrupt you; hear but not really listen?
- Make you feel as if you can't win? Damned if you do, damned if you don't?
- Use drugs and/or alcohol? Are things worse then?
- Incite you to rage, which is "proof" that you are to blame?
- Try to convince you they are "right," while you are "wrong"?
- Frequently say things that are later denied, or accuse you of misunderstanding?
- Treat you like a sex object, or as though sex should be provided on demand regardless of how you feel?

Any of these behaviours are cause for concern. A relationship where three or more of these behaviours is common is clearly unhealthful, and these patterns need to be addressed by yourself and with the person who is acting this way. We will address this in our upcoming work on communication in relationships.

If you read the list and found yourself making excuses for some people in your life; taking responsibility for their abusive behaviour; telling yourself that it's not so bad; telling yourself that it's just too much work or energy to end the relationship; or that they would be too upset/angry/distraught if you were to bring their behaviour to their attention and set boundaries around it, well, take a deep breath and admit to yourself right now that you are in an unhealthful relationship and are co-dependently enmeshed in it. Now the healing can begin.

And know that admitting this doesn't mean you are obliged to do anything about it right now. You can sit in this place of conscious awareness and allow yourself to gather information. Gather support for your budding thoughts about what you need, what you deserve, and about how this relationship impacts you. I strongly encourage you to seek the help of a counsellor who is skilled in the area of co-dependency and abusive relationships. You never have to take any action to change the relationship if you don't want to. This is always your call. The more information you have about what is going on in this relationship and how it impacts you currently, the more you can seek solutions for keeping yourself safe and healthy. These solutions should be a part of your overall life goals.

Notice the abusive patterns in this relationship, and prove to yourself over the next little while how the relationship triggers the use of your coping strategies because of its impact on your needs for safety, comfort, nurturing and reassurance—not to mention esteem! If a change needs to be made, you will make it when you are ready.

Discounting and Denying

Many people assume that, if they are not being physically abused, they are not being abused at all. This is just not true. You may be in a relationship which is draining you emotionally and psychologically, even if you are not being physically harmed. You may not really get this yet on a gut level, but trust me when I say that you absolutely

deserve to feel happy, fulfilled, listened to, and safe in all your relationships. You have the right to take steps to create respect and
safety in your connections with others.

There are three main reasons why you would *discount and deny*
that your experience was/is abusive, even though, on a gut level, you
know it to be true. They are:

1. You don't feel deserving of something better.
2. You don't believe anything better exists.
3. You are co-dependent with this person and believe that you
    are responsible for their feelings and needs. You believe
    you need their approval in order to feel okay taking care of
    yourself.

Let's take some time to look at each of these nasty thought patterns and begin to loosen their grip a bit.

Doubting Your Deservedness

It's not necessary for me to meet you to know, in my soul, that
there is nothing about you (even that worst-ever thing that you keep
beating yourself up with) that is so horrible or so lacking that you
deserve to be treated with disrespect and harmed by others' words
or actions. You just think you do, but it's not true at all. However,
because you have told yourself that it *is* true, you believe you are
deserving of crap or that this is the best you can hope for: you are
settling for mistreatment and a lack of security in your life in some
key relationships, whether they are with your partner, your boss,
your children, your friends or relatives. It doesn't matter who they
are. No one on earth has the right to disrespect you, and you always—ALWAYS—have the right to leave a relationship or take a
break if that person is harming you and not willing to acknowledge
and change their behaviour. **Acknowledgement means nothing
without action**.

Take a trip back a few chapters to the piece on core beliefs.
This is what's going on here. These beliefs about your deservedness and your rights in relation to the rights of others are old core
beliefs—coping strategies from a time when you needed to believe

that the problem lay with you in order to make sense of what was going on around you. What is the core belief which you identified for yourself that may be at play in your discounting and denying patterns? Was it something such as: I am not deserving; I am not good enough; what others think and feel is more important than what *I* think and feel?

What needs did you identify as being unmet at that time in your life which would have led you to buy in to that old core belief in the first place? Whatever these needs are (safety and security, love, acceptance, and belongingness), if you are discounting or dismissing your current or past experience of abuse, there is something about this discussion we are having right now that makes you feel these needs will be unmet if you actually allowed yourself to validate how impactful it was(is) for you.

If this piece fits for you at all, it is understandable that your needs for security and love feel threatened right now. You are thinking about challenging some very old and deep patterns of relating to key people in your life, and you don't yet know what the new way of behaving and feeling in a relationship looks like. That's why you must give yourself the space to do some self-reflection, observe the things we are discussing, and then decide for yourself, when you are ready, what actions you will take. Prove to yourself that the things we are talking about are true for you; not just because I say they are but because you experience them. They are real and happening in your life. Let yourself get to the place where you feel ready to do something about it. Until then, be gentle but conscious!

What If There Is Nothing Better Out There?

We have all had the intrusive ideation that goes like this: What if I end this relationship (leave this job, etc.) and I never find anything as good again? What if I just end up alone? What if I leave this relationship and then I realize that I made a mistake and it's too late? What if it's really all me? What if I really *am* too sensitive or too needy? What if...?

In your current state of mind with a lot of co-dependent training, these thoughts seem very likely if not certain outcomes of asserting your needs and taking care of yourself in an unhealthful relationship. You are still potentially wrapping your head around the concept that it really is an unhealthful relationship. And an even more challenging thought is that you deserve to have only healthful, loving and respectful connections in your life, so of course you have some uncertainty.

The solution here is not to get bogged down in the ideation—those worst-case scenario thoughts—but to acknowledge that they are just coping strategies: ways of keeping you where you are because that situation kind of, sort of, meets your needs for comfort, nurturing, safety, connection, and so on. At least, to your current way of thinking, the current situation is familiar. It is what you know, and that, in and of itself, provides a sort of pseudo-security which may be the best sense of security you have ever known.

Think about the family types from Barbara Colorosso's list. If you were raised in a brick wall-esque or jellyfish-like environment and you haven't done a fair amount of personal growth work, the kind of relationship that you are having with others is very likely reminiscent of those early relationship types. This makes perfect sense. We are drawn to what is familiar.

The solution lies in letting it be okay to change the way you "do" relationship. Acknowledge that you have been confused about what was healthful and acceptable. You didn't know any better. Acknowledge that you are not going to be able to truly meet your needs for security and respect, for example, in this connection as it is now, and you are right to want your relationship(s) to be healthful and respectful, even if you don't exactly know what this looks or feels like for you. The backbone family traits are a good place to become clear on healthful connections, and the upcoming chapter on boundaries is also a good place to enhance your awareness of what you can feel justified in seeking in relationship with yourself and others.

Co-Dependence

In reading over the abusive relationship checklist, was there any part of you that said something like, "So and so would be really mad (or really hurt) if I brought up their behaviour;" or, "So and so wouldn't understand, and they'd just think I'm overreacting or too sensitive, so I'd better not even go there?" If I'm even in the ballpark on this one, this means that you have bought into the co-dependent pattern of actually believing that you are responsible for the other person's feelings and needs; moreover, you believe that, if anything you do or think or feel might stir up some unpleasant feelings in others, you had just better not even think about it!

As we discussed in our work on the three stages of relationships, this type of *I'm responsible for them* thinking is only appropriate when you are dealing with a dependent child, and it should naturally lessen as the child matures and can do more for themselves. As an adult in relationship with an adult, you are not responsible for their feelings or their needs. They are. They (the other person in this relationship) might not know this! They might have a very co-dependent perspective on relationships from their own upbringing and truly believe that it's okay for them to blame you for things that don't go well for them. They might think it is all right to expect you to meet their needs and that you really are bad or mean if you stir up any uncomfortable feelings for them.

This is not at all true. It is, however, a very clear sign that both of you must shift from a co-dependent perspective to interdependence before you will be able to have a safe and healthful relationship with this person. If it is the case that the person you are dealing with believes that their co-dependent perspective is actually normal and "right," it is unrealistic to expect them to understand and support any changes that you need to make in order to meet your needs. They won't get it; at least not without some counselling or being open to some reading on healthful relationships. And as long as you believe that your right to take care of yourself is dependent on their approval and understanding of your right to do this, you are stuck.

This is the External Locus of Control at its worst. When you know what you need to do to take care of yourself but are more focused on getting approval and the good old okey dokey from outside of yourself, you are paralyzed. Hopefully, the work you have done thus far on your relationship with yourself has allowed you to begin to have some sense of an Internal Locus of Control (letting your own feelings and needs determine your choices). Remember that my ideal ratio is 75/25. That's 75% influence from within and 25% from without. And always, your final decision must be one that feels right and peaceful within—one that respects you first and foremost.

The ticket to obtaining this ideal ratio in any harmful relationship you may have is to let go of wanting the approval of the person who is harming you or for whom you feel responsible. Remember, they obviously think that their behaviour is okay and justified in some way, or they wouldn't do it. To expect them to support your desire to change the way you relate with them, when they really do believe that their behaviour is okay, is not realistic. Let go of judging the "rightness" or "wrongness" of your behaviour based on their comfort and approval of it (the External Locus of Control), and let it be okay (offer yourself the reassurance and support that you need) for you to take action solely based on what feels truly honouring and respectful of you.

Courageous conversations are often required when you shift from harmful patterns in relationships to those that are honouring and respectful of you and will ultimately lead you to a feeling of inner peace and groundedness. You must be willing to stand up for yourself and set clear boundaries about what you need, regardless of whether the key people in your life understand and support this. Anything else is still co-dependence and External Locus of Control. This leaves you with very little or no power, needing your old coping strategies and just generally feeling stuck and crappy!

Different Doesn't Mean Wrong

Remember the piece we discussed a while back about it being natural for us to feel awkward and uncertain, even a bit phony, when we are trying a new way of being in relationship with others? It *is* new and different. This is the point. This is what you want! And to expect yourself to feel the same or to feel entirely relaxed and grounded when you are shifting some major old perspectives is an unrealistic expectation. If you allow this expectation to go unchallenged, you will begin to feel that what you are doing is wrong or bad, simply because it feels different from what you are accustomed to. As you are making changes and trying new behaviours, expect some sense of discomfort or difference within. It should not be traumatizing anxiety but a little pitter patter, some butterflies, some flushing of the cheeks and chest area—even some tears would be normal. This is simply because the Drill Sgt. really does believe that you are doing something wrong in advocating for yourself. It goes against the old core belief that he has been reinforcing for decades! So remind yourself and the Drill Sgt. that these sensations of mild discomfort are normal and necessary components of change, and those old beliefs are being triggered right now because of your need for security and reassurance; furthermore, you are going to meet these needs for yourself in a way that doesn't require you to be in a harmful relationship.

The Power of Self-Love

Be very aware that as you grow and take steps to have healthful, interdependent relationship with all the people in your life, you are creating the space for these key people with whom you have had a co-dependent and/or abusive connection to grow as well. The most loving thing you could ever do for anyone who is in your life is to learn to truly love yourself. As you do this, you will forever be able to be a loving presence in your relationships. You will forever only allow respectful loving behaviour in your life. This is a great gift to others because it provides the safe space and the modeling for what a truly healthful and loving relationship can be.

The more we love ourselves, the more we set boundaries with others from a place of quiet confidence, strength, and clarity rather than our initial attempts which are often very defensive, doubt-rid-den and judgemental. When we come from a place of strength and self-love rather than from defensive/protective reaction, it is so much easier for others to hear us.

I invite you to stop looking outside yourself for validation of what you feel and need, and offer yourself a compassionate, trusting and responsive ear. Share your needs with others, and make a conscious choice to spend time and energy with those who naturally support and enhance the healthful and respectful choices you are making for yourself. If you wonder who these people are, they are the ones who do not make you feel awkward or insecure. You rarely use food to cope and are not likely to have bad body thoughts during your time in their presence. If you have even one of these folks in your life, I encourage you to deepen this friendship and spend more time with them (and others like them) and far less time with anyone who triggers you to use your coping strategies before, during, or after a visit with them.

Allow yourself to take an authentic look at what's going on in your relationships right now. Be gentle. Be on the lookout for any of your coping strategies, such as: all-or-nothing thinking, intrusive ideation, and old core beliefs. Just acknowledge them as you look for the underlying unmet need which triggered them. Take steps to acknowledge, validate, and meet those needs as best you can.

21

Boundaries In Action

No doubt the previous chapter on abusive patterns in relationships raised the question, *Okay, so how do I make things different if they aren't the way I want them to be now?* That's a significant question, because it means you are at the determination or perhaps even the action stage of change, and all you need is a solid sense of how to go about creating more respectful and honouring relationships. To this end, we are going to discuss the concept of boundaries. We will look at what a boundary is, what happens when we don't have very strong or healthful boundaries, and how to go about establishing these boundaries in new and existing relationships without alienating everyone in our lives.

The topic of boundaries is key to your recovery from food as a coping strategy. The work we have done so far on your relationship with yourself plays a big part in your sense of deservedness and confidence in setting clear boundaries with others. The last few chapters were meant to support you to have a clear understanding of past and current relationships which may be reinforcing old beliefs and making it difficult for you to feel deserving of the love, security, and respect which you desire in life.

This piece on boundaries will help the Drill Sgt. and your Authentic Self to know what is "normal" in terms of personal boundaries. In other words, you are about to discover what you are entitled to—what you deserve—simply because you exist.

What Are Boundaries And Why Are They Important To Me?

Healthful boundaries are a fundamental piece of creating balance in our lives. The things which we allow and don't allow to happen around us, and to us, tell people a lot about our self-esteem and how we regard ourselves and, ultimately, what they can get away with in their relationship with us!

In other words, if you have good self-esteem, you have strong and healthful boundaries. You feel capable of asking for what you need and letting people know clearly and directly when your needs are unmet. This lets the people in relationship with you know that you expect honesty and integrity from others, and you are willing to bring this to the table yourself. You wouldn't be able or willing to tolerate dishonesty or a lack of responsibility in any relationship. Someone who isn't ready for honesty or directness in their communications with others, or who wants to be able to blame others for their behaviour, wouldn't want to be in a relationship with you because you would be constantly challenging them to take responsibility for their actions. So the clearer you are in your boundaries and what you expect and are willing to accept from others, the more you draw healthful, balanced, responsible people to you: people who have the same goals for honesty and integrity in their relationships as you do.

If your self-esteem is low and you question your worth or deservedness to have what you need and want, you will be less able to clearly ask for what you need and will often feel as though everyone else gets what they want while you don't. You will often beat around the bush, or not say anything, then feel hurt and frustrated when the other person didn't intuit your need. Depending on your level of self-esteem and what you have been taught by role models in your life, you may see getting what you want and need as beyond your control. You may turn the responsibility for your needs, and your life on the whole, to someone else, letting them tell you what you should have or what you can and cannot do or be. Either way, you are a sitting duck, just waiting for someone with a strong need to control and dominate someone else to come along and make you feel "worthy".

The problem with that, of course, is that anyone who has such a strong need to dominate and control your life has even lower self-esteem than you—guaranteed! You are looking for someone to take over because you feel overwhelmed with the responsibility for you. They are looking for someone to dominate because they are over-whelmed with the responsibility for themselves, and they want to be able to focus outside of themselves and blame you for everything that isn't working for them. It may not start out that way; it may seem like the perfect "opposites attract" connection. But soon, when you are not doing what you are "supposed" to do or not behaving in the way this person thinks you should, you will begin to have some power struggles, and it is just a matter of time before you get tired of being told what to do and leave. They may become tired of being "unappreciated" and leave to find someone who will let them run their lives. And that's the best-case scenario this pairing can bring! The worst scenario is when the controller doesn't leave but instead escalates their violence and victimization behaviour

Having a sense of your right to healthful relationships and know-ing how to assert yourself effectively and respectfully is what bound-aries are all about. You may not be able to always get what you need in certain relationships, it's true. But this doesn't mean that your need can't be met—you just need to look for it to be met elsewhere. If it's a fundamental need (safety or security, for example) which is unmet in a particular relationship, you will have to consider whether you want to continue to have this relationship at all and what pur-pose it could possibly serve in your life.

But let's not jump the gun. Let's practice with identifying boundaries that you would like to have in your relationship with yourself and others, and how to go about setting them.

When we have a clear boundary about something, say. . . physical touch from others, we know what kind of touch we are comfortable allowing. This knowledge is very important. Before we can begin to set a clear and effective boundary, we must first be aware of what feels acceptable *to us* and what doesn't. And, a boundary doesn't really exist or count for anything if we aren't going to follow through and uphold it should it be crossed.

A boundary only has meaning when you can trust yourself to uphold it when necessary.

For example, if someone touches you in a way that goes past your comfort level/boundary, you must be able to take steps to meet your needs for safety and trust in yourself, for this boundary to have any meaning at all. Asserting a boundary around being touched can look like anything from inching a little farther away from someone who's standing in your space, to saying, "I'm not comfortable with hugging," to ending a relationship with someone who consistently demonstrates a lack of respect for you and your needs in this area. Whether you choose any of these boundary examples or something else, it depends entirely on your needs at that moment.

Remember, there is no such thing as a right or wrong feeling, there are only needs that you have which are met or unmet. So, if you feel uncomfortable, there's no need to judge it: the thing to do is to recognize that feelings are indicators of needs, and ask yourself what unmet needs are triggering this uncomfortable feeling. And, if the person you are setting the boundary with criticizes or judges you as being "too sensitive," "selfish," and so on, one thing that you know for sure is that their need, whatever it is, is unmet by your boundary setting. This is not your problem. It's not your responsibility, and you don't have to do anything with that at all, aside from reasserting your boundary. Whether anyone outside of yourself validates your need or your right to have a boundary, it is not important.

Taking steps to create a comfortable and respectful environment for your Self is.

If I haven't yet convinced you that boundaries are worth your time and effort, let me say this: as long as you have unclear or un-healthful boundaries, you will continue to use food as a coping strat-egy. This is because as long as you cannot trust yourself to put your needs first when push comes to shove, your fundamental needs for safety and security will be unmet. And, as we've discussed earlier, the primary reason why we restrict or eat when we are not hungry is that we have an unmet need for safety and security.

What Kinds Of Boundaries Do I Have Now?

Healthful boundaries are important because they demonstrate to ourselves and to others that we have high self-esteem and can rec-ognize our right to create the most healthful, respectful relationships we can, and to distance ourselves from people who do not respect our boundaries or meet our needs. As a result, we attract only those people who also love and respect themselves and who honour our right to set boundaries and care for ourselves.

For most of us, old core beliefs borne out of poor treatment, poor modeling and/or misinterpretations of others' behavior in relation to us as children, have led us to respond in one of three ways. All are very harmful to our self-esteem and to our relationship with others.

1. We develop "ultra-rigid" boundaries (those of us who fit this pattern are commonly labeled "control freaks") where things must be *just so*, especially ourselves, and we become very angry, frustrated, and/or impatient (even if we don't express it outwardly) if things don't go as planned and we don't im-mediately get what we expect. We have a strong need for perfectionism in ourselves and others, and we don't tolerate what we perceive as "sub-standard" performance from our-selves or others. It frustrates us to be labeled as controlling or dominating by others when, from our perspective, what we are doing is taking care of ourselves and ensuring things run smoothly.

2. If our boundaries are weak or nonexistent, we consistently send the message to ourselves and others that what we want or need doesn't matter, we have no power, and "things" just happen to us. We believe that we just don't have the right to take care of ourselves if someone else might get mad or their needs are unmet. An example of this may be agreeing to date someone that you don't like so that their feelings aren't hurt; or staying in a relationship that you don't want to be in because you would feel guilt if the other person became upset.

3. Then there's the individual who has ultra-rigid boundaries with themselves but has nonexistent boundaries with others. Most people with disordered eating fall into this category. We expect the world from ourselves—nothing we do is ever good enough—and we can't receive positive feedback from others because we "know" we could have done better. When it comes to our relationship with others, we're the giver! We somehow seem to find ourselves in relationships where we are the one listening, supporting, giving, giving, giving, understanding, compromising, and so on. When we dare to ask for a need to be met, we may get flack and/or feel guilt and shame! This only serves to reinforce the belief that we are undeserving and that it was wrong of us to ask for what we needed at the outset. Because of our old belief system and from our old way of being in relationship with others, we are unable to see that it was perfectly appropriate for us to ask for a need to be met, and it was likely both the way we asked and the fact that our need didn't jive with the needs of the person we were asking which lead to our lack of success. So, rather than asking another way or asking a different person, we take one-hundred percent responsibility for the lack of success with getting our needs met. We blame and internally reprimand ourselves. We then add insult to injury by committing to giving even more, and outwardly we kiss up to the person in an effort to make up for our *transgression* (who did

we think we were, after all?). All this does is reinforce the old belief and make us feel worse, while making the other person acutely aware that they can deny us our needs and we will come back for more.

Whichever of the three patterns above sits closest to your heart and behaviour, the following exploration of boundaries will clarify what must change in your behaviour and your perception of yourself in order to develop the trust in yourself which will lead to a feeling of safety and security within, and to a lasting shift in your relationship with food and body image.

The following checklists of unclear, unhealthful, and life-enhancing boundaries have come to me many times through a variety of workshops, courses, and colleagues over the past 15 or so years. I have no idea where these handouts originated, as there has never been a reference listed. If you know who created these great resources, I welcome hearing from you. I would very much like to credit the originator of these handouts and ensure they are acknowledged for their work.

To help you identify the boundaries which you have that may be impacting your relationship with yourself and others, and ultimately your use of food as a coping strategy, take a look at the lists of unclear and unhealthful boundaries on the next two pages, and make note of the ones that you would say you currently have **most of the time**.

Signs Of Unclear Boundaries

- My good feelings about who I am stem from being liked by you.
- My good feelings about who I am stem from receiving approval from you.
- My mental attention is focused on pleasing you.
- My mental attention is focused on protecting you.
- My self-esteem is bolstered by solving your problems.
- My self-esteem is bolstered by relieving your pain.

- My own hobbies and interests are put aside. My time is spent sharing your interests and hobbies.
- I am not aware of how I feel. I am aware of how you feel.
- I am not aware of what I want. I ask what you want.
- The dreams I have for my future are often linked to you.
- My fear of rejection determines what I say or do.
- My fear of your anger determines what I say or do.
- I use giving as a way of feeling safe in our relationship.
- My social circle diminishes as I involve myself with you.
- I put my values aside in order to connect with you.
- I value your opinion and way of doing things more than my own.
- The quality of my life is in relation to the quality of yours.

Signs of Unhealthful Boundaries
- Telling all.
- Talking at an intimate level on the first meeting.
- Falling in love with anyone who reaches out.
- Falling in love with a new acquaintance.
- Being overwhelmed by or preoccupied with a person.
- Acting on the first sexual impulse.
- Being sexual for your partner, not yourself.
- Going against personal values or rights to please the other.
- Not noticing when someone else displays inappropriate boundaries.
- Not noticing when someone else invades your boundaries.
- Accepting food, gifts, touch or sex that you don't want.
- Touching a person without asking.
- Taking as much as you can get for the sake of getting.
- Giving as much as you can for the sake of giving.
- Allowing someone to take as much as they can from you.
- Letting others direct your life.
- Letting others describe your reality.
- Letting others define you.
- Believing others can anticipate your needs.

- Believing others should read your mind.
- Believing you can read another person's mind.
- Expecting others to fill your needs automatically.
- Falling apart so someone will take care of you.
- Abusing yourself (sexually, physically, emotionally or spiritually).
- Venting your anger on an innocent bystander.

Now that you have a sense of what unhelpful or downright harmful boundaries might be active in your life, take some time and think about your core beliefs:

- Which core beliefs are at play in reinforcing these unhelpful or harmful boundaries?
- When you catch yourself engaging in any of those old patterns of behaviour, what new tools and thoughts would be useful to reinforce and remember?

Also, take a moment and look at each of the items on these lists which you marked as relevant to you in your recent past.

- Ask yourself what coping strategies are triggered in you when this particular boundary violation occurs.

Give yourself the gift of seeing how those experiences, some of which may happen to you daily, trigger you to have bad body thoughts, feel anxious, be depressed, or perhaps to use food to cope.

No doubt you are asking yourself, "What can I do to begin to have strong and healthy boundaries with myself and others?"

In order answer to this question effectively, let's first take a look at some examples of healthful boundaries. As you read, make note of the ones that you can currently trust yourself to enforce, **most of the time**, if they were violated or pressed.

Life-Enhancing Boundaries And Rights
- I have a right to be treated with dignity and respect.
- I have a right to have and express all my feelings.
- I have a right to take care of myself—first.
- I have a right to be listened to and taken seriously.
- I have a right to make mistakes.
- I have a right to say NO! I do not need to justify myself or give reasons.
- I have a right to say NO without feeling guilt.
- I have a right to say NO to anything I feel I am not ready for.
- I have a right to say NO to anything that violates my values.
- I have a right to say NO to anything that I feel is unsafe.
- I have a right to terminate conversations when I feel humiliated or put down, whether the other person is "done" or not.
- I have a right to choose with whom to spend my time.
- I have a right to play and have fun.
- I have a right to set limits for myself.
- I have a right to make my own choices and decisions.
- I have a right to choose my own spiritual beliefs.
- I have a right to physical and emotional privacy.
- I have a right to grieve.
- I have a right to talk about things that are important to me.
- I have a right to be angry.
- I have a right to express my needs.
- I have a right to make noise, to laugh, and to cry out loud.

So, what did you discover about yourself? Do you have some boundaries firmly in place now that you may not have recognized as boundaries? Do you have a better awareness of what life-enhancing boundaries are?

I am aware that I'm about to sound a bit like a broken record, but **these are key points for you to really "get"**:

A. Having clear boundaries means that you have the ability to identify what you need and then take effective and respectful steps to meet this need.

B. Having clear boundaries and being able to assert them when necessary is a key method for getting your needs for security and approval met.

C. Meeting your needs for security and approval consistently in healthful ways is imperative for you to overcome your use of food to cope once and for all.

You will prove the above statements to yourself over the next few weeks, because every time you see yourself violating a boundary or permit someone else to violate a boundary, you will see yourself turning to your harmful coping strategies.

Once you are aware that you have an unmet need, you can ask yourself, "What is the boundary that I can assert right now to meet my need for X in this situation?" Without an awareness of the underlying unmet need, you won't often know what boundary is being pressed or violated and what action is required.

So, with the addition of your newfound awareness of boundaries, the whole picture of attending to your unmet needs looks like this:

a) Notice the coping strategy thought, feeling, or behavior that you are currently engaged in or have just engaged in.

b) Identify the underlying triggering need.

c) Then identify the boundary that you could put in place in order to meet your need.

d) Take action.

Now that you have a better sense of what life-enhancing boundaries look like and how important they are to your overall healing and quality of life, it's time to explore the "take action" part of the picture—how to create clear and strong boundaries in your relationship with others. If you are feeling at all anxious about this and are wanting to skip this part, tune out, eat, distance or detach yourself, it is because your needs for safety and security are unmet when you consider changing the way you currently "do" relationships. That's a great indicator that you really need to explore setting healthful boundaries a.s.a.p! It's also an indicator that you have gone into all-or-nothing thinking. You may be imagining that setting boundaries is equivalent to being a bull in a china shop. Possibly, you imagine yourself alienating everyone in your life and being labeled a supreme bitch or a selfish jerk. Am I getting warm? And, because it can be scary to try a new behaviour and you have the Drill Sgt. going to all-or-nothing extremes, we will take a moment now to discuss any fears, assumptions, and resistance to setting boundaries. Then we will look at *how* to set them once you are a little more relaxed. Okay?

Resistance to Setting Boundaries: Fears and Assumptions

Take a moment to consider your answer to the following question: What thoughts and feelings surface when you consider setting clear boundaries with others? Are you fearing judgement, anger, labeling and such?

In this moment, are you feeling drawn to any of your coping strategies, such as: food, avoidance, old core beliefs, or anxiety? If so, ask yourself: "By looking at my boundaries in this way, what needs do I have that are unmet right now?" Make note of them, and take the time to address your Authentic Self and your Drill Sgt.

If your Authentic Self is feeling at all resistant to exploring boundaries and to the concept of asserting them with others, now is the perfect time to check in with her and ask what needs she fears will be unmet if you begin to explore boundaries in your relationship with yourself and others. Write these fears down, and dialogue with her about each one individually. Do you remember our work on compassionate goal setting? What does she need to know in order to feel safe moving forward in this work?

Likely, one of the needs that she is assuming will be unmet is the fundamental need for security. If so, now is the perfect time to remind her that when you allow your boundaries to be compromised, it doesn't meet *her* needs for security. It is important for you, the Nurturing Parent, to be able to care for her in a way that is respectful and responsible, and that builds a fully-integrated Self. You might choose to remind her that it is the old core belief that is kicking in and creating doubt as to her lovability, acceptability, and right to care for herself. Chances are, after reassuring her in this way, she will be feeling open to moving forward. If there is still some resistance or anxiety (remember that the PLA is all about the all-or-nothing assumptions we are making and our co-dependent training), reassure her that you will take the time to check in with her and identify her needs before you actually assert a boundary with anyone. Commit to checking with her first, and honour that commitment.

The Drill Sgt. will likely be concerned about your need for approval and acceptance and control. He will want to be assured that you can handle setting boundaries in a way that has the greatest likelihood of success and the least likelihood of upsetting others. The Authentic Self will be concerned with upsetting others, too, but often her need is coming more from security than approval. Check in with the Drill Sgt. and ask what needs he has that he fears will be unmet if you learn to set boundaries in your relationship with others and with yourself. Then, for each need, take the time to come up with a way of meeting that need which will work for the Drill Sgt., and allow him to comfortably step aside and let you handle this.

Now, explore the following questions which pertain to specific examples from your past where boundaries were violated. This will give you a crystal-clear understanding of the needs that were or were not met by allowing the violation. You can then take steps to meet them in a more self-respecting way in the future.

1. Think of a recent experience where a boundary of yours was violated and you did not reinforce it.
2. In that situation, what unmet needs led you to feel your boundary was being violated? Offer yourself some empathy

and compassion for the discomfort you experienced in that situation.

3. What needs were being met in choosing not to reinforce your boundary? Offer yourself some empathy and compassion for needing to cope in this way at that time.

4. How could you get those needs met in a way which doesn't compromise your self-esteem?

5. What needs could be met if you were able to reinforce your boundary in those situations?

Come up with a Plan A, B, and C for how you would like to address any future similar situation.

Repeat this exercise three more times for other past boundary violations.

Setting Clear And Effective Boundaries Requires Inner Dialogue

If you have taken the time to run through the above exercise a few times, I'm betting that you have a much stronger sense of what sabotages your boundary setting and how to attend to the underlying needs of the Drill Sgt. and your Authentic Self in ways that respect you. I'm also betting that you have a much better sense of what needs could be met if you were able to consistently reinforce and uphold your boundaries with others.

You may recall that when we talked about trust in yourself, we discussed checking in with your Authentic Self and getting clear on what she needed in order to feel safe and trusting of you in certain situations. In essence, we were talking about inner boundaries at that time. If you have been using the inner dialogue tool at all since then, this is really the same thing but externalized. We are looking at it as boundaries, so it has more of a sense of being in relation to other people rather than just between your Self and you. And the concept is the same. At whatever point you become aware that you have needs which are unmet, whether it is a coping thought, feeling, or behaviour that is surfacing, check in.

In terms of what boundaries you need to have in place in certain situations, your Authentic Self is frequently your best source of clarity. For example, let's say you have the thought that you would like to be in a relationship. You might notice that you start to feel anxious, have some bad body thoughts, or find yourself eating mindlessly. You check in and discover that your Authentic Self has a need for reassurance. She needs to know that you are not going to compromise her need for safety and security to meet your need for relationship. You, the Nurturing Parent, can reassure her that you recognize her need for security and that it is valid. Because of the co-dependent patterns or outright abusive behaviours she has experienced in previous relationships, she has a good reason to question her ability to trust you to take care of her in relationship with someone else. You are just beginning to heal those wounds; therefore, trust in yourself has not yet been developed.

Ask her what she needs to know you will do/won't do that will allow her to feel as though her need for security is being met. And whatever she says, as long as it is reasonable, your first responsibility, just like parent to child, is to her. So, if she says, "If I feel criticized by him, I will call him on it and tell him that isn't okay," and this feels reasonable to you, it is your responsibility to meet her need, honour her boundary, and follow through when push comes to shove, even if part of you feels frightened of rejection or attack.

You will find this kind of commitment to yourself to be very grounding and enhancing of your self-esteem. If the request doesn't seem reasonable to you when presented by your Authentic Self, you can articulate this and negotiate to find a middle ground that will work for both of you. Whatever you do, remember that your Authentic Self is very intuitive. If she is uncomfortable with something, you would do well to acknowledge this and do whatever you can in that moment to create a sense of comfort, even if you don't truly understand her need fully. Trust that your current lack of understanding comes from your old co-dependent training and your alexithymia, and not because there is a lack of credibility to your

Authentic Self's need. For now you must be willing to err on the side of honouring yourself over others, always.

As you develop more empathy and compassion for yourself and begin to validate your needs and feelings more easily and authentically, your ability to assert your boundaries will grow exponentially as will your self-esteem. So for now, even if you don't have a strong sense of what might be creating distress or anxiety for your Authentic Self, if you err on the side of taking her word for it, you will come to a sense of wholeness and integration much more rapidly.

And what about the Drill Sgt.? Let's explore a situation in which you are aware of your need, but the Drill Sgt. tells you that you are not allowed to meet it. Initially, this will happen frequently.

You have a need for rest, for example, and you know it. You have committed to going out with a friend for dinner and a movie. The Drill Sgt. has a mandate to meet your need for approval, externally. He will demand that you go because it's the only way he can imagine your need for approval being met. So in this scenario, the Drill Sgt., in his co-dependency, is badgering you to compromise your own need for rest in order to meet a need for approval. If you consider this in terms of Maslow's hierarchy, the need for love, acceptance, and belongingness does sit below and therefore comes before the need for esteem (which is your own regard and caring for yourself): although I'm sure sleep is a fundamental physiological need and consequently trumps everything. But the Drill Sgt. is relentless. You will need to find a way to meet the Drill Sgt.'s need before you will be able to comfortably honour *your* need and to rest in peace, so to speak. If the Drill Sgt.'s need is for approval, how can you get this need met without compromising your esteem need for rest?

Well, what about calling your friend and saying, "Hi Helen. I know we have a date to meet tonight, but I'm really needing some rest this evening. Would you be willing to postpone our movie night until next week?"

Who's going to say no? Do you truly have any friends that would say, "No. You get your butt out here and have dinner with me now!"? I surely hope not.

Helen may propose that she pop by for a quick cup of tea just to connect. This may feel good to you or it may not. She may ask a few questions just to see if you might want to come but just need a push. Or she may be prone to believe everything is about her and question whether there is something she has done to upset you. If so, that's not your piece of work. It is hers. Your piece is to clearly and respectfully articulate your needs. Respect her enough to trust that she can take care of her own feelings and articulate her own needs. Let it go.

Here is a rule of thumb for every single life situation as you are learning to connect with your Authentic Self and to set boundaries: **Do not commit to anything in the moment of being asked.**

Nothing, nada, zip! No matter how great an idea it seems. No matter how absolutely certain you are that you are going to want to do this thing. If you are being asked to go for coffee as you are walking out of a movie with a friend, respect yourself first. Say, "Let me think about that for a moment." Or, if it's not something that must be decided in ten seconds, and most things aren't, then you could say, "Let me get back to you on that. I'm not sure." Then check in with your Authentic Self. Is there any PLA when you think about that coffee or whatever you are being asked to do? Any at all? If so, there's some all-or-nothing thinking and some co-dependency influencing your decision, and you are best to decline if it is an in-the-moment decision. Or you could take some time to write about your confusion before you respond to the invitation/request.

So, if Helen proposes to come over briefly, you respond with, "Let me think about that and call you back." And then think about it, and call her back. Don't avoid her out of fear. Call her and say, "You know, Helen, I'm just too pooped for company tonight. I'll call you tomorrow and we will set up a new date."

Initially, in this kind of situation, the Drill Sgt. may not fully buy in to your right to rest rather than go out. He may choose to hang on to some anxiety and uncertainty until you connect with Helen again and see that all is well. And if all is not well; if Helen was really disappointed and hasn't let it go, you will be able to talk about it if the friendship is a healthful one. She can express herself and the needs that were unmet. You will be able to hear her, acknowledge this, and validate her need without taking responsibility for it. She feels heard. You don't take it on. All is well. If the friendship is healthful, there will be enough trust and understanding between you for Helen to support you to care for yourself, and she would expect the same from you.

You see, it is okay for Helen to be disappointed about the movie and dinner. Of course she would be, unless she was pooped out too and was happy to stay home. There is nothing wrong with her being disappointed. It is healthful and natural. Let her have her feeling. Don't get in there and try to caretake and prevent her from her authentic experience.

Just because she is upset or disappointed doesn't mean you have done anything wrong. This is a natural response to a sudden shift in a pleasurable plan. Soon you will be able to comfortably say, "I can tell you are disappointed. I was really looking forward to tonight, too." You will be able to name the feeling that you see in the other person. You won't be afraid of it because you know you are not going to feel guilt or be responsible. You won't be saying *don't be disappointed* or *I hope you're not upset*. You will be letting her feel what she feels and acknowledging her feelings.

This is true respect: letting someone feel as they do without your taking responsibility for it or needing to do anything to change how they are feeling. Once you have begun to separate yourself from any old co-dependent training that is within you, you will see for yourself how wonderful it is to witness someone's feelings and not need to do anything about that. And you will begin to see how safe it is for you to share your feelings with others with no expectation that they will feel responsible or need to rescue you. Beautiful friendships emerge out of such respectful behaviour.

22

Social Isolation And Withdrawal

When we discussed boundaries, you may have come face to face with some fear about asking for what you need from others. What you also likely discovered is that you will sometimes choose to isolate yourself, cocoon, and perhaps even risk losing the relationship all together rather than having a direct conversation about a boundary violation or some needs that were unmet in a certain situation. This kind of response, the cocooning rather than attending to the problem, is only a temporary band-aid solution. It will often lead us to use our primary coping strategy (food) to distance ourselves from the feelings that are triggered by the unmet needs for security and approval that we believe we have at that moment. Let's look at how we can make it safer for you to meet your needs in ways that truly demonstrate respect for yourself.

Why Do I Do It?

First, let's explore what leads you to isolate yourself. In short, it's all about how much you trust yourself to set boundaries and to only engage in relationships which are healthful and supportive of you. The degree to which you doubt your ability to assert your needs will be the degree to which you isolate. In other words, if you don't trust yourself to say *no* to others, you will likely refrain from much social interaction, or you will find yourself overloaded with social commitments which are unrewarding and lack depth. You may not even be conscious that this is what motivates you to distance yourself from others. Your Drill Sgt. may have tried to explain your behaviour through his old core-belief perspective, telling you all sorts of stories about how weird and unlikable you are; how no one really cares whether you are around or not; how people are only going to judge you; and how unattractive or unintelligent you are if you go out. None of this is at all true. It's just more of that coping strategy of negative core beliefs and bad body thoughts kicking in. And you now know that this is just an indication of unmet needs for security and acceptance.

As you begin to hone your skill of identifying the unmet needs that drive your coping behaviour, you will be presented with many opportunities, big and small, to strengthen your trust in yourself and create more security by validating your needs, setting clear boundaries, and proving how effectively you can care for yourself. It is likely that at the start of this new way of looking out for yourself you will notice yourself feeling anxious and resistant. There are two key pieces at play here:

1. Somehow, your Authentic Self and not your Nurturing Parent is front and centre trying to navigate this new terrain on her own. This is dangerous, because your Authentic Self is still very young and still needs a lot of reassurance and support to behave in a new way and not buy in to those old core beliefs. She does not have the capacity to rationalize and empathize in the way the Nurturing Parent does. She must not be made to handle scary and stressful situations such as boundary setting. You wouldn't make your five-year-old child go on his own to confront someone about security or approval needs that aren't being met, so you can't expect your Authentic Self to have the courage and ability to do so either.

2. Your Drill Sgt. senses the insecurity, fear, and doubt of the Authentic Self and is doing his "motivation through criti-

cism" to try and get you back in to a "safe" and familiar place. You will likely hear the Drill Sgt. insisting that your needs are not valid or important. You may be aware of him calling you names, such as, weak and needy, when you are experimenting with acknowledging your feelings and needs to others. I encourage you to acknowledge the Drill Sgt.'s comments and then, as we have discussed, ask him what his intent is. Remember: seek to understand.

The solution? Notice the distress and resistance about boundary setting, and call forth your Adult, Nurturing Parent. The Nurturing Parent can then reassure the Authentic Self that her feelings and needs are valid; that she has a right to ask for what she needs and that they, the Nurturing Parent, will take over from here. (Try the hand-on-the-tummy thing here. It really does help to ground you and establish a stronger sense of connection between your Parent and Authentic Self.)

Another key piece for you to "get" about boundary setting is that it doesn't matter if you speak up for yourself *in the moment* of a boundary violation or unmet need, or if you mention it days, weeks or months afterward, there is no statute of limitations on setting a boundary and asking for what you need. Many times we suffer through uncertainty and a lack of security in relationships, or we withdraw from them completely because we fear a certain pattern or experience repeating itself, yet we don't know how to assert our needs and believe it is too late to say anything after the fact. Then it happens again, and we believe we can't say anything because we let it go the first time, and they might wonder why we didn't say anything then. "It will make *them* uncomfortable," we tell ourselves. "They will think I've been thinking about it all this time," or "They will think that I'm really sensitive if I'm bringing this up after so long." We tell ourselves any number of things, but they all come back to some very obvious all-or-nothing thinking that keeps us stuck in our co-dependent pattern of feeling responsible for and worrying about other people's feelings.

It is simply untrue that you can't come back to it later, if you don't say something *in the moment*. And if anyone has tried to tell you so, they are simply trying to avoid either taking responsibility for their behaviour or hearing your side of the experience, or both. If you choose not to respectfully assert your needs because it might make someone else uncomfortable, you are behaving co-dependently and taking responsibility for someone else's needs and feelings without giving them a chance to do so themselves. This is called *enabling*, and it prevents the person from learning to take care of their own needs and feelings. It is neither kind nor caring to enable someone. It stunts their emotional growth; it is a sign of a lack of respect for the individual. In other words, when we caretake or enable someone to behave irresponsibly or ignorantly, we are saying that we don't believe this person is capable of taking care of themselves. This is a significant statement of a lack of respect.

If this is a pattern that pertains to you, you may not have ever thought of it in this light. Don't let the Drill Sgt. do a number on you for not having figured this out or for having engaged in this pattern. Go back to the discussion we had a few chapters ago on dependence and co-dependence, and you will get a prompt reinforcement of the fact that you came by this pattern honestly. Likely, your primary relationship role models taught you to caretake and led you to believe that you were responsible for the needs and feelings of others.

You may have considered yourself to be saving the person distress or saving yourself an argument. You are in a co-dependent connection with this person if your connection is such that you believe you can't respectfully call them on their behavior when your needs are unmet, just because they might get mad or hurt. I encourage you to look at your role in maintaining this co-dependency:

- What part have you played in setting up the relationship to be one in which only "positive" things are brought to this person's attention?
- In what way have you engaged in caretaking behaviour which sent the other person the message that they are not

responsible for their actions or for how they express their feelings?

- What happens within yourself? When you avoid speaking to this person about something which is not working well for you in the relationship, what other behavioural-, thought- or feeling-level coping strategies do you see arising in you? Do you have more negative body thoughts perhaps; reach for food; restrict; over-exercise; drink; shop; feel fearful, angry, depressed; or notice your all-or-nothing thinking about other things stepping up a notch? Maybe even some intrusive ideation kicks in.
- What is the impact on your relationship with this person when you do not speak about what you need? Does it impact how close and connected you feel to them? Do you find yourself feeling resentful or expecting that they will do something for you to "repay" you for not calling them on their behaviour?
- What has happened in the past with this person if you have expressed a need or a feeling in relation to their behaviour toward or around you? Have you been judged, criticized, yelled at or shut down? Has the person chosen to verbalize all the things they don't like about you without really hearing you? If so, it's time to revisit both Chapter 20 on abusive relationships and Chapter 21 on boundaries. Get really clear about what is going on.

Begin to challenge yourself to ask for what you need. Challenge yourself to let this person deal with their own feelings and needs. We will talk more specifically about how to go about this in the next chapter on Communication in Relationships. The reason we are talking about it now is that often we will isolate ourselves physically and/or emotionally (have few deep or intimate connections) because we always seem to find ourselves caretaking for others' feelings and needs, and, frankly, it's exhausting! Therefore, it seems safer to have very few people in our lives or to keep our connections very superficial at best.

A comment I hear very often from my clients, and one I myself uttered to my counsellor all those years ago, is: "No one knows who I truly am, and, if they did, they wouldn't like me." The core belief that we are unlikable, therefore we must keep our true selves hidden away, is behind a giant portion of any isolating behaviour and most of our other coping strategies as well. This belief leads us to take up that "giving" role in our relationships. We are the "great listener"; we are the supporter; and we are often willing to settle for the dregs. Just because someone is spending time with us, we often feel indebted. It's as if they are doing us a favor that we are unworthy of. If this is our belief, we can find it extremely difficult to ask this person for anything. After all, we may believe that they are going out of their way to be our friend. Do we really have the right to ask for more? This is the old core belief talking. It triggers you to feel overwhelmed by the potential for rejection or abandonment, so we settle. Our way of coping with this scenario is often to isolate ourselves both physically and emotionally. Keeping to ourselves often feels the safest course of action.

It is very important to take stock of any relationships that may fit the pattern I have described above, and ask yourself the following:

- Is this person capable of having a more equal relationship with me if I were to ask for what I needed more often?
- Is our relationship as it is because I have allowed it to be one-sided for fear of rejection?
- Is this person someone with whom I like spending time? (Do you look forward to it? And does your use of harmful coping strategies decrease or increase when you are with them?)
- Is this person someone who can be trusted—someone whose actions and words are in alignment?
- Could I let this person be there more for me? How?

Based on your answers to those questions, you may discover that you already have some pretty good friends and that, if you were to share more of yourself with them, you would take the relationship to a whole new level of intimacy. Alternatively, you may discover that you have some relationships which don't have the capacity to grow and allow for you to be a full participant. If this is the case, it's time to clean house. These relationships will only drain your energy due to countless unmet needs, and you will end up compromising yourself by using your harmful coping strategies.

The core belief that *I am unacceptable* or *I am not good enough* may be worded many different ways, but it all boils down to the same thing: There's something wrong with me, and I hope like hell no one figures it out! That bogus old story, in addition to leading us to take the lion's share of the load in relationships, also leads us to a very exhausting pattern of interacting with others. I call it "being ON". When we are *on*, we put a lot of energy into watching everything we say and do. We also criticize, monitor, and assess our every move. While we are in the "public eye," we effect a persona and wear this mask all day. Phew! It's exhausting. No wonder we come home at the end of the day and have nothing left to give to ourselves or anyone. No wonder we feel overwhelmed and that we must decompress with our favorite coping strategy.

No doubt, in our work together and your observations of your interactions with others, you have run up against this pattern. You have likely discovered not only how tiring it is keeping up the appearance of "being together," but also that you have some strong fear around dropping the persona. Your Drill Sgt. might tell you that no one will like you if you do, and you will be rejected. He also told you that, if you asked for a need to be met, you would be abandoned and judged. If you have tried any of the suggestions from the previous chapter, you have most likely discovered that it is possible to set a boundary or meet your needs without being ostracized by the key people in your life. Is it possible that the Drill Sgt. may be incorrect about this, too? Remember, everything the Drill Sgt. does, says, thinks, and feels is based on the skewed perception of your old core beliefs, which are not true now and have never been. If you let him have the last word on anything, it will be defeating and untrue. He believes you to be unacceptable, not good enough, and so forth. If you continue to believe what the Drill Sgt. says and follow his advice, you will only continue to relive old, defeating patterns. It is simply a choice to believe none of what the Drill Sgt. tells you. And you can make this choice.

In summation, your pattern of isolating, to the extent that you find yourself doing this, is your way of coping with the outlay of energy and the stress that comes from buying in to old core beliefs and from not asking for what you need in your relationship with others. It is often evening time (when we are most isolated) that is the most difficult time of day to resist using food to cope. And we know that you are turning your focus to food at this time, because you have needs that are unmet in other areas of your life—often, a whole days' worth of needs and then some! So begin to notice your tendency and desire to isolate, and clue into this indicator of unmet needs. When you find yourself isolating, ask yourself what unmet needs you have at these times. Do what you can to meet these needs then, or reassure yourself that you will meet them at your earliest opportunity.

Now let's explore some common and specific behaviours, thoughts, and feelings which are suggestive of a tendency to isolate, and also some suggestions of how to handle them.

Am I An Isolator?

Let's begin with looking at some signs that will let you know if you use isolation as a coping strategy. I am certain that by the end of this section you will have a clear sense of the ways in which you may isolate yourself as a temporary way of meeting your needs for security and comfort.

These different ways of isolating are offered in no particular order—just the way they came into my head as I'm writing this. You may do one, all, or any combination thereof. It isn't really important how many or which one's you engage in personally. What is key to note is that they are also coping strategies. So invite yourself to be aware of times when you are engaging in these coping behaviours. Then remind yourself that they are simply indicators that you have needs that are unmet. The sooner you recognize your cocooning behaviour and identify the unmet need(s), the less likely you will be to turn to food and feel bad about your body.

Answering The Phone

Do you avoid answering the phone at home? Do you feel as if you are having a mild panic attack by just hearing the phone ring? Do you screen calls, and does it take a major pep talk for you to either answer the phone or return the call, even for people you really like? This is an indication of overwhelm, lack of balance in your life overall, and that you believe some of your needs—security (control) and/or approval, for example—will be unmet if you answer the phone or return the call.

The solution to the phone situation is to allow yourself to screen. This is your right. Check in with the Drill Sgt. and your Authentic Self to see what needs they have that would and would not be met by answering or calling the person back sooner rather than later. And, if just hearing the phone ring stresses you out, allow yourself to turn the ringer off for now, or, if you live with others, let them know that they are not, under any circumstances, to hand the phone to you should someone call. They are to take a message, regardless of whether you are right there or not. Let yourself have as much control and security around this issue as you can for now. You will know when you are ready to answer the phone directly or call people back. And then you will. There's no benefit to letting the Drill Sgt. beat you into compromising your needs for security and comfort just so the person on the other end of the phone gets their need for connection and information met immediately.

Going Out

Okay, what's your experience with "going out"? How well do you enjoy getting dressed up to head out for an evening or a luncheon? Does it matter with whom you are meeting, or is your feeling the same either way? This question alone can tell you a great deal. If your feeling about going out is the same regardless of who will be there and where you are going, then you know it's more your own self-judgement that is impacting you. If your feeling is heightened depending on who's going to be there or where you are going, this tells you something about some co-dependency in your connection with this person, or people, and about your comfort in certain settings.

Going Out On Your Own

There was a time when I was scared to death to go out by myself. I thought for sure people would think I was a loser and had no friends (not far from the truth on the friends part at that time, but anyway...) I was so concerned with what others might think that I chose to stay home and binge rather than go out and see a movie or take myself out to dinner. These are things I do with relish now, but then? Not a hope in hell. I was coming from the External Locus of Control place, and my old core beliefs were yelling that I was unacceptable, not good enough, and undeserving of pretty much anything except breathing! Going out on my own led me to make a lot of assumptions about others: everyone was cooler than I was; everyone had more right to be there than I did; everyone had it "together" but me; and everyone was looking at me and talking about me and pitying me and judging me. Given my headspace at the time, I would have bet you a million bucks these were absolute truths. No wonder I couldn't bring myself to step outside my front door unless I absolutely had to.

New Places

I also recall feeling very anxious about going to new places. Even if I were going out with people I knew well and felt comfortable with, I was very anxious about this. I was certain that I wouldn't fit in or wouldn't be cool enough. I was certain also that the "cool police" were watching, and yes, believe it or not, I worried endlessly that someone at the unknown restaurant or club would approach me upon my arrival and say that I wasn't cool enough, good looking enough, and so forth, and that I must leave! Yes, I really thought that could happen and, of course, in my state of being at that time, I would have believed that not only were they right about my lack of acceptability, but they also had the right to kick me out because of how I looked. And, if they didn't give me the boot, they were only tolerating me. Now I know otherwise, but at that time I felt completely unacceptable (my old core belief) and believed that everyone saw me this way. Therefore, "going out" to new places was absolute torture and definitely high anxiety-producing material. Often, I would feel so overwhelmed that I would back out at the last minute, stay home, eat, and berate my body. You might recall this pattern from Emily's story. You might also have lived it yourself.

The Joy Of Getting Dressed

Then we have the joy of getting dressed to go out. As if we are not uncomfortable (panicked) enough about going out and being "seen"! If you haven't got a lot to choose from in the way of clothes that are comfortable and that you like, you are really in for a stressful experience when you attempt to get dressed and "look nice" for an event. As we spoke of earlier, many of us resist buying clothes until we achieve our "ideal" weight. In the meantime, we are constantly reminded of how uncomfortable we feel in our bodies, and the Drill Sgt. has ample opportunity to remind us of how fat and disgusting we are. We have nothing comfortable in our closets and very little to choose from even then. And of course, **we must look in the mirror!** Isn't that enough to make the Drill Sgt. go on a tirade and for our Authentic Self to beg us to let us stay home, on the couch, with our pj's and some food?

The Solution To Going Out

If you make a commitment to go out, it is important that you are able to meet your needs in this commitment. This means that you should not commit unless you are certain you really want to go, and allow yourself to change your mind about going out—right up to the last minute if need be. This will be a lot easier to do if you tell the person, when you make the commitment, that sometimes social gatherings can be overwhelming for you and you need to play it by ear, and see how you are feeling as it gets closer. And tell the Drill

Sgt. that you won't become a shut-in just because you give yourself a few months to get connected with what you currently do and don't want to do socially.

And how about buying yourself some new clothes (even second-hand ones)? Let's hypothesize that it takes you a few months to begin to see a change in your weight while you are working out the kinks of taking care of the underlying issues. And recall that the key to no longer using food to cope is self-compassion. A most compassionate gesture would be having a handful of outfits that fit and are comfortable. Don't buy what you will fit into in a month. Buy what fits now or something a little larger, for comfort. As I write this, I'm wearing jeans that are a size too big for me because they are comfortable as heck, and that's my criteria above all else now.

Remember that the more uncomfortable you are in your clothing, the more you think negatively about your body; you don't need anymore of the Drill Sgt.'s brand of "motivation through criticism". It hasn't worked in all these years, and it's not about to start working now. So give some serious consideration to biting the bullet and buying some new clothes regardless of how temporary they are. They will, I assure you, be worth their weight in gold. And practice allowing yourself to commit to nothing or to letting people know that, when you do make a commitment to go out, you may need to cancel at the last minute, depending on how you are feeling. Put your needs out there; respect them yourself and others will too.

Travelling

We are talking about a getaway—going on a tropical vacation or going "back home" to visit friends and family. Either way, it can be traumatic when we are laden with bad body thoughts as a coping strategy, and there is strong need for control around our food choices and quantity. For the first period of my recovery process, before I had really grasped the concept of needs or that I even had some, you could guarantee that I would overeat if I went pretty much anywhere farther than my comfort zone of my home and familiar local places. You can shorten your time in this stage of recovery by encouraging yourself to be conscious of your needs throughout your travels. Establish morning and nighttime check-ins with yourself. Then acknowledge and validate the needs you identify, and take steps that day or the next to meet them as best you can. Remember that often the acknowledgment and validation of a need is sufficient to take the PLA that is triggered down a notch or three. So, if for whatever reason you can't meet your need when you identify what it is, just acknowledge it, validate it, and tell yourself *when* you will be meeting it and *how*.

Going Home

What makes it so stressful? We are often not just going for a visit; we are working on reconnecting with some key people and avoiding other ones. Just the thought of going home triggers all sorts of feelings about past experiences, and the need for connection and approval mingle dangerously with the need for security. It is quite common for us to be completely conscious that we don't want to go home or on a particular trip, but we feel absolutely powerless to say no because others might be upset or disappointed in us (a prime example of co-dependency). This does not meet our needs for safety and security at all, and, considering how unsafe emotionally we may feel in that environment, it's likely our needs for connection and approval will also be unmet, given our current state of mind. That's why I strongly encourage you at this time to carefully consider any trips home. If you have identified any co-dependent patterns or abusive patterns in your relationship with the people you would be seeing, it is imperative that you are clear on how you will take care of yourself and how you will set boundaries with these people if they should even hint at any of those old, harmful behaviours. If you question your ability to look after yourself this way in that environment, you are best not to go for now. And if all else fails and you choose to go because you are not able to let go of wanting their approval, let it be okay to take care of yourself with food or any other way you need to cope while you're there, and reassure yourself that you will pick up where you left off when you return.

Please note, I'm not saying that you should never go home for a visit—unless, of course, the connections there are abusive. I'm encouraging you to wait until you are more secure and feeling more confident in your ability to care for yourself in a nurturing way. If we force ourselves to travel to our home (or our spouse's) when we are not feeling grounded in ourselves, we will definitely see a strong need for our coping strategy emerging before, during, and after our visit. And, as many of us want to look our best for the home crowd, the fact that we often overeat, due to the anxiety of our upcoming trip, only serves to reinforce our distress about traveling and provides us with the perfect opportunity to make it about the food. Don't let yourself get away with this, whether before you leave, while you are there, or following your trip (if you ultimately choose to go). Commit yourself to noticing the food and body focus, and to labeling this as your coping strategy. Immediately begin searching for the unmet need. Begin to draw upon your tool kit for identifying when you have an unmet need, what it is, and what you can do to meet it. You will find your travels much less stressful, and you will come home feeling proud of how you cared for yourself.

Tropical Vacations

When we struggle with body image, why do we do this to ourselves? Some people find that their body image concerns disappear when they are in a foreign country with little or no chance of seeing anyone they know. They are the bikini queen in Cuba, but no way would they be caught dead in a T-shirt and shorts on their local beaches. Some even find their relationship with food relaxing significantly. It's not uncommon to hear many clients say, "I hardly thought about food at all while I was away, and I didn't even gain a pound!" Do you know why this is? It's because you gave yourself permission and told the Drill Sgt. you were on vacation; you were going to have what you wanted, when you wanted. Sounds a lot like Natural Eating! Imagine letting yourself bring this mentality to your daily life now. Vacations can be wonderful. It really depends on where you are; how safe you feel; and ultimately, you guessed it, on what needs you have that are unmet by those with whom you are in contact, and with life in general at that time.

Sometimes we resist traveling because we believe we are too fat, and the systems of travel (airplane, in particular) were not designed with overweight people in mind. I know of one lady who took matters into her own hands, following her decision to stop waiting for weight loss to begin her life. She purchased her own personal seat extension and never had to publicly ask for help in that way. It was very liberating for her to realize that she could care for herself while making it safe to travel. Consider the question of what it would take for you to feel safe traveling to places you have always wanted to visit. What needs would have to be met? How can you go about meeting them?

Making Friends

Above, we talked about how we often get into one-sided relationships where we are the giver. We are the one who does the listening and the giving. We know it's one-sided, yet we continue to choose to spend time with this person in that one-sided way. Why? Because we are afraid to face rejection if we ask for some air time, and because we feel guilt asking for what we need based on those lovely old core beliefs. Believe it or not, continuing to play the role of the "listener" or "provider" serves the purpose of allowing you to remain emotionally isolated, and this meets your needs for emotional security. It may seem that you have lots of social connections—you are out and about all the time—but you are still isolated and unknown. Your needs for connection, intimacy, and security are never truly met as long as your relationships remain one-sided and lack depth.

Ask yourself whether this pattern pertains at all to you now. Do you choose relationships with people who are dominant types—those who are wholly self-focused and willing to let the relationship centre around them? When you have accidentally been vulnerable or have exposed more of yourself to a person than you were ready to or comfortable with, regardless of their reaction, do you find yourself withdrawing from this friendship? Check to see how you may be keeping yourself emotionally isolated.

True friendship is a 50/50 affair. Both sides bring themselves to the relationship and share their lives with the other. Both sides take time to hear what the other is doing, feeling, thinking and needing. There may be periods of time when one person takes up a bit more air time due to a stress or life event, but the air time and the sense of engagement in the relationship should be balanced, overall.

You may find yourself being the one who always calls or who always makes the concessions regarding where you go or what you do. This can breed resentment and insecurity. If this pattern is alive in your friendships, ask the other person if they would be willing to share the load, presuming the relationship is important to you. Actually, either way, I would encourage you to have this conversation with the person. If the friendship isn't that important to you, you will have an easier time with the conversation while practicing boundary setting, which is always a good thing. You also may discover that calling the person on their behaviour in the relationship garners more respect, and they will want to engage more fully in the relationship. Now you've got something better than you had before!

If you find that you are the one who takes up most of the air time, ask yourself these questions:

1. Is it because I am afraid of silence and want to keep the conversation going?
2. Is it because I have a lot to say and am waiting for the other person to jump in?
3. Is it because I have never stopped to think that they may have things going on for themselves?

Whatever the reason, monitor yourself in your conversations with others over the next little while, and, regardless of how much you have to share or what is going on for you, make sure you leave space for silence: make sure you ask specifically if there is anything this person wanted to talk about. Try and make the air time as close to a 50/50 split as you can. You will find your needs for sharing and being heard will still be met, and you will discover more about the other person and build a much deeper relationship.

If you step back from carrying the conversation and the other person doesn't fill in the space; if there is a long and lengthy silence or the conversation seems stilted; speak to it by saying: "I notice that when I leave space for you to share things get pretty quiet." See what comes back. I did this some time ago with a very sweet lady with whom I had been attempting to establish a friendship for a year or so. We would get together often enough, but I did all the talking, carried the whole conversation, and, if I were quiet, the silence could last some time! Awkward! Too much room for my Drill Sgt. to roam and make it about me! So one night, in exasperation and fatigue, I said gently and respectfully, "I notice that things get pretty quiet when I leave space for you to share." And to my great surprise, she said: "Yes, I know. I have a really hard time talking about anything to do with myself, and I just don't know how to start or what to say. I've always had a hard time making friends."

Wow! Did you see what just happened there? For months I'd been feeling "less than," "uninteresting," and "not good enough". I'd been making her silence or lack of sharing about *me*. I had been feeling very insecure during and after our visits because of those bogus stories I had been telling myself. I never in a million years would have guessed she would say what she did. In fact, I was braced and expecting to hear, "You know, Michelle, I'm totally bored by you!" I was so tired of holding the whole friendship myself that I was eager to have her thoughts vocalized so I could end it and never have to work so hard again! It was a great lesson for me that yet again everything is not about me! I learned that, when I take the risk to discover what is going on for someone else, there is a new level of depth which is created between the other person and me. And by the way, that *was* many years ago. These days, because I know my worth, what I need in a friendship, and trust myself to speak respectfully to these needs, I would ask my friend our first night out about her quietness. If I had done this then, we would undoubtedly have had a much more pleasant first year as friends!

Remember, friendship should always be a two-way street—pretty close to 50/50—with the allowance for life's ups and downs. You must be willing to not only give of yourself but to also receive. Let people be there for you. Trust that they will be. Be direct in your requests of what you need and want in friendship. Don't make people guess and then be upset because they didn't guess right. Set yourself up for the greatest likelihood for success in your friendships by asking for what you need and only taking 50% of the responsibility for the relationship.

And... A Word About The Grocery Store

Please, never forget that you are the one who is overcoming a food obsession. It's *you* who notices what others eat and look like. It's you who stresses and stews over whether to buy x, y or z just in case you see anyone in the checkout line that you know. Even if you don't, it's stressful. Aside from yourself, the only people who will have any judgement of the food and quantity choices you are making are people who have their own disordered relationship with food. A big piece of your work in healing is that of challenging the pattern of External Locus of Control where you let the opinions of others count for more than your own. When you are compromising your choices by putting in your shopping cart items that you believe would be approved by others versus items that you would really like, remind yourself that this is the ELOC. This is the Drill Sgt., and this pattern only serves to diminish you and your needs. Any guilt, shame, or restrictive behaviour you carry about food will ultimately lead you to use food to cope. By letting it be okay to have what you really want, you will nurture yourself in so many ways.

If the cashier makes a comment about what you are buying, challenge yourself to allow for the possibility that they were just making conversation. She may have wanted to know if those chocolates were good because she's never had them, or she is on a diet and wishes she *could* have them! Remember my rule on assumptions? If you can't let go of an assumption you have made and it is harming you (stirring up bad body thoughts or insecurity), check it out. You will always, always be amazed at what you hear.

How Can I Make It Safe To Step Out Of The Cocoon?

In addition to the specific situations mentioned above, you can make it safer to step out by checking in with your Authentic Self throughout the day and while you are at any social engagements. Ask yourself what you are feeling, and look for any coping-strategy thoughts, feelings, or behaviours. If you find any, ask yourself what needs you have in that moment which are unmet, and what you could do to meet them. Are your needs assumptions, that is, are they real or imagined?

Above all, continue to challenge old beliefs that prevent you from believing you are not good enough, not loveable, not deserving, and not allowed to care for yourself. Yes, it will feel uncomfortable to challenge these old beliefs, but it will be a different kind of discomfort. The discomfort you get from continuing to believe these old messages is a defeating and diminishing kind of discomfort. The discomfort you feel from challenging these old beliefs is an exhilarating, somewhat fearful but excited discomfort, and this is exactly the feeling you want to create the instant you are aware that you are buying in to old beliefs and compromising yourself as a result. Allow yourself to put your needs first. You will be amazed at how people respond with respect and appreciation for your needs if you just ask!

It's Okay To Take Time For Your Self, Too!

And last but not least... let it be okay for you to choose to stay in or isolate emotionally when you need to. Balance is very important, and taking time out just for you is a key component of good health and self-esteem. Choosing to stay in is great, in moderation, and necessary for balance. We all need different amounts of "me time" at different times. So let your own internal needs be the indicator of how much downtime you need. Allow yourself to cocoon, sometimes. For the next few months, you may find that you isolate more than ever as you practice with this tool and let yourself meet your needs for security. This is normal, and that's okay. Allow yourself to do this for as long as you need. Don't compare yourself to anyone else and what they are doing. Just check in with *you*, and ask yourself if you are choosing to isolate because you want a break or because you are avoiding something or someone. You can still choose to avoid that thing or person, but let it be conscious. See if you can find a way to let it be okay to care for yourself without having to hide who you are from the world.

23

Communication In Relationships

I'm choosing to begin this chapter on communication in relationships with a discussion about "assuming versus allowing". This discussion will facilitate you in better understanding some of your patterns in relationships and the use of your new tools in communication, which we are going to speak of shortly.

When I speak of assumption, I am speaking of the interpretation you automatically make through your distorted filters of old core beliefs and all-or-nothing thinking about *why* that person did what you witnessed. When we looked at core beliefs, do you remember our discussion about fact versus interpretation? What physically happened *did* happen. It is a fact. You saw George throw the newspaper. That's a fact. What I am speaking of, when I talk about "allowing," is that you don't know for sure *why* he threw it. You don't know what his intention was or if he even had an intention, other than to get the paper off the chair. He could have just been throwing the newspaper. Allowing means allowing for the possibility that the story you have told yourself about why something happened may not be accurate.

Now I must make it absolutely clear that in the circumstance of any abusive behaviour, the reason *why* someone did what they did is not the main issue. Abuse is unacceptable (in any form), and you should not be sticking around and trying to figure out whether they meant to hurt you or not. You should be protecting yourself. If you choose to do so, you can discuss the reason later, but there is never any legitimate, acceptable excuse for harming another human being (except in self-defense). Please don't confuse the concept of allowing, in the manner I am speaking of, with that of "allowing" yourself to be harmed.

Assuming versus Allowing

When we come from our old Drill Sgt.'s all-or-nothing mindset, we are always making assumptions about what is going on; what people are thinking, feeling, doing; what they really intended to do or say; what they really want from us, and so on. This is such a great shame and also the cause of much of your current distress around any relationships. What makes it worse is that, like so many of your other coping strategies, you have mastered the art of assumption to such a degree that you are unaware that an assumption has been made. To you, it's the absolute truth. In many cases, you will defend your perspective to the death (of the relationship, that is).

Once you lock yourself in to the story that your perception is the truth and that there is no other explanation for a person's actions or any other interpretation for their words, you have done yourself great harm. In essence, you have just said to yourself, and to the person you are in relationship with, that your perspective is the only perspective. You are right and they are wrong. And that's that! You are also sending the message loud and clear that you don't trust this person. You don't believe them.

Where is the other person to go with this? How do they deal with their feelings of hurt, and their needs for trust and safety in the relationship, if there is only one way or one answer and it's yours? What are they to do if your interpretation of them is inaccurate from their perspective—however right it may feel from yours? How does a relationship rebound from an experience where you are unwilling to hear the other person's explanation or to hear that their intention was not as you interpreted it? A relationship can not remain healthful in the face of too many experiences of *I don't care what you say, I am right and you are wrong!*

The only reason relationships ever end badly is that one or both parties are absolutely wedded to their perspective of events and are unwilling to allow for the possibility that their viewpoint is incomplete. The pain of these endings can stay with us for many years, even a lifetime, if we are never willing to let go of our all-or-nothing perspective and see the other person's side.

Life has taught me that there truly, always is more than one way to see a situation. Your perspective has merit. So does theirs. Their perspective may be skewed from their own beliefs and influenced from their past dysfunctional relationship modeling, as yours might be. But the key piece here is that the other person is doing their very best, just as you are, based on the awareness and tools they have at their disposal. The more you open yourself to that truth, the easier life will be, and the more healthful your relationships will be.

When you begin to allow for the possibility that your perspective may not be complete or wholly accurate, while it seems valid to you with the information you have right now, you are saying to the other person that you value them, trust them, and want both of you to feel good about your relationship. Invite them to tell you what their perspective is.

"Allowing" means you are open to the possibility that:

a) Your perspective may be missing some key details.

b) Your perspective may be skewed by your Drill Sgt. and your old core beliefs.

c) Your perspective may be influenced by your energy level and mental state at that moment due to completely unrelated events.

Unless you have taken the time to hear the explanation or intention of the other person, I can guarantee that your perspective is missing a key piece of data which, in my experience, usually diffuses the entire situation once it comes to light. At the very least, it sets the stage for greater understanding on both sides. If you are willing to *allow for the possibility* that what you *think* occurred may *not* have occurred in the way you believe it did, the world becomes a much friendlier place with far more possibilities than ever before. Instead of feeling less secure, you feel more grounded and secure than ever before because your thinking is not as rigid, and therefore you roll more gently with the changes that life brings.

Allowing is both a thought and an action. You allow for the possibility that your immediate interpretation of events may not be accurate, and you take action to ascertain what the other person thinks happened. You put the two stories together, find common ground, and determine the area of confusion. Often, in just uncovering the confusion you will find your hurt or anger dissipating, because now you can see that the other person, just as you did, had a reason for doing what they did or saying what they said, and it wasn't about hurting or disrespecting you.

An example of *assumption* looks like this: You're in the middle of a discussion about something that is very important to you, and the person you are speaking with turns and walks away and starts doing something, let's say, folding laundry. You instantly interpret their actions as dismissive and disrespectful; actions that indicate they don't care what you are saying. You get upset and either terminate the conversation, feeling hurt and angry, or you get louder and more intense to ensure they hear you and to let them know you are not going to drop it! This scenario is leading to a very unpleasant evening and to some damage to the relationship. Depending on whether the other person is an assumer or an allower, things could go either way. If they are an assumer, they will be upset that you are upset. Things will escalate, and neither of you will really know why you are even arguing. If they are an allower, they will ask you why you are raising your voice or why you just stormed out. They will hear your response, acknowledge your hurt, and then share the reason for their actions with you. The ball is back in your court to be heard and believed, or you can continue to assume it was about disrespect and disregard.

An example of *allowing* looks like this: You are in the middle of a discussion about something that is very important to you. The person you are speaking with turns, walks away, and starts folding laundry. You observe this and allow for the possibility that there is a good reason for their behaviour and that it is not because what you are saying is unimportant. You state your observation *with no interpretation and just the facts:* "I notice you've gone to fold laundry while I was in the middle of explaining something to you." Here is where you get to discover whether the other person is an assumer or an allower.

The assumer will be stuck behind the veil of their own core beliefs, co-dependency, and all-or-nothing thinking. They will be prone to becoming defensive when you mention anything about their behaviour. So you might get a response that sounds like "So?" or "What's wrong with that?" At best, you will get "Weren't you done?" as a response.

An allower will say without defensiveness, "Did I. I'm sorry. I didn't realize you weren't finished. What was it you wanted to say?" Or, "I know, I really wanted to get this laundry done, and I thought I could fold while I listen. Do you want me to stop?"

Now the ball is back in your court. In the situation where your pal is an assumer and responds somewhat defensively, you have the choice to go into your old story and feel hurt and wounded and take it personally, or you can come from your new it's-not-all-about-me perspective, remind yourself that you are not responsible for anyone's feelings—just as they are not responsible for yours—and allow for the possibility that they are misinterpreting you. The best solution here is to ask them what they've heard you say—what is creating their defensiveness in that moment—and prove to yourself that it was their own misinterpretation of you that is causing them distress. You then have the choice of asking them if they would like to hear what it is you were trying to say.

As I've said before, if the other person is wedded to their perception of events, there isn't really any place for you to go with this, at least at that moment. Perhaps with some time and distance from the subject, the other person would be willing to hear your experience of things: perhaps not. Being in relationship with a black and white, all-or-nothing thinker is really challenging and makes it difficult to feel safe and trusting enough to share much of yourself with them.

The pattern of assuming that your perception is the "right" one may have helped you to separate from past abusive or co-dependent connections. You may have needed such an all-or-nothing approach to life in the past to be able to stand strong and reinforce your needs with key people in your life. The problem is that the best you can do when you are wedded to the practice of assumption is to be in the independent stage of relationship. Interdependence can not exist with all-or-nothing thinking. It is impossible. At best, you have two strong independent people who have learned to cohabit and keep their distance. At worst, you have a co-dependent connection or abusive relationship where one person consistently gets their way and the other doesn't.

If you have noticed this pattern of assuming in any of your key relationships, now is the time to ask yourself what type of relationship you want with this person. If you want a good, healthful, open, honest and trusting relationship, you must be willing to allow for the possibility that your perspective is not the only one. You must be willing to allow for the possibility that the other person is not out to "get" you or to pull one over on you.

Be willing to allow for the possibility that, if there is confusion or conflict, there has simply been a misunderstanding or that you have misinterpreted their intention in their actions or words.

Without a word of a lie, if you believe this last statement and did absolutely nothing else to heal your communication and relationship with others, you would notice such a positive change in your interactions with everyone in your life that it would truly be like night and day. This is why allowing for the possibility that there has been confusion implies trust in the other person and a willingness to work things out. It implies that you are secure and grounded enough to no longer need the false security of all-or-nothing thinking—of being "right". It is also a sign of your ability to have interdependent connections and to genuinely care about the other person's perspective and needs as well as your own.

Trust In Relationships

At the risk of repeating myself: *relationships are all about communication*. It doesn't matter who the relationship is with or how deep or how fleeting. The method you use to communicate your feelings and needs is fundamental to whether you feel you have had a positive interaction or not. Your relationship with a key person in your life can be blissful and rosy when you are communicating well, feeling understood, and heard. It's as though you are in alignment with your views and needs. And a relationship can turn black and painful very quickly when you feel judged, shut down, unheard, and unimportant.

The most amazing thing about communication in relationships is that, for the most part, the comment or conversation that caused you to go from the first lovely scene to the second sour and dark one results in an unintended outcome. Often, the words or deeds that you find hurtful in your communication with others are perceived this way because of how you interpret them. Your response, from that place of misinterpretation and wounding, is so defensive or angry that it puts the other person in a state of defense themselves, and an argument ensues.

Being willing to trust that you are loved and that the other person's intention would not be to harm you is fundamental to creating and maintaining a healthful relationship. There is no enemy. With the exception of abusive relationships, the other person is not out to get you or hurt you intentionally. Interdependence requires you to be willing to trust that the hurt feelings, which may surface in your relationship with others, are likely from a simple misunderstanding. This trust must be built on a sense of security and trust in yourself first and foremost, then from a sense of trust in the other person.

As we have discussed, trust in yourself is built by taking the time to regularly tune in to what you are feeling, needing, and wanting, then respectfully responding to those signals from within. Trust in others is built by witnessing, over time, a pattern in their behaviour whereby their words and actions match. This is called integrity! They call when they say they will. They follow through on their commitments to themselves and others. They honour the values which are important to you. You see this in their actions as well as their words. The two must coexist, otherwise you have a lot of talk and no action, and you do not have a trustworthy partner for any relationship.

If you are in a relationship where someone's words and actions don't match, what you have is a giant pile of wishful thinking. Allow yourself to step out of your fantasy of what *could* be if that person would just do what they said they would, and invite yourself to see what *actually* is there right now. What is there right now is the truth. What is there right now is what your relationship with this person really is. You can not guarantee that anything about this person will ever change, so the greatest gift you can give yourself is to acknowledge that the truth of the relationship, as it exists now, is all you've got to go by. Anything else is fantasy. It may come true, but you can't bank on it, particularly when the integrity of the other person is in question.

You can't do anything to give someone integrity. You can't force them to grow or even to see where they lack integrity and how it is harmful to your relationship. They must realize this for themselves and want to grow and change for their own self-regard, and then they must actually take steps to do that. It can take some time, and that's assuming this someone is truly committed to their process.

You may have had key players in your development who have made promises and reneged—key players who never took responsibility for ensuring their words and actions aligned. Integrity may be something that seems like a pipe dream, or something which you are not allowed to expect from another human being. The truth is that integrity is fundamental to healthful relationships. How can you possibly feel safe and secure in a relationship and bring everything of yourself to this connection if you can't rely on a person to do what they say they will. A lack of integrity is always a sign of a lack of self-esteem, and it should be considered a great, big red flag if you should see it in your relationship with others.

Trust in relationships takes time to build. You need to spend a fair amount of time with someone, and in a variety of situations, to get a sense of their integrity and whether or not it is safe to trust them. Because those of us who use food to cope also have the coping strategies of alexithymia and co-dependence, you may not even bat an eye at a partner who lies or doesn't follow through on their commitments. It may seem perfectly normal or acceptable to you because you have had this modeled to you, or because you are not as connected to your feelings and therefore are not aware of how stressful this pattern of behaviour is to you. You may even have come into your current relationship through an affair or some other integrity-compromising circumstance. If this is the case, until you have dealt with the integrity issues you both brought to your connection, it is completely unrealistic to feel respectful of yourself, or the other person, and to feel safe in the relationship.

It takes time to be aware of someone's true colours and for genuine trust to build. This is the main reason that people are cautioned against becoming too intimately involved at the start of a relationship. You see, once you share yourself intimately with someone, either emotionally or physically, you begin to feel a sense of bonding and commitment or obligation with this person. Depending on your sense of balance and self-esteem, this bonding can lead you to choose to tune out to red flags which may come up in the relationship (more on flags later). You may have such an interest in maintaining the intimate connection with this person, or in maintaining the feeling you get from them sometimes, that you are willing to look the other way when they compromise your values or don't meet your needs in some way. This can and frequently does lead us to have long-term relationships with people who can never meet our needs; therefore, it can cause us to feel frustrated and diminished and lose self-esteem.

The greatest gift you can give yourself is to allow any new relationship to proceed slowly, giving you time to discover if the person you are connecting with is trustworthy, healthful, and can meet your needs. Six months is a decent amount of time to see most of someone's personality and behavioural traits. Anything less, and you may not have seen enough of their behaviour to judge their stability and integrity accurately, or you may still be blinded by the "honeymoon phase" and willing to overlook things which will become glaring concerns in a short period of time.

My rule of thumb to assess my comfort and trust in a relationship is this: if I can't bring myself to tell someone that I have a certain need in my relationship with them and ask them if they would be willing to meet that need for me, I know that I don't feel safe with this person, and for some reason I don't trust them to respectfully respond to my request. Remember, it is okay for this person to say no—this will happen sometimes. But if I don't trust this person to respect my request enough to listen and try to find a win-win solution (one that meets both our needs), then that tells me a lot about my connection with them at that time.

Sometimes this might simply mean that it's too soon to ask or share that piece of information with this person, and my fear is natural. There has not been enough time to build the trust necessary to safely share this piece of myself with this person. In that case, I can just acknowledge it, and let it be okay to wait until more time has passed and I do feel safe—even if that is weeks away. If I feel such urgency to share something that I am willing to override my sense of comfort and inner security, this is a sign that I am in a co-dependent connection and feel that I must share to meet the other person's need. In this situation, I need to shift my focus from the needs of the other person and bring it back to me. If you do this, you will immediately notice that you feel less anxious and much more grounded.

In the past, I was so desperate to have someone in my life whom I could trust that, even when someone repeatedly showed me they were untrustworthy, I kept giving them chances to prove that I could trust them. They had already shown me in so many ways that I couldn't and shouldn't offer them my trust. They didn't deserve it. I had a hard time seeing this back then because I was caught up in my beliefs that I was unlovable. I was willing to interpret their lack of follow-through or outright abuse as "about me" not being good enough rather than being about them not being capable of integrity at that time in their lives. This was very harmful to me and could never lead to the sense of intimacy and security that I was trying to create. This kind of relationship, where trust is compromised, can never be safe for me or for you.

In any relationship where trust and safety are lacking, you are practically forcing yourself to need your primary coping strategies to both soothe your Self and to tune out to the feelings of distress and insecurity which are naturally and appropriately being triggered. Consider this: if you have made the all-or-nothing assumption that you must either accept what is going on or end the relationship but are not yet ready to do so, what choice do you really have but to tune out with a coping strategy and pretend you are not feeling hurt or unsafe?

The solution? Again, first and foremost, build your sense of self-esteem, and trust in yourself to honour yourself first—always! Then allow yourself to see the full picture of the relationship. Don't tune out to your intuition: those inner ripples that are trying to alert you to something. Stay present, and acknowledge the times when your needs for reliability, trust, dependability, respect, and so on, are unmet. If you don't feel safe enough to express your views, you are in the wrong relationship! Trust me on this one.

I encourage you to first work to change the nature of the relationship with courageous conversations where you state your needs and boundaries clearly. And commit to following through if they are violated. Alternatively, you can move on and enter into only those relationships which are able to meet your fundamental needs for security, trust and respect. Either way, you will benefit from some new communication skills!

There are three key areas that will lead to enhanced communication and more healthful connections in every relationship in your life. They are:
1. Understanding the concept of the message and the meta-message.
2. Clarifying the intention.
3. Seeking to understand.

Let's look at each of these in turn, and how they will make a difference to your relationship with others and with yourself.

The Message And The Meta-Message

I first heard of the concept of the message and the meta-message in a book by Deborah Tannen called *I Only Say This Because I Love You*. This concept is fairly well-known in the field of linguistics and communication, and Deborah Tannen, a linguist of the first order, writes fabulous books for the layperson about how to use the key findings of her research in our everyday communications, specifically with those key people in our lives—siblings, parents and partners. Deborah has another great book that I highly recommend. Its subject matter is mother-daughter relationships and is titled *You're Wearing That?* In fact, I highly recommend any of her work.

Simply put, the concept of the message and meta-message is this:

In every communication we have with another human being, there are two levels of communication taking place simultaneously. One level is the message—these are the actual words we say—everyone in the room would be able to agree (potentially) on the actual words that were spoken. The other level is the meta-message—this is the way we say it! The body language, the tone, even when we choose to bring a thing up, is all meta-message. The meta-message is what gives our conversations significance and spice. It's really all about the meta-message. The meta-message, being unstated, is clearly open to and frequently prone to individual misinterpretation.

This last piece about the significance of the meta-message, coupled with its vulnerability to misinterpretation, is the cause of most arguments. Two people can come away from a conversation having heard the same words but having interpreted their meaning and intention in completely different ways. And, unbeknownst to them both, they carry on with these completely separate understandings and make plans and create stories and have assumptions that are based on their own understanding of the initial conversation. These plans and assumptions serve only to further deepen our sense of "rightness" or accuracy in what we heard.

Here is a good example. A new couple is chatting about their plans for the weekend:

He: "Would you like to have dinner again this weekend?"

She: "That sounds great. I look forward to it. I'll just have to check my work schedule, but we'll have dinner one night."

She walks away from that discussion thinking that she will be seeing him for dinner on the weekend. She plans to work Friday, leaving Saturday open for their get-together.

He walks away thinking that he will be seeing her on Friday unless he hears otherwise. He makes a great dinner on Friday night. She doesn't show! Soon he is calling her on the telephone.

He: "Where are you? I made you dinner."

She: "Oh, I didn't realize we were having dinner tonight. I agreed to work late. I thought you knew."

He: "Why would I have gone to all the trouble of making a special dinner for you if I knew you were going to work late?"

She: "Well, why would I have worked late if I knew we had plans for tonight?"

The Intention

In this case, both are certain that they heard the initial conversation correctly. Both are using their follow-up behaviour based on their obviously different interpretations of the initial conversation as evidence to support that they are the one that heard it accurately! This is so incredibly common and so very unfortunate.

This couple is missing the point. The point isn't who is in the right or who is in the wrong. The point is they misunderstood each other. There is no bad guy: no one is out to get anyone else. So far, the way they are approaching things is from a position of defensiveness where both are looking for the other person to take the "blame," and neither are willing to do so because they believe they are right.

In fact, it is clear in this dialogue that they are both seeking connection and trying in their own way to say, "I value time with you." He, by saying, "I made us dinner." She, by saying, "I wouldn't have chosen to miss dinner with you." These messages can't be heard as long as the couple is stuck in the belief that there is a right and a wrong. This is where the "intention" becomes key. The fact that you are willing to believe that your partner's intention is to love you and be respectful, rather than harm you and be disrespectful, will allow you to trust that there must have been a misunderstanding.

If your automatic assumption is to feel hurt, unimportant, or unloved by your partner's behaviour (or mother's or siblings or coworker's), this tells me that you believe their intention was to harm you and that they consciously chose to do something they knew wouldn't meet your needs. Now ask yourself why you are with this person if you really believe that they intentionally, consciously chose to act in a way they know will offend and hurt you.

Well? If your response was that you don't think they meant to do it, put your money where your mouth is and trust that this is true. Let your actions show that you believe they do not mean harm or disrespect. Trust that their intention is always to build closeness and to enhance your love, and then choose to interpret their behaviour from this place. Notice how the number of stressful interactions between you diminishes overnight!

If you said that you I think they did mean to hurt you, and you are with them because you are too scared to leave and/or I don't think you would ever find anyone else, I implore you to do two things:

1. Offer yourself some compassion for the pain and judgement you are carrying about yourself, then get yourself to a counsellor and begin to work immediately on your self-esteem! Let us support you at the Centre or find another professional to aid you. But do something to heal your perception of yourself. You are being squashed by your bogus beliefs about yourself.

2. Challenge yourself to do the next piece on *Seeking to Understand* five times with your partner over the next week, and see if your feelings about yourself, your partner, and the relationship don't shift significantly.

Seeking To Understand

It's amazing how our old core beliefs taint everything that happens to and around us. The same is true for others, and as I've said before, it is more common for arguments to be borne out of misunderstandings than it is for them to come from true irreconcilable differences of opinion.

Seeking to understand means to ensure you know what the other person is trying to communicate. What is it they need? Then check in about how this fits for you. Can you commit to meeting this need? Does this fit for you? Once you are certain you have heard them correctly and they feel understood by you, you can then seek to be understood yourself.

As Stephen Covey, guru to the masses and author of *7 Habits of Highly Effective People* says, "Seek first to understand, *then* to be understood."

If both people are working at being heard, no one is listening. Someone must be willing to let the other person be heard. Someone must be willing to hold on to their piece and trust that they will also get their chance to be heard after the other person feels heard and understood. If you feel as though you do all the listening in a particular relationship and there is no room for you to be heard when you ask for this, it's time to set some boundaries and ask for what you need. Ask for equal air time. Ask this person if they would be willing to read this chapter of the book. Ask if they would be willing to acknowledge that you do the bulk of the listening when the two of you have a disagreement. They may have a very different perspective on who does what in terms of your conflict resolution, and this could be very important for you to know and understand. It is a sad testament to how deeply-ingrained our old core beliefs have become, when most people would rather leave a relationship than risk the vulnerability of clearly expressing their needs and asking for help in meeting them. If this sounds like you, just allow your focus for the next few months to be on your relationship with yourself. When you are feeling more trusting of your worth and your right to have your needs honoured and met, you can come back to the work on relationship with others.

Let's return for a moment to the couple with the confusion over dinner, and see how seeking to understand benefits them.

Now, imagine that this couple stops arguing for a second, and one of them (he) is willing to trust that the intention of the other would be positive and not to harm. He then holds on to his need to be heard, and seeks to understand what his partner's interpretation of the plan was. He says, "Hold on a second, it seems we misunderstood each other. What did you think our agreement for tonight was?" She immediately feels more relaxed, less defensive, more open and safe to share. She says, "Well, I thought you said we'd see each other this weekend. I didn't understand that you were saying Friday night." He, also now feeling more relaxed, as it's becoming obvious that there was a simple miscommunication, replies, "Oh, so you didn't realize I thought we would be getting together Friday. Well, I thought it would be Friday because we have hooked up the last two Friday's. I thought that was becoming "our" night." To which she replies, "Well, that makes sense. I can see why you'd assume that. I can see that we both got confused about the plan. And I like the idea of us having a night that's just for us."

Hugs and kisses ensue. It's all good, and they go on to have a good time together, trusting that they both care for and respect each other.

In this case, the couple takes the time to seek to understand. They take a moment to find out what the other's perception was, and immediately, as in 99.9% of life's situations, the problem becomes obvious and a solution evident. Plainly, things weren't as clear as they thought they were when they parted from their initial discussion!

Learning to take the time to ensure both people have the same understanding about a discussion before you end it is a great way to prevent this from happening. In other words, make sure that you have interpreted the meta-message accurately. This can be done very simply by saying, "So, as I understand it, we are getting together Friday night at my place for dinner." To which the other responds, "Friday sounds good!" Or, "I may have to work Friday, how about Saturday?" Either way, you're both on the same page!

Try this piece on seeking to understand the other person's perspective, perhaps for five times in the next week, whenever the smallest miscommunication surfaces in your connection with others. You will prove to yourself clearly that it really is all about misunderstanding and not at all about disrespect. When you take time to seek to understand, there is no need for hurt feelings; no need for conflict; no need for food to cope with relationship stress.

Proving this to yourself is a great gift because you learn immediately that there is absolutely nothing whatsoever to fear in open and direct communication. Those old core beliefs, which had you believing someone meant to hurt you with their words, can't exist when you risk a little and check out what their intention was in saying what they said. You will come to see that they meant no harm. There will be no need to run from conversations or to let things go unsaid or unconfirmed. When you challenge yourself to do this just a few times, your self-esteem dramatically improves. You'll see.

And if you are willing to experiment with making sure you are heard clearly when plans are being made, I highly encourage you to do so. It would simply look like this: "So, the agreement is..." And you would do that *before* you end the conversation or hang up the phone. You would wait until the other person fed it back to you. A simple *yes* from the other person doesn't work.

If they have some resistance to playing along here or think you are using some "psycho-babble" tool on them, I encourage you to say this: "Yes, you're right, I am using a tool right now. My intention in doing this is to make our relationship the very best it can be and to ensure we don't have any unnecessary conflict. Are you willing to support me in this?" If the answer is no, you know what to do!

Troubleshooting Communication

If you are imagining certain relationships or recent scenarios where you have interpreted a meta-message inaccurately and ended up in an argument or with some hurt feelings; and if you are fearful or feeling stuck about checking out the other's intention, ask yourself the following questions:

- What am I telling myself about this person and their intention in this situation?
- What am I telling myself will happen if I check out their intention?
- Do I have any core beliefs that might be at play in my interpretation of this person's intention?
- If so, could I allow myself to be open to the possibility that it is my old core beliefs and not this person's intention that have hurt me?
- Could I allow myself to ask this person what their intention was in their words or behaviour? For example, "I wonder what your intention was in saying..."

Give yourself the gift of seeking to understand. Be willing to trust that it is at least possible that you may have misinterpreted this person's intention. Check out your assumption. You will prove to yourself 99.9% of the time that you are safe, that you are loved, that it's not about you, and you can relax!

These pieces of checking out your meta-message assumptions, being open to a positive intention, and seeking to understand the other person's needs and motivation will not only create more healthful relationship with others, but they will also, without a doubt, lead to a more healthful and secure relationship with yourself. This will then lead you to feel more safe being in the present moment and to no longer need your harmful coping strategies!

Nonviolent Communication[1]

Dr. Marshall B. Rosenberg is founder and director of educational services for the Center for Nonviolent Communication, an international, non-profit organization. Nonviolent Communication is a "powerful tool for peacefully resolving differences at personal, professional, and political levels." Dr. Rosenberg has created a wonderful communication tool that, in and of itself, has all of the key pieces you need to transform your interactions with others. I highly recommend that you visit the Center's Web site: www.cnvc.org and, if you get the chance, attend a workshop or ongoing Nonviolent Communication practice group. They are an international organization, and Dr. Rosenberg himself travels the world educating and sharing his great skills.

The model for Nonviolent Communication (NVC) is such a wonderful tool because it allows us to effectively state our feelings and needs without making someone else responsible and, therefore, greatly enhances our chances of being heard and of meeting this need. Conversely, we cannot continue to engage in any co-dependent tendencies we may have and still use that tool because our request is so owned by us. It holds the mirror to our face and forces us to be aware of when we are trying to make someone else responsible for our feelings and needs versus when we are clearly taking responsibility for ourselves and asking someone if they would be willing to meet a need for us.

NVC is a beautifully succinct tool. It has four simple steps. The way to speak non-violently is as follows:

1. **Observation:** State your observation of the situation—no interpretation here—this must be stated in such a way that anyone watching the scene would say the same thing.
2. **Feeling:** I feel...
   What is your feeling about the situation you are experiencing?
3. **Need:** I have a need for...

Identify the needs you have which are unmet in the current situation. Do not say, "I need *you* to..." This turns your statement into a blaming one and puts pressure on the other to meet your need even if it doesn't work for them. So rather than saying, "I need you to stop yelling," try instead to say, "My need for safety isn't met when you raise your voice."

4. **Request.** "Would you be willing to...?

Here you ask the person to support you in meeting your need. If you truly are making a request, they are free to say no. If you would feel resentful, hurt, or angry and take it personally if this person declines your request, then it really wasn't a request. It was a demand, and the person wasn't free to decline. Posing a demand, couched in terms of a request, sets the other person up, and it sets you up to feel disappointed or distressed when the response you wanted isn't forthcoming. It creates mistrust in the relationship because the other person begins to look for the catch in your questions.

If you find this happening, it means you are putting this person in the co-dependent role of being the only one who can meet that particular need for you, and it is exceptionally rare that our needs can only be met by one person. If this person has some co-dependent tendencies themselves and is willing to play along, you *may* get your need met, but it really doesn't benefit the relationship or either of you as individuals. If they don't buy in to the old co-dependent mindset, they will just refuse to be drawn in and made to feel responsible for your need. You will be left to meet it elsewhere or to articulate your need again in a way which gives the other person control over their needs and their response to you.

It really helps, if you are going to make a request of someone using the NVC method, to first be clear in yourself that there are other ways in which you can get your need met if the person declines your request. You can either meet it yourself—the two of you can work to come up with a request they would be comfortable agreeing to—or someone else can meet it for you.

Approaching requests and communication from this perspective is wonderful because you are starting from a place of broad perspective and not all-or-nothing. In essence, you can see the concept of making clear requests as negotiation. And if you want to have a successful negotiation, you may enter it with a clear goal in mind, but you never limit yourself by insisting how that goal will come about or what it will look like. That's the negotiation part.

Here is an example: If you want more time with your partner, you wouldn't enter into a dialogue about this from a you-must-spend-your-weekends-with-me perspective. That is a demand. It doesn't leave room for the other person's needs, and it doesn't allow them to feel as though they are an equal player. If your goal is more time, be clear before approaching your partner about how much more time you need and what that would ideally look like.

Also, be clear about whether there is a lesser amount of time or different day that you would be willing to accept for a few weeks, if there were an understanding that you would come back to the discussion and review how things were going.

You see, this is the difference between co-dependency and independence in relationship versus interdependence. In the first two, there is only one way—yours. Anything else feels as though it is a "compromise" and that this is a bad word: someone has lost, and someone has won. Interdependence means that you are grounded in yourself. You trust yourself to take great care of you, so there is no need to fear hearing what someone else wants and needs: you know you are not going to agree to anything that doesn't work for you. You have also challenged your all-or-nothing thinking to the point where you know there is always more than one way to crack an egg, and you are willing to keep discussing the situation or the needs of each person until both feel they are truly satisfied with the plan. Interdependence means you have trust and security in yourself first and in the relationship second, but the trust is there. It is solid. So there is no rush.

If the other person is willing to work on creating a mutually-satisfying relationship, they will likely seek to meet your request.

If they decline, shift into the seeking-to-understand place and invite them to share what it is about your request that doesn't feel good to them. It's quite possible—in fact, very likely—that they have misinterpreted your request, and, if you ask for clarification of what they heard, you will be able to ensure that you are being heard correctly. What a gift it is for both parties to clarify and seek to understand. Arguments can only occur when you forget this tool.

So all together, the model looks like this:

"I notice you are raising your voice. I feel scared and sad when this happens because my need for safety is not being met. Would you be willing to lower your voice?"

In this scenario, if the person declined your request, you would still be free to meet your need for safety another way. You could remove yourself from the situation, for example. This is where boundaries come into play. Keep in mind, your trust in your rights in relationship are very important in order for you to take good care of yourself and model self-respect for the people with whom you have relationships.

The neat thing about NVC in my perspective, aside from the obvious benefit to relationships from the clarity in my communication, is that often when I stop and think about the request I want to make of someone and begin to frame it in the NVC format, one of two things happens:

1. I realize that I was actually getting stuck in some old co-dependency and wanting to make that person responsible for my "stuff". Framing my thoughts in the NVC model helps me with this because there is no way to make a co-dependent request using the NVC model. So if my request falls apart when I try and run it through the model, I know instantly that I was getting stuck in seeing someone else as responsible for my feelings and needs.

2. I realize that I can meet my need easily enough by myself, and I don't need to ask. I just needed to be clear on what it was that I needed in the first place. You will find this, also. Once you are clear on what you need, often what you are re-

ally looking for is some reassurance and support. It is absolutely okay to ask others for this. In fact, a direct request for reassurance is one of the most self-esteem- and relationship-enhancing things you can do. And, you will find that most of the time your own acknowledgement of your need, and your own reassurance that you are doing okay or have a right to feel what you feel, is more than enough to meet your need.

The Flag System

I am sharing with you a concept that is not in and of itself a communication tool. However, it is a fundamental tool for assessing the information you are receiving verbally and non-verbally from people in your life. Once you have assessed this information, you will be in a stronger and clearer place to determine for yourself how you want and need to proceed. By that, I mean whether or not you need to speak to the other person; if so, what you need to say.

All of our communications with others can be categorized in terms of flags: red, yellow, and green. In our ideal relationships, we have tons of green, a few yellow (which get immediately changed to green with some seeking to understand and open sharing) and almost never a red one.

Red flags indicate any words or actions which can be found on both the list of Unclear and Unhealthful Boundaries (Chapter 21) and on the list of Signs of an Emotional Abusive Relationship (Chapter 20). Red flags are dangerous to have in any relationship. Your sense of security and trust in the relationship will be compromised as long as any red flag is there. Also, if you hold certain values high, such as: monogamy, no use of drugs, and spiritual growth, these values should be on your list of red flags in order for you to feel safe and respected in your relationship.

Yellow flags would be any non-red behaviours or words which make you feel uncomfortable or concerned about the values or intention of the person. They do not compromise your sense of physical safety, but they do make you question the integrity of the person or make you wonder if you are getting the whole story. A yellow flag creates a momentary doubt about your suitability and/or about the trustworthiness of the other person. Yellow flags can also speak to whether the other is a match for you in terms of hobbies and interests.

Green flags are fabulous. Their communication is in alignment with their actions, and your values are aligned as well. There is no part of you saying, "Oh, I'm not certain about that. I sure hope he doesn't do that with me!" It's all good. It's all a "go". You feel peaceful and easy with this person, and things just seem to flow.

Red Flag Example

This is an example of a red flag in action: You are in a conversation with someone you are just getting to know, and you are telling them something that is very important to you and that you are quite proud of in yourself. The other person starts laughing and makes a derogatory comment about how silly your pursuit is and how they don't *get* how anyone can waste their time on it. RED FLAG! RED FLAG! Criticism, judgement, contempt, ridicule, disrespect! Not good. Fortunately, you have some options:

1. You can say nothing. End the conversation, and never speak to this person again. I support this option!
2. You can say, "I find your response to my sharing disrespectful and rude. I wonder what your intention is in saying that?" They better have a damned good response that lets you know without a doubt that they misunderstood your sharing, such as, "Oh, I'm really sorry. I thought you were saying you didn't like that either." Even then, you clearly have a serious communication problem and you are best to move on. Now would be the time to make it clear to that person that you love that pursuit, you respect it, and you couldn't be in a relationship with anyone who didn't. I fully, one-hundred percent, support this action as well. I'm all about courageous, self-respecting conversations. They are so good for your self-esteem and for building healthful connections. If the other person comes back to you with anything other than

a sincere apology and a total change in their tune, you would be compromising yourself to continue in the relationship in any form.

3. *Caution! This option should be used* only *if you do not want to have healthful self-esteem and a life free from food and body-image focus.* You can continue in the relationship as is. You do have this option, but the consequences are great, and this is just the beginning! You see, to remain silent in that moment would be to send the other person a loud and clear message that they can ridicule you any time they want, and you will keep coming back for more. Not a good start. I do not support this option at all.

A trait or character flaw which is noticed at the beginning of a relationship will stand out even more as you get to know each other. That's why any red flags, unclear boundaries, or major value differences need to be addressed as soon as they arise. You must set the tone for a respectful and healthful relationship by establishing clear boundaries about the things which raise a red flag from the outset. Any harmful, unhealthful, or abusive behaviour that you witness in the other early on should be seen as a cue to distance yourself from the other person, and you should not proceed with the relationship at that time—if ever.

My rule of thumb around red flags is this: If I hear or see anything in the other person that is a red flag, I speak to it instantly, assuming it is not an abusive behaviour—there is no room in my life for that—and, while I might tell the person what I've witnessed, I would not be open to discussing any further connection with them.

The answer I get when I speak to a red flag, assuming it is not abusive, tells me:

a) If this is an unconscious pattern the other person is unaware of and unwilling to look at. If so, end of story, end of connection.

b) If it is a conscious pattern that the person is actively working on healing. If so, I set a clear boundary with the person about what my needs are and what I will and won't accept in my relationship with them, and they get one more chance, that's it. *One more chance.* I know all too well how much energy unhealthful connections take, and I respect myself too highly to have anyone in my life that is disrespectful or unsafe. I far prefer my own company to someone who is critical of me, demeaning, or untrustworthy.

So I give one more chance, assuming there are some wonderful green flag things about this person that make me see a huge benefit in the connection. I commit myself to following through. If the violation occurs one more time, that's it. End of story, end of connection. I don't need to articulate why I have ended the connection, although I can if I choose to. But it isn't open for discussion. It was a red flag; therefore, this person/behaviour can't be allowed to be in my life. There are far too many wonderful green flag people out there, and the more time you or I spend with red flag ones, the less time and energy you will have for the life-enhancing ones.

I mentioned earlier that fundamental value differences, such as: monogamy, spiritual beliefs (if they are important to you or the other person), substance use, and racial prejudices are red flag issues. If you need a monogamous partner and discover early on that your potential partner has had affairs in his last two relationships, this is about as big as a red flag gets. It needs to be spoken to, and you must know that he has had some time between his last relationship and the one with you to heal this pattern. You have the right to ask what he has done to ensure this behaviour will not be repeated in his relationship with you. If he hasn't done a big piece of work in understanding and healing this pattern, you are far better off just being friends. Don't wait for him to "prove" that he has changed. Come to think of it, why would you want him in your circle of friends when his fundamental values differ vastly from yours? You see, if the pattern isn't troublesome enough for him to be willing to work hard to change it, he doesn't have the same value system as you and probably thinks it's no big deal. Listen to this.

Pay attention to the red flags which you see and hear in the other person, friend, potential partner, colleague or teacher. All of the above are relationships and need to be approached from the perspective of only the green flags get to go forward! Otherwise, keep your distance until the red flag is removed and it's a green. This will happen either by the other person actively changing their behaviour, or by you removing yourself from the relationship.

Yellow Flag Example

An example of a yellow flag is this: You are having a chat with someone in the lineup at the supermarket. You start to wonder if you might form a friendship, possibly a partnership with this person, and then they say, "Yeah, I went heli-skiing yesterday, I'm going parachuting tomorrow, and next week my buddy and I are off to trek the Himalayas." Well, unless you are an extreme-sport-mega-outdoor kind of person, you are not going to have a lot in common. This is a yellow flag.

It doesn't mean they are a bad person or that you or they are lacking in some way. A yellow flag is more a representation of the difference between likes and dislikes which, if they are too big or too many, make a relationship a lot of work and very little fun. Noticing yellow flags doesn't mean that you have to end the relationship, and it doesn't necessarily say anything about the wellness of the other person. It just speaks to differences that need to be acknowledged and clarified before you can decide whether to proceed in the relationship.

Going back to the supermarket example... Let's say you were interested in the guy in the check-out lineup, and then he says those things about his activities. If you were to honour your Authentic Self, which would be saying *"I don't like those activities or that much intensive activity,"* you might say: "Wow! It sounds as though you really enjoy being active and doing extreme things." He may say, "Yes!" And you now know that the two of you are not a match. You can like him, you can find him sexy, you can think he's a great guy, and you can know that he's not right for you because of the yellow flag that isn't going away.

Or he may say, "Actually, I don't really. My friend and I won this contest, and they take you on all these adventures for two weeks. Normally, I just go for a bike ride if I want some exercise." You happen to love cycling, and now you're talking! The yellow flag has been removed from the road, and it's all green (for now anyway).

So, yellow flags are meant to spur you to clarify what you are hearing and witnessing, and then compare this new, clarified data with who you know yourself to be and what you like. If you don't like clubbing but someone you just met and like goes dancing each evening until 3:00 a.m., this is a big yellow flag, and you are best to either have a very casual friendship or nothing at all. This person is not relationship material for you, as a friend or partner.

As soon as you notice a yellow flag, you must check it out. In any relationship, save yourself time and energy by speaking to what you see that concerns you. The way the other person responds will either clarify the issue—making the road all green flags again—or show you that there is cause for concern. If the latter is the case, you would discuss this with the person, and the two of you would discuss how to navigate this concern in the relationship. If you can't come to an agreement, I encourage you to seek an outside support person: a couples' counsellor, for example. Clear up these yellow flags, a.s.a.p. Most marriage counselling fails, not because the counsellors aren't skilled, but because the couple waits too long to seek help—typically seven years after an issue has become contentious. The sad thing is that many of the issues that break up marriages are yellow flag issues and not red ones, but they've been left for so long, and there is such an emotional charge around them, that they have become red flags and are hard to overcome.

So, if you are already in a committed relationship, start speaking to anything which you experience that doesn't feel good or comfortable to you, and anything which makes you think that it doesn't feel quite right. Name it to the other person. Use some of the communication tools in your tool kit and get talking. You may never have had one, but you absolutely deserve a green flag relationship. And if yellow flags surface in a green flag relationship, they are dealt with immediately and respectfully, and you are quickly back to all green again.

In a healthful interdependent relationship, yellow flags will surface but not very often. You are two separate individuals from two different backgrounds. There are bound to be some differences and some confusion from time to time. What makes the difference between a safe and healthful place to be and one that will only bring you more of the old harmful patterns and co-dependency is that in the safe and healthful place, you are free to speak to your yellow flags and to have your concerns acknowledged, respected and attended to. In the old harmful pattern, you do not feel free to share what isn't working for you, and there is no respect and acknowledgment of your needs and feelings when you do.

One last piece that is absolutely fundamental:

Just because you have a partner or friend who is able to hear you when you share your concerns, this doesn't mean the yellow flag or red flag is gone. Their behaviour absolutely must change as well. The ability to hear concerns and respond respectfully is a good sign for sure, but it doesn't count for anything if the person is going to keep doing the same thing the same way. Often times, if we are challenging old beliefs and co-dependent patterns in our relationships, the simple act of asking for what we need is so frightening that, when we do receive a reasonably respectful response and feel heard by the other person rather than judged and criticized, we feel so relieved that we think the job is done. It isn't. You still must *see* the behaviour of the other person change—consistently, not just for a while. Otherwise, they are simply paying lip service to your concerns and not really "getting" it.

I look at the Flag system as part one of a three-part process:
- Part one is the identification of a red or yellow flag; first to yourself and then to your friend/partner.
- Part two is the respectful receiving of your sharing by the other and the mutual creation of a plan for how this need

will be met or, in other words, how this behaviour will be changed and when. This is the boundary-setting part where you let the other person know exactly what you need and what you expect in order to make this flag turn to green. To do this most effectively, use Non Violent Communication or the concept of Intention and Seeking to Understand.

• Part three is the actual change of the behaviour.

Remember, all of the pieces must be there in order to turn a red or yellow flag to green.

I had the experience of beginning to build a friendship with someone who was over an hour late the first two times we got together. Not good. Mega red flag for me in the respect, dependability, and reliability department. How can I trust this person to be there for me if that is how they are in the first two meetings. Of course, they had very great and legitimate reasons both times, but that's not the point. I could also find a great and legitimate reason to be an hour late for everything I do if I wanted to. The point is that timeliness is important to me, and it indicates many other things as well. The first time I was willing to allow for the possibility that it was a miscommunication as to when we were expected to meet. So, I let that go. However, I absolutely spoke to it the second time it happened. The person was a great listener and did a wonderful job of feeding back to me that they heard me. I felt respected and understood. It was great; we had a lovely visit and made plans to get together again. Guess what? Yup! One-and-a-half hours late this time! Amazing! That was that. There was and is no room in my life for disrespect and unreliability. There was clearly a great lack of integrity in our relationship. This person's words and actions were far from alignment, and I was not interested in settling for that in any friendship.

In summary: Communication in relationships is *everything* to creating a healthful and balanced connection with someone. Your skill at knowing what you feel and need, then articulating that clearly, will go a long way to creating healthful, respectful relationship with others.

After years of working with these tools myself, I would say that healthful communication boils down to this:

1. Be as respectful, direct, honest, and brief as possible when asking for needs to be met and setting boundaries. The simpler and clearer the message, the less room for misunderstanding and confusion. So try to state your needs and request statement in 2 sentences max.
2. Allow, rather than assume.
3. Take the time to seek to understand the intention and needs of the other person.

And remember this: you absolutely deserve to have only respectful, loving connections in your life. It is up to you to create them. Now you know how.

* A note from the Centre for Nonviolent Communication:

"We share our material freely and we appreciate donations. A contribution that reflects your appreciation of what we offer and the value you receive will be used to further the development and distribution of Nonviolent Communication. We hope that you will find enough value to want to support the work we are doing and those of us doing it. There is, however, no obligation, regardless of how many copies you print or distribute, unless you are using the information for profit. If you would like to use this information for profit, please contact us regarding licensing the material."

The Center for Nonviolent Communication
2428 Foothill Blvd. Suite E
La Crescenta, CA 91214
www.cnvc.org +1.818.957.9393

A Few Last Words

Congratulations! You did it. We have covered all the key pieces in your recovery process.

We have discussed the myriad coping strategies which may be a part of your current repertoire. We have explored why you may be drawn to certain harmful coping strategies and how they impact you. We have discussed a variety of tools for you to use for each of those old, harmful coping strategies so that you can be more conscious of the times you want to use them. And we have looked at numerous new, life-enhancing ways of responding in those situations.

We have looked at your relationship with yourself: why it is the way it is, and how you can strengthen and deepen your connection with yourself. We have also just finished exploring your connections with others: what is healthful and honouring of you and what is harmful and destructive to your life. You are now armed with a hefty tool kit with which to approach any life situation.

Over the next little while, all that remains is your consistent conscious effort to reinforce new ways of coping and to shed your old beliefs and unhelpful behaviours. I assure you that your consistent effort in this regard will be rewarded with a life that is free from food and body-image focus, and full of love and peace. It may be hard to trust in this from where you sit now, but I know it is true. Allow yourself to read and re-read pieces of this book throughout the next few months and beyond. If you do, the material herein will carry you through your entire recovery process and then some.

Let's wrap up our work together with a quick look at the original Coping Strategy Flow Chart (from Chapter 7), and then we will look at a coping strategy flow chart that is loaded with your new tools. At a glance, you will be able to see what stands as old patterns you will want to change. You will also have at your disposal a short list of the new tools you can use to make these changes as simple and smooth as possible.

I couldn't fit all the new bits and pieces onto the new coping strategy flow chart, so I settled for some of the key ones. Notice how much material we have covered. Notice how great your new awareness is of old patterns and new ones. Notice that there are many tools at your fingertips to attend to any concerns with food, with yourself, and with others. Celebrate your new-found awareness. It is a permanent and key step in healing your use of food to cope.

You have many new ways to approach your life now. When you practice your new tools, situations with others will not have the power to overwhelm you and lead to food-coping behaviour as they once did. Your regard for yourself and overall sense of well-being can only continue to grow when you respectfully acknowledge your feelings and needs.

THE OLD:

Behavioural-Level Coping Strategies   **Behaviour(s)**

Overeating; restriction; purging through exercise,
        laxatives or vomiting
Shopping
Drinking, Television, Internet, Computer Games
Drugs
Sex
Relationship addiction
Co-dependency
Isolation
Avoidance
Procrastination
Perfectionism
Sleeping (a lot)
Busywork
Passive-aggression
Raging
Blaming
Cutting

Feeling-Level Coping Strategies   **Feelings(s)**

Alexithymia
Permeating Level of Anxiety
Depression
Anxiety
Anger
Sadness
Frustration
Resentment
Insecurity
Overwhelm
Hopelessness and Despair

Thought-Level Coping Strategies   **Thought(s)**

The Drill Sergeant:
Bad body thoughts
Negative self-talk (put downs and harmful core beliefs)
All or nothing thinking
Intrusive Ideation
Discounting, Dismissing and Denying

Unmet Needs

Food, Air, Water / Safety and Security, Love, Acceptance, and Belongingness /
Esteem / Self-Actualization

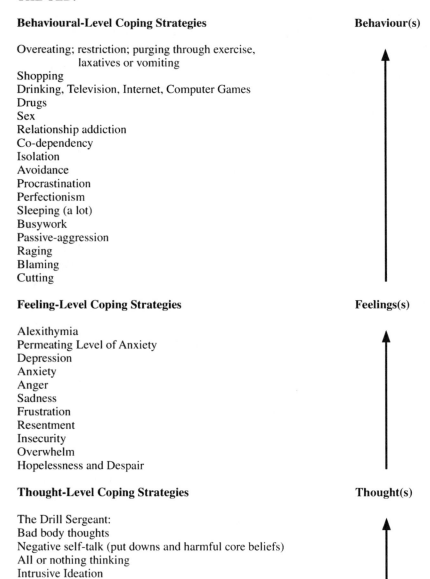

THE NEW:

Life-Enhancing Behaviours

Checking in with your Authentic Self: Identifying Feelings and Needs
List of Stressors
Boundary Setting
Self-Care
Compassionate Goal Setting
Tackling Unfinished Business
Natural Eating
Acting As-If
Letter of Fact
Plan A, B and C
Your Personal Mission Statement
Seeking to Understand
NVC
Allowing For the Possibility

Life-Enhancing Feelings

Compassion
Empathy
Respect
Fear
Anger
Sadness

Life- Enhancing Thoughts

Awareness of any resistance/readiness to change
Awareness of the Drill Sgt. and his intentions
Awareness of and respect for your needs
New Core Beliefs
The Matrix: Am I in the Past/Present/Future/Thinking/Feeling/Doing?
Awareness of the PLA
Awareness of the Diet Mentality
ILOC
Awareness of Family Structures and Developmental Stages
Allowing versus Assuming
Awareness of Meta-Messages
Awareness of Red Flags, Yellow Flags and Green Flags

Unmet Needs

Food, Air, Water / Safety and Security / Love, Acceptance, and Belongingness /
Esteem / Self-Actualization

Recall The Process of Lasting Change

Repeated patterns are a window to your needs. For every pattern you repeat, such as: overeating, purging, or restriction, there is a need that is being met within you. Your inability to change the undesirable pattern has nothing to do with lack of willpower or discipline. The pattern is merely a symptom of a deeper problem. As we discussed earlier, if you direct your efforts only at attempting to eliminate the symptom without putting effort into understanding and dissolving its cause, you are setting yourself up for a very fatiguing and defeating battle.

Awareness is the first step in changing any behaviour. You must first become aware that you are doing something that is detrimental to your values and life plan in order to effect change. Resistance is often your immediate reaction to becoming aware of what you are doing and why. This makes perfect sense. You have lived your life with a certain set of behaviours and beliefs. Given this, change, even if desired on some level, often feels less like innovation and more like annihilation of your entire existence as you know it. You wonder what will be left of you, your relationships, and the life you know, when you have made the changes necessary to free yourself of this debilitating behaviour. Which really means that when you are fully aware of the underlying need that leads you to execute this behaviour, will you still choose the people and things you have chosen so far? From this perspective, change can look very scary and the outcome very lonely. This is why so many of us have to hit our own personal "rock bottom" before we are ready to challenge old, harmful patterns of thoughts and behaviours. You must reach a place where you say, "I don't care what the outcome is. Just make it stop!"

And yet, questioning what life will look like when you are "done" is a wise and significant thing to do. It implies that you know you can change, and on some level you know that your current behaviour is providing you with a way of remaining in an uncomfortable situation without having to fully feel the discomfort being generated. In other words, you know that you are numbing yourself to certain aspects of your life, and, because you have chosen this approach to problems for so many years, it is a little scary to imagine being fully present and aware. You are saying that you want your life to be different, but you are fearful of how this change might appear. This sounds reasonable, from the perspective of the person who has yet to experience the benefits of the change and can only imagine the void which will remain by the removal of the old behaviour. Until you have experienced the pleasure and freedom that is created by letting go of the old pattern, you are naturally going to have some discomfort and doubt about the change.

It is human nature to seek familiarity and feel comforted by it. Often, even when the familiar behaviour is harmful to your essence and prevents you from fulfilling your dreams, you will cling to it because of the comfort provided by the familiarity. This very normal tendency in all humans is why lasting change must happen gradually.

When you demand immediate and complete change, you deny yourself time to learn the lessons that the problem or situation you have created is meant to teach. And you certainly don't have a solid base or foundation in place to feel secure as you move into unfamiliar territory. This means you are likely to flounder and find yourself returning to your old familiar behaviour when things get a little challenging. This can leave you feeling defeated and hopeless.

Just think of any diet or "nutritional plan" you have tried. You no doubt discovered that your attempts to heal your relationship with food and body-image focus, prior to understanding the cause, set you up to have short-term success. Your success could last only for as long as you did not require those coping strategies, that is, as long as nothing in day-to-day life upset your apple cart! This is why, at the pinnacle of our Diet Mentality, many of us can stick to a diet or some form of restrictive behaviour for only about 12 hours! Max! You can be "good" during the day when you are busy, out and about, or in front of others, but when you get home or the chores of the day are mostly attended to, you decompress with food, and the whole cycle repeats itself. If the underlying trigger that leads you to use food to cope is unattended, you will be in trouble when something happens that you hadn't planned for, or it didn't happen the way you had hoped. The feelings and unmet needs, which naturally and appropriately get triggered in those life situations, currently drive you to restrict, binge, or purge to cope.

To be successful in changing an old coping strategy, you must have the confidence of knowing that a nurturing force is standing by, ready to catch you when you start to naturally default into those old patterns. And this force must be predominantly found within. Building a solid, nurturing, supportive, and understanding relationship with yourself can take some time, as it would with others; however, you will begin to see the immediate benefits of this stronger and more supportive internal relationship in your awareness of what you are thinking, feeling, and needing in that moment, and in your ability to respond to those thoughts, feelings, and needs respectfully and appropriately.

With a greater sense of trust, security, and awareness of yourself rather than the impatience your Drill Sgt. was throwing your way, you will feel a sense of relief which allows you to relax and trust yourself to make life-enhancing and dignified choices around food, yourself, and others.

And know this as well: you own this process of change. It does not own you. You can take it as fast or as slow as you like, and as you have time and space for. You can look at as much "stuff" and be as aware as you want at any given time, and you can make as many changes as you wish; furthermore, you can return to your previous comforting behaviour whenever you feel the need for the old numbing peace that it brings. Soon, you will naturally find that the old, comfortable coping behaviour no longer fits. It just doesn't feel right any more. It is not who or where you want to be, nor will you really feel the need to find "security" this way. You will naturally choose not to use it, opting to engage in thoughts, feelings, and behaviours which you have had some practice with and that are coming to feel so much more respectful, natural, and "right" on a gut level than that old coping strategy ever did or ever could. You have found yourself. You have found peace.

A Few More Last Words

Please know that I welcome your questions and sharing about this process. Feel free to e-mail me with your experience at mmorand@islandnet.com. *Food is not the Problem II* is in the works and will offer a deeper exploration of some of the key pieces we have discussed in this book. Keep in mind the CEDRIC Centre has a free weekly newsletter and blog that has a new *Tools for Recovery* article each week, in addition to other great bits and pieces to aid you in your healing journey. To sign up, just visit our Web page @ www.cedriccentre.com and click on the Newsletter heading.

I urge you to take time with this process. In our work on compassionate goal setting, I showed you a simple and clear way to set goals around your healing and life in general. Allow yourself to set goals in that way for this process. Let yourself commit to the next six months, or a year, to be fully engaged in this process. Challenge yourself to pick one or two key pieces and focus on them; set goals around them *compassionately*. Give yourself every chance for success. Prove to yourself that you can change those old patterns of thought and behaviour which brought you to this place. I know you can, because I see it happen each day with both male and female clients of the CEDRIC Centre.

You can supplement your work on the material in this book with one of our on-line or in-house groups; our intensive weekend workshops; or a full semi-residential healing plan at our centre in Victoria, B.C., Canada. As with any new skill, the more support you receive early in the process, the speedier and more smoothly it will progress.

It doesn't matter what you have already tried or how many times something hasn't worked, you have most likely been trying the wrong thing. Remember, you have spent many years mastering those old coping strategies. You will need to put some conscious effort into mastering your new ones. But that's all they are; new thoughts and behaviours. And the old ones are just old thoughts and behaviours. They are not truths. They are not who you are. You can let them go and move forward to create a life filled with love, respect, and dignity for yourself.

You have a right to peace and love as the norm in your life. Allowing for the possibility that I may be right is all you need to do!

Love, Michelle

REFERENCES

CHAPTER ONE: FOOD IS NOT THE PROBLEM
Barbara Sher, *I Could Do Anything If Only I Knew What It Was*.
Dell, August 5, 1995.

CHAPTER TWO: READINESS FOR CHANGE
Prochaska and DiClemente, *Stages of Readiness for Change*.
Transtheoretical Therapy, 1982.

CHAPTER FOUR: THE MATRIX
Bennett, E. and Hastings, P. *The Bennett-Hastings Process of Counselling Matrix* (permission for adaptation granted in 2006 via personal communication). Matrix first shared at Gonzaga University, Spokane WA in Counselling Practicum class 2000.

CHAPTER FIVE: BASIC NEEDS
Maslow, Abraham. *Hierarchy of Basic Human Needs*: Hergenhan et al.

CHAPTER NINE: POST TRAUMATIC STRESS DISORDER
Hendryx, M., Haviland, M., and Shaw D. *Dimensions of Alexithymia and Their Relationships to Anxiety and Depression* 1991; and Taylor, Bagby, Parker & Ryan, 1990.

CHAPTER NINETEEN: DEVELOPMENTAL STAGES
Bowlby, J., as quoted by Susan Johnson, *Psychology* Today, March 01, 1994.

NB: The above references are in addition to those noted within the text of this book.

WHO AND WHAT IS THE CEDRIC CENTRE?

The CEDRIC Centre is a counselling centre situated in beautiful Victoria, British Columbia, Canada, which specializes in supporting people worldwide to heal from their use of food as a coping strategy.

Our Primary Counsellors Are:

Michelle L. Morand, MA, Founder and Director.

Karen Stein, Counsellor.

Beth Burton-Krahn, MA, Counsellor.

Visit our Web site @ www.cedriccentre.com for a full listing of our staff, services and skill set.

WHAT DO WE OFFER?

- We offer a semi-residential program that provides our clients with the tools they need to experience a happy and fulfilling life that is free from the use of food as a coping strategy. Visit our Web site for more details on how we can make your dreams a reality.
- Individual and group counselling anywhere in the world via telephone and internet.
- Intensive weekend workshops and healing retreats.
- A free weekly newsletter containing information on the recovery process as well as tools to aid you in your healing journey.
- Our blog: www.cedriccentre.com/blog
- A series of WORKBOOKS and CD'S designed to supplement your work, or to be used as tools in the privacy and comfort of your own home during your process of recovery.

For more information on any of these services, please visit our Web site at www.cedriccentre.com

We welcome the opportunity to create a healing plan that is specific to your individual goals and needs. Let us know how we can support you in liberating yourself from the use of food to cope.

AVAILABLE ON CD

Natural Eating

This CD covers all the basics of why you use food to cope and what you can do to bring greater awareness and choice to your underlying triggers. If you are ready to challenge your existing patterns around food and begin to have a free and easy relationship with food, this is the place to begin.

Michelle Morand, Founder and Director of the CEDRIC Centre, shares the basic principles of recovery from Disordered Eating and the Diet Mentality. With clear and simple information and tools, you will immediately begin to understand and change your stressful and undermining thoughts, feelings, and behaviours around food.

Running Time: 60 minutes

$24.99

Compassion Is The Key

Compassion is often the key missing ingredient in our relationship with ourselves. As such, we seek motivation through criticism and fear, which only serves to drive us back to food to cope. In order to truly be free from food as a coping strategy, regardless of whether you overeat, purge, or restrict, the first step is beginning to have empathy and compassion for yourself. No, this doesn't mean anything like settling for where you are now. It means respecting and appreciating yourself enough to want to be the best you can be and live the life you were meant to live. Compassion is the key.

In this CD, Michelle Morand, Founder and Director of the CEDRIC Centre, will share key information on why you may resist self-compassion; why it is so important to your freedom from food to cope; and what you can begin to do today to gently, compassion-ately, and successfully begin to challenge your Diet Mentality once and for all!

Running Time: 60 minutes

$24.99

Healthy Relationships

The patterns we have learned regarding how to be in a relation-ship with another person are often a key element in our use of food to cope. Those old, harmful ways of thinking about relationships and the role we play in them are a significant impediment and fre-quently thwart our recovery. This doesn't speak to your "significant other" necessarily: it may be colleagues, parents, kids, friends, the grocery store clerk, and so on. It doesn't matter who it is. If you're in the habit of looking outside of yourself for validation and approval of who you are and what you're worth, you will, to some extent, be stuck in the insecurity of the "External Locus of Control." This is a very vulnerable place to be when you're at home, and it's highly unlikely that you can avoid using a behavioural coping strategy, such as: food, alcohol, shopping, or co-dependency. It's impossible to feel safe and secure in your world when it is (or at least seems to be) ruled by everyone else; their moods; their whims and needs at the moment.

Michelle Morand, Founder and Director of the CEDRIC Centre, will give you the tools to assess the relationship issues that may lead you to use food to cope, and what you can do specifically to begin to think, feel, and act differently in those situations to bring about more healthful and more authentic connections with everyone in your life. If you just froze in your tracks at the thought of authentic commu-nication in your relationship with some key people in your life, this CD is a *must have* for you! Conquer those old patterns now, before they get any deeper into your relationships. Authentic communica-tion is actually much simpler than what you're doing now, and it creates much, much, much less distress within you and with others than do some of your current communication patterns.

Join Michelle for one hour that can change forever the way you think, feel, and act in your relationships.
Running Time: 60 minutes
$24.99

WORKBOOKS

The CEDRIC Centre is pleased to offer two key resources in the form of our Natural Eating and Core Beliefs workbooks.

The workbooks include many exercises and opportunities to fully explore your relationship with food and with yourself. Consciousness is key in changing any unwanted behavioural pattern. The more you understand why you personally use food to cope and what you can do to change this behaviour, the more you will be in a position to effect real and lasting change when you notice yourself wanting to use food to cope in your day-to-day existence. These workbooks are geared toward creating greater awareness within you, while giving you clear and concrete tools to change the thoughts, feelings, and behaviours that keep you stuck using food to cope.

Natural Eating

This workbook covers the basics of what sets us up to use food to cope and how your current thoughts, feelings, and behaviours perpetuate this pattern. If you are eager to learn what drives your use of food to cope, this workbook is an invaluable resource.
52 Pages
$20.00

Core Beliefs

This workbook provides you with information and tools specific to your relationship with yourself and how your belief systems impact your use of food to cope. With the exercises in this workbook, you will uncover, explore, and begin to heal the old beliefs and life experiences that keep you trapped in your use of food to cope.
35 Pages
$20.00

We would be pleased to mail any or all of our CD's and work-books. Note that all prices quoted are in **Canadian funds**. Applicable taxes and shipping are not included in quoted price of workbooks and CD's.

Lightning Source UK Ltd.
Milton Keynes UK
27 September 2010

160432UK00001B/113/A